Peace in the Holy Land

By the same author

A SOLDIER WITH THE ARABS

THE STORY OF THE ARAB LEGION

BRITAIN AND THE ARABS

WAR IN THE DESERT

THE GREAT ARAB CONQUESTS

THE EMPIRE OF THE ARABS

THE COURSE OF EMPIRE

THE MIDDLE EAST CRISIS

THE LOST CENTURIES

A SHORT HISTORY OF THE ARAB PEOPLES

THE LIFE AND TIMES OF MUHAMMAD

PEACE IN THE HOLY LAND

An Historical Analysis of the Palestine Problem

BY

JOHN BAGOT GLUBB

HODDER AND STOUGHTON
LONDON SYDNEY AUCKLAND TORONTO

Copyright © 1971 by J. B. G. Ltd.

First printed 1971

ISBN 0 340 10639 5

All rights reserved. No part of this publication may be reproduced or transmitted in any form or by any means, electronic or mechanical including photocopy, recording, or any information storage and retrieval system, without permission in writing from the publisher.

Printed in Great Britain for Hodder and Stoughton Limited, St. Paul's House, Warwick Lane, London, E.C.4, by Ebenezer Baylis and Son Limited, Worcester, and London

At the wicket gate that leads to the kingdom of the tranquil and serene are barred all those in whom hatred, revenge, jealousy, greed, envy, anger or lust has gained dominion. But . . . defenders of the oppressed find ready admittance. There is a special type of nobility attached to those who devote themselves to the oppressed, the persecuted and the downtrodden. Victims of oppression and discrimination are rarely able to defend themselves. They are scarcely ever even given a hearing. They desperately need defenders.

JOHN A. O'BRIEN, *Eternal Answers for an Anxious Age*

The *true*, the *real* trouble we are in, my dear friends, consists quite simply in the fact that man is as he is and cannot make himself different. He is the cause of his own trouble. He suffers from himself.

KARL BARTH, *Call for God*

If there is ever to be a happy and peaceful world we have all of us got to learn to understand and to love the difficult, the exasperating and the unlovable.

J. B. PHILIPS, *Good News*

Introduction

AN arrogant contempt for the past seems to be characteristic of modern times. Our success in developing chemical, electronic and mechanical devices has produced in us an idea that no one before us was of any importance. In fact, however, human nature has changed little in the last four thousand years and the history of these four millennia teems with situations similar to those which confront us today.

Another factor essential to the comprehension of modern problems is the realisation of the influence still exerted today on our mentality by events which occurred many centuries ago. The Old Testament, for example, still profoundly affects our psychology. For these reasons, I am surprised at the immense number of books written about the Palestine Problem, which commence in 1917 or 1920.

In this book, I have tried to expose the human and the historical causes of the present conflict. I have also endeavoured to write rationally and without emotion, for it is the violent passions which this problem has aroused which make it so difficult to solve.

Finally, I would like to add that we are not entirely justified in laying the blame on the intractable mentality of "Arabs" and "Jews". For a great part of our difficulties are due to the age in which we live, to our own materialism, our cynicism and our unscrupulous politics, which, in their turn, are traceable to our abandonment of belief in God. For men, if they lose sight of the Spiritual, behave to one another like wild beasts.

J.B.G.

Mayfield,
Sussex.

Contents

		PAGE
	Introduction	7
	Author's Note	15
I	Patriarchs and Shepherds	17
II	The Lord Yahweh	31
III	The Conquest	43
IV	Glorious Days	55
V	Decline and Decadence	71
VI	Isolation or Internationalism	87
VII	Jews Fill the World	107
VIII	The Herodians	123
IX	The Collapse of Militancy	141
X	The Tragedy	157
XI	The Arab Hurricane	171
XII	The Middle Ages	191
XIII	Blood-soaked Centuries	207
XIV	Middle East Martyrdom	221
XV	The Consequences of Contempt	239
XVI	The Coming of Zionism	255
XVII	The Mandate	271
XVIII	The Slide to Anarchy	287
XIX	The Psychology of Suffering	305
XX	By Force Alone	325
XXI	The Middle East—Key to World Power	341
XXII	An Outline Solution	355
	Appendix I	363
	Appendix II	364
	Bibliography	368
	Index	371

List of Maps

		PAGE
1	The Levant Topographical	18
2	Sinai and the Exodus	27
3	The Invasion	40
4	The Conquest	49
5	Palestine at the Time of Saul	58
6	Palestine under David and Solomon	63
7	Palestine in the Time of the Kingdoms of Israel and Judah	75
8	The Assyrian and Babylonian Empires	83
9	Palestine after the Return from Babylon	91
10	The Empires of Seleucus and Ptolemy	98
11	Judaea under the early Hasmonaeans	102
12	The Roman Empire	112
13	Areas overrun by Alexander Jannaeus	126
14	Pompey's Settlement	128
15	Dominions of Herod the Great	133
16	Palestine at the Time of Christ	137
17	Operations of Vespasian	146
18	The Capture of Jerusalem by Titus	149
19	The Byzantine and Persian Empires in A.D. 630	172
20	Trade Routes from the Orient	174
21	Operations in Syria 634	180
22	The Progress of Arab Conquest	182
23	The Muslim-Christian Border	194
24	Jewish Migrations and Expulsions	210
25	Seljuqs and Crusaders	224
26	The Mongols in the Middle East	226

27	The Campaigns of Tamerlane	231
28	Illustration of Article in *Der Orient*	248
29	The Royal Commission Partition Plan 1937	283
30	The United Nations Partition Plan	295
31	Jewish Population in 1944	297
32	To show that Syrian, Iraqi armies and the Arab Legion did not invade Israel	308
33	To show U.N. Partition and additional areas seized by Israel	311
34	The Rhodes Armistice Demarcation Line	313
35	Sharm al Shaikh and the Gulf of Aqaba	331
36	The Middle East—Key to World Power	344
37	The Arab and Muslim Worlds (reproduced by permission of *Affari Esteri*, Rome)	351
38	An Outline Solution	360

List of Genealogical Trees

	PAGE
The Seleucids	97
The Hasmonaeans	100
The Herodians	130
Quraish	176
The Seljuqs	222

Author's Note

A BOOK covering four thousand years inevitably encounters a problem of names, which change frequently. Either the name disappears and a new name replaces it, or else the old name remains, but now signifies something quite different.

As regards geographic names, I have used the designation "Palestine" throughout the book, simply because everyone knows what it means. This is not propaganda intended to suggest that Israel does not exist. For the same reason, I have in places used such names as Judaea, Samaria and Galilee, because they are familiar.

Names which refer to human communities are even more confusing, because ancient names are still in use, but now carry quite different meanings. The names Jew and Arab are the most frequent example.

Words are equally deceptive. "Nation", for example, can mean the inhabitants of a certain area, which is controlled by one government. This political use of "nation" then has no ethnic significance. But "nation" is also used in the opposite sense to indicate an ethnic group, people all descended from the same ancestors, although not all under one government. The word "people" is even more confusing. I recently heard a lecture given by a Jew, whose object was to prove that the Jews today are a "people", not a "nation". He appeared to mean that they were a definite community, though not of one ethnic origin. But a German writer complains that the German "people" are now divided up in several different countries. He presumably meant the word "people" to signify a single ethnic stock.

These vague words are of particular importance in the Palestine dispute because both sides have frequently used them with different meanings, sometimes with the deliberate intention to mislead. All I can do is to assure the reader that I have not used such verbal quibbles in order to deceive, but have tried as far as possible to make my meaning clear.

I

Patriarchs and Shepherds

The word of Yahweh was spoken to Abram in a vision, "Have no fear, Abram, I am your shield". "My Lord Yahweh", Abram replied, "what do you intend to give me? I go childless . . ." And then this word of Yahweh was spoken to him . . . "Your heir shall be of your own flesh . . ." Then taking him outside he said, "Look up to heaven and count the stars if you can."

Genesis XV Jerusalem Bible

The Bible mentions the antipathy felt by the Egyptians . . . toward the bedouins who tended flocks of sheep and goats . . . east of the Delta, but bedouins have kept their flocks in that general area throughout history. Even today, Arab bedouin regularly appear.

C. F. PFEIFFER, *Egypt and the Exodus*

The history of Egypt is traditionally divided into thirty dynasties, from . . . Menes (*c.* 2980 B.C.) to Alexander's conquest (332 B.C.)

C. F. PFEIFFER, *Egypt and the Exodus*

Too much effort has been made to place the history of Jews on a strange, mystifying level and too little effort made to explain it in terms of the forces that have moved and are still moving through all human history.

RABBI ELMER BERGER, *The Jewish Dilemna*

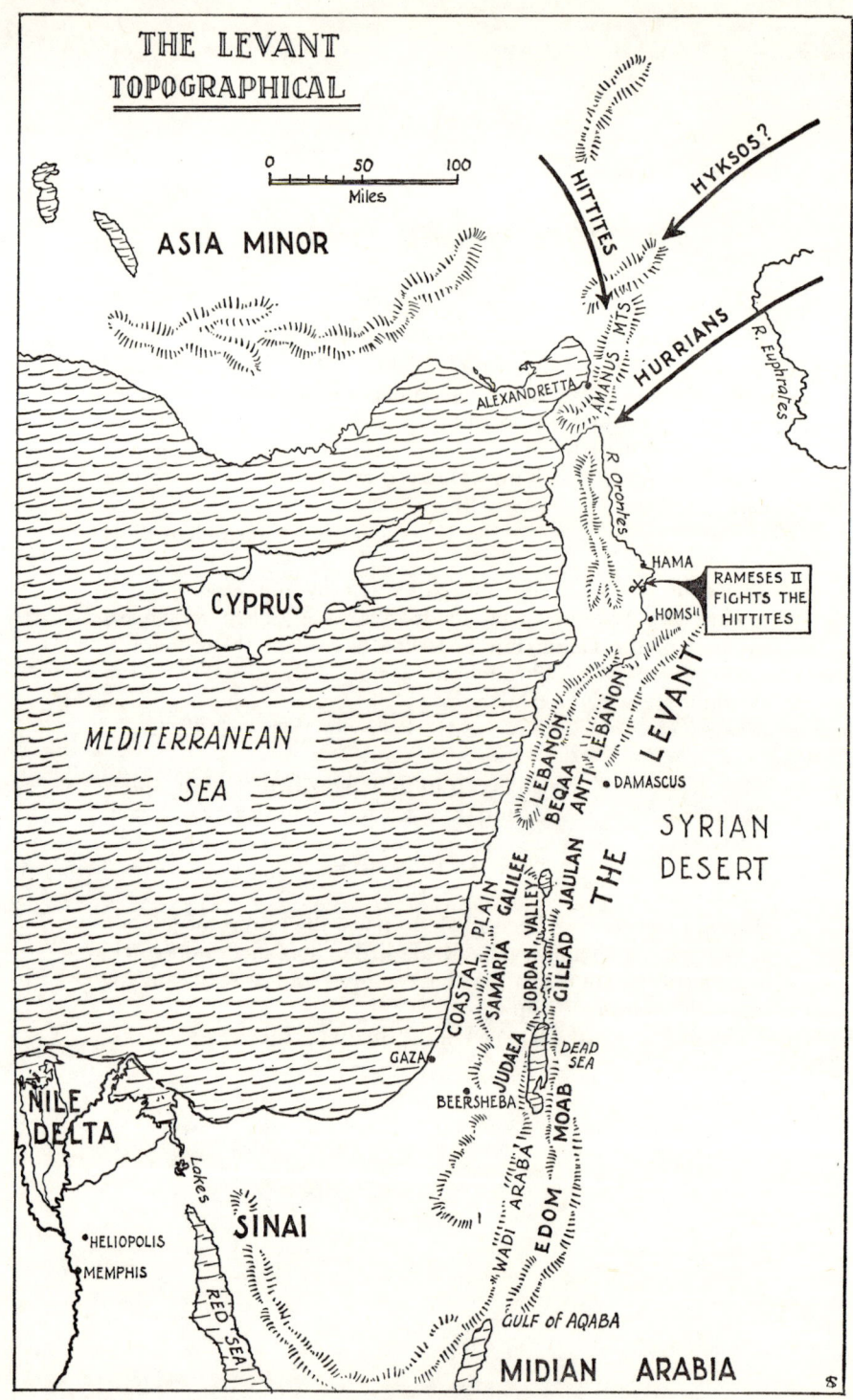

MAP 1

I

THE Levant, the land at the eastern end of the Mediterranean which we divide into Lebanon, Syria, Palestine and Jordan, constitutes one geographical area. Bounded on the west by the Mediterranean and on the east by the Syrian Desert, it measures some five hundred miles from north to south but only about eighty miles from west to east.

This area is divided into sharply marked strips, running from north to south. On the west lies the coastal plain, from (modern) Alexandretta to Gaza. Next, and parallel to it, a range of mountains, Amanus, Lebanon, Galilee, Samaria and Judaea. East of these mountains there is a deep rift, the Orontes, the Beqaa, the Jordan valley, the Wadi Araba, the Gulf of Aqaba and the Red Sea. At the Dead Sea, the rift is 1,300 feet below sea level.

East of the rift valley lies another range of mountains, Anti-Lebanon, the Jaulan, Gilead, Moab and Edom, to use biblical names. While these ranges present steep slopes and cliffs to the west, they fall away only gradually to the east into the high plateau of the Syrian Desert.

* * *

Recently, archaelogists have told us of the existence in Palestine of towns and, therefore, of organized political communities, as early as 7000 B.C., though flint instruments dating from Palaeolithic times are plentiful.

The north-and-south ranges of mountains and the intervening rift valley have had a profound influence on the population, for these barriers were only with difficulty passable to nomadic tribes from the eastern desert. Migrating nations coming from the north, however, could move down the coastal plain or the rift valley without encountering any physical barriers. The flint users seem to have been overrun by a copper-using people from the north, who in their turn were conquered, about 3200 B.C., by bronze-using invaders, probably originating from the Caucasus or the Caspian.[1] According to Flinders Petrie, these people were highly civilised, articles imported from as far afield as Ireland and India being found with their remains.

[1] Sir Flinders Petrie, *Palestine and Israel*.

The Horites, or Hurrians, seem to have arrived in northern Syria from north Persia or Turkestan. They were followed by the Hittites, who had been living on the plateau of Asia Minor and were probably related to the modern Armenians. Their features were distinguished by the large nose which we associate with the Jews. In fact, this peculiarity is still to be seen among Armenians and "Arabs" in Syria, but not in Arabia. Moscati[2] says that there are two distinct racial types in the Levant, the "oriental" in Arabia and Persia, and the Armenoid, with the prominent nose. The word Semitic originally denoted a group of languages. The extremely mixed origins of the inhabitants of the Levant make it impossible to call them collectively "Semitic peoples".

* * *

Before proceeding to discuss the Old Testament narrative, it may be useful if I make my own position clear. I am a Christian and I am not attempting to discredit the Old Testament. The situation, however, is not a simple alternative--to believe or to disbelieve. The problem is how to interpret the meaning.

Man, I suggest, is growing and his capacity for appreciating God expands as he grows. The earliest men thought of gods who resembled their own chiefs, who were pleased or angry or perplexed, who gave rewards to their supporters and tried to revenge themselves on their enemies. This does not, of course, mean that God ever was like that, but that that was the only way in which the minds of primitive men could visualize Him.

In the same way, small children see their father as strong, and feel safe holding his hand. But when they grow older, they may fear and dislike him for trying to control them. As adolescents, they consider him stupid and old fashioned, but later in life they will tell their own children what a splendid father they had. Father was the same person all the time but the children saw him under different aspects as their own minds developed. God, of course, is always the same but the minds of men in different ages have imagined Him in many different guises.

In Old Testament times, primitive men visualised their god as a mighty warrior, who hated his enemies and was pleased when they were killed. At a later stage, they criticised him and thought that they could do his work better, as adolescents think of their parents.

But the good God was too loving to take His children to task for

---

[2] Sabatino Moscati, *Ancient Semitic Civilizations*.

their infantile illusions. "He knew what was in man." But when He saw a man willing to serve Him without hope of gain, He touched him with His Spirit and fired him with devotion and the strength to serve. Intellectually, of course, this dedicated servant was a man of his time, with the limited conceptions of his contemporaries, but his loyal devotion could be used by God, even if his mentality were puerile.

If, therefore, we read that God wished the Israelites to massacre the Canaanites, I believe that we are free to think that this was the picture of a god which occurred to these simple men. In the same way, a school teacher will accept a small child's statement that her daddy is the most important man in the world, even if she herself knows that he is in reality an unskilled labourer.

To query the views about God expressed in the Old Testament is not necessarily to be an atheist, to deny the "truth" of the Old Testament or to disbelieve in "miracles". The fact that the Divine Spirit can fire the hearts of men is the greatest of miracles. All life is a miracle and a mystery, but I think we must be convinced that the God of the Universe is a Spirit, and is not inspired by the human lust to win battles and kill enemies.

Indeed, many of the troubles encountered by religions are due to the attempt of well-meaning people to claim that some statement made by a man four thousand years ago is sacred for all time, although it appears to bear the stamp of the age in which he lived, and is contrary to the morality which we respect today. With this preface, we will proceed to study the narrative.

* * *

Modern scholars believe that Abraham lived about 1850 to 1800 B.C. Egypt, Palestine, Syria and Babylonia were already very old civilisations when he arrived from Mesopotamia. From a period thousands of years before Christ down to our own times, a type of tent-dwelling tribes has always moved along the edge of the cultivation in the Levant countries. These people are sometimes called semi-nomads or donkey bedouins. They cannot move far into the desert, not having camels. Their tents and possessions are carried on donkeys, and they live by their sheep and goats or by helping in the fields at harvest. Abraham was the headman of a small group of this kind.

* * *

In the 1920s, I often rode on horseback through Arab tribes. Round the camp fire, I was told stories of the origin of the tribe.

These took the form of an account of the exploits of their original ancestor, and of his sons and perhaps his grandsons. Thereafter, the stories ceased. After three generations, the number of actors had become so great that the story-tellers could no longer remember them all.

The stories of the original heroes had become highly stylised, including verbatim speeches, poems recited by the ancestors of the tribe, or ballads celebrating their victories. If pressed for more, the narrator would produce incidents of the time of his own father, many centuries later. The stories of the patriarchs in Genesis seem to me exactly to resemble this form. It is unlikely that the story of Abraham was written until some nine hundred years after his death. The account, as we now have it, was probably only finalised some fifteen hundred years after Abraham. Frequently re-edited, the narrative shows insertions here and there, expressing the sentiments of many centuries later.

In Genesis XVIII, 25, Abraham asks, "Shall not the Judge of all the earth do right?", an apparent proof that Abraham was a monotheist. But much evidence goes to prove that he did not believe in only one God. We are thus obliged to presume that the passage was inserted by an editor, perhaps twelve hundred years later, when belief in monotheism was spreading.

Primitive (and indeed not so primitive) people tend to think of their god as a man. The god of Abraham visits the latter in his tent, has dinner and invites him to come outside and look at the stars. Then he says goodbye to his host and continues his journey.

To most of us, "home" suggests a place. To moving nomads, home is a group of people. The god of the nomad was the protector of the family. We are so used to the phrase "the god of Abraham, Isaac and Jacob" that we do not pause to analyse it, but if we do so, the expression does suggest the protector of one family. It seems unlikely that Abraham ever gave much thought to the whole world, of which he can have had no conception.

While nomad gods were necessarily themselves nomadic, settled peoples believed in local gods, who protected their towns and their lands. Abraham, we are told, pitched his tent at Mamre (Hebron), where a shrine existed to the local god. Such territorial gods were looked upon like land owners. If Abraham wished to camp in the Hebron area, it would be necessary to secure the agreement of the local god. The word Al Shaddai,[3] the mountain god, is used in places

---

[3] Genesis XVII, 1.

as the god who spoke to Abraham. The name would be suitable for the god of Hebron, which is the highest place in Palestine. The ritual described in Genesis XV, 9 to 18, was a common heathen ceremony. Sacrificial animals were cut in half, and those taking the oath walked between the two halves.[4] The description of this pagan rite might be thought to suggest that Abraham made a covenant with the local god of the Hebron area.

Many modern historians and Bible commentators express the opinion that the dearest wish of every nomad is to obtain land on which to settle. This is entirely erroneous, for nomadism is a way of life deeply engrained in such people. Even in our own times, many governments have made great efforts to settle nomads, but have met with obstinate resistance. There is no reason to believe that Abraham or his family had the least desire to settle down. John Bright, in his fine *History of Israel*, says that the clan of Abraham roamed the land "supported by the promises of their God that it would one day belong to their posterity". Yet nearly a thousand years later, after the conquest of Canaan, they apparently still preferred to live in tents.

Abraham wanted to graze his sheep in the Beersheba area. But, in summer, surface pools of rainwater dried up and the sheep had to drink from wells. Abraham, I surmise, did not want to settle down as a farmer but he wanted to own some wells.[5] Later he bought a cave to bury his family, but he and his descendants continued to live in tents.

Scholars agree that the Abrahamic promises were not written down for some nine hundred years (as long as from William the Conqueror to us). At that time, the Davidic kingdom *did* aspire to rule all Palestine. The possibility, therefore, arises that the editors who compiled our version of Genesis may have attributed their own ambitions to old Abraham, the donkey bedouin. If we are prepared, then, to consider the possibility that Abraham was not the first monotheist, but that he sought gods to protect his family, we must ask ourselves how the belief later arose that the god who spoke to Abraham was the Spiritual Creator of the Universe.

We do not know who were the gods of Abraham, but several centuries after his death, Yahweh came to be recognised as the God of Israel. Perhaps the priestly editors of our Old Testament substituted Yahweh for other names used for Abraham's god in the original narrative. Our translators lost the significance of the various names used, by translating them all as the Lord God. As we associate this

---

[4] Cf. Ronald Clements, *Abraham and David*. Rev. R. E. Clements, M.A., Ph.D., is an ordained Baptist minister.
[5] Genesis XXI, 30.

phrase with the Spiritual Creator of the Universe, Christians assumed that it was He who dined in Abraham's tent and who argued with the patriarch over the fate of Sodom.[6]

After the Patriarchs, some four hundred years are passed over in silence. Meanwhile, about 1720 B.C., the Hyksos, an Asian people, conquered Syria, Palestine and Egypt. The Hyksos were, perhaps, Turks, for their average height was only five feet.[7] Moreover, they introduced horses, and the Central Asian Turks were great horse breeders.[8] Perhaps the Pharaoh who promoted Joseph was a Hyksos ruler. The Hyksos might well trust the Palestinian nomads, who were foreigners like themselves, rather than the native Egyptians whom they had conquered.

The peculiar conditions of the Nile delta enable us to visualise the reasons for the sojourn in Egypt. The wealth of that country did not come from rain. The prosperity of Egypt came solely from the Nile. Land submerged by the Nile flood was phenomenally fertile. Land a few inches higher, not covered by the Nile, was bare desert.

Sinai, Beersheba and northern Arabia supported a population of sheep and camel breeders. But the climate is liable to wide variations in rainfall. When the rains fail, the flocks die. A shepherd who has lost all his sheep has lost all his capital. Years of good rainfall are, thereafter, no use to him, for he has no sheep to breed from. He must obtain money in order to buy sheep and start business again.

To the bankrupt shepherd, Egypt, for thousands of years, has supplied the answer. Abraham, in a bad year, had gone down there.[9] The desert comes so close to the cultivation that the nomad can pitch his poor tent on gravelly desert and walk into the towns to earn wages. These he uses to buy sheep and donkeys, until the family is again viable. Then they set out once more to the east and resume their traditional way of life.

It was doubtless under such circumstances that many poor Syrian shepherds camped on the eastern edge of the delta between 1720 and 1280 B.C. About 1568 B.C., an Egyptian patriotic movement finally drove out the Hyksos and established the eighteenth dynasty. It often occurs that when a conquered people regains its freedom, it passes straight over to a period of military aggression and sets out to conquer someone else.

The eighteenth dynasty, accordingly, embarked on an era of

[6] Genesis XVIII, 16 to 33.
[7] Sir Flinders Petrie, *Palestine and Israel*.
[8] Pfeiffer believes they were mixed Semites, Hurrians and Hittites. C. F. Pfeiffer, *Egypt and the Exodus*.
[9] Genesis XIII, 10.

conquest in Palestine and Syria. About 1310 B.C., however, Egypt suffered a period of weakness, owing to the collapse of the eighteenth dynasty, but Rameses I (1310–1309 B.C.) restored order and founded the nineteenth dynasty. Rameses II (1290–1224 B.C.) fought a pitched battle with the Hittites on the Orontes,[10] and stabilised the frontier north of Damascus. The rest of his reign was a period of peace and plenty.

The old Egyptian capitals had been at Thebes or Memphis. The Hyksos built their capital at Avaris, later called Tanis. The eighteenth dynasty moved again to Memphis but Rameses II brought the capital back to Avaris. In this area, he built large fortified cities, using forced labour. Egyptian governments had always used unpaid labour, a system only abolished by the British administration at the beginning of the present century.

A contemporary Egyptian inscription records that Rameses II used prisoners-of-war taken on his expeditions to Syria. If they were from eastern Syria, they would be of the same type as the indigent shepherds on the fringe of the delta, whose young men would probably also be conscripted. Forced labour was usually supplied by the Egyptians themselves, but an imperialist Pharaoh would take pleasure in using foreigners rather than his own subjects. The Egyptians have always been hostile to nomads. "Every shepherd is an abomination to the Egyptians"[11]—a dislike which still persists.

Prisoners-of-war could expect no better, but the usual gatherings of impoverished shepherds must have been greatly exasperated. They had come to earn wages, and it must have been frustrating to have to work for nothing. But this "bondage" cannot really be called slavery. Before leaving Egypt, the Israelites[12] borrowed from the Egyptians "jewels of silver and jewels of gold" in order to steal them. "Yahweh gave the people such prestige in the eyes of the Egyptians that they gave them what they asked. So they plundered the Egyptians."[13] Yahweh is here seen, not as God of the Universe, but as the god of Israel, defrauding the Egyptians. However, the fact that the Egyptians were willing to lend their valuables to the Israelites does not suggest slavery, as we visualise it, but neighbourly friendliness. Morever, when conditions were hard later on, the Israelites were to regret the loss of the fleshpots (we should say—the high standard of living) of Egypt.

[10] Map 1, p. 18.
[11] Genesis XLVI, 31.
[12] I call the ancient Israelites by that name, as opposed to the modern Israelis.
[13] Exodus XII, 36. Jerusalem Bible.

Moses was allegedly born an Israelite, but was adopted by Pharaoh's daughter and given a princely education, probably with the Egyptian priests of Heliopolis. Manetho, an Egyptian priest-historian, who wrote in the third century B.C., says that he actually became a priest.[14] However, he sympathised with the poor shepherds on forced labour, killed an Egyptian foreman, and escaped to Sinai. Here he was hospitably received by Jethro, described as the priest of Midian,[15] whose daughter he married.

Moses worked as a shepherd for Jethro. One day, when out with the sheep, he received his first spiritual call, known as the incident of the Burning Bush. If Moses was educated as a polytheist, can he have received his first knowledge of a spiritual God from his father-in-law? There does not seem to be any reason to doubt that this was a genuine spiritual experience.

Moses is told to go and lead his people out of Egypt, but asks what is the name of the god who orders this. The reply is, "*I am* has sent you." (The name Yahweh, is believed to mean "he is".) Exodus VI states that this was the first time the name Yahweh was revealed. Apparently the Israelites had never before heard of Yahweh. Moses obtains leave from Jethro and, taking his wife and his two sons with him, sets out for Egypt. "On the journey, when Moses had halted for the night, Yahweh came to meet him and tried to kill him."[16] Just when the reader feels that Moses had had a spiritual vision, and that the story is comprehensible and even inspiring, he is perplexed by a mysterious verse like this.

* * *

Our reconstruction of the life of the poor shepherds on the eastern border of Egypt obviously suggests that there had been a constant coming and going of such people since the first arrival of Jacob and his family four hundred years earlier. The brief biblical account states that Jacob had migrated to Egypt with seventy persons belonging to his family,[17] whose descendants, in the ensuing four hundred years, had increased in numbers, without mixing with any other stock. In fact, they must have consisted of mixed groups of donkey bedouins from Palestine and Syria. Whether any, or how many of them, were descended from Abraham cannot now be guessed.

[14] Cf. Pfeiffer, op. cit.
[15] Midian was the northern Hejaz. Map 1, p. 18.
[16] Exodus IV, 24. Jerusalem Bible.
[17] Genesis XLVI, 27.

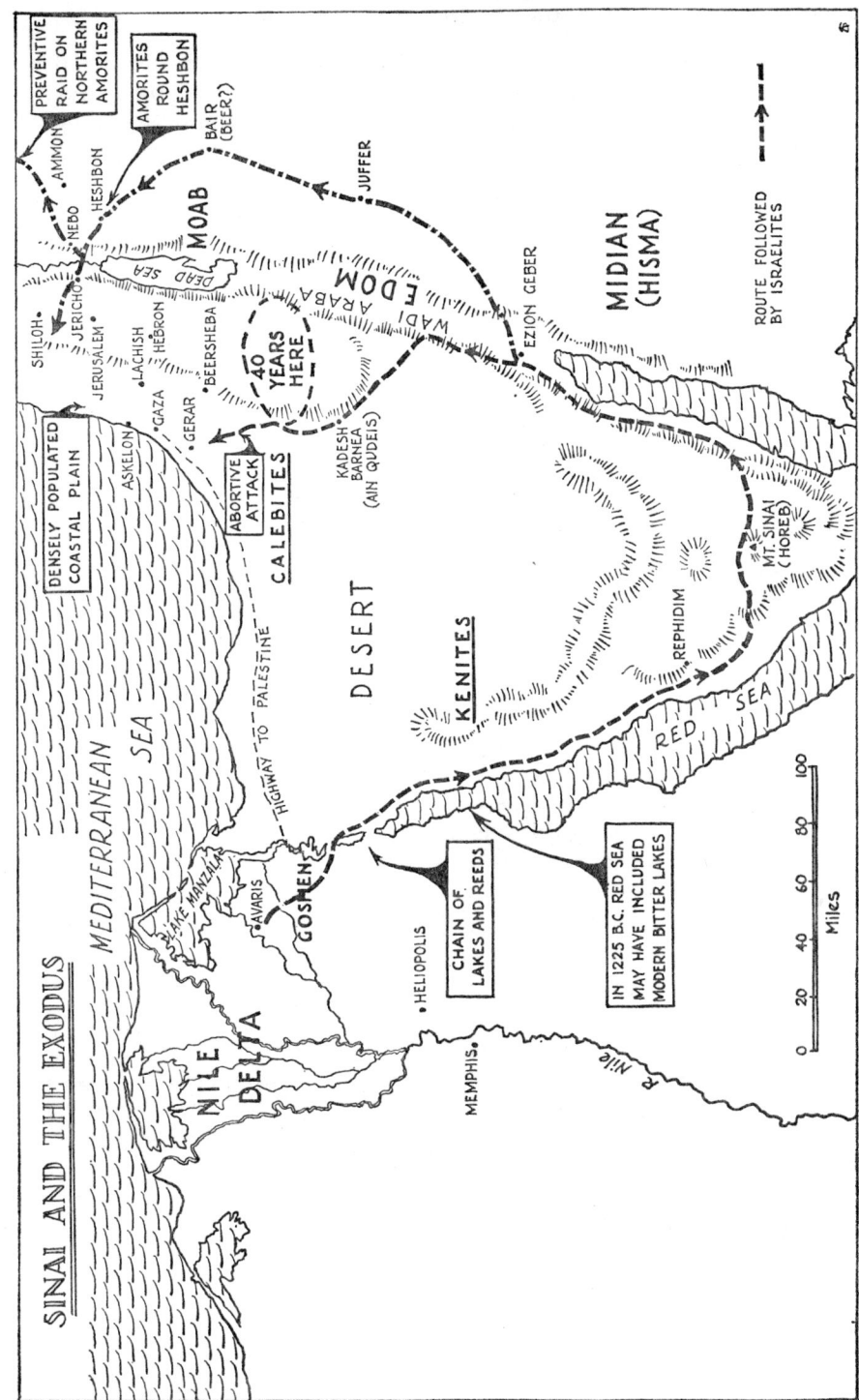

MAP 2

Led by Moses, some of the shepherds seem to have escaped about 1222 B.C. Rameses II died in 1225 B.C.[18] Perhaps the confusion caused by the death of this great ruler provided the opportunity. The shepherd community must have been familiar with Egypt and with her army. Chariots, the use of which the Egyptians had learned from the Hyksos, now dominated the battlefield, as tanks have done in our time. Moses had lived for years in Sinai and was familiar with the ground. He must have discussed plans for the escape with the shepherd elders.

Against chariots, men on foot would have little hope unless they could operate on marshy soil or in mountains. The same situation has arisen in our own wars between infantry and tanks. The Egyptian delta is a flat area made by the Nile silt. Ground level is little above that of the sea and the country has many lakes and marshes. The Suez Canal has changed the eastern side of the delta which may, in 1222 B.C., have consisted of a chain of lakes and marshes connecting the present Bitter Lakes with Lake Manzala.

This line of marshy land must have appeared to the Israelites to be a possible refuge from the chariots. Scholars tell us that the words used in Exodus do not mean the Red Sea but the Reed Sea, suggesting a lake with rushes in it. Beyond the marshes, it is scarcely more than thirty miles to the mountains of Sinai, equally unsuitable for vehicles.

It is true that the objective of the shepherds was Beersheba. But Beersheba was a hundred and fifty miles away across a sandy plain. If a column of chariots pursued them, the refugees would be exterminated in these plains. The shepherds, therefore, escaped southwards down the line of lakes, passing east of modern Suez, whence they crossed to the mountains. They probably often moved out in spring to graze their sheep and would have been familiar with the country. The pursuing column blundered into marshy ground, where the vehicles sank up to their axles.

We may notice also that, when the Israelites escaped, they were accompanied by a "mixed multitude", probably different groups of Syrian and Palestinian shepherds. There were with them also "flocks and herds, even very much cattle".[19] Cattle must mean sheep, as cows could not live in Sinai. This passage, in the Jerusalem Bible, is translated, "People of various sorts joined them in great numbers; there were flocks too and herds in immense droves."

When the fugitives reached the mountains of southern Sinai, they were safe from the chariots but the area is extremely arid, with no

---

[18] Exodus II, 23.
[19] Exodus XII, 38.

towns. They had brought some flour with them on their donkeys but, when they reached Sinai, most of it had been eaten. In spring, shepherds may almost live on the milk of their flocks for a week or two, but at other times they need bread.

Barley or wheat can only be obtained from a farming area. As a result, shepherds have to move to such a district at intervals. Here they sell some lambs or wool and with the proceeds they buy barley or wheat. But there are no villages in southern Sinai, so they turned on Moses and demanded bread. To the shepherd, his sheep are his capital and cannot, except rarely, be killed for food.

While they were in southern Sinai, Moses retired to one of the mountain peaks to meditate and once again received a divine revelation. As a result, he recorded the ten commandments on tablets of stone, the only writing material available. If Moses had been educated by the priests of Heliopolis, he may well have been able to write. An Ark was made in which the tablets of stone were deposited and which was carried with the people when they moved camp. The Ark is of interest because archaeologists state that Egyptian priests also carried the symbols of their gods in arks, on the occasion of religious processions. Moses may have copied this Egyptian practice.

We close this chapter, leaving our refugees in the mountains of Sinai, safe from the fighting vehicles indeed, but with little food or water.

NOTABLE DATES

Abraham *circa* 1850–1800 B.C.
The Exodus *circa* 1222 B.C.

CONCLUSIONS

(1) It seems doubtful whether Abraham and his donkey bedouins really wanted land. They were still in tents nine hundred years after him. The present account was probably written some nine hundred years after Abraham.
(2) Impoverished nomads still camp along the east side of the Delta, but the Suez Canal has changed the topography.
(3) There are no records for a period of four hundred years from the Patriarchs to Moses. We cannot know if the Israelites of Moses' time were descended from Abraham. He was, doubtless, the theoretical ancestor of the tribe but a

good deal of intermarriage must have taken place. Joseph, for example, had an Egyptian wife.

(4) Rameses II, like every ruler of Egypt until Lord Cromer, used forced labour on public works.

(5) Moses had a genuine spiritual experience at the Burning Bush. Before this, the Israelites had never heard of Yahweh, who was to become the god of Israel. Again on Mount Sinai, Moses had a spiritual visitation.

II

The Lord Yahweh

To anticipate somewhat at this point, I would maintain that Israel's religion can best be typified by one word, by a name: Yahweh. It is this that dominates completely all the source material that we possess ... This name occurs more frequently than any other noun or verb in the book. It has been calculated that it is used more than 6800 times, as against the 2500 occurrences of the general word for "god", Elohim.
    Th. C. Vriezen, *The Religion of Ancient Israel*

An emphasis upon ties of kinship, and a lack of attachment to fixed sanctuaries, are reasonable assumptions for the religion of an unsettled group of semi-nomads.
    R. E. Clements, *Abraham and David*

II

WHEN the Israelites reached Sinai, Jethro came to greet Moses, bringing his wife and children. Moses told him all that Yahweh had done in rescuing Israel from Egypt. And Jethro replied, " 'Now I know that Yahweh is greater than all the gods ... ' Then Jethro ... offered a holocaust and sacrifices to God; and Aaron came with all the elders of Israel to share the meal with [Jethro]."[1] This passage suggests that Jethro, the priest of Midian, was senior to Moses in the worship of Yahweh. He conducts the service, while Moses, Aaron and the elders constitute the congregation. It will be recalled that Moses was living with Jethro when he saw the Burning Bush.

We are told that the Israelites had never heard of Yahweh before the Burning Bush.[2] It seems, therefore, possible that Moses heard of Yahweh from Jethro. It may be argued that Jethro learned about Yahweh from Moses, but then Moses would have been the authority and Jethro his disciple. Yet, when the thanksgiving service was offered, it was Jethro who officiated and Moses joined the congregation.

William Neil[3] comments upon this account, "many scholars have noted that the impression left by this narrative is that Jethro is represented, not so much as a humble convert to the worship of Yahweh ... but rather as a religious dignitary who is treated with marked respect by Moses ... If Yahweh were the god of Sinai, worshipped by the Midianites or the Kenites, and if Jethro was his chief priest, Moses' father-in-law would be receiving no more than his due if he were treated with the utmost respect by all the Israelites."

But in the next paragraph, William Neil seems to be alarmed at his own temerity. "The Old Testament ... singles out Moses," he writes, "as the creative mind which God used to mediate a new conception of himself, albeit under an old name, to the people of his choice. At the Burning Bush, Moses was singled out not by an imaginary tribal deity of an obscure Midianite clan, but by the Lord of Creation." I could not omit this passage owing to its delightful human snobbishness.

---

[1] Exodus XVIII, 8 to 12. Jerusalem Bible.
[2] Exodus VI, 3.
[3] Rev. William Neil, *One Volume Bible Commentary*.

What a pity Jethro was not related to Pharaoh. But the Lord of Creation has a way of using obscure people. On a subsequent occasion, He even chose a village Carpenter in preference to Caesar Augustus.

Can Israelite monotheism have been evolved from pagan polytheism, asks a modern Bible commentator,[4] and answers in the negative. Therefore, it is argued, it must have been revealed directly by God to Moses alone, and by him to Israel alone. Archaeology, we are told, has shown that the surrounding nations were all polytheistic. This is indisputable, but archaeology deals in cities and inscriptions, and cannot tell us about the religion of the tent dwellers of Sinai. William Neil himself later on tells us that the prophets and psalmists always looked back to the desert days as the high water mark of Israel's obedience to God, when "a simple faith in Yahweh walked hand in hand with an austere code of morality".[5] He continues, "the life of a bedouin tribe, with its simple demands, its communal ownership of the necessities of life, its wholesome attitude to sex and generally uncomplicated existence was one in which such provisions as those contained in the Decalogue would seem in no sense unrealistic. Indeed, we may hazard a guess that part of the background of Moses' call to the service of Yahweh was the glaring contrast presented to his mind between the sensuous and amoral polytheism, which he had come to know at close quarters in Egypt, and the healthy piety and morality which he found among the Kenite worshippers of Yahweh."

This passage seems perfectly reasonable, though generally unwelcome to clerical writers, for it reflects on the belief that God first revealed Himself to Moses, who thereby made his followers into "God's people". It does not appear to me that this question affects the Christian religion. Some churches, however, having accepted that God's revelation to Moses was original and unique, the truth of Christianity is now sometimes thought to depend on this point. Many commentators have agreed that early Israelite religion took its origin from the desert. "There are indications," writes Ronald Clements, "that Kadesh was the centre of the cult of Yahweh, who was venerated in pre-Israelite times as the God of Sinai—Horeb."[6]

The possibility that the religion of Israel came from the desert is

---

[4] G. E. Wright, *The Old Testament against its environment.*
[5] Rev. William Neil, *One Volume Bible Commentary.*
[6] R. E. Clements, *Abraham and David*, quoting J. Gray, *The Desert Sojourn of the Hebrews and the Sinai-Horeb tradition.*

increased by some findings of Sir Flinders Petrie.[7] At Tel al Ajjul (old Gaza), he found a number of small single rooms, "isolated from other buildings, entirely plastered and whitewashed, without any decoration or colour, nor image or place for an image. Marking the purpose of such rooms, there is outside the door a raised bench about a foot high, the top of which, a yard square, is covered with white sea shells, embedded; it slopes to a drain ... Such a place is obviously for washing the feet before entering the shrine, and from the bench the worshipper could step on to the white plastered floor of the shrine." Sir Flinders dates these shrines without idols at between 2000 B.C. and 1600 B.C., that is between four and eight hundred years before Moses.

A more exciting find was Serabit al Khadim in Sinai, a few miles from the ancient Rephidim, where Jethro met Moses. It was the remains of a temple, estimated at about 1500 B.C., or three centuries before Moses.[8] "A square tank of stone stood outside the door. In the square court there was a circular basin of stone, surrounded by four pillars which carried a roof over it. A third tank was in a further court, also surrounded by four pillars. Here is the prototype of the Brazen Sea in the court of the Jewish temple,[9] and of the Hanafiyeh tank in the court of an Islamic mosque.

"None of these provisions for ablution belong to any Egyptian temples, nor to temples or shrines north of Gaza; this is an Arabian system which has survived for 4000 years or more, without any images or sculpture ...

"Further, in the Serabit temple there were innumerable burnt offerings from which a deep layer of ashes was thrown out; but no bones were with these, so the ashes were from scarifices consumed by the worshippers, and not from whole burnt offerings. In the shrines of Serabit three incense altars were found ... Thus it is fruitless to try to delimit the beginning of ablutions or altars of incense in the Jewish system, for the cognate Arab tribes were using them before the Exodus ... This prototype in the North Arabian shrines removes any need of debate as to when Israel renounced images for worship; they were never in that system, though readily adopted later from Canaanite customs."[10]

The discovery of this imageless place of worship, of the same design as the later temple of Jerusalem, at the place where Jethro met Moses

---

[7] Sir Flinders Petrie, *Palestine and Israel*.
[8] Map 2, p. 27.
[9] II Kings XXV, 13.
[10] Sir Flinders Petrie, *Palestine and Israel*.

coming out of Egypt, increases the probability that it was his father-in-law who was God's instrument in converting Moses to the idol-less worship of Yahweh. Perhaps Jethro, the priest of Midian, made his burnt offerings, subsequently eaten by Aaron and the elders of Israel, in this very temple.

But perhaps the most dramatic feature of the resemblance of north Arabian religion to that of the early Israelites is that the shrine in Mecca consisted of a small cube-shaped building, containing no idol or image, like the Holy of Holies in Jerusalem. Another resemblance was that Israelites and desert Arabs both practised circumcision. Abraham, coming from northern Syria, only learned about circumcision when he arrived south of Hebron.

Unfortunately, while Moses lived about 1225 B.C., the first detailed knowledge we have of Arabian religion is at the time of Muhammad, nearly two thousand years later. One Bible commentator rejects the idea that the Sinai religion came from Arabia on the grounds that, in Muhammad's time, the Arabians were "typical polytheists".

This is not entirely accurate. Firstly, our knowledge of Arabian religion is two thousand years after Moses, as long as from the life of Christ to ourselves. Secondly, Arabian religion did not carve stones to imitate living beings, except perhaps for a few statues brought from Roman Syria. The "gods" of Mecca were spirits, who could act as intermediaries between God and man. Muhammad never calls his enemies idolaters, but always "associaters". They associated minor spirits with the one God.

The minor spirits, however, never married nor did the supreme God, whereas most, if not all polytheistic systems, made their gods marry and have children. In this absence of sex, the Arabian religion resembled that of Sinai.

Further evidence is provided by the Book of Job, a monotheistic discussion which never mentions Israel. The raiding of Job's camels presupposes a desert country. It has been suggested that Job may have been a resident of Tebuk or Teima.[11] Other preachers of monotheism in Arabia are also mentioned by Muhammad in the Qoran.

It seems possible, therefore, that the religion of Sinai was not a sudden new revelation, but the result of a long process of development, dating back for centuries in northern Arabia. Such a hypothesis is in accordance with the method of God's working throughout all history. The alternative theory states that the revelation made to

[11] Map 20, p. 174.

Moses was original and unique—a sudden leap forward in human development.

* * *

I believe that Moses underwent a genuine religious experience on Sinai. History is full of such spiritual calls, resulting in the complete rededication of the lives of the people concerned. To Christians, the conversion of St. Paul and of St. Francis of Assisi are perhaps the best known. When Moses came down from Sinai, "the skin on his face shone so much that they would not venture near him". This luminosity is a known peculiarity of ecstasy. When St. Teresa of Avila had been in ecstasy, we are told "her face shone like candles".

* * *

When considering the religion of ancient Israel, we have to remember two things. Firstly, while Moses may have been a saint and a genius, the tribesmen were ignorant shepherds. Whatever revelations Moses may have received, the ordinary Israelite thought of Yahweh as the god of the tribe, who would go up with them personally to battle against other tribes, whose gods would, of course, fight for them.

Secondly, the general condition of mental and spiritual development among the shepherds was very different from that of the prophets five hundred years later, and from that of the Jerusalem priests, who ultimately edited and produced our version of the Old Testament. It is absurd, to say "Israel in Sinai believed this or that", and to quote Amos or Isaiah to prove it. It would be no more ridiculous to claim that the English, in William the Conqueror's time, knew that the earth was a globe, and to quote Sir Isaac Newton as proof.

The idea that "Judaism" was revealed in its spiritual completeness to Moses is contrary to all human experience. Everything in life grows and changes continuously. The argument is that Moses received a revelation from God, which must have been final and complete, for God cannot change. In fact, however, the recipient of a revelation, as we have seen, can only absorb as much as his knowledge permits.

But the intellectual is the least important aspect of revelation. An ignorant man can be set on fire by a touch of the Divine Spirit, even though his *intellectual* conception of God is entirely wrong. I suggest that Moses was a spiritual genius, but that the shepherds were just men of their time and country. A little of the genius of Moses touched some of them, just as happened to the contemporaries of St. Francis or of Wesley.

I see no proof in the narrative that the Sinai shepherds thought themselves to be superior to any other tribes. The narrative records an agreement between Yahweh and these shepherds, who regarded him henceforward as their tribal god, just as Chemosh was the god of the Moabites. The misunderstanding, if such it be, occurred a thousand years later, when the word Yahweh was changed to "the Lord", as we shall see.

* * *

It is not surprising that it took forty years for Moses to mould this heterogeneous gathering of shepherds into a cohesive group. Exodus tells us that, when they left Egypt, they were a mixed multitude, though the "sons of Israel", Moses' own clan, took the lead.

Unfortunately, from Exodus XXI to Numbers XX,[12] there are seventy-eight chapters apparently describing the ritual and furniture of the Jerusalem temple before the Babylonian Captivity, with a great deal of legislation, applicable to agricultural life. After the destruction of the Temple, the priests recorded these details, to preserve them for a future revival. This mass of extraneous material conceals the vivid and natural impression of the narrative of the shepherds in Sinai.

Shepherds, as we have seen, grazed along the verges of the cultivation. In spring, they moved into the villages, sold their lambs, wool, butter and oil, and bought in return grain to make bread. There were no agricultural communities in Sinai, so they soon had no bread. The nearest area producing grain was Beersheba. They consequently moved to that area, probably watering in the Wadi Araba on the way.[13] They camped, we are told, at Kadesh Barnea, thought to be the modern Ain Qudeis.

A stele of Pharaoh Merneptah, the son of Rameses II, has been discovered in Egypt, describing an expedition to Palestine. The Pharaoh claims to have defeated the Hittites, the Canaanites and the Hurrians, adding, "Israel is scattered, his seed is not." In the case of the other peoples, their cities are mentioned, but no town accompanies the reference to Israel. This is the first mention of Israel outside the Old Testament. The date may be about 1220 B.C.

[12] Except for Numbers X-XIV, which returns to the narrative.
[13] Map 2, p. 27. Araba has three short syllables.

It seems that, no towns being given, Israel was still in tents in Sinai. Having camped in the Beersheba plains to buy grain, the shepherds may have been surprised and overrun by the Egyptian chariots. I have seen shepherd camps overrun by such mounted charges. Everybody scatters wildly, making for any hills or ravines. The sheep, the donkeys and the tents are abandoned. But charioteers could not load up sheep or tents. At night the shepherds would return and round up what animals were left. The camps would, in any case, be widely spread for better grazing, and many of them would escape unnoticed.

The tribes in the area were Kenites, Jethro's tribe, Kenizzites and Calebites, who may have been worshippers of Yahweh before the Israelites. Kenites are later found with Israelites in Palestine. The Calebites also threw in their lot with Israel, and eventually took Hebron, and were incorporated in Judah.

It may be remarked that at Kadesh Barnea, Israel was in "Abraham country". According to Genesis, as we now have it, this area had been promised to Abraham. Yet in the part of the narrative describing the arrival of the community south of Hebron, there is no reference at all to Abraham. Were the Israelites at this time unaware of the promises to Abraham?

Some scholars have pointed out that, from the end of Genesis to the Babylonian Captivity, Abraham is scarcely mentioned. Only when Israel had ceased to exist did the promises to Abraham assume importance.

* * *

The Old Testament attributes the abandonment of the attack in the south to orders from Yahweh. The southern coastal plain was the most densely populated and progressive area in Palestine. The mountains from Judaea to Samaria (to use later names), however, were poor and thinly populated. An attack from the east would, therefore, be easier. The Israelite shepherds may well have spent forty years as nomads in the Kadesh Barnea–Wadi Araba area. No details are included in the narrative.

A new generation had then grown up in the desert. The hardness of their lives, the leadership of Moses and their belief in Yahweh as a war leader, had consolidated them. Moses decided to move northwards and try again. Edom and Moab being unfriendly they made a detour to the east. In Hisma (modern name), they were bitten by serpents. The area still has a reputation today for poisonous snakes.[14]

[14] Map 2, p. 27. See Numbers XXI, 6 to 9.

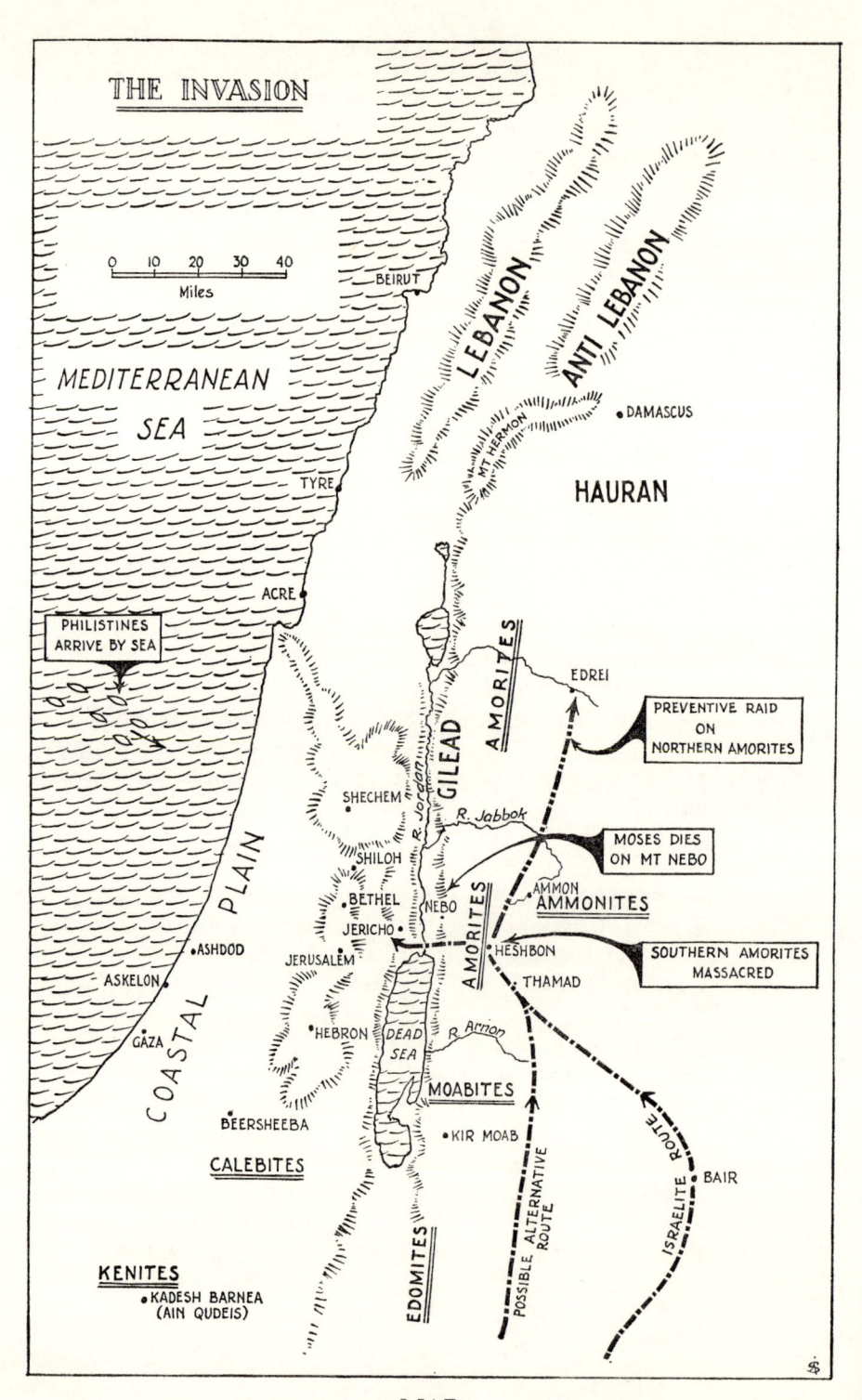

MAP 3

Many places cannot be identified but Beer could be Bair, a well in the right position. When I was in Jordan, a desert fort was built on this well, which is exactly as described.[15] Being in the bed of a narrow valley, it silts up when not in use and has to be re-dug by the next arrivals.

The range of mountains east of the Jordan valley was at the time divided between a number of tribal groups. There were Amorites in the Hauran, and on the mountains of Gilead as far south as the Arnon. East of them were the Ammonites, round modern Amman. South of the Arnon was the smaller tribal group of Moab, and then Edom. The Israelites overran the southern Amorite group, the name of whose "king" (or tribal shaikh) was Sihon, who lived at Heshbon (modern Hesban). By this means, they reached the crest of the mountains, overlooking the Jordan valley.

The country south of Damascus was also inhabited by Amorites, who might come to the help of their kinsmen. The Israelites, therefore, turned quickly northwards and raided them before they could prepare. The Amorites were defeated at Edrei, the modern Deraa. All of them were apparently massacred.

Moab was alarmed and their chief sent for Balaam, a prophet who seems to have been living on the Euphrates in northern Syria. It is interesting to hear that he was a priest of Yahweh, a fact which suggests once more that Yahweh was the god of desert tribes. As the Israelites were also worshippers of Yahweh, Balaam could not curse them.

Deuteronomy summarises the narrative from Egypt to the arrival in Moab, in the form of speeches attributed to Moses. Further legislation follows and then two more discourses by Moses. Most of this material is now believed to date from some five hundred years later. The only writing materials at this period were slabs of stone or baked bricks, impossible to carry about on donkeys.

Moses died and was buried on Mount Nebo.[16] The Israelites then descended the steep slopes of the mountains, a drop of nearly four thousand feet, and camped on the floor of the rift valley, opposite Jericho.

The Old Testament says that Israel had six hundred thousand men of military age, which would give a total population of two millions. Flinders Petrie explains the difficulty by comparing the numerals used in 1220 B.C. with those employed some five centuries later. He traces certain numerals used in the early period and finds them

---

[15] Numbers XXI, 16 to 19.
[16] Map 3, p. 40.

closely to resemble those employed at the later date with quite a different meaning. Making the necessary corrections, he reduces the ages of the patriarchs and the numbers of the Israelites to normal proportions.

However the errors occurred, most modern scholars believe that the Israelites had some five thousand fighting men, giving a total population of fifteen or sixteen thousand. Seeing that they could all drink from one well, and that they marched round Jericho seven times in one morning, there can scarcely have been more.

CONCLUSIONS

(1) There seem to be many indications that the simple worship of Yahweh was practised in Sinai, and perhaps in all northern Arabia, before the Exodus, and that Moses learned it from Jethro. My own belief is that Moses received a genuine spiritual visitation at the Burning Bush, but that he attributed it to Yahweh. Intellectual misconceptions do not invalidate a spiritual experience.

(2) Yahweh worship was simple, as was inevitably the case with nomads. A distinctive feature of his cult was the prohibition of images. Temples dedicated to him included a holy, cube-shaped building, empty of images. Complicated temples, idols and statues could not be carried by nomads.

(3) Moses was doubtless a religious genius, and his visions at the Burning Bush and on Sinai were genuine spiritual experiences. The ordinary Israelites, however, thought of Yahweh as their war chief who would lead them in battle. In Sinai, they met the Kenites, who had long worshipped Yahweh and who probably recommended him to the Israelites as a commander. It is difficult for us to understand the uncomplicated ideas of such simple people.

(4) The whole narrative from Egypt to Moab is extraordinarily fresh and vivid. It is, however, complicated by large blocks of later material describing the cult of the Jerusalem temple and the laws governing an agricultural community.

III

The Conquest

"My angel will go before you and lead you to where the Amorites are and the Hittites, the Perizzites, the Canaanites, the Hivites, the Jebusites; I shall exterminate these . . . I shall spread panic ahead of you; I shall throw into confusion all the people you encounter; I shall make all your enemies turn and run from you . . . yes, I shall deliver the inhabitants of the country into your hands, and you will drive them out before you . . . Moses went and told the people all the commands of Yahweh . . . All the people said with one voice, 'We will observe all the commands that Yahweh has decreed.' "

Exodus XXIII, 23 to 32, XXIV, 3
Jerusalem Bible

"When Israel had finished killing all the inhabitants of Ai in the open ground . . . all Israel returned to Ai and slaughtered all its people. The number of those who fell that day, men and women together, was twelve thousand."

Joshua VIII, 24, 25

III

WE may pause here in the narrative to consider the meanings of the various names used for God. The Hebrew name Yahweh is that most often employed. Many centuries later, perhaps about 300 B.C., Israelite elders decided that the word Yahweh was too sacred for daily use. They replaced it by Adonai, which means lord. When, soon afterwards, the Pentateuch was translated into Greek, Adonai was translated as *kyrios*, which means literally "lord". In Latin, *kyrios* became *dominus*. In English translations, *kyrios* and *dominus* became the Lord, a term unquestioningly accepted as meaning the Creator of the Universe.

In their new translation, published in 1966, the Dominican Fathers have returned to the use of Yahweh. To me, the impression produced by their Jerusalem Bible was overwhelming. Where he is addressing Moses or the Israelites, the phrase used is, "I am Yahweh, your god." In the third person, he is "Yahweh, the god of Israel." The shepherds seemed to regard Yahweh as a god who had chosen them, and had promised to march at their head to destroy other tribes, each, of course, under command of its own god.

We have already agreed that Moses probably had a genuine spiritual experience. How could this happen, it may be asked, if he thought he was speaking to a local tribal god? I venture to suggest that God may be indifferent to our *intellectual* conceptions, although we attribute great importance to them. After all, the minds of men compared to God are infinitely smaller than the minds of mosquitoes compared to men. Might not God reveal Himself to a man who is prepared to give dedicated service, even if his *intellectual* idea of God was ridiculous?

But whatever Moses himself believed, the shepherds visualised Yahweh as their war leader. The Christian today, however, is perplexed to read of "the Lord" ordering the massacre of every living thing. In the description of the fall of Jericho, we are told that everything alive in the town was killed, "men and women, young and old, even the oxen and sheep and donkeys, massacring them all".[1] The same story is repeated again and again. Can these endless massacres and brutalities have been specifically ordered by that God whose very nature is Love?

[1] Joshua VI, 21. Jerusalem Bible.

By changing the name Yahweh into "the Lord", the translators have placed Christians in a dilemma ever since. Christian apologists have been hard put to it to explain away this apparent paradox. "The Canaanites were very wicked," is the most usual line of approach. "Such people deserved to be exterminated." It is impossible now to estimate the degree of their "wickedness". But even if they were sexually immoral—the usual charge—it would fare ill for us today if all persons with lax sexual morals were to be massacred.

The so-called ritual prostitution practised in Palestine in 1200 B.C. was common to many agricultural peoples of the time. It was based on imitative magic. To produce an effect, it was necessary to simulate it. The rain-maker sprinkled water on the ground in imitation of rain. Human sexual relations similarly stimulated the fertility of the fields. I have told elsewhere[2] of a pious Muslim in Spain who, in the twelfth century A.D. wrote a book on agriculture. "In former times", he says, "it was believed that if a man slept with a virgin underneath a barren tree, it would bear a heavy crop of fruit." Although Abu Zakariya hastens to disclaim any such superstitions, the idea must have persisted for two thousand years after Joshua or he could not have heard of it. The Canaanites and the Amorites were thus in error as to the facts of agriculture, in common with most of their farming contemporaries. Did their error merit a policy of genocide?

In the preface to the 1952 edition of the Revised Standard Version of the Bible, the committee of translators explained why they continued to use the expression "the Lord", in preference to the original Hebrew word "Yahweh". "The use of any proper name for the one and only God, as though there were other gods from whom He had to be distinguished, was discontinued in Judaism before the Christian era and is entirely inappropriate for the universal faith of the Christian Church."

The solution adopted by the translators was to change the name of the tribal god to that of the Creator of the Universe, thereby attributing to the God of Love the savage mentality which the nomads imparted to their tribal deity. To read the Pentateuch in the Jerusalem Bible is, to me, to receive the overwhelming impression that the originators of these traditions had no conception of the God of the Universe.

Their world was limited by Egypt, Syria, the Euphrates and the desert. If the world stretched beyond that, they were not interested. To let the sheep eat their fill, to care for the lambs, to milk the

[2] J. B. Glubb, *The Lost Centuries*.

ewes, to keep the wolves at bay—these duties, not theology, occupied their waking hours. They praised Yahweh their god when things went well, and grumbled against him when times were bad. I doubt if their religion went further.

The nomadic life is incredibly bare. A rough tent little larger than a double bed. No artificial lighting or lamps. The whole population is illiterate and no writing materials exist. To such people dogma is impossible. Cult and ritual need buildings. Theology cannot exist where no one can read or write.

"How is it that Yahweh, the only God, is the God of Israel," asks the introduction to the Jerusalem Bible. "That among all the nations of the earth Israel should be his people? The Pentateuch answers: because to Israel the divine promise was made." But this is no answer at all. "God chose Israel because He had promised to choose Israel."

Conscientious Christians have considered themselves obliged to justify the actions of these shepherds, "God's Chosen People", "The People of God". They express an admiration for their faithfulness in the desert which does not seem to be justified by the Pentateuch, which continually denounces their faithlessness.

We are told that the qualities of the early Israelites were unique in the ancient world. Their consideration for the poor is said to be without parallel. "Other religions, Zoroastrianism and Muhammadanism for example, know of the Divine power, holiness and goodness. But a righteousness that loves the weak and the outcast, a mercy and righteousness directed towards those whom the world passes by—that is phenomenal and unique."[3]

In so far as Islam is concerned, this sweeping generalisation seems to me completely erroneous. Chapter XC of the Qoran, verse 13 onwards, describes the conduct which earns God's favour. "It is the setting free of a slave, or the giving of food in a day of hunger to an orphan who draws near, or to the poor man lying in the dust." So considerate is Islam for the poor and the weak that some modern writers have seen it as a revolt of the poor against the rich.

These well-meant attempts to justify God's "choice" by depicting the early Israelites as uniquely virtuous in a wicked world seem quite unbiblical. In Deuteronomy IX, 6, we read, "Be in fact sure, then, that it is not for any goodness of yours that Yahweh gives you this rich land to possess, for you are a headstrong people. Remember; never forget how you provoked Yahweh your god in the wilderness."

[3] G. Ernest Wright, *The Old Testament against its environment*.

Having been taught from childhood that the primitive Israelites in Sinai were "God's own people", it is difficult now to be objective. With all humility, I can only submit my own impressions. Having lived with such nomads, I find the Exodus account so true, so vivid, and so natural, that I am obliged to accept it. There is no need to explain it by miracles, divine intervention, or a chosen people of God.

* * *

Just before the arrival of the Israelites at Jericho, the Philistines had established themselves on the southern coastal plain. They were sea-borne invaders from Crete and the Aegean, probably driven out by a northern conquering race, the Dorians. Other groups arrived in Egypt and Lebanon at the same time. The Philistines were considerably more advanced than the Israelites.

* * *

The Book of Joshua seems to be a saga, written perhaps long afterwards, in praise of the hero. The Book of Judges gives a different and more factual account. After the capture of Jericho, a village of less than two thousand inhabitants, covering some six acres, the Israelites moved up a spur of the mountains above Jericho to Bethel. This spur is still the only easy way up the mountains, between almost unbroken cliff faces on the north and south. The top of the mountain range from Bethel (the modern Beitin) to Gibeon (modern Al Jib) is more flat and open than most of the chain of mountains from Hebron to Shechem, and was well cultivated with numerous villages. Some of these belonged to the Gibeonites, a clan which had come to an agreement with Joshua, while he was still in Jericho. Opposite the sloping spur leading up to Bethel was a correspondingly easy way down the western slope of the mountains through Beth Horon (now Beit Aur) to the coastal plain. At the head of this descent to Beth Horon was Gibeon, which was thus strategically placed. This well populated little plain formed a certain barrier between the more arid and rocky mountains to the south and the country extending northwards to Shechem, the modern Nablus.

Joshua X states that the Jebusite King of Jerusalem called upon the rulers of the Hebron area and of Lachish and Eglon in the western foothills and went up to attack Gibeon, an important centre of communications, which had literally sold the pass by making a separate treaty with the Israelites. Joshua, however, came to the aid of his new allies and defeated the southern chiefs, pursuing them

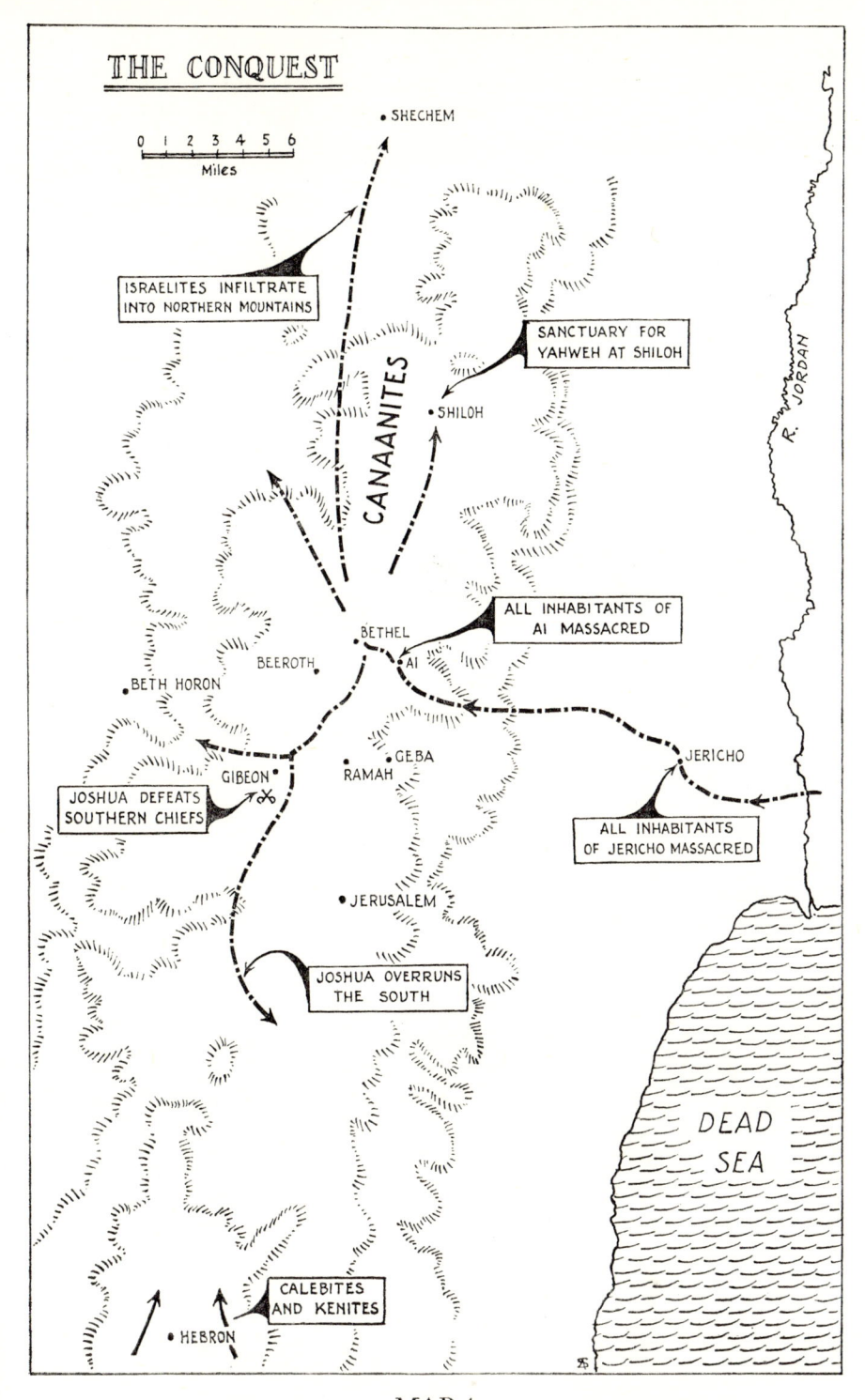

MAP 4

down the descent of Beth Horon. These Hebron tribes are, in Joshua X, described as Amorites. Profiting by this victory, he overran the hill country to the south.

Either before this incident, or at about the same time, the Kenites, the tribe of Moses' father-in-law, and the followers of Caleb,[4] invaded Hebron from the south. These tribes, it will be remembered, were semi-nomadic in the Beersheba-Sinai area, and were probably worshippers of Yahweh before the Exodus. Hereafter, though not present at Mount Sinai, they became integrated into the tribe of Judah, which occupied the Hebron area.

Whereas the Book of Joshua depicts him as having conquered all the mountain range from Hebron to Shechem, and as then surveying it and dividing it up between the tribes, the Book of Judges tells a more realistic story. It depicts the various tribes, each acting independently and trying to seize an area for itself, often by coming to an agreement with the existing inhabitants. Judges I, 29, for example, says, "Ephraim did not drive out the Canaanites who dwelt in Gezer; but the Canaanites dwelt in Gezer among them." And again, "Asher did not drive out the Canaanites, but the Asherites dwelt among the Canaanites, the inhabitants of the land." In most translations, the people of the land are said to have been subjected to forced labour. Ronald Knox,[5] however, translates, surely more correctly, "they forced them to pay tribute".

The majority of modern scholars believe that there was little or no fighting north of Bethel at this stage. The Israelites infiltrated into the country and came to terms with the inhabitants. This may have been, in some cases, because the villagers preferred to pay tribute to the nomads and be able to cultivate their fields. Such arrangements have existed from time immemorial in the Middle East and indeed were only superseded in the 1920s. Nomads, though few in numbers, had a great potential for causing trouble. Farmers, who wanted to scatter over their fields to work, were often prepared to pay tribute in return for freedom to carry on their activities unmolested.

Scholars in a settled and organised society (even under Solomon, but much more so in modern Europe) assume a much greater degree of organisation than could exist in a nomadic community. A federation of twelve tribes, they say, presupposes a treaty.[6] The Book of Joshua describes him as allotting land and fixing tribal boundaries—

---

[4] p. 39.
[5] Holy Bible, trans. by Ronald Knox.
[6] John Bright, *A History of Israel*.

ideas current in a settled agricultural community but incompatible with nomadic life. Like so much else in the Pentateuch, these passages must have been written centuries later. The best description of nomadic society is in the last verse of Judges, "In those days there was no king in Israel and every man did as he pleased."

* * *

We have seen that, before the Exodus, Egypt had frequently intervened in Palestine and had, indeed, ruled Syria for several periods. Just before the Israelite invasion, however, Egypt, owing to the collapse of the nineteenth dynasty, had fallen into anarchy and evacuated Palestine.

Henceforward, there was no unifying force to organise an army, and each little tribe or village was left to provide for its own defence. In the absence of a central government, nomads possessed the extraordinary advantage of mobility. Accustomed to travel across the desert with their flocks and families, they could move like a single mobile division. The settled population, grouped in towns and villages with no common leader, were unable to put a joint force in the field. Thus the nomads, though few in numbers, could always achieve numerical superiority at any one point.

There are, of course, no census figures and our estimates are no more than guesses, but the population of Palestine could perhaps have been half a million. Most of these would have been in the coastal plain but we might allot a hundred thousand to the mountains. The Israelites had only five thousand fighting men, making them a small minority compared to the settled peoples. The inhabitants of Jericho, fighting alone, were probably less than two thousand, against whom the invaders could bring five thousand men. Thus, moving forward in a group, they were able to overwhelm each little town or tribe in succession.

I happened to live for several years in a district of southern Iraq, where a similar phenomenon had occurred. The old Arab historians reported the existence of a nomadic tribe called the Muntifik, in the desert south of the Euphrates in the twelfth century A.D. In A.D. 1124, for example, they raided Basra. Probably in the thirteenth or fourteenth century A.D., they crossed the Euphrates into the cultivated area. The nomads, who were only a fraction of the settled population, conquered one small tribe after another. Camping on the fringe of the cultivation, or on waste land between villages, they obliged the cultivators to pay them tribute.

About 1600, the Muntfik were the undisputed rulers of the area and were spoken of as princes. They rebelled against Ottoman rule and the cultivators fought under the command of the Muntfik "dynasty". These former nomads, however, still remained in their tents, looking down with some condescension on their subjects. In 1922, I myself went to live in the Muntifik area. The nomads were still living in tents and collecting tribute from the cultivators. This was some five hundred years after their original arrival from the desert. The system has only broken down in the last forty years.

The Beni Sakhr tribe was nomadic in the Hejaz in the fourteenth century A.D., when they are mentioned there as paying tribute to the Mamlooks of Egypt. In the fifteenth or sixteenth centuries, they appeared in the desert east of the Jordan. Today, perhaps four hundred years after their arrival, they own the villages along the fringe of the desert, which they cultivate with agricultural labourers from the settled area. The majority of Beni Sakhr are still nomadic and live in tents.

Many other similar examples could be quoted. In each case, the number of the nomads is very small compared to that of the settled peoples, but their mobility and close integration enable them to conquer the cultivators, group by group. They then often give their tribal name to the area, although ethnically they form only a small fraction of the inhabitants. They do not quickly take to cultivation, but they continue for centuries to live in their tents, on the tribute they collect from the villagers.

The Israelite invasion of Palestine seems to me to have been one of innumerable such events from pre-historic times down to our own days. I am convinced that the narrative is true because I have seen the same thing happening. If this view be correct, the Israelite invasion was not a unique divine intervention made on behalf of a nomadic group, whom the God of the Universe preferred to all other human beings.

Judges III, 5, puts the resulting situation in a nutshell. "The Israelites lived among the Canaanites, the Hittites, the Amorites, the Perizzites, the Hivites and the Jebusites. They married the daughters of these peoples and gave their own daughters in marriage to their sons, and served their gods."

The phrase, "they dwelt among them", may refer to the fact that they pitched their tents between the villages, as the Muntifik did in Iraq. It also implies that the Israelites were fewer than the "people of the land". We can say that, in the United States, the Red Indians live among the white population, but we cannot say that the whites live among the Red Indians, because the latter are fewer.

Scholars have commented on the fact that, while there seems to have been fighting south of a line from Jericho to Beth Horon, the ridge from Bethel to Shechem seems to have been penetrated without a battle. Some deduce that the tribes in this area were similar to the Israelites and joined them voluntarily. This is doubtless possible, for we saw that the "Israelites" in Egypt were probably a mixed group.

It is equally possible that these farmers preferred to pay tribute and be allowed to go on with their work. In some cases, according to Judges I, the Amorites pushed the invaders back, in others they were obliged to pay tribute, sometimes they just all settled in together. A sanctuary was built for Yahweh in Shiloh and there the Ark was deposited.

The word "judges" does not, of course, mean judicial officials, but war leaders. Henceforward, there is no more fighting with the Canaanites on the mountain range. The Israelites were already integrating with them. War leaders arose when the area was attacked by external neighbours. Normally such local campaigns involved only one or two Israelite tribes under a local war chief, whom most English translations call judges. Except when such a crisis arose, "every man did as he pleased", an idyllic state of society in the opinion of most tribesmen.

CONCLUSIONS

It seems possible that:

(1) The god of Israel, from the Exodus onwards, was Yahweh, who was already worshipped in Sinai and elsewhere, chiefly by desert dwellers.

(2) Nomads were unable to make or carry images, and consequently Yahweh worship did not involve images.

(3) Moses did enjoy spiritual visitations, which we may probably recognise as being from the Divine Spirit, who reveals Himself to all who are willing to serve.

(4) The Israelite tribesmen, however, thought of Yahweh as a warrior, who, in person, would lead them to victory. They were fortunate to have been "chosen" by so efficient a warrior god.

(5) This simple, logical and natural story, if I may say so in all humility, seems to me to have been concealed from us by the fact that the translators rendered Yahweh as "the Lord".

IV

Glorious Days

There is no reason to doubt that the belief in a covenant between Yahweh and David arose very early . . . It was a piece of court theology which proved to be eminently successful in establishing the claims of the Davidic house. The assertions of the divine election of Mount Zion as Yahweh's dwelling place and of David's house to provide Israel's kings, became central features of the religious traditions of Jerusalem.
                        R. E. CLEMENTS, *Abraham and David*

We can hardly look back on any . . . of the kings and priests with much admiration or pride. But the whole world will forever remember the names of Amos, Hosea, Isaiah, Jeremiah, Micah . . . It is the immortal spirit of dauntless moral independence that we revere in the prophets, not the old political independence fought over endlessly, sometimes in self-defence, and sometimes in offensive wars to carve out more territory, to rule over more slaves, to be richer at the expense of neighbours.
                MOSHE MENUHIN, *The Decadence of Judaism in our Time*

IV

THE Philistines were sea-borne invaders from Crete and the Aegean, who established themselves in the coastal plain, as the Israelites had in the mountains. Industrially more advanced than the Israelites, they possessed iron, which they used, with brass and bronze, to make chariots, swords, spears and ploughshares. They rapidly amalgamated with the people of the land, as the Israelites had done in the mountains. Having mastered the southern coastal plain, they moved into the plain of Esdraelon also.[1] Presumably to conciliate the native inhabitants, the Philistines became worshippers of the local god, Dagon. By the middle of the eleventh century B.C., they were forcing their way up into the mountains.

Soon after 1050 B.C., a force of Philistines arrived at Afek in the foothills. The Israelites were driven back in a first skirmish, so they sent for the Ark of Yahweh, which was kept at Shiloh, some twenty-seven miles away.[2] In spite of these precautions, Israel was utterly defeated, and the Ark of Yahweh was captured by the enemy. The Philistines then overran the northern half of the mountains, destroying the shrine at Shiloh. Their force, like that of the Israelites, consisted of unpaid tribal levies, who could turn out for a short campaign, but, after that, must disband themselves to follow their normal avocations. They did not possess a regular army to garrison conquered territory, but seem to have left a few outposts in the mountains.

The Philistines took the Ark of Yahweh to Ashdod, but soon afterwards the people of the town were afflicted with tumours, probably bubonic plague. The Ark was moved to Gath, but there also the people of the town developed tumours. As a propitiation of Yahweh, the Philistines sent away the Ark and with it, as an offering, five model tumours and five rats, all made of gold.[3] It is interesting that the Philistines associated bubonic plague with rats. Europe did not discover the connection until nearly three thousand years later.

In this crisis, the prophet Samuel rose to fame. A man of outstanding character, he lived at Ramah, where he built an altar to Yahweh, after the destruction of Shiloh. Calling on Yahweh for help, he roused in the Israelites the spirit of resistance. Nevertheless,

[1] Map 5, p. 58. [2] I Samuel IV. [3] I Samuel VI

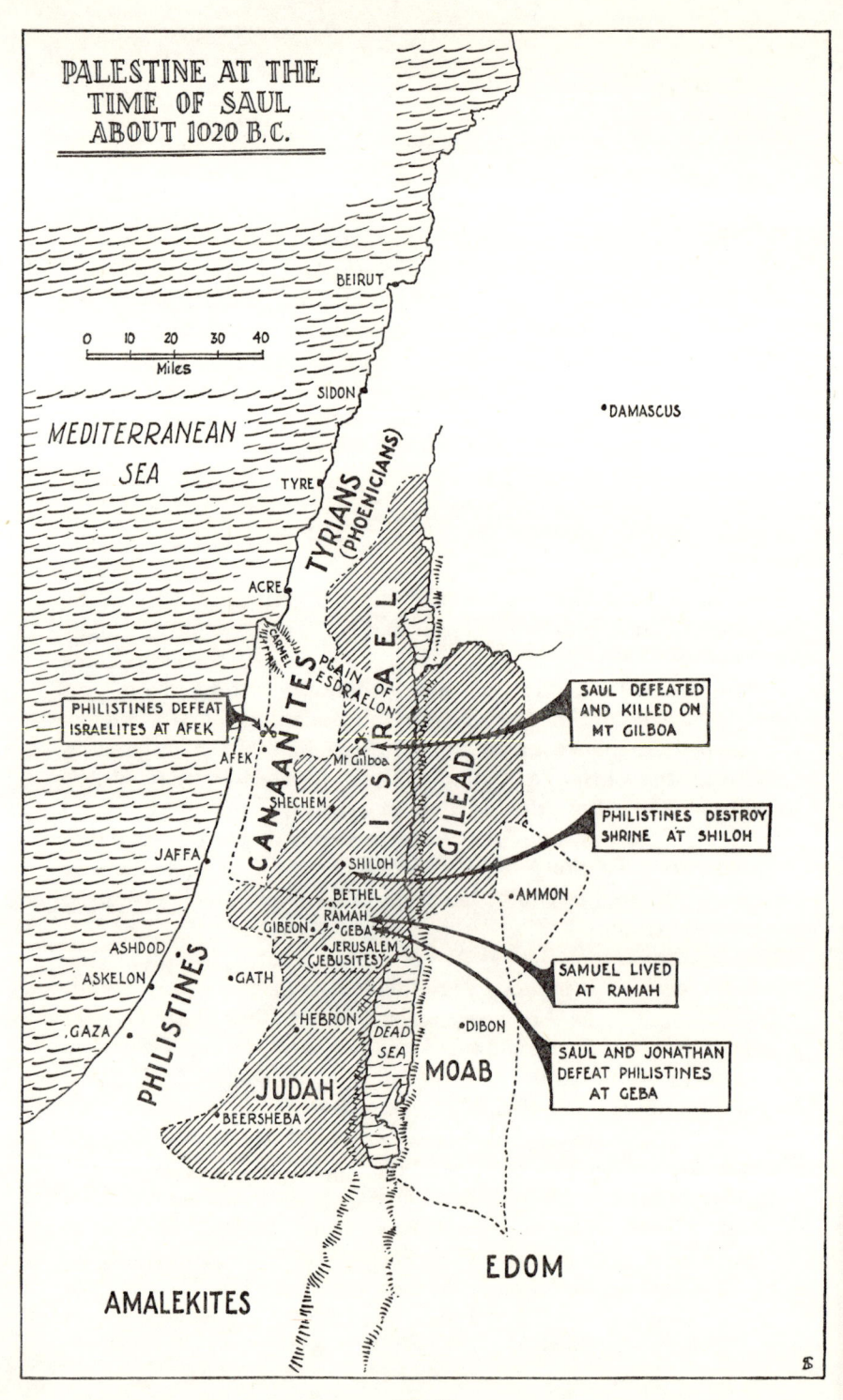

MAP 5

there was no central figure to take the lead. Many tribes had not come at all to the Afek battle. Samuel was growing old and his sons were obviously incapable. As a result, the elders went to Samuel and demanded a king to lead them. I Samuel VIII represents the prophet warning the people against a king. The next chapter, however, represents Samuel as receiving an order from Yahweh to anoint a king.

In Chapter XII, the first attitude reappears, and Samuel tells the people, "what a very wicked thing you have done in the sight of Yahweh by asking to have a king."[4] These contradictory viewpoints, written perhaps a century later, seem to represent, on the one hand, the views of an old tribesman, longing for the old nomadic freedom and, on the other, a royalist, perhaps under Solomon, seeking to represent Yahweh as favourable to monarchy. A later editor combined the two opposing viewpoints.

Saul was, at the time, a splendid young man. Anointed by Samuel, he begins by defeating the Ammonites, but against the Philistines, he can only employ guerrilla tactics. I Samuel XIII, 15, tells us that he had only six hundred men. Largely owing to the initiative of his son, Jonathan, however, he defeats a Philistine force at Geba, five miles north of Jerusalem. This success seems to have loosened the hold of the Philistines in the mountains north of Jerusalem, and allowed Saul to consolidate his position.

Samuel then came to Saul and told him that Yahweh wished to revenge himself on the Amalekites, who had raided the Israelites two hundred years before when they left Egypt. Yahweh, said Samuel, ordered that every man, woman and child be massacred, and also every living animal, ox and sheep, camel and donkey. Saul defeated the Amalekites and killed every human being, regardless of age or sex, with the sole exception of the chief, whom he brought back as a prisoner. He also spared the best of the sheep and the cattle.

Samuel came to meet Saul and denounced his disobedience, because Agag, the Amalekite king, was still alive, and because all the animals had not been slaughtered. "Since you have rejected the word of Yahweh, he has rejected you as king," he said. Samuel then sent for Agag and butchered him with his own hands. This incident is one of those with which Christians are confronted, for most English translations say that the Lord insisted on the massacre.

On the stele of Mesha, King of Moab, found at Dibon (modern

---

[4] I Samuel XII 17. Jerusalem Bible

Dhiban),[5] we read that Chemosh, the god of Moab, was angry because the Moabites had neglected his worship. As a result, he allowed Israel to conquer most of the country. But later he relented and gave the victory to Moab, who captured Ataroth and Nebo, massacring all the inhabitants of both places as an offering to Chemosh.

"One can see that what the Moabites believed about their god offers important parallels to what the Israelites believed about theirs," writes Vriezen. He adds in a note "the researches of Breckelmans would indicate that (as far as we know) this (general massacre) was known in the ancient world—apart from Israel—only in Moab." If this statement be true, it would appear that Israel and Moab were more brutal than any other ancient community. How are we to reconcile this view with that expressed by Dr. G. Ernest Wright, that "a righteousness that loves the weak and the outcast" was peculiar and unique to the ancient Israelites?

Discoveries at Ugarit, near modern Latakiya in Syria, show that here, as in Israel, sheep and oxen were sacrificed, and that such animals had to be without blemish. There were burnt offerings and sacrifices as in Israel, and temple officials, including a high priest. In Ugarit, also, there was an attitude of reverence and "an affectionate attachment to the godhead".[6]

Thus we see that, superficially at least, the religion of the ancient Israelites was, in some ways, like those of the surrounding nations. But we must remember that the religion of Israel itself was always changing, so that the most we can do is to try and describe it at a given moment. The sacrifices of sheep and oxen can only have been introduced under agricultural conditions, because oxen cannot live in the desert. These sacrifices, therefore, were probably copied from the "people of the land".

The religion of the desert days was characterised by the absence of images, by complete devotion to Yahweh and by the absence of sex in the attributes of Yahweh. These, however, may have been characteristics of all simple desert religions of the time. Perhaps the Israelites were more single-minded in their devotion to Yahweh, than, let us say, the Ammonites to Milcom or the Philistines to Dagon. This single-mindedness may have been the seed of monotheism to come. But the corollary of this single-mindedness was intolerance, which, if Vriezen be right, they shared only with Moab.

This peculiar intolerance was to lead to the extraordinary anomaly

---

[5] Map 5, p. 58.
[6] Th. C. Vriezen, *The Religion of Ancient Israel*.

that Christianity, admitting the Old Testament to be inspired as well as the New, was to become a persecuting religion, though all the precepts of Christ were precisely the opposite. We even see the perpetuation of the same intolerance in modern Israel.

With these speculations may be contrasted the view expressed by Rev. William Neil. "The Israelites are a peculiar people unlike any other. Their call and their covenant single them out from any other nation as the chosen instruments of God's purpose."[7] When we reach the end of the narrative, in the rise of rabbinical Judaism and of Christianity, we can look back at the whole story and wonder at its development. But it seems to me wrong to depict the primitive Israelite invaders as peculiarly virtuous.

* * *

From this stage onwards, the problem which becomes increasingly insistent is that of the integration of the descendants of the shepherds of Sinai with the natives of Palestine. William Neil himself, two pages after the passage above quoted, has the following paragraph: "Now the situation has changed. The Canaanites, who were after all Semites[8] like the Hebrews and had merely arrived earlier than the Israelites, are now no longer mentioned as enemies or indeed as rivals. The two strains have amalgamated. Canaanites and Israelites are one. By inter-marriage, treaty and trade the fusion is more or less complete. Israel has become the dominant partner in the transaction and the military leader. In the process many Canaanite customs have become Israelite customs and in particular much of Canaanite religion has been incorporated into the religion of Yahweh."

The great majority of modern biblical scholars agree with this lucid passage. But how does this fit into the previous statement that the Israelites are peculiar people unlike any other, singled out as the chosen instruments of God? The invading shepherds in the days of Joshua were only some five thousand men. As a result, the amalgam resulting from the fusion of the Israelites with the inhabitants of the mountains (for they had not yet reached the coastal plain) was considerably more Canaanite than Israelite from the ethnic viewpoint.

[7] Rev. William Neil, *One Volume Bible Commentary*.
[8] This is an oversimplification. The Palestinians in 1200 B.C. were, as we have seen, composed of many races, some of them from Asia Minor, Greece, or Central Asia. Canaanites may have been a collective term for Palestinians, with no ethnic significance.

What had happened was identical with what occurred two hundred years after the Norman conquest of England. The leading Norman families formed a military caste in power, but the rest of their followers disappeared into the population of England.

* * *

Saul's position was undermined by Samuel, who anointed David as a rival king. The latter, pursued by Saul, complained, "They have driven me out so that I have no share in the heritage of Yahweh. They have said, 'Go and serve other gods.' "[9] The Jerusalem Bible here has a footnote, "The land of Israel was God's inheritance ... It was thought impossible to worship Yahweh in another land where alien gods held sway." In view of this passage, it is difficult to claim that David (not to mention Abraham) was a monotheist.

Saul, frustrated and embittered, was eventually killed in battle with the Philistines on Mount Gilboa.[10]

David was first accepted as king by Judah alone and ruled for seven and a half years in Hebron, while a descendant of Saul reigned in the north. David, an astute politician, maintained cordial relations with the Philistines. When the latter went to fight the Israelites —the campaign in which Saul was killed—Achish, King of Gath, asked David to go with him.

This incident shows that Judah, which was partly composed of Kenites, Kenizzites and other tribes, was already distinct from the northern tribes and ready to join the Philistines against them. Even after David united the north and south, the distinction between them remained.

For some years, David in Hebron was at war with Ishbaal, the son of Saul. Eventually Abner, the commander of Ishbaal's army, went over to David but was murdered by Joab, David's commander, who saw in him a potential rival. Ishbaal was then also assassinated and the northern tribes submitted to David in about 1000 B.C. He was to rule for thirty-three years.

David was a man of exceptional gifts, a born leader, a gifted strategist and an acute politician. As long as David in Hebron was at war with Saul's son, the Philistines were pleased to assist him. But when he united all Israel, they realised that their supremacy was threatened. They attacked him but were repulsed.

Although some two hundred and fifty years had elapsed since

[9] I Samuel XXVI, 19. Jerusalem Bible.
[10] Map 5, p. 58.

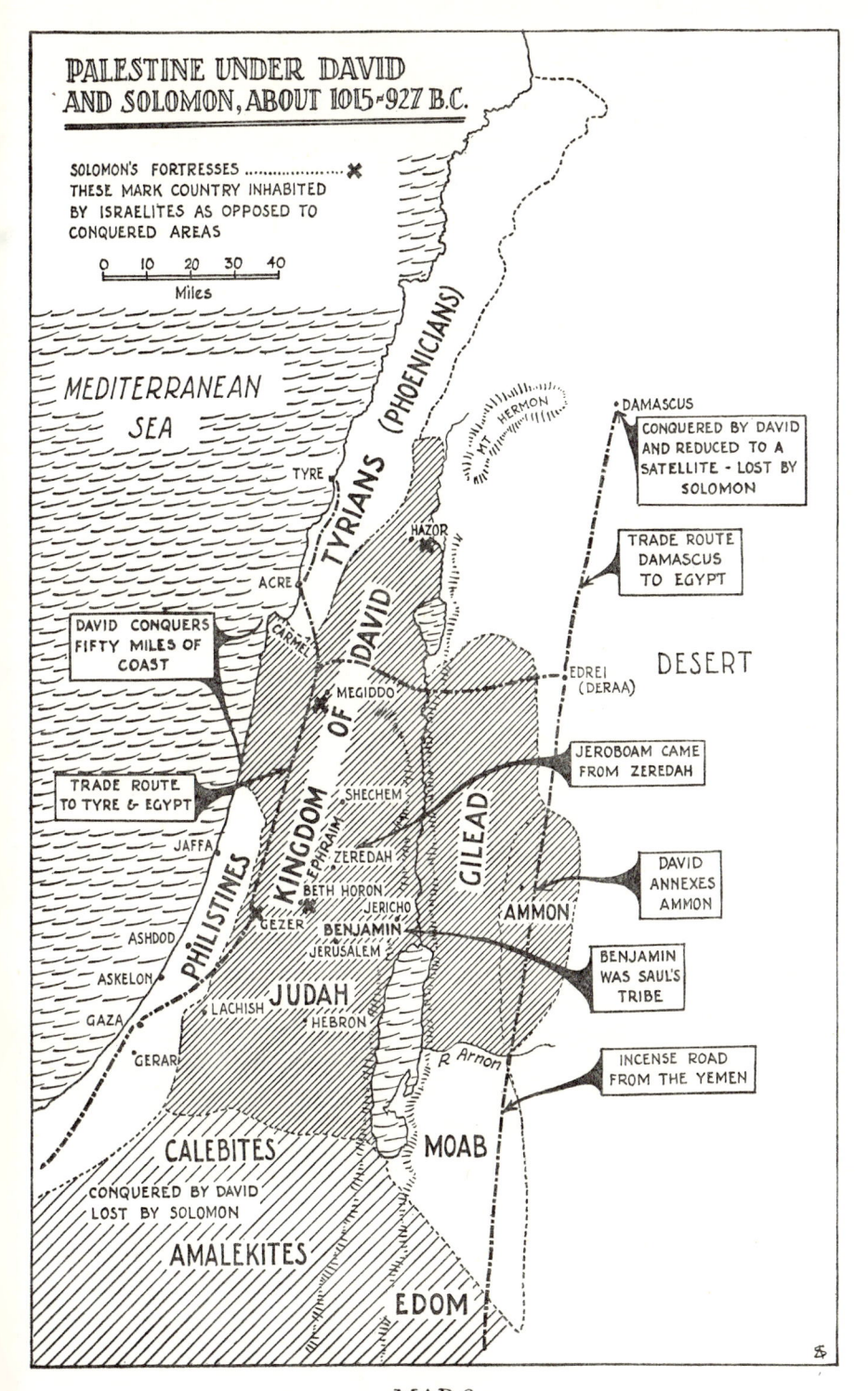

MAP 6

Joshua's invasion, Jerusalem still belonged to the Jebusites. Its presence on the northern border of Judah, together with that of the Gibeonites and other non-Israelite towns on the plain up to Beeroth and Bethel[11] had tended to isolate Judah from the northern tribes. In addition, it had the reputation of being an impregnable fortress. David saw that Jerusalem, being centrally placed, would constitute a splendid capital for a united Israel. It also had the advantage of being "neutral", as between Judah and the north.

David accordingly seized the city and moved his residence there. The Jebusites, however, seem to have remained a majority in the town, as they still were at the time of the Babylonian Captivity. The Jebusites had a tradition of priest-kings at least eight hundred years old, for Genesis XIV, 17 to 24, mentions Melchizadek, King of Salem, a priest of the Most High God, who was called El Elyon. It seems probable that this Jebusite tradition may have inspired the idea of David and his special covenant with Yahweh.

To gain yet further religious prestige for his new capital, David brought up to it the Ark, which had lain neglected in a village since its return from the Philistines. Royalist propaganda suggested that Yahweh had made a special covenant with David, whose dynasty was to rule for ever. Jerusalem, a Jebusite town, was alleged to be the special residence of Yahweh. Such statements are frequent in the Psalms[12] and elsewhere. This royalist propaganda was to change world history but, at the time, the northern tribes were not deceived. They remained loyal to their older local shrines, and made little of David's "new" shrine in Jerusalem.

Having thus consolidated his position, David embarked on campaigns of conquest. First he attacked Moab and then marched against the Aramaean King of Damascus, and placed a governor and a garrison in the city. Returning to Jerusalem, he defeated the Edomites, south of the Dead Sea, and appointed governors over them also. "Wherever David went, Yahweh gave him victory."[13]

The next victims of David's expansionist policy were the Ammonites. While the army was besieging Ammon (Amman), David committed adultery with Bathsheba, the wife of Uriah the Hittite, who was away at the war. The king sent orders to Joab, the commander of the army, to arrange for Uriah to be killed, whereupon David married his widow. Bathsheba, who was to be the mother of

---

[11] Map 4, p. 49.
[12] Psalms LXXII; LXXVI; LXVII, 67-72; LXXXVII; XCVII, 8; XCIX, 1, and others.
[13] II Samuel VIII, 14.

Solomon, was a Hittite woman. David's own grandmother had been a Moabitess.

Hitherto the Israelites had been tribal levies, who fought best in their own mountains. To conquer Damascus, David raised a regular army of mercenaries. The majority, the Cherethites and the Pelethites, seem to have been Philistines, but it is also claimed that he employed Gauls. For the first time, Israel used a force of chariots.

In the mountains, the Israelites and the Canaanites were now one people. Indeed Yahweh was now often called Baal. But David had now conquered other countries, the inhabitants of which he encouraged to integrate with the Israelites. His retainers include such names as Ahimelech the Hittite, Doeg the Edomite and Uriah the Hittite. The Philistines retained their independence, but were pleased to serve as mercenaries in David's army. The conquered areas, Edom, Moab and Damascus, were not settled by Israelites.

The sudden rise of Israel to this dominating position among her neighbours had transformed the Israelites. Hitherto a group of backward mountain tribes, they had now marched to Damascus and to Edom. The citizens of these states came to pay their court in Jerusalem. David had also conquered fifty miles of the coastline south of Haifa, down which lay the great trade route from Damascus to Egypt.[14]

The Middle East has always derived part of its wealth from the transit trade from the Indian Ocean to the Mediterranean. Another valuable commerce was the import of incense by camel caravan from the Yemen to Egypt and Syria. His control over Edom enabled David to impose transit dues on this valuable merchandise.

The history of Israel, from Sinai to the Captivity, forms, in miniature, a sample of the lives of nations, "a panorama of human life and hopes on a midget stage."[15] The reign of David was for Israel the military stage in her life history. The same phenomenon occurred in Britain from A.D. 1700 to 1815, and in France from Louis XIV to Napoleon. Inevitably imperial expansion led to an influx of foreigners and to the loss of the pious, but narrow spirit of the "good old days".

This outward glory, however, was marred by bitter hatreds among the members of David's family. His son Amnon raped his own sister and was murdered by another son Absalom, who subsequently rebelled and tried to kill his father.[16] Eventually Absalom was also

---

[14] Map 6, p. 63.
[15] William Neil, Introduction to A. Parmelee, *A Guide Book to the Bible*.
[16] II Samuel XVII, 4.

killed but these internal feuds triggered off another rebellion, this time by Sheba the son of Bichri of Benjamin, Saul's tribe, who cried " 'We have no share in David... Every man to his tents, O Israel'. At this all the men of Israel deserted David and followed Sheba. But the men of Judah stayed with their king."[17] The union of all Israel, brought about by David, was suddenly seen to be only skin-deep.

II Samuel XXI tells how there was a famine caused by the failure of the rains. David enquired of Yahweh and was told that the reason was that a blood feud between Saul and the Gibeonites was not settled. The Gibeonites were Amorites, allies of Israel since Joshua. David, we are told, asked them how they wished to settle the feud and they demanded the lives of seven of Saul's descendants. David gave seven of Saul's sons and grandsons to the Gibeonites, who impaled them on a hill outside their village.[18] Are we to believe that the God of Love insisted on the death of these seven innocent men? Or was David disposing of the remnant of Saul's dynasty?

Even in the last few days of David's life, the royal family were torn by hatreds. Adonijah, Absalom's brother, attempted a coup d'état. David hastily proclaimed Solomon his successor, and the latter, supported by the foreign mercenaries, mounted the throne. On his deathbed, David urged Solomon to have Joab murdered. No sooner was David dead (*c.* 970–960 B.C.) than Solomon caused his elder brother Adonijah and other potential rivals to be assassinated, including Joab.

* * *

As in the case of most nations, the military phase under David was followed by the commercial age under Solomon, corresponding to the Victorian era in Britain. Solomon wanted peace, and sought for it partly by foreign marriages. It might be said of him, as it was of the Habsburgs, "Others wage war; thou, happy Austria, weddest." Solomon's most important bride was a daughter of one of the last feeble Pharaohs of the twenty-first dynasty.

His closest ally was Tyre, modern Lebanon, which extended south as far as Carmel. Its Greek name was Phoenicia but the people called themselves Tyrians. They were probably of mixed Greek descent, were efficient seamen and they traded to the whole

---

[17] II Samuel XX, 1 and 2.
[18] II Samuel XXI. The Jerusalem Bible says "impaled". The Revised Standard Version has "hanged".

Mediterranean. They were already planting colonies in Cyprus, Sardinia, Sicily and North Africa.

Solomon knew that those who desire peace should prepare for war. While David relied chiefly on his mercenary infantry, his son built up a large force of chariots. He also established a number of fortresses around the mountain homeland of Israel at Hazor, Megiddo, Beth Horon and Gezer.[19] These bases were garrisoned by a paid regular army. Solomon does not appear to have ever called out the old tribal levy.

Damascus soon revolted and regained her independence. The territory ruled by David shrank slowly but surely. Solomon devoted more attention to commerce and industry than to war. Among other activities, he bought horses in Asia Minor and sold them in Egypt. A main trade route ran from Damascus through Edrei (now Deraa), up the Vale of Esdraelon, over the hills by Megiddo and down the Palestine coast to Egypt.[20] A long section of this route now ran through territory controlled by Solomon. In addition, his friendship with Tyre, the world's largest commercial port, brought much business. The northern tribes devoted themselves more and more to commerce, though Judah was much less affected.

Solomon established firm control over Edom down to the Gulf of (modern) Aqaba. A commercial fleet, manned by Tyrian sailors, traded down the Red Sea. Near Ezion Geber,[21] he mined and smelted copper and perhaps iron. Solomon became very rich, but there was also a general rise in material prosperity and in wages.

Solomon's control of Aqaba enabled him to charge heavy dues on the Yemenite incense caravans. The object of the famous visit of the Queen of Sheba may have been to protest against the extortionate demands of Solomon's officials. But if the king's business acumen brought in money, his extravagance and love of ostentation cost more.

The most famous building erected by him was the Temple, the layout of which followed the pattern of the temple at Serabit al Khadim. A small cube-shaped building was called the Holy of Holies. The Temple was only one of many buildings built in the royal compound, which included several palaces and an armoury. To carry out all his building works, Solomon used unpaid labour "from all Israel",[22] as Rameses II had done in Egypt. Even with such methods, however, the country fell into debt and Solomon was obliged to sell twenty towns on his northern border to the King of Tyre.

[19] Map 6, p. 63.   [20] Map 6, p. 63.
[21] Map 2, p. 27.   [22] I Kings V, 27.

Jeroboam was a young man from Zeredah, possibly modern Surdah, eleven miles north of Jerusalem. Being educated, he was made a foreman in charge of the forced labour employed on the Temple, and witnessed the oppression of the poor. Presumably he was denounced as an agitator, for his arrest was ordered, but he escaped to Egypt.

The Old Testament blames Solomon for religious laxity, and attributes to him seven hundred wives. Many of these were from neighbouring countries and wished for shrines in which to worship their respective gods. To please them, Solomon built "high places" on the neighbouring hills. To worship on hilltops had long been a feature of Syrio-Palestinian religion. Even in Israel, the worship of Baal and Yahweh had become so amalgamated that we find Samuel sacrificing on a "high place".

It is, indeed, no longer possible to assess the meaning of the word Israelite. Free intermarriage with the people of the land continued at all levels. "A careful reading of the Old Testament itself makes it clear that their [the Israelites'] unit was both politically and racially extremely vague. The religion of Yahweh was not the religion of a particular geographic area: it was the religion of a military and priestly aristocracy and was never ... the only religion to be found within the borders of Israelite domination."[23] But if we cannot find what Israelites were nor separate them from other groups, how were they a unique and chosen people, different from anyone else?

* * *

Solomon died about 927 B.C. Like Louis XIV in France, he had raised his country to a high level of wealth, but to do so he had grievously oppressed the people. The death of the Israelite *Roi Soleil* was also followed by the deluge.

NOTABLE DATES

David's reign About 1000 B.C. to 967 B.C.
Solomon's reign About 967 B.C. to 927 B.C.

CONCLUSIONS

(1) The reigns of David and Solomon are typical of the development of primitive peoples, from tribal freedom to

[23] J. Parkes, *The Conflict of the Church and the Synagogue.*

royal autocracy, and from militarism to commercialism.
(2) The period covers profound social changes, the growth of luxury and the oppression of the peasants. Ethnically the descendants of the shepherds of Sinai have become indistinguishably integrated with the people of the land. From the religious viewpoint, Yahweh worship is the state religion, but every form of mixture with the local religions is practised by the people.
(3) The royal family is extremely corrupt. The sons of David constantly assassinated one another or rebelled. Solomon had all his brothers murdered.

Unhappy mankind is constantly building up, in imagination, Golden Ages past and future, to relieve the pain and anxiety of the present. The reigns of David and Solomon have been thus idealised as Glorious Days. But, in fact, David's reign was a long succession of rebellions, wars and assassinations. At the end of Solomon's life, the country was seething with revolt, which broke out immediately after his death.

V

Decline and Decadence

Since I have called and you have refused me,
Since I have beckoned and no one has taken notice,
Since you have ignored all my advice
And rejected all my warnings,
I, for my part, will laugh at your distress,
I will jeer at you when calamity comes...
For the errors of the ignorant lead to their death,
And the complacency of fools works their own ruin;
But whoever listens to me may live secure,
He will have quiet, fearing no mischance.
Proverbs I, 24 to 33

> The merry tambourines are silent,
> The sound of revelling is over,
> The merry lyre is silent . . .
> The city of emptiness is in ruins,
> The entrance to every house is shut.
> There is lamentation in the streets:
> No wine, joy quite gone,
> Gladness banished from the country.
> Nothing but rubble in the city,
> The gate smashed to pieces.
> *Isaiah XXIV, 8 to 12*
> Jerusalem Bible

V

"SAUL had failed: David had failed: Solomon had failed. The kings and the kingdom had been weighed in the balance and found wanting. From the death of Solomon and the end of the undivided kingdom of Israel the story is a sad and sordid one of disruption, intrigue, war and corruption until finally the remnant of the high hopes of Israel crashed with the ruins of Jerusalem less than five hundred years after Saul became its first king. Israel had paid the price for playing at power politics, for aping the common run of nations, for mistaking culture for covenant, for becoming indistinguishable from any other of the petty principalities that staggered from one crisis to another in the ancient Mediterranean world ... Even the emergence of a Hezekiah or a Josiah could not arrest the headlong career of a people that had entrusted themselves to the wrong kind of leadership and that failed to see that the pursuit of wealth, power and prestige, and the fake security that these things bring was not the path that the people of God must follow ... But the Israelites were the people of God, a people with a call and a mission."[1]

Down to the last sentence, this passage seems to me an admirable summary of the history of ancient Israel. They *were* just one more petty principality, staggering from crisis to crisis. Like every other nation which has risen and fallen, they did entrust themselves to the wrong kind of leadership, they did fail to see that the pursuit of wealth, power and prestige brought a false sense of security.

The admirably clear Old Testament narrative of the rise and fall of Israel presented a plain lesson to all the subsequent nations of mankind—wealth, power and prestige are not the things that matter. But we have been careful to close our eyes to the lesson, and have taken refuge in myth and in miracle—the Spiritual Ruler of the Universe, we are told, chose one primitive tribe, which He loved more than the remainder of the human race. In fact, He took pleasure in seeing them massacre the other tribes. This paradox has never ceased to perplex Christians—how could the God of Love order genocide? Yet it is difficult to free our minds from the beliefs of our ancestors.

Thus Rev. William Neil, at the end of a lucid summary of the

[1] Rev. William Neil, *One Volume Bible Commentary*.

history of ancient Israel, ends up, "But the Israelites were the people of God."

* * *

The story of the revolt against Rehoboam is well known and is magnificently told in I Kings XII. We may note in passing that, as in the rebellion of Sheba the son of Bichri against David, the rebels are reported to have cried, "To your tents, O Israel," suggesting that many, if not all, Israel were still tent dwellers.

Jeroboam returned from Egypt and was chosen as ruler of the northern kingdom. The modern flavour in this incident is almost laughable. How often, in our own times, have we seen disgruntled demagogues from these countries take political asylum in Egypt, only to return later and become little dictators in their countries.

Judah remained loyal to the House of David, which was after all a clan of their own tribe. We have already seen that Judah had been strongly differentiated from the northern tribes, ever since the conquest. The territory of Judah was poor and mountainous, and many of the people remained simple shepherds.

The northern kingdom was more productive and supported many more "Canaanite" inhabitants before the conquest. These were not killed by the Israelite invaders. Two hundred years later, the Israelites had become assimilated to the Canaanites and Yahweh had become largely identified with Baal.

The contrast between Israel and Judah was further emphasised in the reign of Solomon, when the country was opened up to the more civilised states of Tyre and Syria. The people of the ten northern tribes took an increasing part in business activity. When Ahab was killed in 850 B.C., the order issued to the army was, "Every man to his city and to his own country." There is no longer any mention of Israelite tents. The assimilation of the northern Israelites into the urban commercial life of Syria was completed.

Jeroboam had many problems to face. Seventy years of royalist propaganda had convinced many people that Jerusalem was the only place where Yahweh could be worshipped, and the royal Temple services included references to Yahweh's perpetual covenant with the House of David.

Jeroboam consequently set up shrines in the north to which pilgrimages were to be made. In this, he was not entirely unjustified. Three hundred years had elapsed since the conquest and only in the last fifty years had Jerusalem become holy.

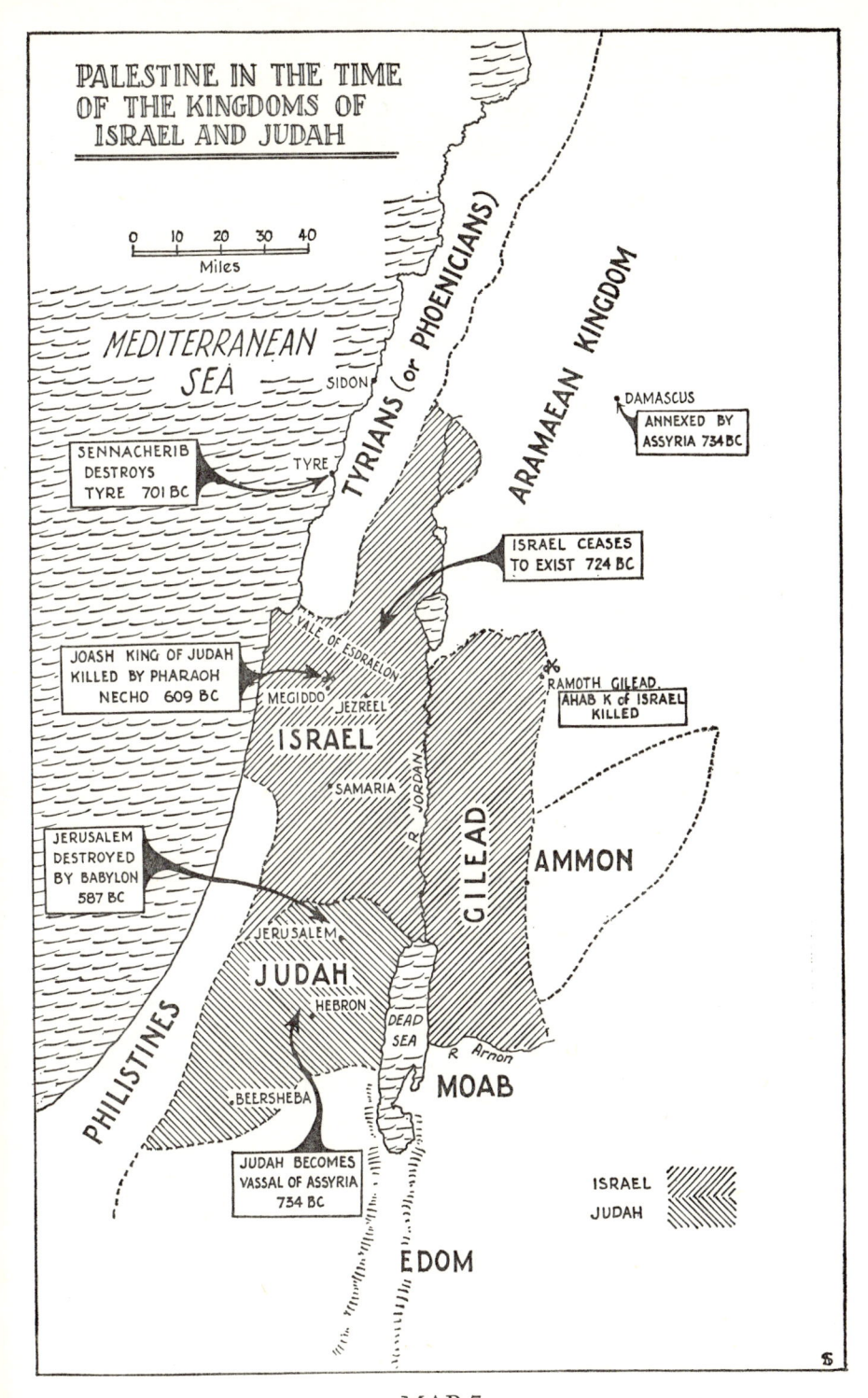

MAP 7

We must always remember that our Old Testament was completely re-edited by the priests of Jerusalem, when Israel had ceased to exist. Although they incorporated some material from the north—the so-called E narrative—they were free to reject any material they did not like and thereby to slant the whole story. There are even scholars who believe that some of the psalms were borrowed by the Jerusalem priests from Canaanite worship. The whole situation was so fluid that it is difficult to draw rigid distinctions.

* * *

The northern kingdom was as unstable as Syria has been since 1945. Jeroboam was succeeded by his son, who was assassinated within the year by Baasha (900–877 B.C.), who made himself ruler. He was succeeded by his son Elah (877–876 B.C.), who, a few months later, was murdered by Zimri. Within a week, another coup d'état placed Omri (876–869), an army officer, on the throne.

Omri was a man of exceptional ability. Seventy-two years of anarchy from Jeroboam to Omri had reduced Israel to impotence and the King of Damascus had become the most influential ruler in Syria. The basis of Omri's policy was alliance with Tyre, then at the height of its commercial prosperity. Its colony of Carthage was to be founded a few years later. Living on overseas trade, Tyre purchased agricultural produce from Israel. Omri cemented the alliance by the marriage of his son Ahab with Jezebel, the daughter of the King of Tyre. Omri also made peace with Judah. Tyre, Israel and Judah then combined to resist Damascus. The Judah-Israel peace enabled both to embark on local campaigns. Judah reasserted her lost supremacy over Edom and Israel compelled Moab to pay tribute.

Soon, however, these endless petty rivalries were overshadowed by the fear of Assyria. About 874 B.C., Asshur-nasir-pal II (883–859) invaded northern Syria and reached the Mediterranean. In 859 B.C., Shalmaneser III (859–824) returned to Syria and Hamath (modern Hama), Damascus, Israel, Ammon and others united to oppose him. In 853, a drawn battle was fought at Qarqar on the Orontes, and the Assyrians withdrew.

Israel under Ahab grew rapidly in wealth and prosperity. Ahab built a splendid new capital at Samaria, with apparently another palace at Jezreel, twenty-five miles away.[2] But the transformation

[2] Map 7, p. 75.

of the agricultural population into a commercial state produced the usual consequences. The businessmen became very rich, but the poorer classes grew poorer still. The rich lived in luxury and used their capital, gained in commerce, to buy up country estates. Small farmers were eliminated and the rural population became wage labourers. Once again, we are impressed by the absolute normality of these developments. Britain, France and the United States have all faced these problems, or are facing them now.

These conditions, so contrary to the early "Israelite dream" of freedom and equality, gave rise to a succession of "prophets", who denounced the vices of the age. One of the first of them was Elijah. I Kings attributes Elijah's opposition to Ahab to the import of Melqart, the Baal of Tyre, by Jezebel. Reading the story, we are horrified by the wickedness of Ahab and Jezebel.

But are we not doing the same? Would there not be an outcry if Jews and Muslims were forbidden to have mosques and synagogues in Britain? Would not such a policy be called reactionary, medieval or, even worse, bad for business? The problems of Israel are the same as have faced all nations. Rural conditions guard a simple faith and high morals. Urbanisation leads to wealth, luxury and materialism, which end in national catastrophe. This was to happen to Israel and to many nations after her and is happening to us today.

Elijah was a native of Trans-Jordan, not of luxurious Samaria. He was utterly devoted to Yahweh and believed in the massacre of his enemies.[3] The fact that, when pursued by Jezebel, he fled to Sinai is significant. For Sinai was the embodiment of the old, free tribal tradition. Here Elijah underwent a spiritual experience, and heard a still small voice which recalled him to his duty.

About 850 B.C., Ahab was killed in a battle with the King of Damascus at Ramoth-Gilead, the modern Rimtha.[4] In spite of the increasing threat of Assyrian conquest, these typical Syrians continued to quarrel among themselves. Ahab was succeeded by his son who, eight years later, was killed in a coup d'état led by an army officer called Jehu. Elisha was involved in the plot, which was ostensibly against the luxury of the court and the influence of Tyre.[5] Wholesale massacres resulted.

The chief of the Rechabites was privy to the conspiracy.[6] The Rechabites were a nomad clan who had refused to give up their

---

[3] I Kings XVIII, 40.
[4] Map 7, p. 75.
[5] II Kings, IX and X.
[6] II Kings X, 15 to 17.

tents, take up agriculture, drink wine or indulge in the fashionable luxuries. They remained shepherds because they believed that the pure religion of Yahweh could only be maintained under nomad conditions. It is interesting to compare this passage with that in which Yahweh refuses leave to David to build him a house. "I have never stayed in a house," Yahweh said, "but have always led a wanderer's life in a tent."[7] There speaks the real nomad chief.

Jeremiah XXXV also praises the way of life of the Rechabites and holds them up as an example to Judah. Yet they were not Israelites but Kenites, who may have been worshippers of Yahweh before Moses. Yet I find it of deep interest to note that the final spiritualisation of Judaism was not to come through these puritans, but through the collapse of the cultured and wealthy, and through the new religious outlook which emerged from the catastrophe. If we can see the meaning of the Old Testament, instead of saying that every word was written by God, new religious and historical lessons are on every page.

Hereafter the descent of Israel to ruin was rapid. After a recovery under Jeroboam II (783–743) a succession of coups d'état brought chaos. In spite of this, Israel and Damascus attacked Judah, who appealed to Assyria. In 734, Tiglath-Pileser conquered all Syria as far south as the Plain of Esdraelon. The population of Galilee was deported, the King of Judah became a vassal, the Kingdom of Damascus was annexed by Assyria.

In 724, Shalmeneser V (727–722) invaded Palestine and took Samaria. After two hundred years, the northern kingdom ceased to exist. The population was deported, some to northern Iraq and some to Persia, where they disappeared into the local inhabitants. They were replaced by the importation of new, mixed populations. Homogeneous national groups were liable to rebel. Assyrian policy was, therefore, to "scramble" all the populations of their empire, leaving no homogeneous communities.

* * *

In these years occurred a new and highly significant development —the appearance of the prophets. These were not soothsayers whose task it was to foretell the future. We should perhaps call them "revivalists". At the height of Israel's wealth, corruption and decadence, they called for a return to God. In them, almost for the first time, we find genuine moral issues. The historical books—

---

[7] II Samuel VII, 6. Jerusalem Bible.

Samuel, Kings and Chronicles—give a normal picture of violence, bloodshed, plunder and hatred, common to all the petty Middle Eastern states, ten centuries before Christ.

The appearance of the prophets at the height of a period of decadence is intensely encouraging. Beneath the surface of cruelty and murder, this quiet spiritual progress must have been going on—a comforting hope for us when we read our daily newspapers. The prophets were not able to prevent the crash of Israel's permissive society. But after the catastrophe their words were remembered and led to advances in spiritual thinking which changed the world.

> By the help of your God, return to him,
> Hold fast to kindness and justice,
> And put your trust continually in your God . . .
> And does Ephraim say, Yes, but I have grown rich,
> I have made myself wealthy?

But Hosea does not only call for a return to God, he promises also that God will forgive.

> I will heal their unfaithfulness,
> I will love them with all my heart,
> Now that my anger has turned away from them.[8]

If we read the Old Testament with unprejudiced minds, we find a most wonderful account of the rise, decadence, fall and revival of a community, with continual applications to our daily life. But the applicability is based on the belief that these were ordinary people like us. As soon as we say that these were unique, chosen people, unlike any other race, we lose interest. We are ordinary people, so obviously none of all this applies to us.

* * *

Since the death of Solomon, we have confined ourselves to the ten northern tribes. The situation in Judah was simpler. Firstly, the soil was poorer and many men continued to be shepherds, the original status of the Yahweh worshippers. Secondly, no international trade route crossed Judah, bringing rich merchants and foreign ideas. Thirdly, the surviving prestige of David provided a stable dynasty.

[8] J. B. Philips, *Four Prophets*.

It is true that the reigns of David and Solomon brought money to Jerusalem and a "higher standard of living". But when Jerusalem became the capital of the tiny kingdom of Judah alone, the situation reverted to what it had been. Judah retained a precarious hold over a part of Edom, a poor country with no corrupting influences. There were periods of religious laxity and then revivals, as under Hezekiah. Gradually corruption seeped into Judah also, though these factors enabled her to survive for a hundred and thirty-five years longer than the northern kingdom. Ahaz, King of Judah (735–715) had, as we have seen, become a tributary of Assyria, and was obliged to pay homage to Tiglath-Pileser in Damascus.

Isaiah describes the anarchy of the times. Referring to Judah, he says:

> His land is full of silver and gold
> And treasures beyond counting;
> His land is full of horses
> And chariots without number.
> His land is full of idols . . .
> The people oppress each other, man exploiting man,
> Yes, every man his neighbour.
> A youth can insult an old man,
> And a lout abuse a man of high repute . . .
> My people are oppressed by boys
> And ruled by women.[9]

It is interesting to note that Isaiah cites as two signs of social disintegration the revolt of youth and a female share in government.

In 715 B.C., Hezekiah became King of Judah. There seemed to be a faint hope of escape from subjection to Assyria. The prophets had attributed the fall of Israel to her desertion of Yahweh. A religious reform might save Judah. Babylonia had revolted against Assyria and Sargon II was also at war with Midas, King of Phrygia.[10] Egypt had been torn by civil wars, but in 716 B.C.[11] the twenty-fifth dynasty was established. The Judaeans hoped to play politics, setting off Egypt and Assyria against one another.

In 703 B.C., Tyre, Judah and part of Philistia rebelled against Assyria with Egyptian encouragement. In 701, Sennacherib arrived and crushed Tyre, which never recovered. He then went on to

---
[9] From Isaiah, II and III. Various translations.
[10] Map 8, p. 83.
[11] John Bright, *A History of Israel*.

Philistia, destroying several outlying Judaean towns on the way. On the advice of Isaiah, Hezekiah sued for peace. Sennacherib agreed but increased the tribute and annexed a number of Judaean towns to Philistia.[12]

Sennacherib returned thirteen years later, about 688 B.C. The famous scene in *II Kings XVIII*, 17 to 35, probably took place on this occasion. But "the angel of Yahweh went out and struck down a hundred and eighty-five thousand men in the Assyrian camp."[13] Herodotus mentions the incident and says that the Assyrians were overrun by a plague of rats. Hezekiah soon after developed bubons also. Perhaps, once again, we have an epidemic of bubonic plague.

* * *

We must here insert a brief note on the contemporary prophets, first Isaiah, and Micah. Isaiah received a spiritual experience,[14] though it is told in contemporary poetic phraseology. It is true that he visualised the call as coming from Yahweh, but, as we have already remarked, God's spiritual calls to us do not depend (as we are inclined to think) on the accuracy of our intellectual conceptions.

Judah was following in the path of Israel. The rich men oppressed the poor and the judges were open to bribes. The free democracy of tribal and desert tradition had gone. Judah, moreover, suffered from one delusion which had not affected Israel. The royalist political propaganda had disseminated two ideas, firstly, that Jerusalem was the residence of Yahweh and would never be conquered. Secondly, that the House of David would rule for ever.

No conditions were attached, in the popular mind, to these promises. The people felt confident that Yahweh would defend Jerusalem, regardless of the immorality of the public. Meanwhile, the ritual of the Temple became more elaborate, the vestments more gorgeous, the sacrifices more lavish, but no moral reformation resulted. This situation is eloquently denounced by *Micah, VI 6*:

How shall I come into the presence of Yahweh,
And bow down before God on high?
Shall I approach him with burnt offerings—with calves a year old?

---

[12] II Kings XVIII, 13 to 16.
[13] John Bright, *A History of Israel*.
[14] Isaiah VI.

> Will he be pleased with thousands of rams,
> With ten thousand rivers of oil?
> Shall I give my first born for my own misdeeds—
> The fruit of my body for the sin of my soul?

But Yahweh answers:

> You know well enough, Man, what is good!
> For what does Yahweh ask of you,
> But to be just, to love mercy,
> And to walk humbly with your God.

Isaiah, who had access to the king, initiated two ideas which are still affecting our own times. He believed the contemporary doctrine that Yahweh had his dwelling place in Jerusalem. But the worldly attitude of the public and the political threat of Assyria convinced him that a catastrophe could not be avoided. How could these paradoxical beliefs be reconciled?

His solution was, firstly, that a catastrophe would be brought about by Yahweh himself, who would use Assyria to punish faithless Judah. Secondly, that Jerusalem was, none the less, the dwelling place of Yahweh. A purified remnant would survive, and a scion of the House of David would arise and bring justice and victory. We see here the seeds of two doctrines—the perpetual sanctity of Jerusalem and the coming of the Messiah.

* * *

The message is of vital significance to us today. The moral state of our country resembles that of Judah in Isaiah's time. Materialism holds sway, but, under the surface, is malaise verging on despair. The end of all this may be a national catastrophe, but Isaiah's message brings us hope. For catastrophe is a means of purification. The best is yet to come.

* * *

Manasseh (687–642 B.C.), the son of Hezekiah, reversed his father's policy and became a servile dependent of Assyria. But Assyria herself was over-extended. Babylon and Egypt rebelled again. Migrating Indo-Aryan races pressed in from the north. The Medes were already established south of the Caspian.

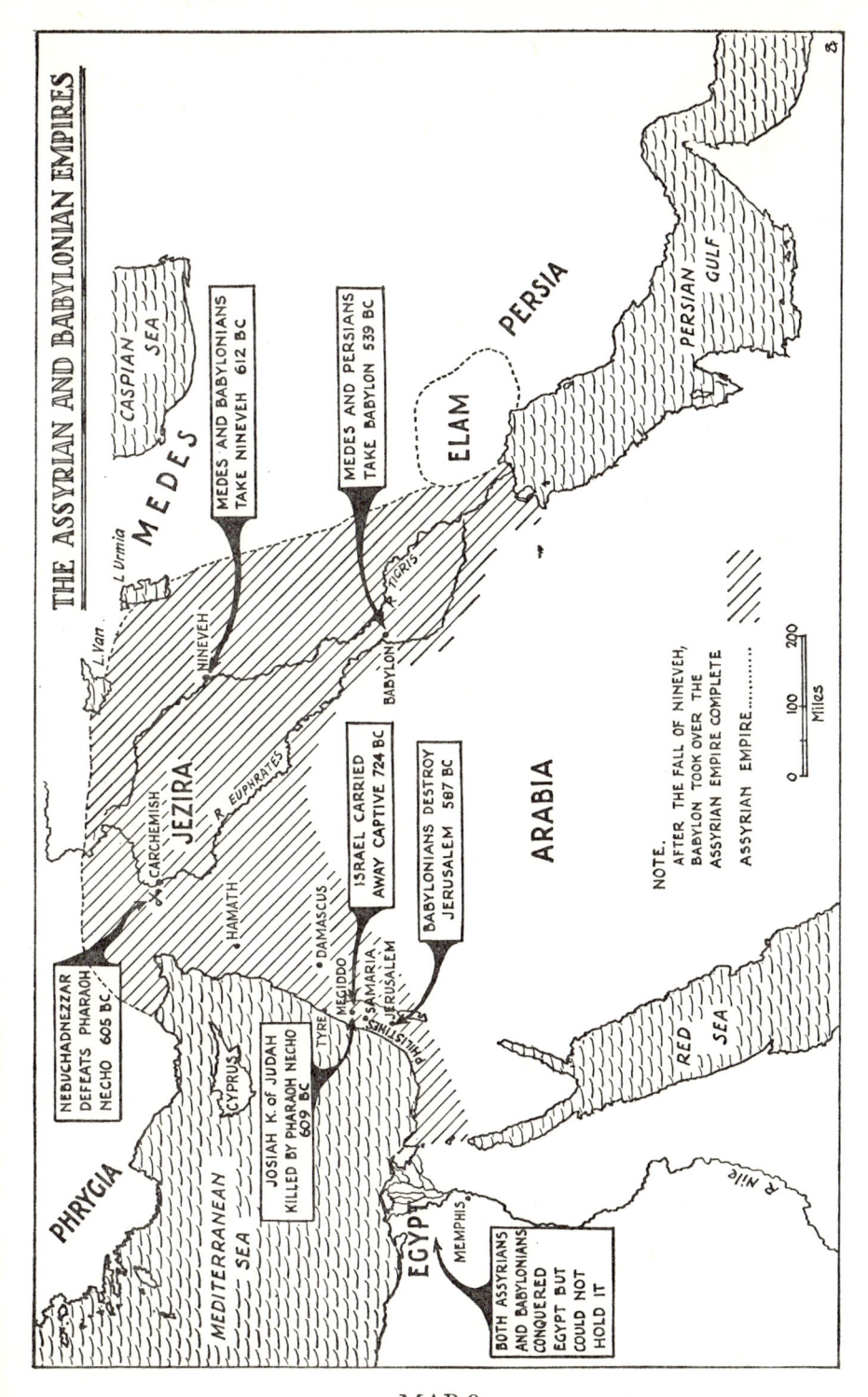

MAP 8

Ashurbanipal, the last great Assyrian king, fought back fiercely. When he died, in 633 B.C., Assyria seemed once again victorious. Twenty years later, in 612 B.C., the allied Medes and Babylonians took Nineveh and Assyria ceased to exist.

* * *

Under King Josiah (640–609 B.C.), Judah enjoyed a last Indian summer. The collapse of Assyria made her independent, without any effort on her part. In 622 B.C., a book was "found" in the Temple, which some scholars believe to have been our Book of Deuteronomy. The sensation caused by this discovery seems to imply that the Mosaic Law had been forgotten.

Presumably to avoid local heresies, Josiah forbade worship in any of the many shrines which dotted the country. Only the priests of Jerusalem were to be recognised, all country priests being simply dismissed. This restriction of worship to Jerusalem denied religious activity to country people, who had little spare time to visit the capital.

In 609 B.C., Pharaoh Necho (609–593) swept across Palestine and Syria to Carchemish on the Euphrates.[15] For some reason unknown to us, Josiah tried to stop him at Megiddo, but was killed and his army destroyed. His son, Jehoiakim, became king as a vassal of Egypt. The independence of Judah ended after twenty years, just as the independence of Egypt was ended by the arrival of the Russians in 1967, twenty years after the withdrawal of Britain. Josiah's religious reform, as it had not prevented this disaster, was abandoned.

In 605 B.C., Nebuchadnezzar of Babylon fell upon the Egyptian army at Carchemish and destroyed it. In 604, Nebuchadnezzar arrived in Philistia. Jehoiakim transferred his allegiance and became a vassal of Babylon. In 601, he rebelled but died in 598. In 597, the Babylonians arrived and Jerusalem surrendered. The king, the principal citizens and part of the population were carried off to Babylon. Zedekiah, the king's uncle, was installed by the conquerors.

But Judah was still torn by faction. In 589, the Judaeans, still buoyed by the belief that Jerusalem was Yahweh's dwelling place, rebelled again, in spite of the protests of Jeremiah. In 588, the Babylonians returned and blockaded Jerusalem. They then systematically destroyed all Judaea, demolishing every town.

In 587, Jerusalem fell. Zedekiah was blinded, his sons executed.

[15] Map 8, p. 83.

Jerusalem was razed to the ground. A further party of citizens was deported to Babylon. Many Judaeans escaped to Egypt, including Jeremiah. Some fled to Syria, Ammon or Moab. Judaea was left depopulated.

NOTABLE DATES

Death of Solomon	927 B.C.
Disappearance of the northern Kingdom of Israel	724 B.C.
Disappearance of Judah	587 B.C.

CONCLUSIONS

(1) To me, the clear narrative of the Old Testament is an epitome of the lives of all nations, teaching us how to avoid the catastrophe which befell Israel. The belief that the Israelites were unique, different from any other race, destroys the significance of this splendid parable.

(2) Those who believe that the Israelites were a unique people, face the problem of who the Israelites were. In their five hundred years of existence, they had become integrated with the other races of the Levant.

(3) Yahweh was a desert god, whose worship was inevitably simple in nomad days. The early Israelites worshipped him, though they admitted the existence of other gods.

(4) Even in the era of materialism, revival preachers gradually taught that God must rule the world and that He required morality, not slaughtered animals.

(5) Materialism ended in tragedy, from which emerged a clearer and more spiritual conception of God.

VI

Isolation or Internationalism

"The people of Israel . . . have not broken with the native of the countries . . . but have found wives among these foreign women for themselves and their sons: the holy race has been mingling with the natives of the countries" . . . At this news I tore my garment and my cloak, I tore hair from my head and beard . . . I stretched out my hands to Yahweh my god.

Ezra IX, part of verses 1 to 6

Jonah was very indignant at this; he fell into a rage. He prayed to Yahweh and said, "Yahweh, please take away my life." Yahweh replied, "Are you right to be angry? . . . Am I not to feel sorry for Nineveh, the great city, in which there are more than a hundred and twenty thousand people, who cannot tell their right hand from their left, to say nothing of all the animals."

Jonah IV, Jerusalem Bible

In Canaan, of course, as a result of the struggle for Yahweh and against other gods, the exclusive status of Yahweh as God centred more and more on Yahweh's relations with Israel, although Amos clearly puts the matter otherwise. It was this that engendered the strong tension between what we call particularism and universalism.

Th. C. VRIEZEN, *The Religion of Ancient Israel*

VI

IN Judah, the Babylonian conquest seemed to be unmitigated disaster. All the towns were rased to the ground and their populations massacred. This was not a persecution of the Jews. The Assyrians and Babylonians always treated rebellious provinces this way. Judaea was left desolate and uninhabited.

The upper classes were deported to Babylonia. The remainder scattered to Ammon, Moab, Edom, Syria and especially Egypt, constituting the beginning of the Dispersion.

Once arrived in Babylon, the treatment of the exiles was good. They were free to farm, take up business and practise their religion. Life in Babylonia was more spacious than in the rocky hills of tiny Judaea. After a period of nostalgia, the exiles threw themselves into this new life of opportunity. Some became very rich.

Great numbers of Judaeans fled to Egypt, many of them settling in the capital, Memphis. A Judaean military colony was founded about 588 B.C. at Elephantine, at the first cataract on the Nile.

The old Judaean beliefs had been shattered. Yahweh had not defended Zion and the House of David had not ruled for ever. The exiles found in Egypt and Babylon cultures far superior to their own. Living in these great empires made them realise how tiny Judaea had been. Could so small a country be the choice of a really great god?

Second Isaiah, who seems to have lived at this time, strikes a new note in describing Yahweh as the Creator of the whole world.[1] Out of the depth of disaster, we see the beginning of spiritual Judaism, from which Christianity and Islam were to grow. Deprived of the Temple as a geographical rallying point, observance of the Law became the sign of a Jew.[2] Great intellectual activity characterised the Babylonian community. The Pentateuch was re-edited, Leviticus being inserted to record the ritual of the ruined Temple.

After the death of Nebuchadnezzar, internal schisms broke out in Babylon and the throne changed hands three times in seven years. Finally, in 539 B.C., Cyrus the Persian took Babylon and her whole empire. "Cyrus was one of the truly enlightened rulers of ancient times."[3] He declared universal religious toleration and restored the

---
[1] Isaiah XL, 12; XLIV, 6 et seq.
[2] From this point onwards, we can speak of Jews, an abbreviation of course for Judah.
[3] John Bright, *A History of Israel*.

gods of Babylon. In 538, he authorised the restoration of the Temple in Jerusalem. His policy was the exact opposite of Assyrian and Babylonian brutality. The Judaean exiles also gained spiritual knowledge from the Persians, who were not polytheists and did not worship idols. They believed the world to be divided by a constant struggle between the spiritual powers of Good and Evil. From Persia also the Jews derived their eschatology, some of which has come down to us.[4]

The first party to return to Jerusalem was a small one. "Yet did many of them stay at Babylon, as not willing to leave their possessions."[5] Bright estimates the population of Judah at this time at twenty thousand, but this included also a number of Gentile groups. Not until 516 B.C. about twenty years after the first return, was the Temple rebuilt. Thereafter, we know nothing of events in Judah for seventy years. Syria and Palestine together formed one province out of twenty in the vast Persian Empire. The tiny Jerusalem community was ruled by the high priest.

By contrast, the Judaean community in Babylonia and Persia flourished greatly. Many of its members were rich, while others held important posts in the administration or at court. In Egypt also the number of Jews continued to increase, and there were Jewish communities in Asia Minor.

The population of Judah in 445 B.C. was perhaps some fifty thousand. Three or four provincial towns had been rebuilt but there were few inhabitants in Jerusalem.

Nowadays, popular ethnology visualises humanity as divided into "races". It is often assumed that the members of each race are descendants of those with the same name two thousand years ago. This is scarcely ever true. In 55 B.C., Julius Caesar invaded Britain and was opposed by the Britons. Rome stayed for some four hundred years, then came the Picts, Scots, Angles, Jutes, Saxons, Danes and Normans. The Britons of today can be only slightly related to the Britons of two thousand years ago.

The Sinai shepherds invaded Palestine in 1200 B.C. They were a minority in the mountains, and they never settled in the coastal plains. For seven hundred years, they inter-married with the people of the land. The human race does not live in water-tight compartments, and ethnic names centuries old change their significance.

* * *

[4] Rabbi Raisin, *Gentile Reactions to Jewish Ideals*.
[5] Flavius Josephus, *Antiquities of the Jews*, Book XI.

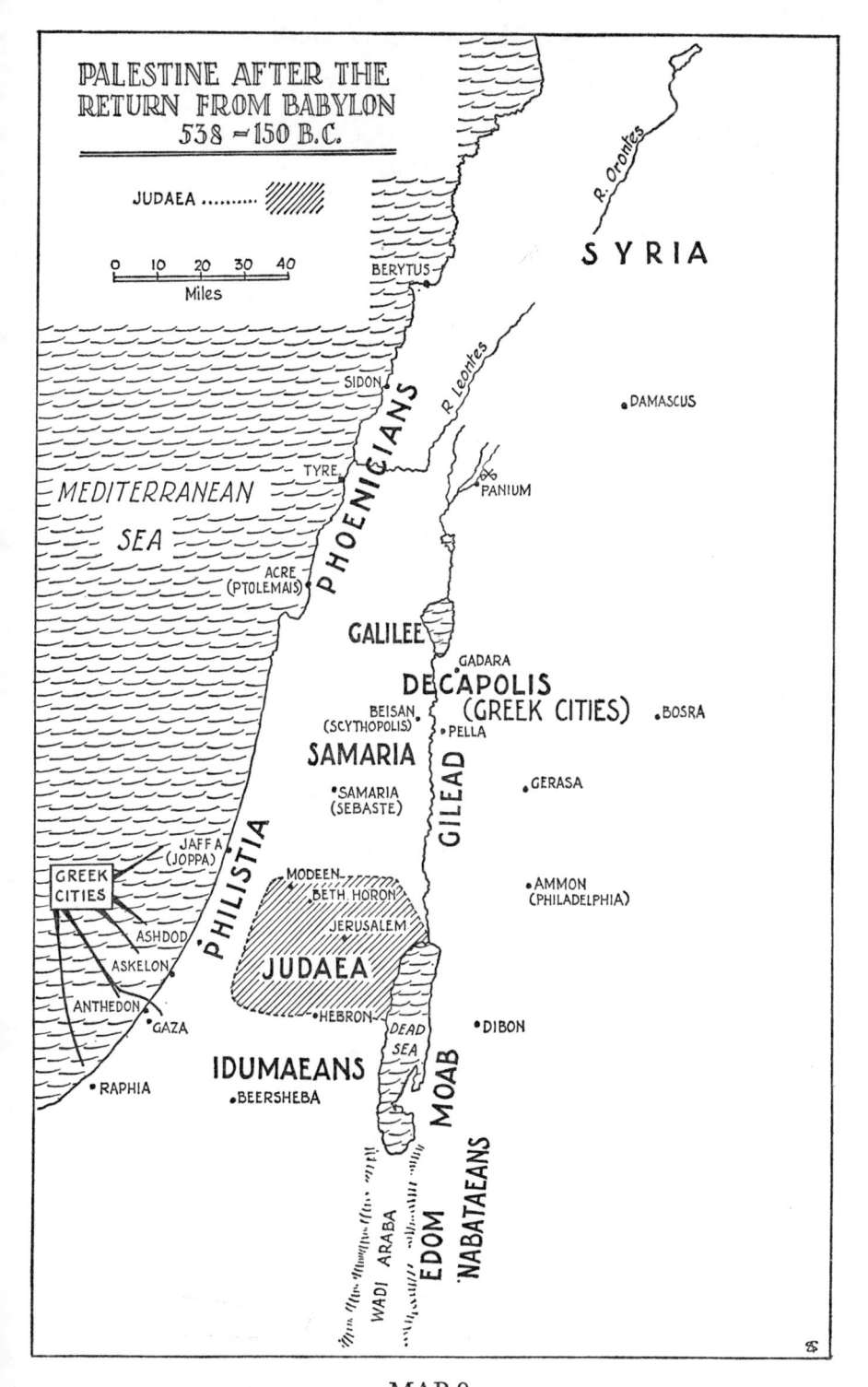

MAP 9

Nehemiah was cup-bearer to Artaxerxes I (464–424 B.C.). The vivid account of how he obtained leave to rebuild the walls of Jerusalem is told in Nehemiah II. With letters from the king and a military escort, he travelled to Jerusalem, about 440 B.C. A natural leader, he collected the people of the district and repaired the city walls. Judaea had been divided between Samaria, Idumaea and Philistia, the governors of which objected to losing part of their territory. Nevertheless, it appears that Judaea was reconstituted into a separate district and Nehemiah was made governor. The date of his death is not recorded, but we know that, in 411 B.C., the governor of Judaea was a Persian official.

But it was Ezra, not Nehemiah, who changed the history of Judah. Probably about 397 B.C., he arrived in Jerusalem with the royal authority to reform the religion of Yahweh. He was an expert in the Law. The Pentateuch he used was not quite the same as ours, but was probably largely similar.

The principal emphasis in Ezra's reform was on the prohibition of marriage between Jews and the rest of humanity. The "holy race" was henceforward to be isolated from mankind. Many Bible commentators loyally acclaim the reforms of Ezra, but Rev. William Neil goes so far as to call him "a holy bigot". Even Rabbi Raisin condemns his narrowness. The movement which he originated, however, is still with us today.

The prohibition of intermarriage was an entirely new idea. The Israelites had been freely intermarrying with the people of the land for eight hundred years. He seems to have been a "reactionary", to use a modern term, who wished to recreate the times of Joshua, trying to revive the original conquerors' contempt for the "natives".

Ezra's reforms were completely opposed to public opinion today. The idea of a superior race, the blood of which would be contaminated by intermixture with others, is no longer popular. Hitler was not original in his conception of a "master race". Aristotle is said to have told the young Alexander that the relationship between Greeks and people of other races was like that between human beings and animals. The narrow pride of a single community, believing itself superior to the rest of humanity, has a never-ending appeal to human vanity.

Ezra shows the same confusion between "race" and religion as still befogs Jewry. He was speaking inaccurately in describing the Jews as "a holy race", for ethnically they were a mixture of many Levantine peoples. The distinction lay between those who served Yahweh or did not.

Ezra's marriage reform was rigidly enforced, "foreign" wives were divorced and their children disowned. What became of the victims of these "broken homes" is not explained. Thereby originated that isolationism which gradually produced an ever-growing hedge of rules and prohibitions, intended to separate those who professed Judaism from the rest of humanity.

But we must not forget that Judaism was no longer limited to Judah, or even to Palestine. It is probable that the number of Jews outside Palestine already exceeded the population of Judah. Since then, Judaism has often shown two conflicting tendencies. Jews scattered in the world became the advocates of a liberal attitude to all peoples, while others insisted on the narrow isolationism of "the holy nation".

Biblical commentators sometimes quote Leviticus XIX, 18, "You shall love your neighbour as yourself", as proving the unique morality of the early Israelites as "God's people". Among Arab tribes, the word neighbour means "fellow tribesman". The full text of Leviticus XIX, 18, is, "You shall not take vengeance or bear any grudge against the sons of your own people, but you shall love your neighbour as yourself."[6] Thus the verse appears, not as benevolence towards humanity, but as a safeguard of tribal solidarity against the world.

As Judaism became more spiritual, the meaning of neighbour seems to have caused doubt, as illustrated by the question addressed by the Scribe to Our Lord.[7] By replying with the parable of the Good Samaritan, Christ made it clear that *He* interpreted neighbour as all mankind. But it was from these same Samaritans that Ezra demanded complete isolation.

Judaism, Islam and Christianity alike insist on compassion, love and humility. Sincere believers in all three religions practise these virtues *within their own communities*. But for two thousand years they have interpreted "neighbours" as their co-religionists only. Jews regarded Christians as savage brutes, Christians visualised Muslims as fierce fanatics. How different the world would be if they had interpreted neighbours as all the human race. The Good Samaritan seems to be one of the most important and least observed of the Gospel parables.

*   *   *

[6] Revised Standard Version.
[7] Luke X, 29.

Ezra's isolationism was not unopposed, even in Judaea. The Book of Ruth seems to be an anti-apartheid pamphlet, written at about this time, the heroine being a Moabitess, the grandmother of David.

More striking, however, is the Book of Jonah. Our complete misunderstanding of this lovely parable is typical of the sterile literalism of our scientific age, for our attention is concentrated on whether or not a whale could swallow a man.

Jonah, whose name means dove, a traditional symbol for Israel,[8] is told to preach to wicked Nineveh. He thus represents Israel, charged to make God known to the world. He does not wish to do so, tries to escape, is thrown into the sea and swallowed by a whale—the Babylonian Captivity. Restored by a miracle to his own country, he goes to Nineveh, which immediately repents. The moral is obvious—if Israel had been obedient, the whole world could have been converted. But the isolationists in Jerusalem were going in the opposite direction, cutting themselves off from the outside world. These two strands were likewise to persist in Judaism, the passion to proselytise and the urge towards isolationism.

But the most penetrating insight into human psychology follows the conversion of Nineveh. When his preaching was successful, Jonah was angry. It is more gratifying to our pride to feel ourselves to be the chosen ones, superior to all other men, than to see the world converted and equal to us. This mentality was not limited to the Jews. The history of the Church shows us innumerable instances of this same sanctimonious pride.

The Book of Jonah ends by pointing out that God loves all His creatures, not only the wicked people of Nineveh but even their cattle. "We are here on the threshold of the Gospels."[9] Such was the answer of liberal Judaism to the narrow isolationism of Ezra.

* * *

The reign of Artaxerxes I (464–424) coincided in Greece with the age of Socrates, Phidias, Plato, Pericles, and Aeschylus, the Golden Age of Greek culture. Already Greek merchants were establishing themselves in the Levant and Greek ideas were beginning to impinge on Syrian thought. Meanwhile, the Persian Empire was growing decadent.

But the chaotic nature of Greek democracy made any extension of Greek power impossible. Only when Philip of Macedon dominated the Greek republics did foreign conquest become feasible. In 334 B.C.,

---

[8] Rev. William Neil, *One Volume Bible Commentary*.
[9] Introduction to the Prophets in the Jerusalem Bible.

Alexander, the son of Philip, crossed into Asia Minor and defeated Darius III at Issus.[10] But he did not pursue the fleeing Persian Army. He realised (and Russia today has not forgotten) that world empire required naval command of the eastern Mediterranean. Marching down the coast, he took the seaports of Tyre and Gaza, occupying Egypt almost unopposed. During the winter of 332–331, he founded another great seaport at Alexandria. In 331, he returned northwards, destroyed the Persian army at Arbela, and annexed the whole Persian Empire. The tiny district of Judah passed unnoticed from Persian to Greek rule.

When, in 323 B.C., Alexander the Great died in Babylon at the age of thirty-three, his vast empire fell apart. Two empires finally emerged. Seleucus I Nicator, a Greek army commander, became the ruler of Persia, Babylonia, Syria and Asia Minor with his capital at Antioch. His rival, another Macedonian officer called Ptolemy, made himself emperor of Egypt, Libya, Cyprus and Palestine.

For nearly three centuries, the Seleucid and Ptolemaic dynasties were to be rivals. The Seleucid was a great land empire, the Ptolemaic a sea power, with naval command of the eastern Mediterranean. Judah, claimed by both sides, found herself a disputed frontier zone, as she had been between Egypt and Assyria. From 301 to 198 B.C., she remained under Egypt.

The most remarkable fact about Alexander had been, not his victories, but the breadth of his ideas. He was strongly opposed to local nationalisms, and urged his men to marry Persian women and fuse the two races. He was not only tolerant, but active in his efforts to end religious and communal hates. The Ptolemies and the Seleucids likewise granted toleration to all religions, and the Judaeans were free to live and worship as they wished.

Both empires tried to persuade Greeks to emigrate to Syria and Egypt. The Greek phalanx was the backbone of both armies. Greek businessmen and settlers poured into the Middle East, building cities inhabited almost entirely by Greeks.

Ptolemy V Epiphanes[11] (204–181 B.C.) came to the throne at the age of five, his Seleucid contemporary being Antiochus III, the Great. In 198 B.C., Ptolemy's army was defeated at Panium, the modern Banias, and Palestine was annexed by the Seleucids.

But a new power was already advancing from the west. In 190 B.C., Antiochus was defeated by the Romans at Magnesia. He retired east of the Taurus, and the states of Asia Minor became Roman satellites.

[10] Map 10, p. 98
[11] For a list of the Ptolemies see p. 104.

Worse still, the Seleucids were obliged to pay so heavy an indemnity as to make their empire virtually bankrupt. Thereafter, the Romans, avoiding war, endeavoured to destroy the Seleucids by intrigue.

The son of Antiochus III, Seleucus IV Philopator, was obliged to send his son Demetrius as a hostage to Rome. In 176 B.C., Seleucus IV was murdered and his brother, Antiochus IV Epiphanes, mounted the throne. An intelligent ruler with charming manners, he enjoyed intellectual conversation. He faced the formidable task of keeping his heterogeneous empire intact while he paid off the indemnity to Rome. The latter played a double game, demanding more money while urging Antiochus' subjects to rebel against the heavy taxation needed to pay the indemnity.

Antiochus Epiphanes sought to hold his empire together by the common bond of Greek culture. Northern Syria was the heart of the empire, from the coast and the Orontes to the Euphrates, including the Greek cities of Antioch, Seleucia, Laodicea (now Latakia) and Apamea.[12] In Palestine, the coastal plain was almost entirely hellenised, with Greek cities at Ptolemais (now Acre), Appolonia, Joppa (Jaffa), Azotus (the Philistine Ashdod, Arabic Isdood), Askelon. Anthedon, Gaza and Raphia (now Rafa). Scythopolis (Beisan) had a large Greek population. Sebaste (Samaria) had been rebuilt as a Greek city.

In Trans-Jordan were the ten Greek cities (the Decapolis), Philadelphia (Ammon, now Amman), Philoteria, Arsinoe, Pella (now Kharbet al Fahal), Dion, Gerasa (now Jerash), Gadara (Umm Qeis), Hippos and Bosra.[12] This extraordinary influx of Greeks changed the ethnic composition of Syria, Lebanon and the coastal plain of Palestine, down to our own times.[13]

Judaea was a Temple state, of which there were others in the empire. The high priest farmed the imperial taxes from the Seleucid king. Seleucid interference was due to a local Judaean intrigue. One Simon, a Temple official, quarrelled with Onias II, the high priest, and suggested to the Seleucid government the seizure of the Temple treasure. The officer sent to enquire into the matter was assaulted and injured.

Meanwhile, the hellenisation of Jerusalem had been started by the Jews themselves. This was not treason against Judaism. The Greeks were the leading nation, as the United States was after the Second World War. To imitate them was modern, not to do so was old fashioned.

---

[12] Map 10, p. 98. Map 11, p. 102.
[13] *Cambridge Ancient History*, Vol. VII, ch. 5.

THE SELEUCIDS

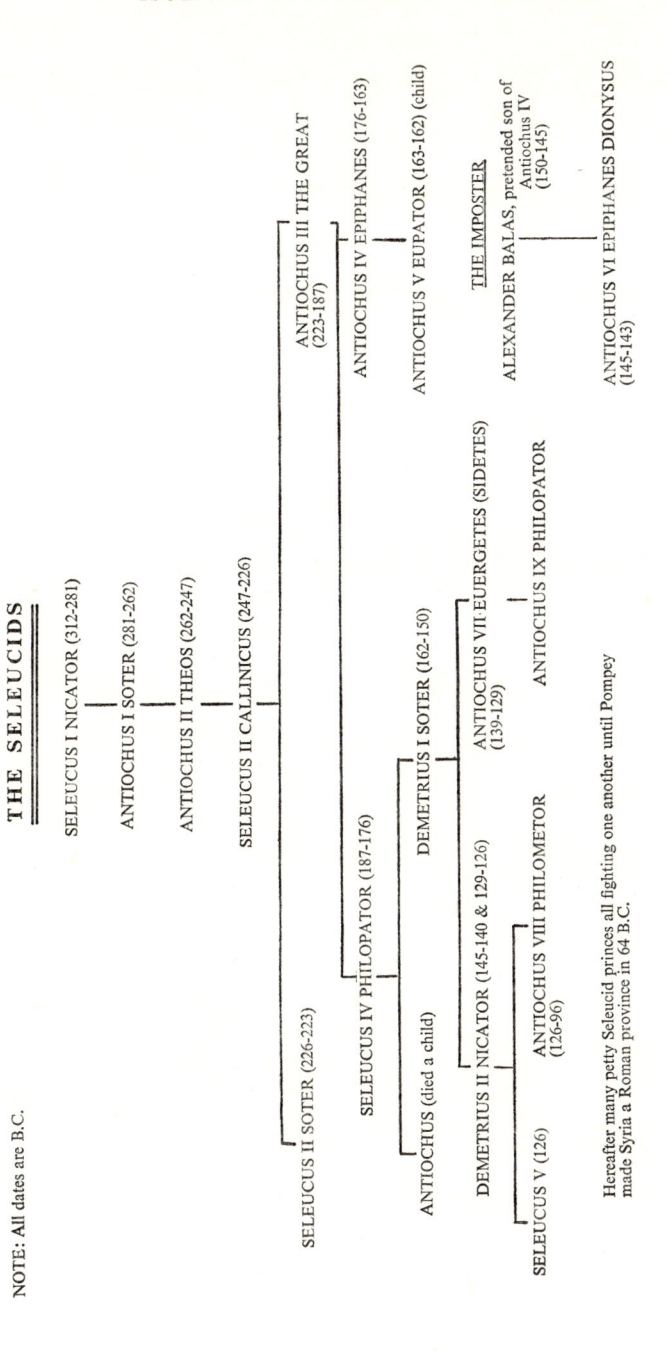

NOTE: All dates are B.C.

- SELEUCUS I NICATOR (312-281)
  - ANTIOCHUS I SOTER (281-262)
    - ANTIOCHUS II THEOS (262-247)
      - SELEUCUS II CALLINICUS (247-226)
        - SELEUCUS II SOTER (226-223)
        - ANTIOCHUS III THE GREAT (223-187)
          - SELEUCUS IV PHILOPATOR (187-176)
            - ANTIOCHUS (died a child)
            - DEMETRIUS I SOTER (162-150)
              - DEMETRIUS II NICATOR (145-140 & 129-126)
                - SELEUCUS V (126)
                - ANTIOCHUS VIII PHILOMETOR (126-96)
              - ANTIOCHUS VII EUERGETES (SIDETES) (139-129)
                - ANTIOCHUS IX PHILOPATOR
          - ANTIOCHUS IV EPIPHANES (176-163)
            - ANTIOCHUS V EUPATOR (163-162) (child)
            - THE IMPOSTER
              ALEXANDER BALAS, pretended son of Antiochus IV (150-145)
              - ANTIOCHUS VI EPIPHANES DIONYSUS (145-143)

Hereafter many petty Seleucid princes all fighting one another until Pompey made Syria a Roman province in 64 B.C.

Demetrius II Nicator and Antiochus VI Epiphanes Dionysus were both reigning from 145 to 143, engaged in civil war.

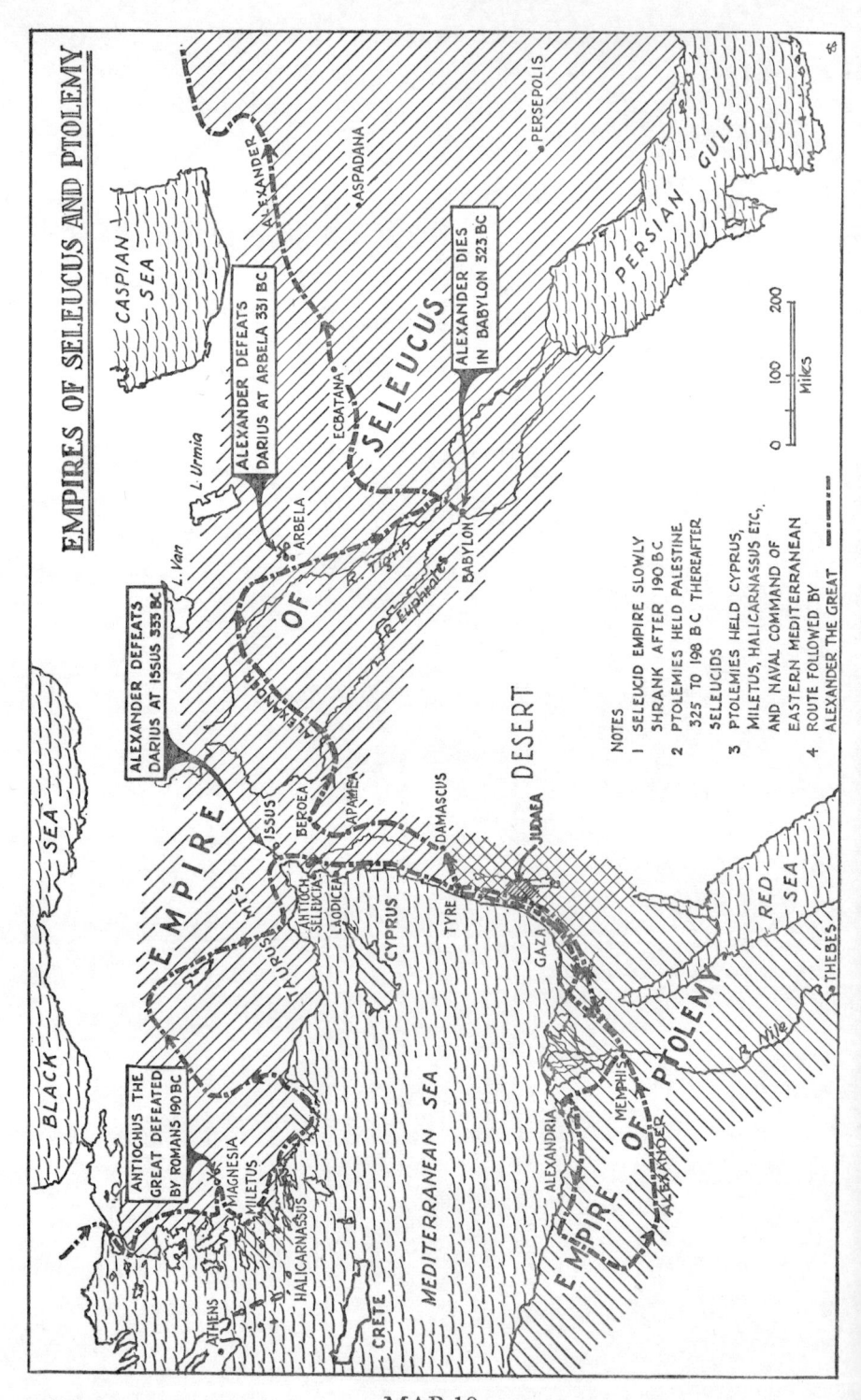

MAP 10

Soon another intrigue began. Jason (note the Greek names), the brother of Onias II, persuaded the Seleucid government to make him high priest in place of his brother. In return, he supported the hellenisers in Jerusalem. Young Jews wore Greek hats and exercised naked in the gymnasium, to the indignation of conservative Jews, for Middle Eastern peoples have always been modest in exposing their bodies. A Jewish deputation took part in the festival of Heracles in Tyre. (Heracles was our old friend Melqart, Jezebel's god, with a nice new Greek name.) "The initiative in the attempt to hellenise Jerusalem was not taken by Antiochus; it was taken by a certain section of the Jews themselves."[14]

Antiochus Epiphanes, in 172 B.C., was threatened with war by Ptolemy and moved to Joppa with an army. He visited Jerusalem, where Jason welcomed him royally with a torchlight procession. New intrigues rent Jerusalem. In 169 B.C., one Menelaus, the brother of Simon already mentioned, persuaded the government to make him high priest, though he was not even of the tribe of Levi. Jason fled to Ammon.

While Antiochus was campaigning in Egypt, in 169 B.C., Jason returned, seized Jerusalem and massacred the adherents of Menelaus. Antiochus was worried by these disturbances behind him, especially as there was a pro-Egyptian party in Jerusalem.

Usually a friendly man, the king made a tragic mistake. The empire included many small religious groups who were loyal to the empire, but in Judah it seemed that religion fomented disloyalty. Not, it seemed, a very admirable religion, for all the disturbances were caused by rival claimants to the post of high priest. As there was already a strong hellenising party in Jerusalem, Antiochus resolved to expedite hellenisation by force. With this, he combined an attempt to suppress Judaism. If he had supported hellenisation and left religion alone, he might have succeeded. But with Rome standing over him, he was in a hurry.

Troops occupied a fort on Mount Zion. Circumcision was forbidden and it was made an offence to refuse to eat pork. In December 167 B.C., the daily temple sacrifices ceased and a statue of Olympian Zeus was set up in the Temple. This action was religious persecution, not because Antiochus favoured any other religion, but because he thought that Judaism was the source of political disturbances.

A village priest, Mattathiah, of the Hasmon family, in the village of Modeen,[15] killed a government official who was offering a pagan

---
[14] *Cambridge Ancient History*, Vol. VIII.
[15] Map 11, p. 102.

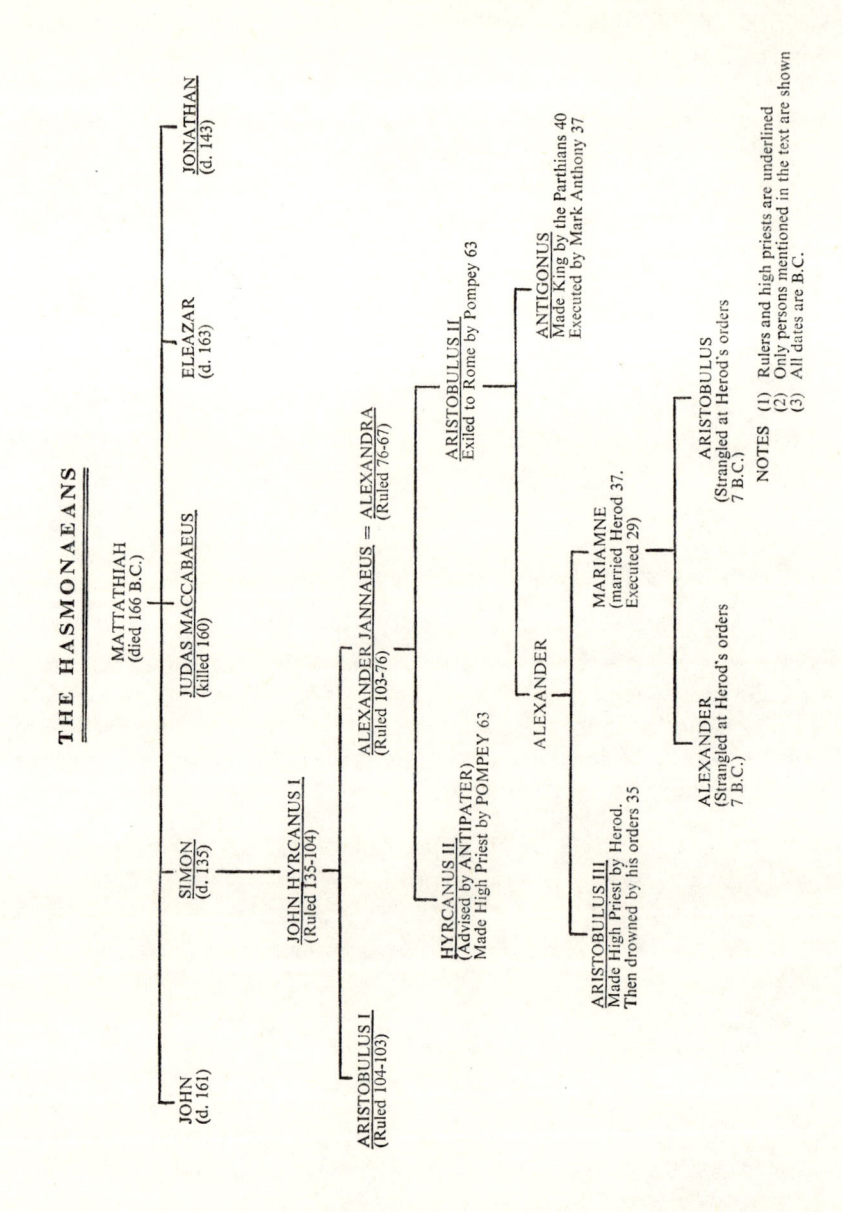

THE HASMONAEANS

```
                        MATTATHIAH
                        (died 166 B.C.)
                             |
        ┌────────────┬───────┴────────┬──────────────┐
        |            |                |              |
      JOHN        SIMON           JUDAS           ELEAZAR        JONATHAN
     (d. 161)     (d. 135)       MACCABAEUS       (d. 163)       (d. 143)
                    |            (killed 160)
                    |
        ┌───────────┴─────────────┐
        |                         |
   ARISTOBULUS I             JOHN HYRCANUS I
   (Ruled 104-103)           (Ruled 135-104)
                                  |
                         ALEXANDER JANNAEUS = ALEXANDRA
                           (Ruled 103-76)     (Ruled 76-67)
                                  |
                    ┌─────────────┴─────────────┐
                    |                           |
                HYRCANUS II                ARISTOBULUS II
                (Advised by ANTIPATER)     Exiled to Rome by Pompey 63
                Made High Priest by              |
                POMPEY 63              ┌────────┴────────┐
                    |                  |                 |
              ALEXANDER           ALEXANDER         ANTIGONUS
                    |                                Made King by the Parthians 40
          ARISTOBULUS III        MARIAMNE            Executed by Mark Anthony 37
          Made High Priest       (married Herod 37.
          by Herod.              Executed 29)
          Then drowned by                |
          his orders 35        ┌─────────┴─────────┐
                               |                   |
                           ALEXANDER          ARISTOBULUS
                           (Strangled at      (Strangled at
                           Herod's orders     Herod's orders
                           7 B.C.)            7 B.C.)
```

NOTES (1) Rulers and high priests are underlined
       (2) Only persons mentioned in the text are shown
       (3) All dates are B.C.

sacrifice. He and his five sons then took to the hills and raided other villages, killing hellenised Jews. In 166 or 165 B.C., Mattathiah died and his third son, Judas, nicknamed Maccabaeus, assumed command. The "Jewish" peasants of 160 B.C. were much the same people as the "Arab" peasants of today. Writing more than two hundred years later, Josephus was able to say, "We are not a commercial people."

The Book of Daniel is thought to have been written at this time. The "little horn" was meant for Antiochus, the Abomination of Desolation for the statue of Zeus in the Temple.[16] The sufferings of Judah also produced the first mention of immortality in Jewish writing.[17]

Antiochus died at Isfahan in 163 B.C. Meanwhile, the regent Lycias made a compromise settlement with Judaea. Eliakim (Greek Alcimus) became high priest and temple services were resumed. Antiochus Eupator became king.

In 162 however, Demetrius arrived from Rome, killed Eupator and mounted the throne.[18] Alcimus, the high priest, sent an embassy to Demetrius to complain against the Hasmonaeans, whose guerrillas, under Judas Maccabaeus, continued their activities. The Hasmonaeans sent a deputation to Rome where they secured an equivocal treaty, a Roman intrigue to undermine the Seleucids.

In Jerusalem, the situation appeared normal and religious toleration had returned. The Hasmonaean guerrillas, however, were still at large and ambushed a Seleucid force at Beth Horon. Demetrius quickly sent troops, the guerrillas were defeated and Judas Maccabaeus was killed. Only two of the sons of Mattathiah now survived, Simon and Jonathan.

Demetrius was too capable to please the Romans, who sent an impostor, Alexander Balas, to claim the Seleucid throne. Demetrius and Balas both sought the help of Jonathan the Hasmonaean who, from being a rebel, suddenly found himself courted by kings. Jonathan supported Alexander, who made him high priest. Alexander had the advantage of being incapable, while Demetrius was brave and efficient. In 150 B.C., Demetrius fell fighting and Alexander Balas became king. Demetrius II, the son of Demetrius I, however, defeated Alexander and himself became king in 145 B.C. He won the support of Jonathan, who took advantage of the confusion to massacre the Jewish supporters of the Seleucids. The crumbling

---

[16] Daniel VIII onwards.
[17] Daniel XII, 2 and 3.
[18] Genealogical Tree, p. 97.

JUDAEA UNDER THE EARLY HASMONAEANS 168-135 B.C.

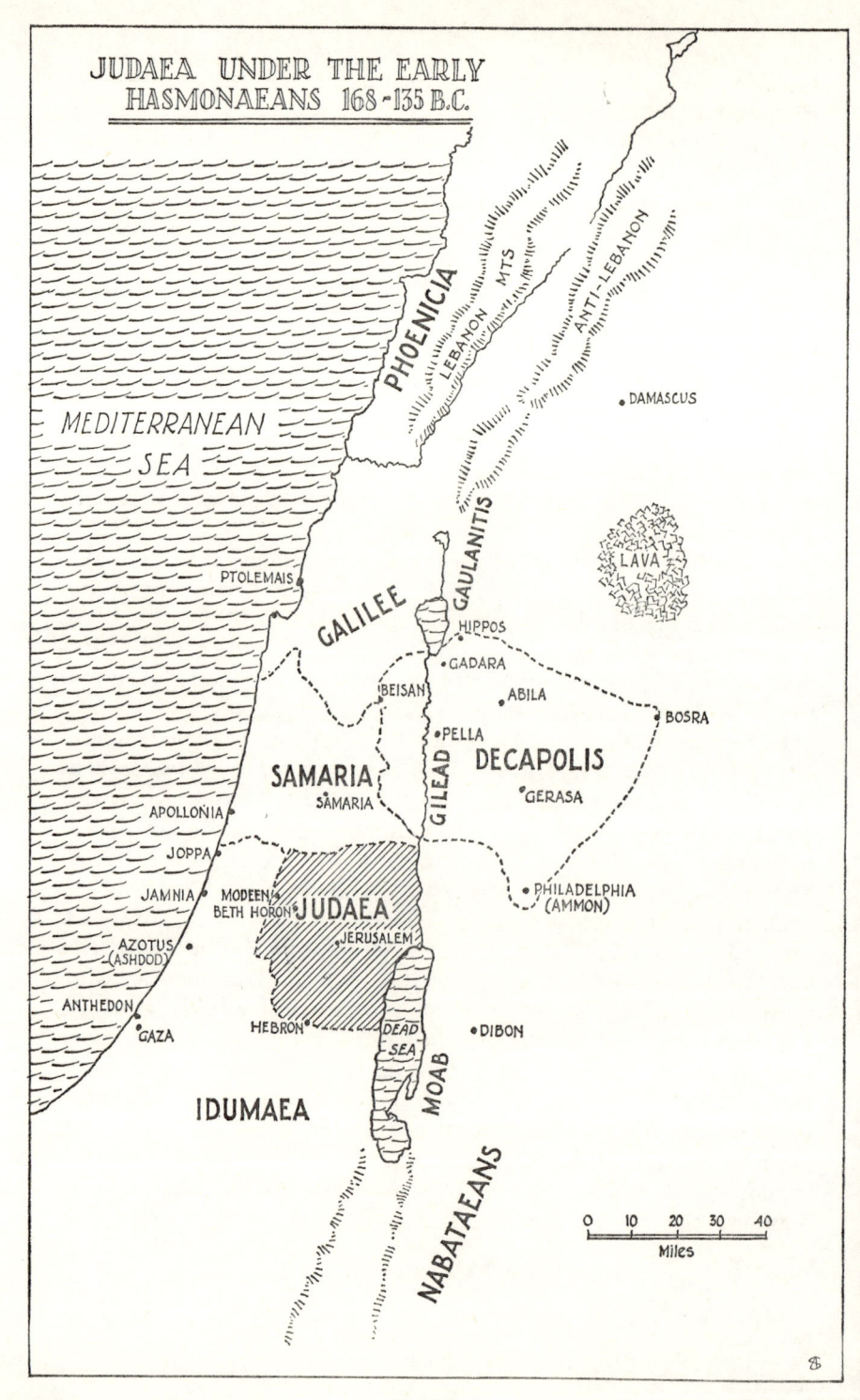

MAP 11

empire had abandoned its own friends to support the extreme nationalists—a process familiar to our own times.

In 145 B.C. the son of Balas rebelled, and Jonathan transferred his support to him. In return, Jonathan's brother Simon was made governor of southern Syria and used Seleucid troops to increase the territory of his new dynasty. In 142 B.C. an adventurer called Tryphon made himself dictator of Syria. Seizing Jonathan on a visit to Ptolemais, he put him to death. Simon assumed control in Judaea and offered his services to Demetrius II.

In May 141 B.C., the Seleucid garrison in Jerusalem surrendered and Judaea found herself independent. In September 140 B.C. the Jewish assembly vested the hereditary high priesthood in the Hasmonaean family. Simon was proclaimed "high priest, commander-in-chief and prince of the people of God". The Greek city of Joppa was conquered and annexed.

In 138 B.C. Simon was assassinated by his son-in-law, but his son, John Hyrcanus, seized power. In the same year, a new Seleucid, Antiochus VII, retook Joppa and then Jerusalem, but allowed Judaea to retain Joppa. In 129 B.C. Antiochus VII was killed and the empire fell into anarchy. Many of the Greek cities became independent. The Nabataeans, an Arab trading community based on Petra, assumed control of Trans-Jordan.

The Hasmonaeans were to rule Judaea until 38 B.C. Though they had started as a religious revolt, their era was to be marked by increasing antagonism between them and the pious Jews, hitherto called Chasidim, but now becoming known as Pharisees.

Just as the Nazi persecution produced the present aggressive military state of Israel, so the originally heroic resistance to Antiochus Epiphanes transformed Judaea into a fanatical and aggressive military principality. John Hyrcanus attacked all his neighbours who, hitherto mere districts of the Seleucid empire, had no military organisation. In the south, he conquered the Idumaeans (formerly called Edomites), who had settled in Hebron. To increase his army, he forcibly converted the Idumaeans to Judaism—a new policy further invalidating any Jewish claim to ethnic unity.

In about 108 B.C., he took the predominantly Greek city of Samaria, massacring the whole population. Scythopolis (Beisan), also chiefly peopled by Greeks, met the same fate. John Hyrcanus died in 104 B.C.

* * *

Judaea under the Hasmonaeans enjoyed a brief spell of independence between empires, much as the Middle East did in our times between the British and the Russians. Enthusiasts hailed the end of imperialism and the independence of small nations. The small nations, then as now, used their independence to attack their neighbours.

"Not the Maccabees or the Parthians conquered the Seleucids but Rome."[19] Indeed the part played by Russia today resembles that of Rome from 200 to 64 B.C. Never fighting but endlessly fomenting wars, Rome reduced the Middle East to chaos before moving in herself.

NOTABLE DATES

The Babylonian Conquest	587 B.C.
Permission given by Cyrus to rebuild the Temple	538 B.C.
Nehemiah governor of Judah	440 B.C.
Ezra's reforms	about 397 B.C.
Alexander occupies Egypt	332 B.C.
Palestine under the Ptolemies	301–198 B.C.
Antiochus Epiphanes tries to suppress Judaism	169 B.C.
Hasmonaean Rebellion	166 B.C.
Death of Judas Maccabaeus	160 B.C.
Disintegration of the Seleucid empire	150–64 B.C.

THE PTOLEMIES

Ptolemy I Soter	(323–283 B.C.)
Ptolemy II Philadelphus	(283–246)
Ptolemy III Euergetes	(246–221)
Ptolemy IV Philopator	(221–204)
Ptolemy V Epiphanes	(204–181)
Ptolemy VI Philometor	(181–145)
Ptolemy VII Euergetes (Physcon)	(170–116)
Ptolemy VIII Soter (Lathyrus)	(116–108 and 88–80)
Ptolemy IX Alexander	(108–88)
Ptolemy X Alexander	(80)
Ptolemy XI Philopator Philadelphus Neos (Auletes)	(80–51)
Ptolemy XII Philopator and his sister Cleopatra	(51–47)
Ptolemy XIII Philopator with Cleopatra	(47–44)
Ptolemy XIV Caesarion with his mother Cleopatra (He was allegedly the son of Cleopatra and Julius Caesar)	(44–30)
Egypt becomes a Roman province	30 B.C.

[19] *Cambridge Ancient History*, Vols. VII and VIII.

CONCLUSIONS

(1) The Dispersion of the Jews began in 587 B.C. with the Babylonian Conquest.

(2) Three generations in Babylon changed the Judaeans from peasants to men of the world.

(3) Ezra originated the idea of "the holy nation", the blood of which would be contaminated by intermarriage with the rest of humanity.

(4) Ever since, Jewry has been divided between isolationists and internationalists.

(5) The priestly aristocracy soon became corrupt. Their intrigues were the cause of Seleucid intervention.

(6) The rebellion of Judas Maccabaeus makes stirring reading, but, when successful, it degenerated into cruel and aggressive militarism.

VII

Jews Fill the World

Thus saith the Lord of hosts, the God of Israel unto all ...
Whom I have caused to be carried away from Jerusalem ...
"Build ye houses and dwell in them and plant gardens and eat
the fruit of them; take ye wives and beget sons and daughters
... and seek the peace of the city whither I have caused you to
be carried away captives, and pray unto the Lord for it; for in
the peace thereof, shall ye have peace."

Jeremiah XXIX, 5 to 7

Jewish life in Babylonia flourished economically and spiritually;
and in Egypt there developed a prosperous and happy Jewish
community that reached one million in the first century of the
Christian era. The centre of Jewish life had long since shifted
to Babylonia and Egypt.

MOSHE MENUHIN, *The Decadence of Judaism in our Time*

Their dispersion along all the Mediterranean coast and the use
of the Greek language, which they adopted when out of
Palestine prepared the way for a propagandism of which
ancient societies ... had till then offered no example ...
Judaism became the true religion in an absolute sense: to all
who wished, the right of entering it was given, and it soon
became a work of piety to bring into it the greatest number
possible.

RENAN, *Life of Jesus*

VII

EVENTS in tiny Judaea tend to command attention to the neglect of Jews in other countries. To redress the balance, we must leave Judaea for a while and consider the Jews of the world.

The Dispersion commenced with the Babylonian Conquest in 587 B.C. (Ten out of the theoretical twelve tribes had, of course, ceased to exist in 722 B.C. with the Assyrian conquest.) The Babylonian conquest left Judaea depopulated. The ruling class was deported, but many Judaeans fled to Egypt, where they settled, some in the capital, Memphis, and some in the provinces. Many intermarried freely with Egyptians.

The conquest of Egypt by Alexander, in 332 B.C., resulted in increased migration from Judah. Josephus[1] states that, "Alexander having received from the Jews very active support against the Egyptians, granted them, as a reward for their assistance, permission to reside in the city [Alexandria] on terms of equality with the Greeks.

"This privilege was confirmed by his successors who, moreover, assigned them a quarter of their own, in order that, through mixing less with aliens, they might be free to observe their rules more strictly; and they were also permitted to take the title of Macedonians." They were allowed their own administration, and their own judicial system. "The Jewish community was in fact a city within a city with powers practically equal to those of the Alexandrines."[2]

It may be noted (in connection with later ghettos) that, in 300 B.C., Jews preferred to live in a Jewish community at a time when, far from being oppressed, they enjoyed special privileges.

The population of Alexandria was graded in four categories:

(a) The Macedonians, a privileged class, presumably Alexander's veterans.

(b) Alexandrines—Greeks living in Alexandria.

(c) Resident foreigners, such as Persians.

(d) Native Egyptians—artisans and labourers. These were not citizens.

---

[1] Flavius Josephus, *Wars of the Jews*, Book II.
[2] H. I. Bell, *Jews and Christians in Egypt*.

Alexandria was an independent city, in which citizenship was a privilege. There were Jews in all four categories. Jewish "Macedonians" were the descendants of those who had assisted in the Greek conquest. Jews in category (d) might have been those already integrated with Egyptians, or Egyptian converts to Judaism.

The Ptolemies continued the privileges accorded by Alexander. They also employed Jews in their armies, some rising to high rank. Seleucus I likewise granted Jews citizenship on an equality with Greeks. Before Alexander, Greeks despised other races as barbarians just as the Jews looked down upon the rest of the human race as Gentiles, but Alexander had been strongly opposed to racial prejudice.

When the Greeks first met the Jews, they were interested. They thought "that their founder Moses, a man of extraordinary sagacity and courage, had deliberately made their customs unlike those of other peoples in order to keep them a nation apart."[3]

When the Greeks came to know the Jews, friction arose. The Jews abstained from all the social amenities of Greek city life, the theatre, the gymnasium and the public festivals. This unsociability provoked resentment. Christianity has been accused of hating Jews, but the same factors existed in 300 B.C.

After 330 B.C., the Middle East was sprinkled with Greek cities. These colonies inclined to be democratic and to annoy emperors and kings. The Jews normally supported the dynasties and not the democracies, provided that they were free to observe their own customs. Where there was a large Jewish community in a Greek city, they built a synagogue and lived together, often being allowed to establish their own judicial system, according to traditional Middle East custom.

Jews often made a speciality of securing important official positions. Perhaps, as an unpopular minority, they hoped thereby to gain security. Under the Ptolemies, many Jews were tax collectors. In Alexandria, by their own choice, the Jewish quarter was near the royal palace. In Judah itself, Hebrew was a dead language, and the Judaeans spoke Aramaic. Under the Ptolemies and the Seleucids the Jews spoke Greek as their native tongue. Commencing under Ptolemy Philadelphus (283–246 B.C.) the Septuagint, the first Greek translation of the Old Testament, was gradually produced in Alexandria.

It was just before this time that the elders in Judaea substituted the name Adonai for Yahweh. (Yahweh was slowly coming to be thought of as the universal, not as a tribal God.) In the Septuagint,

[3] Hecataeus, *Apud Diodorus Siculus*, quoted by S. Davis. In fact, it was not Moses, but Ezra.

Adonai was translated *kyrios*, lord. Thus, all unnoticed, did the chosen people of Yahweh become the Chosen People of God.

Jews in Egypt and Syria lived in a Greek atmosphere and studied Greek philosophy. While the majority continued to observe the Law, their minds were saturated with Greek culture, and they shared less and less the narrow outlook of the Judaeans. Their devotion to Greek thought gave them a tendency to universalism. Yet the intellectual predominance of the Greeks went with a polytheistic religion. Judaism as a religion, combined with Greek culture, would, the Jews felt, produce an ideal society. The Jews of the Dispersion, accordingly, set themselves to convert the Greek world.

No one in the ancient world was interested in ethnology. It is, therefore, impossible for us to discover who the Jews of the Dispersion were. The Graeco-Roman geographer, Strabo (born 63 B.C.), says that by 87 B.C. the whole world was full of Jews. "It would be difficult to find a place in the whole world which did not have a large and influential Jewish community."

Speaking in 59 B.C., Cicero, in defence of Flaccus, said in Rome, "You know how large a group they [the Jews] are, how unanimously they stick together, how influential they are in politics."

Estimates of the numbers of Jews in the outside world to those in Judaea shortly before the time of Christ vary as widely as statements that, "the Jews of the Dispersion were at least as numerous as those in Judaea", to "Jews of the Dispersion may well have been ten times as numerous". Perhaps four or five times would be a likely guess. "Judaeans flowed in a steady stream into other countries", writes Rabbi Raisin, speaking of Hasmonaean times (166 B.C. to 38 B.C.). "The multitude of Jews all over the world on the eve of the Roman invasion of Palestine," he continues, "was not the result of abnormal fecundity. A very large proportion of them were converted Gentiles."[4]

Jean Juster refers to the "fury of proselytisation" which seized the Jews from 200 B.C. to A.D. 300.[5] Rabbi Raisin again refers to "a rising tide of proselytisation" in the two centuries before Christ. For five hundred years—300 B.C. to A.D. 200—the Jews were spiritually more advanced than the Greeks and the Romans. Roman religion became more and more a state ritual. By contrast, the new Judaism, with its monotheism and its appeal to the individual, deeply impressed the masses.

The chief obstacle to conversion was the Law, which meant

---

[4] Rabbi Raisin, *Gentile Reactions to Jewish Ideals*.
[5] Jean Juster, *Les Juifs sous L'Empire Romain*.

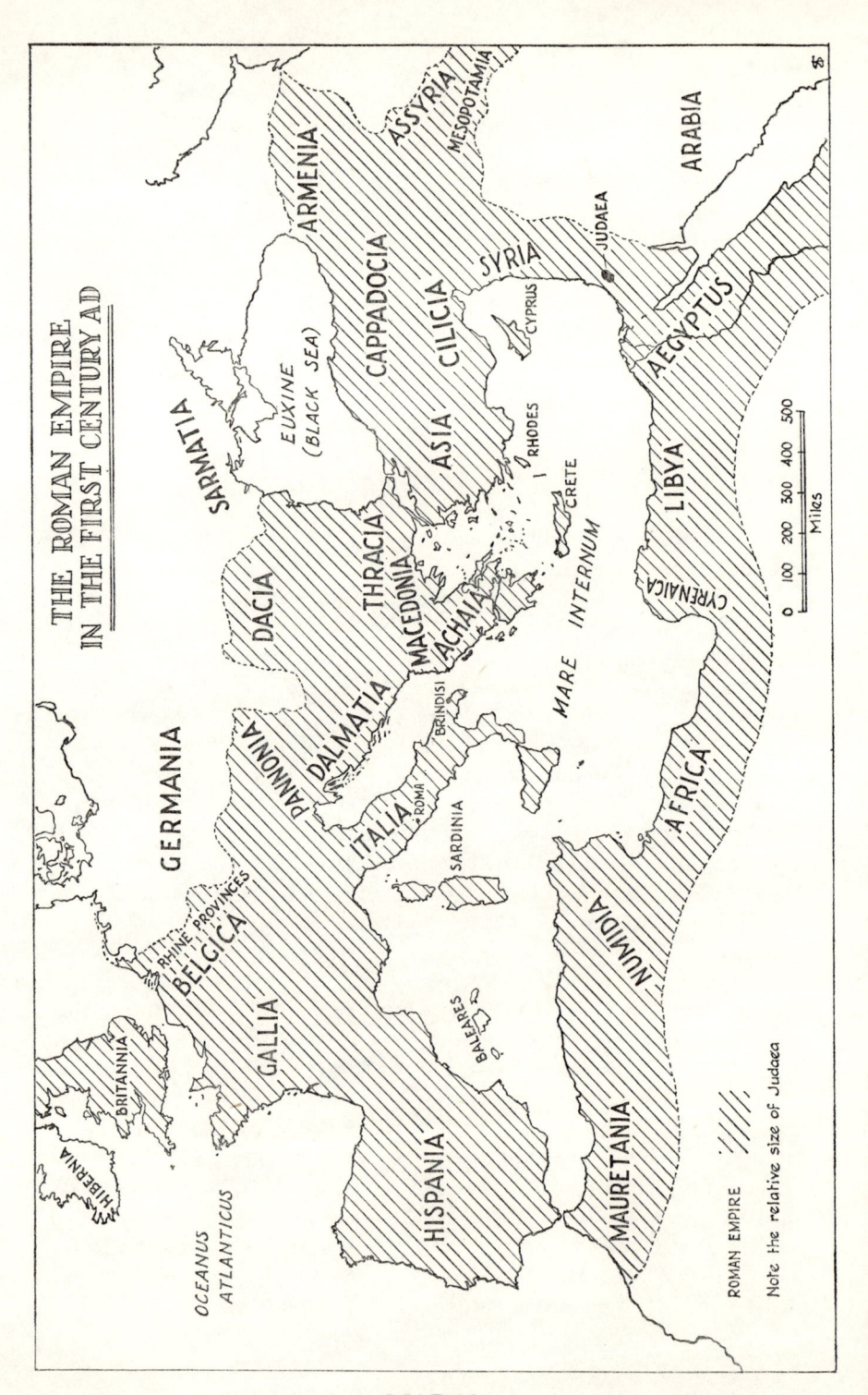

MAP 12

circumcision, Sabbath observance and the dietary laws. Circumcision was a deterrent to men, but Sabbath observance was popular. The dietary laws obliged a proselyte to leave his family and friends, and move into a Jewish community. In no other way could he obtain Jewish food. In view of the agony of such a decision it is remarkable how many proselytes were made.

The attraction of Judaism to pagans was its spiritual quality and its intimate appeal to the individual worshipper. Compared with these essentials, the insistence on innumerable rules about food seems to us trivial. The Jews, however, were adamant. Converts must live as Jews among Jews and cut themselves off completely from the Gentile world—they could not be Jews, and also Greeks or Persians.

The result was the appearance of a class of half-Jews, known as "God-fearers". These people were drawn by the monotheism and the spiritual appeal of Judaism, but would not or could not comply with all the dietary laws. Juster estimates the number of "God-fearers" to have been equal to that of full converts. Their combined numbers must have constituted a formidable proportion of the population of the empire. This rapid rate of conversion is not so surprising when we think that in three hundred years—say A.D. 32 to A.D. 325—Christianity was to convert the whole Roman Empire.

The fact is that the Greeks and the Romans, with all their intellectual triumphs, were suffering from spiritual starvation. Every human being has a longing for God, even if it be subconscious. If this thirst for God were stimulated, the whole earth could be flooded with the knowledge of God, as the waters cover the sea.

Juster has made studies of the cities in which Jews formed an important community in Roman times. It includes almost every city in France, Italy, Sicily, Sardinia, Spain, the Balearics, Greece, Thrace, Pannonia, Dalmatia, Macedonia, Asia Minor, Syria, Armenia, Mesopotamia, Assyria, Babylonia, north and south Persia, Arabia, the Yemen, Egypt, Ethiopia, Cyrenaica, Libya, Africa down to Mauretania, and the Rhine provinces of Germany. He compiled his list from inscriptions, Jewish cemeteries and literary sources.

Philo, the Jewish philosopher of Alexandria, claimed that "half the human race" were Jews. Other sources allege that, at the time of Christ, there were a million Jews in Egypt out of seven million people, or fourteen per cent. In Cyrenaica, the proportion was the same. In Rome under Tiberius (42 B.C.–A.D. 37) there were sixty thousand Jews out of eight hundred thousand, or seven and a half per cent. The population of the empire under Augustus has been estimated at fifty-five million, of whom nearly five million were Jews, or about nine per cent. Bar Hebraeus (*c.* 1270) a Jew converted to Christianity, says that there were seven million Jews under Claudius (A.D. 41–54), which would give twelve and a half per cent of the population of the empire.

If we accept Juster's estimate that God-fearers were as numerous as Jews, it will be seen that the Jews constituted an extremely serious problem for the Romans. The above figures do not, of course, include the Jews in Persia, Babylonia or Arabia, outside the Roman Empire.

Of the million Jews in Egypt under the Ptolemies, some were very rich and many were tax-collectors. It seems, therefore, that the traditional connection of Jews with finance had already begun in Alexandria before the time of Christ. When Josephus wrote, after A.D. 70, that the Jews were not a commercial people, he was referring only to the Judaeans. An interesting comparison may perhaps be drawn with the Irish in the last three centuries. Ireland was a country of poor peasants, yet Irish emigrants often rose to fame, when they moved to Britain or to the United States.

The Jews of Alexandria had served the Ptolemies for nearly three centuries but when the Romans arrived they abandoned the Greeks and helped the new conquerors, receiving special favours from the Roman emperors in return.[6] Augustus withdrew the democratic independence of the Alexandrines but confirmed the Jewish privileges. The Greeks of Alexandria consequently disliked the Jews as the pampered minions of their Roman conquerors. The Jews seemed always to succeed in being on the winning side.

In the summer of A.D. 38, Agrippa I,[7] coming from Rome, landed at Alexandria and was given a royal reception by the Jews. The Greeks, to show their resentment at Roman favouritism of the Jews, parodied the Jewish celebrations by dressing up an idiot in royal robes. Violent riots followed, Jewish premises were sacked and Jews killed. Both sides sent deputations to Rome, but the infamous Caligula was emperor and neither party obtained satisfaction.

Later, rioting recommenced, the Jews this time being the aggressors. "The Alexandrine Jews were not all Platonising philosophers (like Philo), nor shrinking and persecuted martyrs, but for the most part a violent and turbulent rabble as likely to institute a pogrom as to suffer one."[8]

[6] H. I. Bell, *Jews and Christians in Egypt*.
[7] See next chapter.
[8] S. Davis, *Race Relations in Ancient Egypt*.

On 24th January, A.D. 41, Caligula was assassinated and Claudius became emperor. Both sides again sent deputations to Rome. Claudius' reply is still extant. Couched in carefully measured terms, the letter reprimands the Greeks for their hatred of the Jews and confirms all the privileges enjoyed by the latter. "I must reserve for myself," he writes, "an unyielding indignation against whoever caused this renewed outbreak; but I tell you plainly that if you do not desist from this baneful and obstinate hostility, I shall perforce be compelled to show what a benevolent prince can be, when turned to just indignation . . . I bid the Jews to profit by what they possess . . . an abundance of all good things. And not to invite Jews . . . from Syria . . . thus compelling me to conceive a greater suspicion. Otherwise I will by all means take vengeance on them as fomenting a general plague for the whole world."[9]

The Alexandrian riots are of interest for several reasons:

They disprove the charge that hostility to Jews was originated by Christianity. The same phenomenon existed in pre-Christian times.

The Alexandrian riots are, conversely, sometimes quoted to prove that the unhappy Jews have always been persecuted. In Alexandria, however, the Jews were the favourites of the government. Many Alexandrian Jews held important offices in the financial departments of the administration. This situation gave them power, but was not calculated to make them popular.

Space does not allow of separate discussion of the Jews in every country, but perhaps the following extract from Renan may be taken as typical. Jews, he says, arrived very early in Gaul, long before the birth of Christ. They were well received and made many converts. "There were groups of people, who attached themselves to Judaism by conversion, who did not have a single ancestor in Palestine. And when one remembers that the Jewries of England and Germany have come from France, we regret that we do not possess more data. One would probably see that the Jew of Gaul at the time of Gontran or Chilperic (died A.D. 584) was more often only a Gaul professing the Israelitish religion."

* * *

In the previous chapter, we left Judaea, in 104 B.C., under John Hyrcanus, and we shall resume the narrative in the next chapter. We will now break off the historical narrative and write a few words

[9] H. I. Bell, *Jews and Christians in Egypt.*

on the religious development of Judaism, which made it so attractive to pagans in the Roman Empire.

*　　*　　*

We have seen how, before the Babylonian conquest, the ordinary Israelite believed Yahweh to be the tribal god of Israel. He had no conception of the whole world, still less of the universe. This, in my humble opinion, did not prevent Moses, Isaiah and the prophets from receiving genuine spiritual experiences for, fortunately for us, God does not limit His mercies to those whose theology is *intellectually* correct.

The Israelite religion of Yahweh, it is true, commanded them to worship only one god, but it did not exclude the existence of other gods. But when the Israelites became integrated with the people of the land and grew wealthy, their religion too became elaborate. Their increasing commercialism led to the inevitable results which can be seen today in western Europe and North America—materialism and self-seeking. As always occurs in such circumstances, catastrophe followed.

But it was from that very catastrophe that spiritual Judaism arose. All the material factors on which religion had relied were gone. Something vaster, more spiritual and more enduring began slowly to emerge.

Jewish records pass lightly over the period from Ezra to Antiochus, but in this period Judaism had quietly attained new ethical levels.[10] It now began to be preached that God should be worshipped for Himself, and not for reward. About 200 B.C. appeared the Book of Jesus, the son of Sirach, called in our Apochrypha, Ecclesiasticus.

> My son, be gentle in carrying out your business,
> And you will be better loved than a lavish giver.
> The greater you are, the more you should behave humbly,
> And then you will find favour with the Lord.
>
> Many are the arrogant and renowned,
> But the humble are those to whom he reveals his secrets.
> For great though the power of the Lord is,
> He accepts the homage of the humble.[11]

---

[10] G. F. Moore, *Judaism*.
[11] Ecclesiasticus III, 17 to 21. Jerusalem Bible.

What long centuries of quiet growth divide this poem from Samuel's demand for the utter extermination of the Amalekites.

* * *

In the case of individuals, suffering can produce two alternative results. It may deepen the character of the sufferer making him more gentle, more kind and more sympathetic to other people. Or it may embitter him against God and man, and produce a narrow fanatic, seeking only for revenge. Job's wife urged him to curse God and die, but he replied, "Shall we receive good at the hand of the Lord and shall we not receive evil?"

The Jews seem to me to have reacted in the same manner. The terrible catastrophe of the Babylonian conquest produced two results. Some of them became saints, while others grew into narrow, bitter fanatics. Both types were to continue side by side.

* * *

It is not possible to say that "the Jews", at any given moment, believed this or that—human affairs are much too complicated. In about 200 B.C., however, the following trends may be indicated:

The great majority of "Jews" were no longer in Judaea but filling the world, many of them being Gentile proselytes.

Secondly, in Judaea, the priestly aristocracy (soon to be called Sadducees) were largely hellenised and extremely venal.

Thirdly, many quiet thinkers were beginning to conceive of God as Ruler of the world, not only of Israel.

Fourthly, before Babylon, Israelite thinking had been tribal, that is to say, communal. The prophets declared that Israel had sinned and would be punished. The whole community was responsible. The disappearance of Judah and the Temple, and the emigration to other countries, made individuals responsible for their own piety.

The gradual perception that Yahweh (or Adonai as He was beginning to be called) was the God of the whole world led to the uncomfortable suspicion that Israel might not be the *sole* recipient of His mercy. "The belief that the true religion must in the end be the universal religion of itself made Judaism a missionary religion.[12]

"The exclusive worship of one god alone ... by the law of a national religion, is not monotheism at all," continues G. F. Moore.

[12] G. F. Moore, *Judaism*.

Monotheism is the belief that only one God exists. As the implications of monotheism "were recognised they were found to collide with the exclusiveness of the reciprocal relationship between God and Israel." The Jews, consequently, set out zealously to convert the world.

Nevertheless, they still hankered to keep for themselves the principal rôle. Thus a conflict appeared between the idea of world conversion to Judaism, on the one hand, and the continued pre-eminence of the Jews on the other. The solution was that a Gentile convert must be "adopted" into the Jewish community, as sons and daughters were adopted into families in classical times. The adopted son only became a full member of his new family by completely renouncing the old.

While this provision must have deterred many would-be converts, it ensured the retention of the peculiarities of the Jewish community, independent of ethnic origins. Thus Judaism did not become an international religion but remained a distinctive community. In many countries, the "Palestinian-Jewish" ethnic element was so small as to be negligible, yet the community retained the typical peculiarities of Jewish life.

The insistence that Gentile proselytes must become in every respect Jews (abandoning their former nationalities, ties and families and living in a Jewish community), was decisive. It was the key to the phenomenon of how Jews can in many ways be so alike and yet belong to innumerable ethnic stocks.

Judaism claimed to have been revealed by God to Moses. Nothing thereafter could, in theory, be changed without implying that the original revelation was wrong. Yet, in fact, Judaism had changed completely. This was effected by the religious leaders, who deduced a new, spiritual faith from verses here and there in the Old Testament. They themselves also made new rulings which were rigidly enforced. The belief in immortality did not appear until about 150 B.C., but even then Judaism looked rather to a Millennium on earth than to a future life.

The Babylonian Conquest, by destroying the Temple, gave birth to the synagogue, wherever Jews collected. The synagogue was originally a school for instruction in the Law, and only later became a place of worship. The school was everywhere the sign of the Jewish community. The pagans had no religious schools and no organized method of teaching religion.

The synagogue school was the chief instrument for effecting conversions. They were open to anyone and, as the teaching was in

Greek and other local languages, many Gentiles went to listen. Great numbers, in that decadent and despairing world, were impressed by what they heard.

"At the time of Judas Maccabaeus, for example, there were virtually no Jews in Galilee," says G. F. Moore. "A century later, Jews were in a majority." Some of these, as we shall see, had been converted by force, but some were voluntary Gentile converts.

"There is no way of estimating statistically the results of Jewish propaganda (to secure converts) in the centuries that fall within the limits of our enquiry, but they were indisputably very large. The converts were of many races and of all ranks in society."[13] Some of the most eminent scholars of the second century A.D. were of Gentile origin, including the famous Rabbi Akiba.

* * *

Entering, as we now are, the Roman era, a few words may be useful on the Jewish privileges, which have already been mentioned. Religious toleration was sincerely respected in antiquity. The gods of the nations were courteous to one another. Only the God of Israel was "fierce and unsociable. He refused to reciprocate the toleration which other religions were willing to give Him."[14] To pagans, He seemed always jealous, refusing to allow his servants to perform many actions which were compulsory by law.

To other governments, the Jews were a problem. Either they must be compelled to obey the laws—which, they would complain, was religious persecution, an idea uncongenial to the ancients; or else they must be given privileges, making them alone immune from the laws. The Greeks and Romans did not punish people for their beliefs, but only for their actions.

Among the many privileges accorded to Jews alone was exemption from military service, and from work on Saturdays. In Rome, when a distribution of food was made to the poor on a Saturday, Jews could draw theirs on Sunday. If the food was of a kind they refused to eat, they could have the value in cash. The export of gold was forbidden. Jews only could collect gold and send it to Jerusalem.

In some places, Jews had their own food markets, their own police and their own judges, who could try both civil and criminal cases and inflict punishments. They could hold public meetings, form associations, collect and spend money. No other community had the

---

[13] G. F. Moore, *Judaism*.
[14] Jean Juster, *Les Juifs sous l'Empire Romain*.

right to do these things. Polygamy was illegal under Roman Law, but Jews could have as many wives as they wished.

Government officials were compelled to attend public festivals. The oath taken by an official on assuming office included a reference to the divine qualities of the emperor. On some occasions, Jews were refused office because they would not take the oath, on others the formality was waived, for Jews only, or a different formula employed. At any rate, many Jews achieved the rank of Roman knights, and there were Jewish members of the Senate. It is not surprising that other communities complained that Jews received the same rewards as other citizens, but were excused most of the duties.

The rebellions in Judaea caused no curtailment of these privileges throughout the empire. After a rebellion, many Judaeans were taken to Rome as slaves, part of whom worked in the imperial palace. As the years passed they were gradually freed. Jewish freedmen in the palace were known to the emperor, and were sent to the provinces as his personal representatives, to deliver secret letters or to enquire into abuses. Poppaea, the mistress, and later the wife of Nero, was believed to be a "God-fearer", and used her immense influence to assist the Jews.

Augustus sent costly gifts to the Temple in Jerusalem. His wife, Livia, had a Jewish maid. The children of the Herodian family[15] lived for many years in Rome, on familiar terms with the imperial family. "Jewish practices had penetrated into pagan Roman circles, perhaps even into the higher social orders... The Jews were aggressive in securing converts to their religious views and practices."[16]

It was their aggressive proselytisation which occasionally got them into trouble in Rome, especially when their converts were in "the higher social orders". Complaints of the terrible persecutions of Jews by the Romans can scarcely be called historical.

NOTABLE DATES

The Babylonian Conquest	587 B.C.
Alexander the Great	336–323 B.C.
Alexander's Conquest of Egypt	332 B.C.
Substitution of Adonai for Yahweh	about 300 B.C.
Commencement of the Septuagint	about 280 B.C.

---

[15] See next chapter.
[16] Henry J. Leon, *The Jews of Ancient Rome*.

CONCLUSIONS

(1) The Dispersion began with the Babylonian Conquest in 587 B.C.

(2) The Judaeans found life more spacious in Babylon, Egypt, Syria and Greece and few returned to Judaea.

(3) After about 300 B.C., great numbers of Gentiles were converted to Judaism.

(4) The Babylonian disaster produced two opposite results.
- (a) A spiritualisation of Judaism, envisaging a single God of all mankind.
- (b) A narrow, fanatical nationalism, demanding isolation from all the human race who were not Jews.

VIII

The Herodians

Herod was not all monster... In his younger years, he was attractive; his charm could cast a spell over men and women. The man who could become the friend of Antony and of Augustus... cannot have been an empty or an immeritorious man. Everyone flattered these men, particularly their clients; but only Herod won their friendship, only Herod became the confidant of Agrippa, only Herod was appointed by Augustus official adviser to the Roman governor of Syria. All this argues ... outstanding ability. That Herod possessed it was proved by his administrative ability... They knew that they could rely upon him absolutely. The country was at peace during his reign, trade flourished, cities were restored and new ones built.

STEWART PEROWNE, *The Life and Times of Herod the Great*

VIII

THE Seleucid collapse left the Levant in anarchy, as it is today (1970). In Judaea, the Maccabaean revolt had resulted in an outburst of aggressive militarism. "The object now quite evidently was no longer the protection of the Jewish faith, but the strengthening and extending of Jewish power."[1]

Under John Hyrcanus, who died in 104 B.C., antagonism between the Hasmonaeans and the Pharisees had greatly increased, together with the growth of aggressive nationalism, showing itself in territorial expansion by conquest. Hyrcanus, hated at home, used mercenaries recruited in Asia Minor. After conquering Idumaea, he had seized Marisa and Adora in Philistia, again forcibly circumcising the inhabitants. Since the Babylonian captivity, the urge to convert the world to Judaism had been growing. The Hasmonaeans, though not religious, were aggressive nationalists and used forcible conversion.

John Hyrcanus was succeeded by his son Judah, called in Greek Aristobulus (104–103 B.C.). He was popular with the Greeks although, according to Josephus, he murdered his mother and his brother. He conquered Galilee, which was inhabited by a people called the Ituraeans, whom he circumcised by force.

At the time of Judas Maccabaeus, there had been virtually no Jews in Galilee.[2] Isaiah had called it "Galilee of the Gentiles". "The Galileans of the time of Jesus Christ must have had largely heathen ancestors."[3] Many Christians may be startled to hear that some of the Twelve Apostles may not have been ethnically Jews.

Aristobulus was succeeded by his brother, Alexander Jannaeus (193–76 B.C.), who took the title of king. "The new priest-king proved to be a savage ruffian. His reign was filled with fighting. His arms extended the Jewish kingdom till it practically coincided with the Kingdom of David."[4]

He attacked Ptolemais, but met with a bloody repulse. Turning east, he seized the Greek city of Gadara. In 96 B.C. he invaded the hellenised coastal plain, and took and burnt Gaza. Thence he invaded Gaulonitis.[5] He suffered a crushing defeat and arrived back

---

[1] Emil Schurer, *A History of the Jewish People*.
[2] G. F. Moore, *Judaism*.
[3] *Cambridge Ancient History*, Vol. IX.
[4] *Cambridge Ancient History*, Vol. IX.
  Jaulan or Golan, seized by the modern state of Israel in 1967.

MAP 13

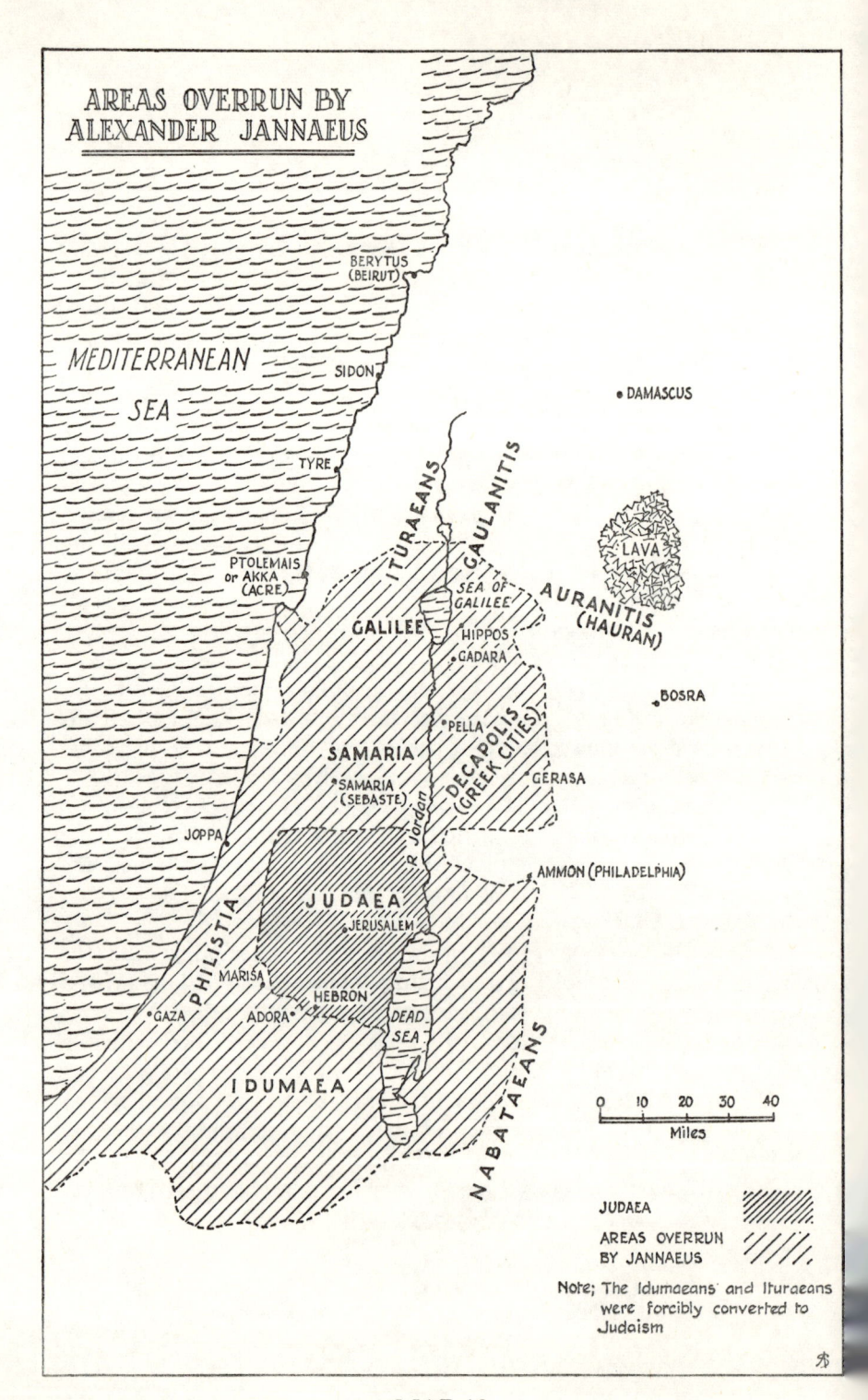

in Judaea as a fugitive in 90 B.C. This disaster was the sign for a rebellion, instigated by the Pharisees. Two years of civil war used up the resources of Jannaeus and he asked for terms, but the rebels insisted on his death. Fighting continued, the rebels being assisted by a Seleucid prince, Demetrius III, great-great-great nephew of Antiochus Epiphanes. Again Jannaeus was defeated.

But many Judaeans were alarmed at the sight of a Seleucid. Jannaeus gained support and suppressed the revolt after six years of savage civil war. He celebrated his victory with one of the most barbarous actions in history. "As he was feasting with his concubines in the sight of all the city," writes the Jewish historian, Josephus, "he ordered about eight hundred of them [the rebels] to be crucified, and while they were still living he ordered the throats of their children and wives to be cut before their eyes. This was by way of revenge for the injuries they had done him."[6]

No sooner was his authority restored than Jannaeus resumed his aggressive wars. While besieging a fortress near Gerasa (Jerash), he died, in 76 B.C., of alcoholism, from which he had been suffering for three years. "Over the hellenised cities of southern Syria, the conquests of a barbarian like Jannaeus passed like a devastating storm. Once populous districts went back to wilderness."[7]

He was succeeded by his wife, Salome Alexandra, who reigned nine years. Female rulers were rare in Israel but common in Egyptian and Hellenistic dynasties. Jannaeus, on his death bed, advised his wife to reverse his policy and to ally herself with the Pharisees.[8] This the queen did sincerely, her reign passing peacefully, for the Pharisees enjoyed wide popular support. Her son, Hyrcanus II, a weak man under the thumb of the Pharisees, was made high priest. Her second son, Aristobulus II, had the fierce spirit of his father. When Alexandra died in 67 B.C., civil war broke out between the brothers, Aristobulus II being supported by the Sadducees.

Antipater, an Idumaean, had been made governor of Marisa and Adora by John Hyrcanus. His son, Antipater II, married an heiress of Petra, who bore four sons, Phasael, Herod, Joseph and Pheroras. Ethnically Idumaeans (Edomites) the family had been forcibly Judaised by John Hyrcanus.[9]

Antipater II took service under the weak Hyrcanus II, who was soon forced to retire by his fierce brother, Aristobulus, who made

---

[6] Flavius Josephus, *Antiquities of the Jews*, Book XIII.
[7] *Cambridge Ancient History*.
[8] Flavius Josephus, *Antiquities of the Jews*
[9] Genealogical Tree 3, p. 120

MAP 14

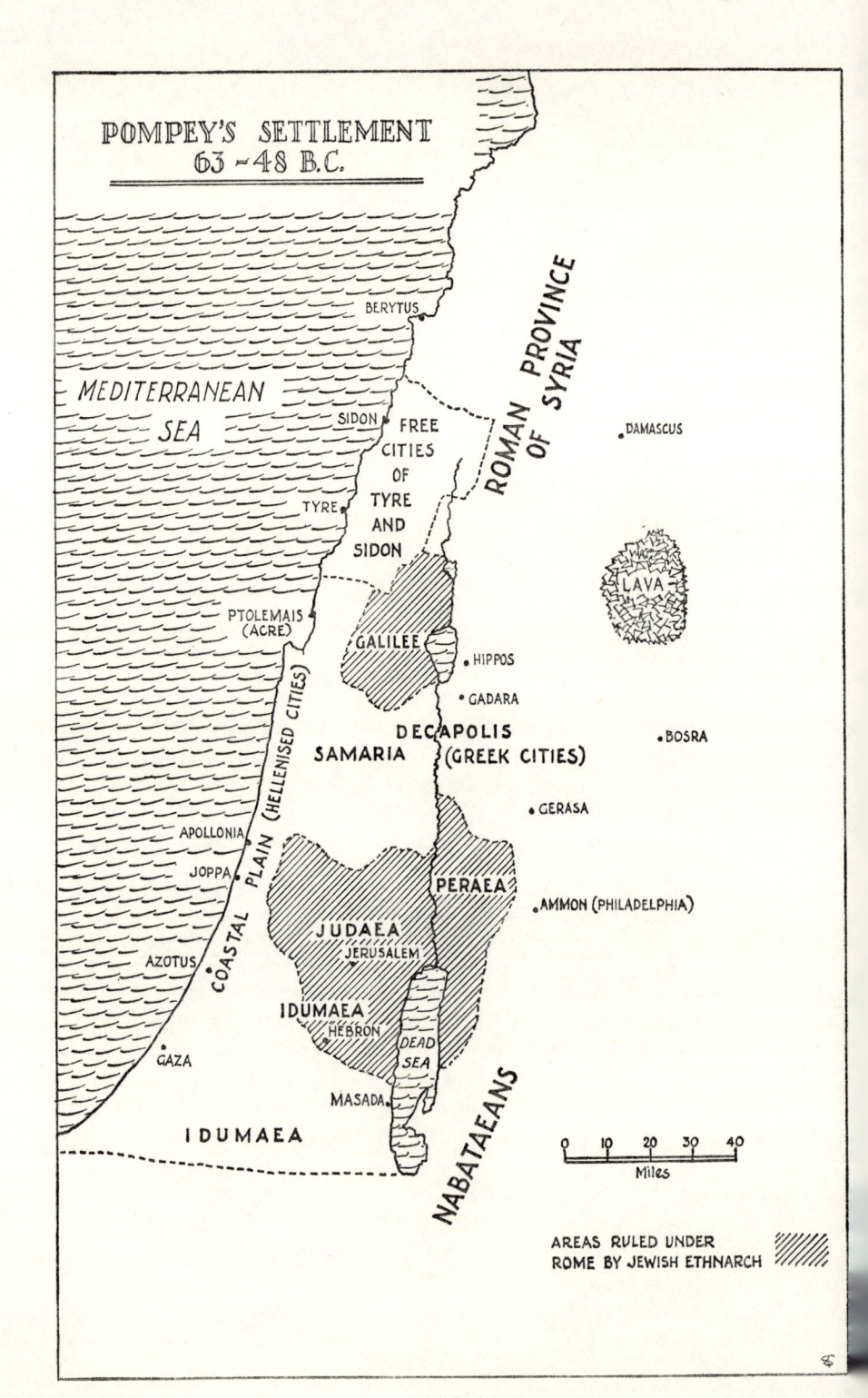

himself high priest. But Antipater induced the Nabataeans to support Hyrcanus II and Aristobulus was besieged in the Temple.

Meanwhile, in 66 B.C., the Roman Senate sent Pompey as commander-in-chief in the East. In 63 B.C. he arrived in Damascus, where he received three rival Judaean deputations, one from Hyrcanus led by Antipater, one from Aristobulus and one from the people of Judaea, who begged for the removal of all the Hasmonaeans. Pompey took Jerusalem and entered the Holy of Holies, but, unlike Antiochus Epiphanes, he did not seize the treasure. Aristobulus was sent to Rome to grace Pompey's triumph. The diplomacy of Antipater secured Hyrcanus II in the succession with the title of ethnarch.

The Greek cities conquered by the Hasmonaeans were liberated by Pompey, including all the coastal plain. Judaea retained part of Idumaea, Galilee, and part of Peraea, the inhabitants of which had been forcibly Judaised. But Judaea itself, with its ethnarch, was placed under the Roman proconsul of Syria. Just as high priestly rivalries had brought the Seleucids to Jerusalem, so the Hasmonaean civil wars brought the Romans.

In Jerusalem, Antipater was the real power behind Hyrcanus. Alexander, the son of Aristobulus II, raised guerrillas but was suppressed. Herod, the second son of Antipater, made a devoted friendship with a young Roman officer called Mark Antony.

Rome was now torn by the civl war between Pompey and Caesar. In August 48 B.C., Pompey, defeated at Pharsalus, fled to Egypt, but was assassinated on landing. Caesar, with a small force, arrived soon after, but found his position precarious, the Roman garrison being for Pompey. Antipater, Pompey's friend, quickly transferred his loyalty to Caesar. With three thousand Judaeans, he marched to help Caesar in Egypt, persuading the Nabataean king to send his cavalry. Caesar was deeply grateful and showed marked favour to the Jews. In return, he allowed Hyrcanus to annex the Greek city of Joppa, liberated by Pompey, but which was Jerusalem's only outlet to the sea.

Antipater persuaded the Jews in Egypt to support Caesar, as those of Rome had already done. Under Caesar, Rome soon recovered her prestige. Antipater had skilfully transferred to the winning side. Caesar declared the descendants of Hyrcanus to be hereditary high priests. Antipater was made a Roman citizen and was authorised to rebuild the walls of Jerusalem. These measures were decided by Caesar at Antioch between 13th and 18th July, 47 B.C.[10] Judaea was made to pay a quarter of her corn crop to Rome. Antipater not only

[10] Stewart Perowne, *The Life and Times of Herod the Great*.

THE HERODIANS

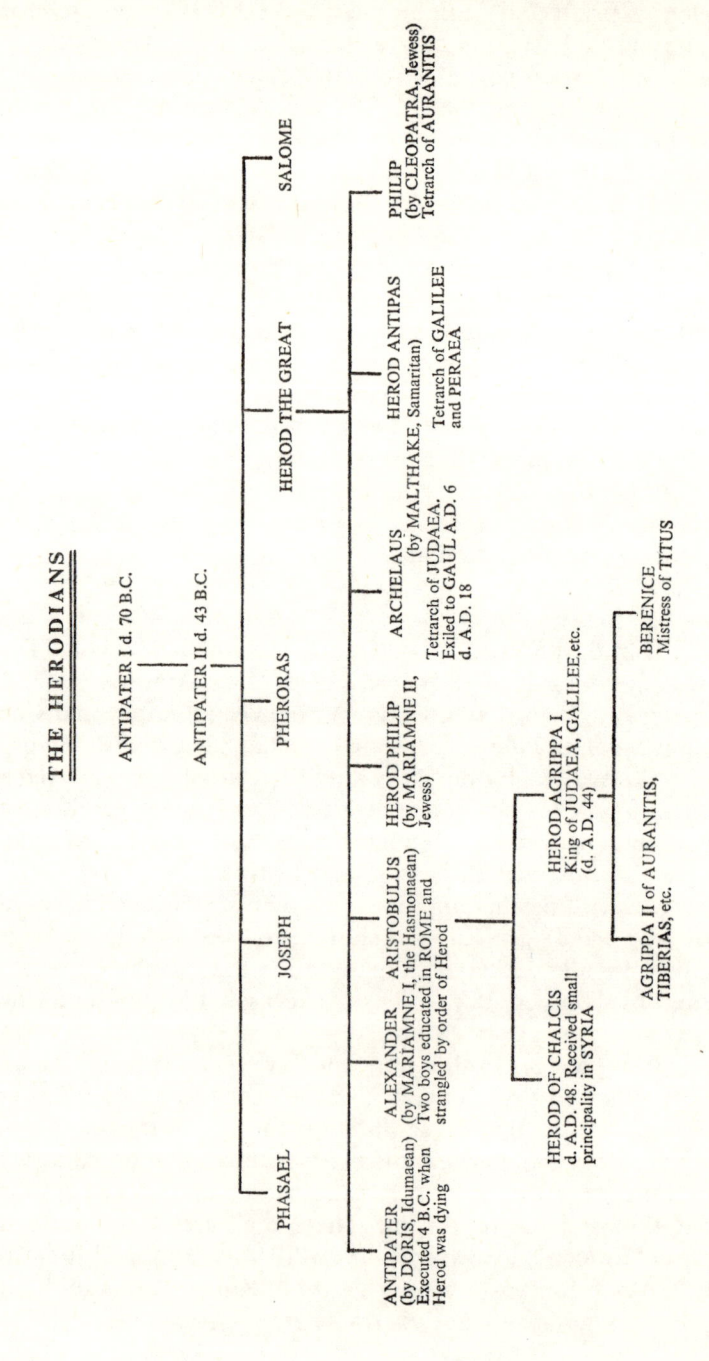

ANTIPATER I d. 70 B.C.
│
ANTIPATER II d. 43 B.C.
│
├── PHASAEL
├── JOSEPH
├── PHERORAS
├── HEROD THE GREAT
│   ├── ANTIPATER (by DORIS, Idumaean) Executed 4 B.C. when Herod was dying
│   ├── ALEXANDER ARISTOBULUS (by MARIAMNE I, the Hasmonaean) Two boys educated in ROME and strangled by order of Herod
│   │   ├── HEROD OF CHALCIS d. A.D. 48. Received small principality in SYRIA
│   │   └── HEROD AGRIPPA I King of JUDAEA, GALILEE, etc. (d. A.D. 44)
│   │   ├── AGRIPPA II of AURANITIS, TIBERIAS, etc.
│   │   └── BERENICE Mistress of TITUS
│   ├── HEROD PHILIP (by MARIAMNE II, Jewess)
│   ├── ARCHELAUS (by MALTHAKE, Samaritan) Tetrarch of JUDAEA. Exiled to GAUL A.D. 6 d. A.D. 18
│   ├── HEROD ANTIPAS Tetrarch of GALILEE and PERAEA
│   └── PHILIP (by CLEOPATRA, Jewess) Tetrarch of AURANITIS
└── SALOME

rebuilt the walls of Jerusalem, but added a new outer wall on the vulnerable north side.[11]

Antipater's second son, Herod, was now twenty-six, tall and handsome, with captivating manners. On familiar terms with Jews, Arabs, Greeks, Romans and Egyptians, he was also hardened by living amidst the endless civil wars, treachery, murder and bloodshed of Judaea. A certain Ezekias raised Jewish guerrillas in Galilee. Herod, sent to quell the revolt, rounded up the rebels and killed Ezekias.

The increasing power of this Idumaean family roused the jealousy of the priestly aristocrats. The feeble Hyrcanus was persuaded to order the trial of Herod by the Sanhedrin, a body consisting of Pharisees, Sadducees and notables. It was obvious that the Sanhedrin would execute Herod for killing Ezekias. He accordingly escaped to Sextus Caesar, proconsul of Syria, who made him governor of southern Syria and Samaria. The incident convinced Herod of the unreliability of the Judaeans and of the necessity of reliance on the friendship of Rome.

The Roman civil wars were not over. Sextus Caesar was murdered by Pompey's faction, which called in the Parthians. On 15th March, 44 B.C., Caesar himself was murdered in Rome. Suetonius[12] describes the wild grief of the Jews of Rome on whom he had bestowed many favours. He had confirmed their right to practise their religion, to absent themselves from state ceremonies, to collect and send money to Jerusalem, and he had exempted them from military service.

Cassius, one of Caesar's murderers, came as proconsul to Syria in 43 B.C. Antipater, Caesar's friend, did another volte face. Cassius needed money, so Antipater raised him a large sum in Judaea. At this crisis, Antipater was poisoned by his rivals in Jerusalem. But Cassius had been won just in time, and sent help to Herod, still governor of southern Syria. Anarchy reigned in Judaea. Hyrcanus II was senile and encouraged Herod's enemies. A deadly sub-war of intrigue and murder kept Judaea in confusion.

The rival Roman armies moved towards one another in Greece. Caesar's party was led by Mark Antony and Octavian, the future Augustus, the republicans by Brutus and Cassius. Herod had a close friend on both sides—Mark Antony and Cassius, whom he had carefully cultivated in Syria. Herod, already aspiring to succeed Hyrcanus, became betrothed to Mariamne, the old man's granddaughter, hoping thereby to insinuate himself into the royal

[11] Map 18, p. 149.
[12] Suetonius, *Lives of the Caesars*.

family. He already had a wife, but Judaism allowed polygamy.

In October 42 B.C., Mark Antony and Octavian defeated Brutus and Cassius at Philippi. In 41 B.C., Mark Antony came to Tyre, where he was greeted by his old friend Herod. Deputations also came from Judaea to complain against Herod, but their importunity angered Antony, who ordered their arrest. Herod and his brother, Phasael, received the title of tetrarch.

Unfortunately Antony went on to Egypt where he was captivated by Cleopatra, with whom he spent the winter of 41–40 B.C. The Parthians invaded Syria unopposed, bringing with them Antigonus, the son of Aristobulus II, the grandson of Alexander Jannaeus.[13] Hyrcanus II and Phasael were invited to a conference and treacherously seized. Phasael was killed, Hyrcanus deported to Babylon. Antigonus became king and high priest.

Six months before the honoured friend of the rulers of Rome, Herod suddenly found himself surrounded by enemies. Escaping from Jerusalem, he left his family in the fortress of Masada and fled to Egypt. Mark Antony had left for Rome and Cleopatra invited the handsome young Herod to pass the winter with her.

Herod refused to waste time in dalliance, though it was already winter and sea travel was risky. Sailing for Rhodes, his ship was almost wrecked, and he landed destitute and bedraggled. Such, however, was his personal charm that he raised enough money in Rhodes to equip a splendid trireme and arrived in regal state at Brindisi. In Rome he was welcomed by Mark Antony and won the friendship of the young Octavian. The Senate passed a unanimous resolution appointing him King of Judaea.

It was fortunate for Herod that Antigonus, his Hasmonaean rival, was identified with the Parthians, thereby ensuring for Herod the undivided support of Rome. Even so, his instant success was an extraordinary tribute to his personality. "Herod had conquered Rome: King Herod still had to conquer Jerusalem."[14] Meanwhile, the Parthians had withdrawn, leaving Antigonus King of Judaea.

Suddenly, early in 39 B.C., Herod landed at Ptolemais. A quick visit to Galilee, of which he had formerly been governor, enabled him to obtain recruits. Then marching swiftly down the coastal plain, he seized Joppa, then on to Idumaea, where he relieved his family, besieged in Masada by Antigonus. Without resting, he moved up from the south and laid siege to Jerusalem. Meanwhile, Samaria, which had been brutally devastated by the Hasmonaeans, declared

[13] Genealogical Tree, p. 100.
[14] Stewart Perowne, *The Life and Times of Herod the Great.*

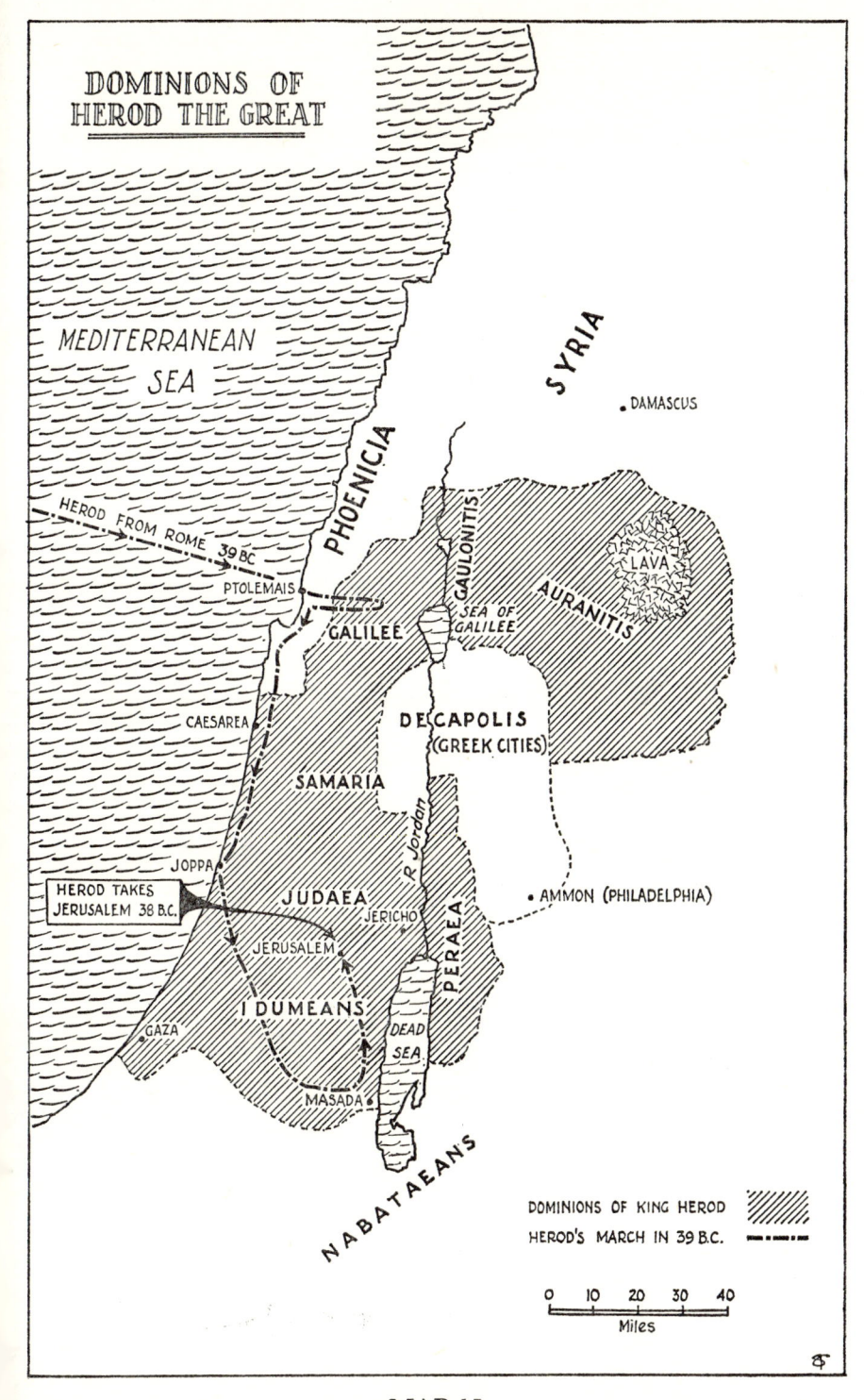

MAP 15

for Herod. Jerusalem, now surrounded, held out desperately and Herod could not take it.

Fortunately for him, Mark Antony landed in Syria in 38 B.C. The two friends greeted each other enthusiastically and Herod borrowed two legions. Amid scenes of violence and bloodshed, Jerusalem was carried by assault. Antigonus was executed and Herod proclaimed king. Ever since the rebellion of Judas Maccabaeus in 166 B.C., Palestine for a hundred and twenty-eight years had been torn by violence and soaked in blood.

In 32 B.C., Antony, who was living with Cleopatra, broke with Octavian. The queen, who hated Herod because, in 40 B.C., he had rejected her advances, persuaded Antony to give her Syria, Samaria and even Jericho. On 2nd September, 31 B.C., however, Antony was defeated by Octavian at Actium and died soon afterwards. Herod, the close friend of Antony, had to change sides. He sailed to meet the victorious Octavian in Rhodes. Once more, his magnetism won the day and Octavian confirmed him in his kingship.

Octavian came to Syria and rode down to Egypt with Herod at his side, amid the acclamations of the public. (There were, of course, no Jewish cities on the coastal plain.) Well might Herod's enemies despair. In an age of endless wars, he was always on the winning side.

From 30 B.C. onwards, Judaea under Herod enjoyed wealth and security for the first time in a hundred and thirty-six years. He succeeded owing to his policy of friendship with Rome and through his personal liaison with Augustus.

Herod's kingdom was important to Rome. It was half-way between Syria and Egypt, two of the most wealthy provinces of the empire. Secondly, Parthia was Rome's most powerful rival and it was vital that the Levant be kept loyal to Rome. Thirdly, the rich oriental trade was carried by caravan from Aden to Egypt and Syria, passing through the country of the Nabataeans, Herod's relatives through his mother.

Judaea had caused endless trouble, but under Herod was stable and loyal. As a result, the country was left alone, with a minimum of imperial interference. Herod was an excellent administrator as well as a politician. His civil service was less corrupt than that of Rome. The roads were safe, commerce flourished and Judaea prospered. Herod covered the Levant with cities, theatres and castles. He constructed a splendid new city and port at Caesarea, for Palestine lacks natural harbours. The climax of his work was the rebuilding of the Temple in Jerusalem.

Herod's public career had been brilliant but his family life was tragic. Perhaps he had married Mariamne to insinuate himself into the Hasmonaean family, but he also loved her. She did not return his love, but thought only of a Hasmonaean restoration. She persuaded Herod to make her brother, Aristobulus III,[15] high priest, hoping to use him to destroy her husband. Herod, mad with jealousy at Mariamne's intrigues, contrived the drowning of Aristobulus in Jericho.

Life in the palace became fiendish. Herod adored Mariamne, who hated him with a cold hatred. Salome, Herod's sister, loathed Mariamne and persuaded her brother that she was unfaithful, which was false. Before a packed court, she was sentenced to death and executed. Herod, who loved her passionately, became almost insane, a gloomy and suspicious tyrant—one of the most melodramatic tragedies in history.

The Judaeans also hated Herod for co-operating with Rome, although he had thereby brought them peace and prosperity. If we forget our neat labels of "Jews" and "Arabs", we see the extraordinary resemblance of the Palestinians of today to the subjects of Herod, who gained security and wealth for his country by "co-operating with the Mandatory Power". King Abdulla did the same and was assassinated in Jerusalem, as Herod would have been if he had not been protected by his bodyguard of four hundred Gauls.[16]

The Arabs of Arabia are realists. They do not show this quality of unreasoning—and yet heroic—narrowness, which from time to time breaks out in the Palestinians, whether we call them Jews or Arabs. I am peculiarly aware of this quality for I came in contact with it. No matter how strong the enemy, any "reasonable" compromise is denounced as treachery. Such was the spirit of the Hasmonaeans and we shall encounter it again.

In addition to his bodyguard, Herod maintained a regular army of mercenaries, including Thracians, Germans, Idumaeans and natives of Asia Minor. He built military colonies for these veterans, thereby adding a few more strange ingredients to the ethnic mixture in Palestine.

In 21 B.C., Augustus visited Antioch, whither Herod went to pay his court. There had been disorders in Auranitis (Hauran) south of Damascus. To the annoyance of the Nabataeans, Augustus gave the whole area to his friend Herod.[17] Nationalism was of no interest to the Romans. There were no Jews in Auranitis, but Herod was loyal and a good administrator. Then Herod paid a state visit to Rome,

---

[15] Genealogical Tree, p. 100.
[16] Rabbi Raisin, *Gentile Reactions to Jewish Ideals*.
[17] Map 15, p. 133.

where he received a magnificent reception. He brought back with him Alexander and Aristobulus, his two surviving sons by Mariamne. The boys had been educated in Rome.

Herod's last years were increasingly tragic. He had had ten wives, whose children loathed one another. Most active of all in intrigue were Alexander and Aristobulus, the sons of Mariamne. Eventually they were strangled by the old king's orders.

Herod was suffering from a disease which had affected his reason. He was in constant pain and the lower part of his body was infected with gangrene. The palace became a bedlam. His eldest son, Antipater was denounced to him and Herod, himself at death's door, ordered his execution. It must have been at this time, while he lay dying perhaps in partial delirium and extreme physical agony, that he gave the order which made him infamous—for the massacre of the Innocents in Bethlehem.

Herod died in Jericho in April 4 B.C., at the age of seventy. The Judaeans hated him. What he did for them can best be judged by what occurred after his death.

*   *   *

In 1969, a book was published, which seemed to prove that the alleged madness of George III was due to porphyria, an illness discovered during this century.[18] The disease is due to a defect in the chemistry of the body, resulting in the accumulation of toxic substances which damage the nervous system. At the height of an attack, patients are described as "ill, paralysed, delirious and in agonising pain." The descriptions of the symptoms of George III seem remarkably similar to those of Herod. Certainly the metamorphosis of the charming, suave, and diplomatic young Herod into the fierce ogre calling for the execution of his own children, while himself convulsed in agony, seems to require some explanation other than just wickedness.

I accordingly wrote to Dr. Hunter, giving him Josephus' description of the symptoms of Herod's fatal illness. He replied most courteously saying that Herod's illness did not suggest porphyria, but seemed to be an intestinal disease, probably cancer. "You would certainly be on very safe ground to assume that he must have been delirious," he added.

*   *   *

[18] I. Macalpine and R. Hunter, *George III and the Mad-Business*.

PALESTINE AT THE TIME OF CHRIST

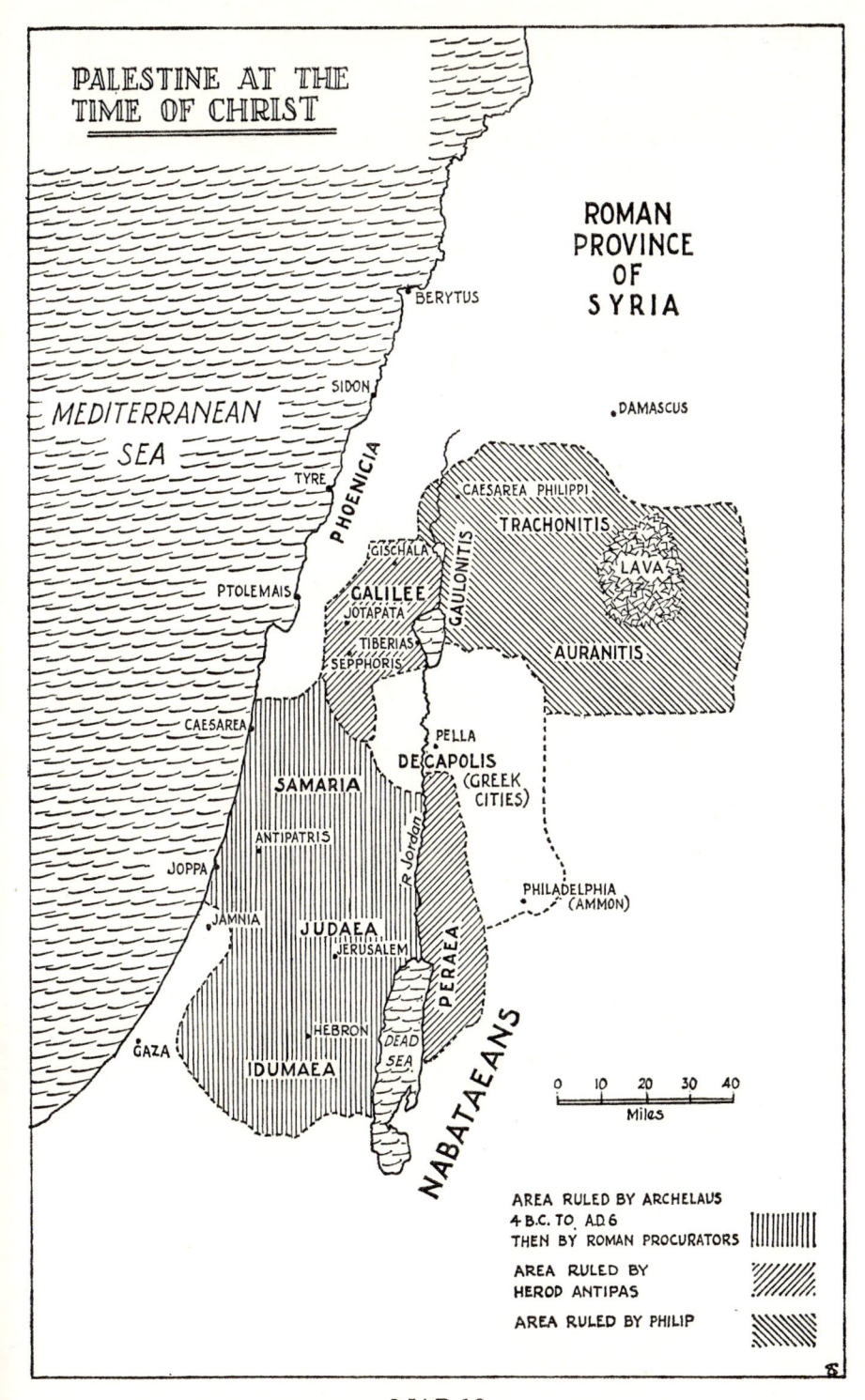

MAP 16

In his will, Herod left Judaea to his son Archelaus, whose mother had been a Samaritan.[19] Herod Antipas, brother of Archelaus, received Galilee and Peraea. Philip, whose mother was a Jewess, received Gaulonitis, Auranitis, and Trachonitis. A popular delegation from Judaea went to Rome to beg for direct Roman rule and the exclusion of Herod's family, but Augustus confirmed the will. Archelaus, however, ruled so badly that, in A.D. 6, he was exiled by Augustus to Gaul. Judaea passed under direct Roman rule, as the popular delegation had requested. Herod Antipas and Philip retained their provinces. The Roman procurator of Judaea chose Herod's new Greek city of Caesarea as his headquarters. In A.D. 27 Pontius Pilate was appointed procurator and remained for ten years. He was an energetic administrator, less corrupt than his predecessors.[20] Nevertheless, the Judaeans opposed him bitterly. He gave Jerusalem a regular water supply, which was a crying necessity, by building an aqueduct thirty-seven miles long. "The Jews," writes Josephus, "were extremely angry at the steps which he had taken to supply them with water."[21]

He had used money from the Temple treasure for the purpose. The continual and often captious complaints which they made to Tiberias against Pilate, may have made him hesitate to release Jesus. "If you release this man you are not Caesar's friend" would thus be a threat to send another complaint to Rome.[22]

Herod Antipas proved competent as tetrarch of Galilee and Peraea. He had married a daughter of the Nabataean king but, in A.D. 26, his incestuous marriage to Herodias offended both his subjects and the Nabataeans. It was Herod Antipas who beheaded John the Baptist and who, with his soldiers, mocked Christ on the morning of the Crucifixion.

Philip died in A.D. 33 after thirty-seven years of quiet rule over his tetrarchy, which contained very few Jews. As he left no son, his small territory was reincorporated in the Roman province of Syria.

NOTABLE DATES

John Hyrcanus	135–104 B.C.
Alexander Jannaeus	103–76 B.C.
Herod the Great	39–4 B.C.

---

[19] Matthew II, 22.
[20] F. M. Abel, *Histoire de la Palestine*.
[21] Josephus, *Antiquities of the Jews*, Book XVIII.
[22] John XIX, 12.

CONCLUSIONS

(1) The "Jews" did not hold Palestine from the Return from Babylon to the destruction of the Temple in A.D. 70. They only held the small territory of Judaea.

(2) The Hasmonaeans, however, conquered and forcibly circumcised the Idumaeans and the Galileans, who became "Jews" by religion but not by ethnic origin. The Jews never occupied the coastal plain.

(3) The original revolt of Judas Maccabaeus evokes our sympathy, even our enthusiasm.

(4) The later Hasmonaeans became savage ruffians.

(5) Herod the Great gave the Holy Land thirty-four years of peace. He died of an agonising disease, accompanied by delirium and acute nervous disorders.

(6) From 166 B.C. to A.D. 135, a period of three centuries, Palestine was drenched in blood, largely due to Judaean military aggressiveness. Yet, with a paradoxical duality which seems to haunt the whole story, in the heart of this savagery was growing a tiny seed, which was to lead the world to spiritual gentleness.

It was from the utter catastrophe which these fanatics largely brought on themselves, that the conception of a single God of Love was to emerge. This is the Lord's doing and it is marvellous in our eyes.

IX

The Collapse of Militancy

For who shall have pity upon thee, O Jerusalem? or who shall bemoan thee? or who shall go aside to ask how thou doest?
Jeremiah XV, 5 Authorized Version

Indeed what can it be that hath stirred up an army of Romans against our nation? Is it not the impiety of the inhabitants? Whence did our servitude commence? Was it not derived from the seditions that were among our forefathers, when the madness of Aristobulus and Hyrcanus, and our mutual quarrels, brought Pompey upon this city, and when God reduced those under subjection to the Romans, who were unworthy of the liberty they had enjoyed? ... Such as inhabit this holy place ought to commit the disposal of all things to God ... As for you what have you done? ... thefts and treacherous plots against men, and adulteries. You are quarrelling about rapines and murders. The Temple itself ... is polluted by the hands of those of our own country.
Josephus' Appeal to the Defenders of Jerusalem.
FLAVIUS JOSEPHUS, *Wars of the Jews,* Book V. Chapter 9

IX

HEROD AGRIPPA, a grandson of Herod the Great, had been to school in Rome, where Claudius and the father of Caligula were his classmates. In A.D. 23, he returned to the Levant when his extravagant Roman habits soon reduced him to penury. After some years drifting here and there borrowing money, he returned to Rome where he soon found himself in prison.

With the death of Tiberius in A.D. 37, however, everything in Rome was reversed. The friends of Tiberius were degraded, his enemies promoted. Caligula, the new emperor, accordingly took Agrippa out of prison and made him king of Philip's former tetrarchy.[1] Soon after, Herod Antipas was exiled to Gaul for intrigue, and his dominions were added to those of Agrippa. In A.D. 39 Caligula wished to place his statue in the Temple, but Agrippa rendered a valuable service by dissuading him.

Agrippa was still in Rome in January A.D. 40, when Caligula was assassinated. Hastily trimming his sails, he helped to raise his old schoolmate, Claudius, to the purple. The latter, in gratitude, added Judaea to his kingdom, making it coterminous with that of Herod I.

To atone for his old disreputable life, Agrippa settled in Jerusalem, where he daily sacrificed in the Temple. He is the Herod mentioned in Acts XII, 1 to 3, who beheaded James, the brother of John and imprisoned Peter. But Agrippa, pious in Jerusalem, was a man of the world in Beirut and Caesarea, where he held games in honour of Claudius. He was taken ill during a speech at these games in the spring of 44 and died five days later.[2] On his death, a Roman procurator was again appointed to Judaea.

In 53, his son, Agrippa II, was given the former tetrarchy of Philip. Nero, who donned the purple in 54, added to his territory Tiberias and fourteen villages in Galilee. The Herodians had become professional kings, even in areas where there were no Jews.

Meanwhile, conditions in Judaea were deteriorating. Robbers roamed the country and the Sicarii, assassins with long knives hidden in their clothes, murdered whom they would. In A.D. 64,

---

[1] Map 16, p. 137.
[2] Acts XII, 20 to 23.

Florus, a protégé of Nero's mistress, Poppaea, was nominated procurator of Judaea. He immediately set about lining his pockets. In May 66, he seized seventeen talents from the Temple treasury, to pay the imperial taxes, which were overdue. A riot ensued, causing many deaths. Agrippa II arrived and addressed the crowd on the folly of rebellion against Rome. But he was abused and stoned, and left hastily for his northern kingdom.

The nationalists were now out of hand. They seized Masada, Herod's former stronghold, and massacred the garrison. In Jerusalem, the moderates and the Sadducees begged Florus to act quickly but in vain.

King Agrippa II sent two thousand of his cavalry, who occupied the upper city, the rebels being in the lower city and the Temple. Fierce fighting ensued. Agrippa's men eventually withdrew but the Roman auxiliaries—mostly non-Jewish Palestinians—were killed to a man. The massive Antonia, overlooking the Temple, was taken and its garrison exterminated. In retaliation, the Greeks in Caesarea massacred their Jews.

All over the country, the Jews murdered the Gentiles, who retaliated when the occasion offered. Terror reigned in Palestine. The governor of Syria, Cestius Gallus, was obliged to act. He had four legions in Syria but only took one, the Twelfth, though he added considerable numbers of local auxiliaries.

Though it was October and the rains were due to break, he moved slowly, camping a thousand yards north of Jerusalem. The Twelfth Legion attacked, quickly carried the outer wall and reached the Antonia, which they began to undermine. According to Josephus, if Gallus had pressed on, the city was his. Instead, he lost his nerve, called off the attack and retreated.

To retire is often disastrous when fighting an irregular enemy. The Jews, who had been about to surrender, swarmed out of the city in wild excitement and overtook the Romans as they straggled down the narrow valley of Beth Horon. Gathering on the mountains, the Jews rolled down boulders and poured a stream of missiles into the column.[3]

Some six thousand soldiers were killed in the disaster. Gallus abandoned his baggage and his siege train. A demoralised mob took refuge in Antipatris. In the eyes of the rebels, drunk with victory, the Roman Empire had ceased to exist. Every trace of Rome was removed from Judaea.

Palestine was in chaos. Josephus says that "many of the most

[3] Map 17, p. 146.

eminent Jews" foresaw the end and quietly left Jerusalem. The small Christian community, remembering perhaps that their Master had given His blessing to peacemakers, moved to Pella, beyond the Jordan, a city of the Greek Decapolis.

In Jerusalem, the rebels set up a government. Ananus, the high priest, was declared head of the state, with Ben Gurion as his assistant. Our historian, Josephus, went as governor of Galilee, with his headquarters at Sepphoris.[4]

But, as always in Palestine, the rebels fell out among themselves. Every bandit who could raise a gang became an independent commander. The bandit leaders in Galilee were jealous of Josephus, and a vicious gang war broke out between him and one John of Gischala.

In February 67, Nero appointed Vespasian as Commander-in-Chief in Judaea. (He had made his name by capturing the Isle of Wight, during Claudius' campaign in Britain in 43.) Vespasian, who was fifty-eight years old, dressed like a common soldier. He was careful and thorough rather than brilliant. He would not, like Gallus, expose himself to a disaster. He knew that the relentless advance of a regular army was demoralising to irregulars. His son, Titus, twenty-seven years old, was on his staff.

Josephus says that Vespasian had three legions,[5] some eighteen or twenty thousand men, with an even greater number of auxiliaries—Gentile Palestinians, Nebataeans and Syrians.

After re-occupying Galilee, Vespasian laid siege to Jotapata, a fortified town nearly surrounded by precipices and defended by the governor, Josephus. After a stout resistance for forty-seven days, the place was taken, Titus having crept in with a few men before dawn, and opened the gates. Most of the defenders were killed, but Josephus was taken prisoner and became a personal friend of Titus, who was his own age.

The summer of 67 passed in these operations and in the occupation of Tiberias, Tarichae and Joppa. Finally the Romans took Gischala. The local gangster, John of Gischala, escaped to Jerusalem, where he secured a large following by boasting of his prowess against the Romans.

Jerusalem was in anarchy. Cut-throats from the whole country had flocked into the city to plunder the respectable citizens. "Those who were desirous of war," writes Josephus, "by their youth and boldness were too hard for the aged and the prudent men ... They

---

[4] Josephus, *Wars of the Jews*. Map 17, p. 146.
[5] Suetonius writes that Vespasian had "two extra legions".

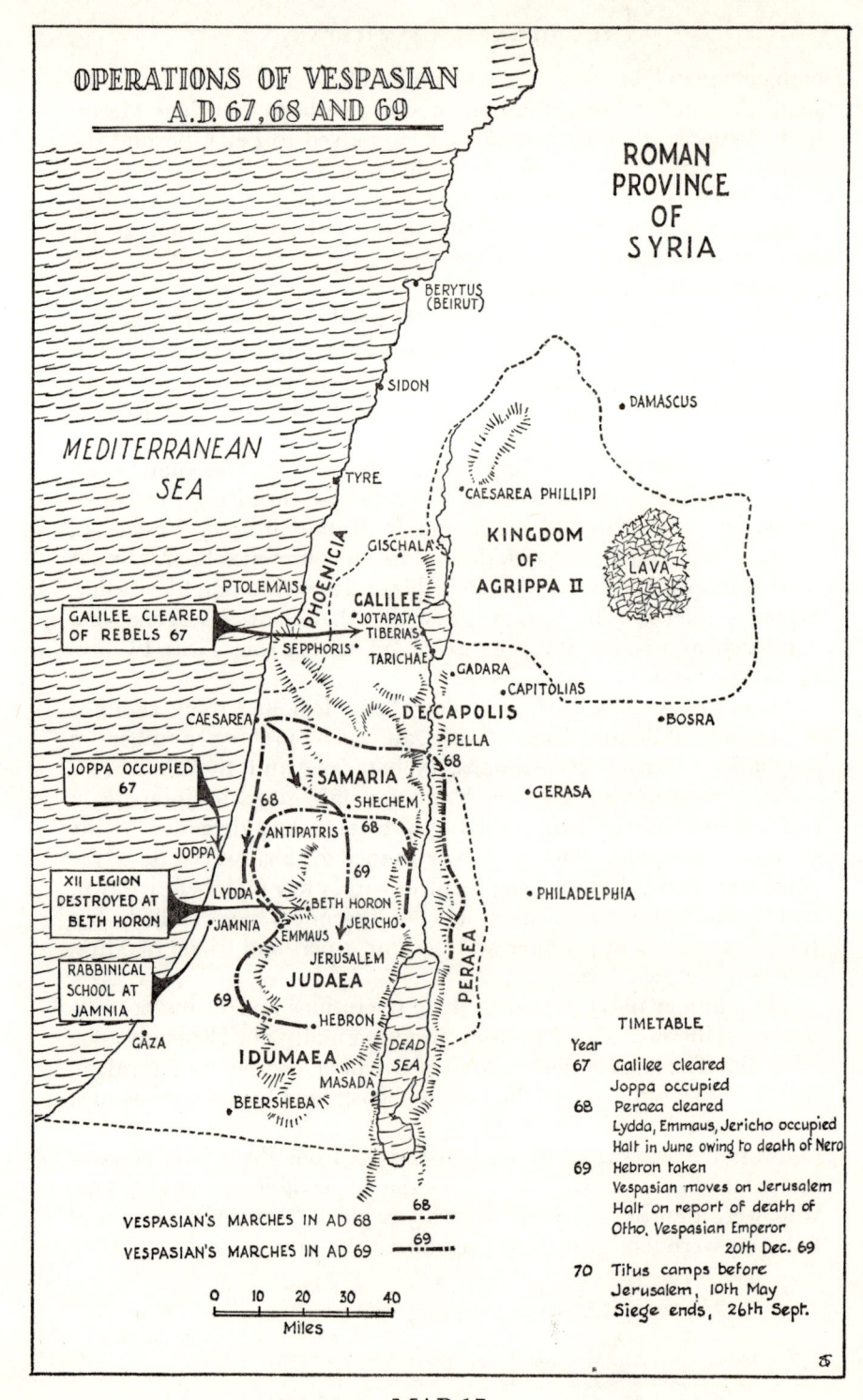

MAP 17

got together to rob the people of the country, insomuch that for barbarity and iniquity those of the same nation did in no way differ from the Romans."

The Zealots, or extreme nationalists, found an ignorant peasant, dressed him in robes and, amid much laughter, declared him high priest. They established themselves in the Temple, which they made into a fortress. Ananus called on the people to expel the Zealots. The public wished to obey but were defeated by the gangsters, who killed many of them.

The Zealots then sent for the Idumaeans, who broke into the city, looted houses and killed numbers of people, including Ananus, the high priest. Two-thirds of the gangs in Jerusalem seem to have been Idumaeans, Galileans or Peraeans, who had been forcibly Judaised by the Hasmonaeans.

* * *

Early in 68, a Roman column cleared the country east of the Jordan. Hearing of a rebellion in Gaul against Nero, and fearing a civil war, Vespasian hastened his operations. Moving out from Caesarea, he took Lydda and established the Tenth Legion at Emmaus.

Then, crossing the mountains by Shechem, he took and fortified Jericho. In June 68, he was ready to move on Jerusalem, when he heard of the death of Nero and of Galba's acceptance of the empire. He thereupon halted the advance and sent Titus to Rome to seek orders from the new emperor.

When Titus reached Corinth, he heard of Galba's murder in January 69 and of Otho's acceptance of the purple. Titus returned to his father who, thinking the civil war over, resumed the advance through Samaria and camped ten miles north of Jerusalem. The Fifth Legion seized Hebron.

One of the most respected rabbis of the time, Johanan ben Zakkai, determined to escape from Jerusalem. Fearing the gangs, he feigned death and was carried out in a coffin on the shoulders of his disciples. Once clear of the city, he went to Vespasian and obtained permission to open a school to study the Law at Jamnia (Yavneh, Yibna) on the coastal plain. His action was to change the history of Judaism, and, indeed, of the world.

In the early summer of 69, all was ready for the attack on Jerusalem, when news came of the defeat of Otho and the march of Vitellius on Rome. Vespasian again called a halt.

But the German legions who had come with Vitellius were savages. Rome was disgusted with her new emperor, a man, according to Suetonius, "stained by every sort of baseness"—he had been a favourite of Nero. The legions on the Danube refused their allegiance.

On 1st July, 69, the two legions in Egypt declared for Vespasian, followed, the next day, by four legions in Syria under Mucianus. Vespasian himself had three legions. Though now acclaimed as emperor, Vespasian continued his usual routine, showing neither pride nor elation.[6] A grand council was held in Beirut, where it was decided that Mucianus would march on Rome, Vespasian wait in Egypt and Titus finish the Judaean war.

On 20th December, 69, Rome declared for Vespasian and Vitellius was killed. Vespasian waited at Alexandria till the summer of 70, when the sea was safe for navigation, before sailing for Rome.

* * *

For many months, while operations were halted to await the result of the imperial struggle, the Jews did not prepare for the coming war, but continued to fight one another.

In Jerusalem, John of Gischala and the Galileans held the upper city, while the Zealots held the Temple. A vicious sub-war of knifings and stabbings made the narrow streets run with blood. One Simon bar Giora with his gang was living by plundering the people of the Hebron area. The citizens of Jerusalem invited Simon to their city, to protect them from John of Gischala and the Zealots. Simon occupied the lower city with his bands and confusion became worse confounded.

All the gangs now began to use artillery (ballistae) throwing large rocks which came humming over the roof-tops and crashed into the buildings. Most of the provisions, accumulated for a siege, were looted by the gangs.

* * *

In April 70, Titus advanced from Caesarea on Jerusalem. His army consisted of the three legions formerly under Vespasian—the Fifth at Emmaus, the Tenth at Jericho and the Fifteenth in the north. To these was added the Twelfth, eager to retrieve their

---

[6] Tacitus, *Histories*.

MAP 18

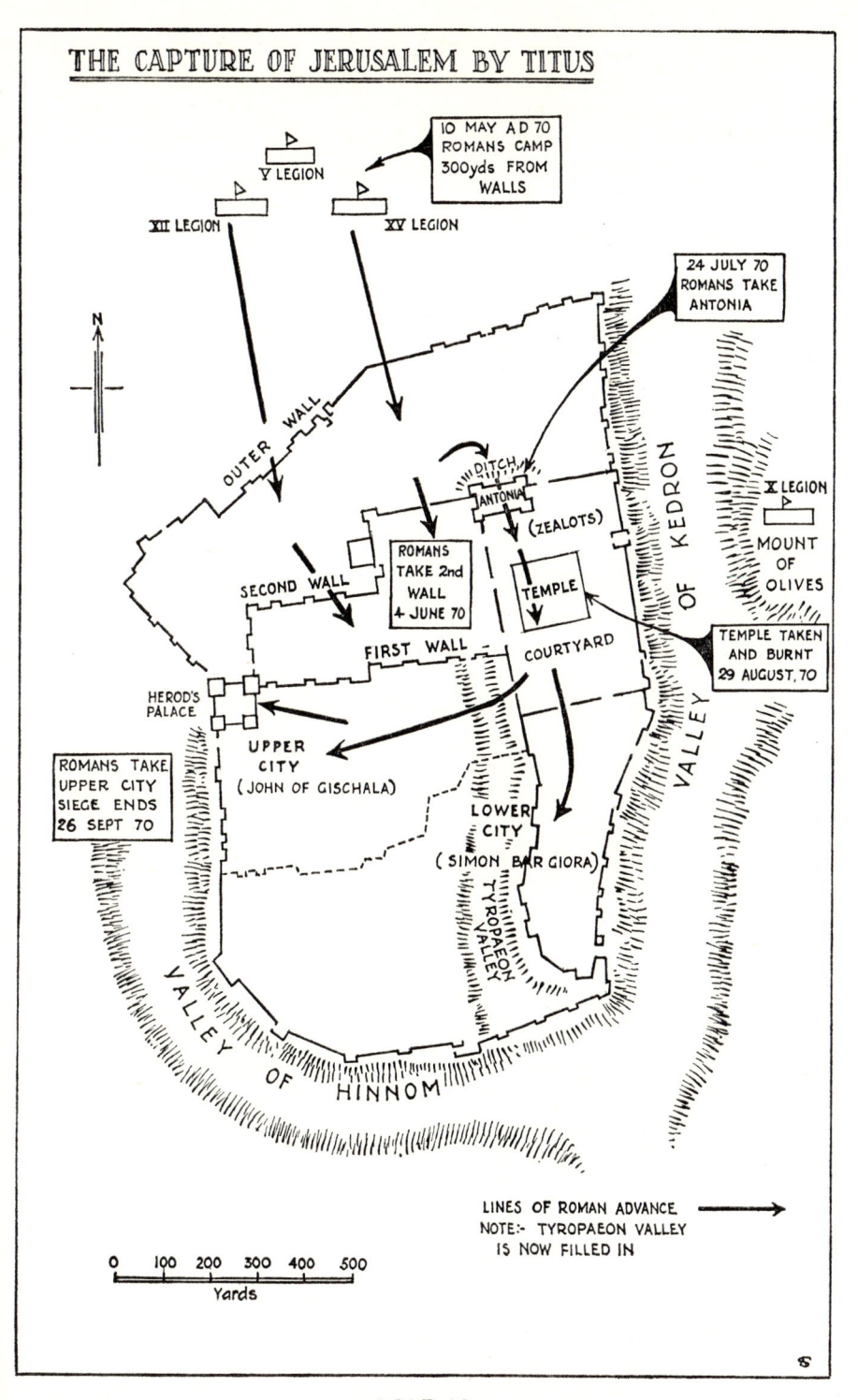

disgrace under Gallus. Two thousand reinforcements from Egypt and three thousand from Syria, made a total, with local auxiliaries, of some sixty-five thousand men.[7]

Titus, reconnoitring on horseback, was nearly captured by a sally from the city. On 10th May, 70, the Romans moved up to within three hundred yards from the walls. The Twelfth and Fifteenth legions were in the front line, with the Fifth in reserve. The Tenth, from Jericho, occupied the Mount of Olives.

Although John of Gischala, Simon bar Giora and Eleazar the Zealot had at first united to resist the Romans, they now resumed their private wars, knifing one another in the narrow alleyways, while the Roman engines battered the walls. "They suffered nothing worse from the Romans than they made each other suffer."[8]

The Romans soon broke through the outer wall and moved up to the second. Simon held the western half of this line and John of Gischala the eastern and the Antonia. On 4th June, after twenty-five days of the siege, the Romans took the second wall. The east, south and west approaches to the city were protected by ravines. The Antonia fortress commanded the area across which the Romans must advance. The attackers, working like ants, began to fill in the ditch to enable them to bring their mobile towers and battering rams up to the walls of the Antonia. The Jews, in a furious sally, burnt the mobile wooden towers.

Titus decided to surround the whole city with a nine-foot breastwork, five miles long, which was done in the amazingly short time of three days. Roman soldiers were tremendous workers. Neither food nor reinforcements could now reach the doomed city. Some, now that it was too late, tried to escape, but were caught and crucified within sight of the defenders.

The attack on the Antonia was renewed. At three in the morning of 24th July, twelve legionaries, with a trumpeter and the standard-bearer of the Fifth, crawled through the ruins of the Antonia and emerged on the walls. The trumpet sounded, the legions advanced, and Titus with his bodyguard ran through the ruined fortress to the gates of the Temple, where the attackers were stopped in a desperate sword and dagger struggle with the Zealots.[9]

Titus, wishing to save the Temple, sent Josephus to summon the defenders to surrender. With other Jewish leaders, including two former high priests who were with the Romans, he begged the gangs

---

[7] Stewart Perowne, *The Later Herods*.
[8] Josephus, *Wars of the Jews*.
[9] Josephus, *Wars of the Jews*.

to accept terms, but they replied only with mockery. Fighting was resumed and the Temple gates set on fire.

Titus again ordered the preservation of the Temple, but, in a mêlée in the court, a soldier threw a torch and, in a few minutes, Herod's masterpiece was wrapped in flames. It was 29th August, 70. Herod Agrippa II and his army were fighting for the Romans. His sister, Berenice, was Titus' mistress. Perhaps they and Josephus and the many prominent Jews in the Roman camp persuaded Titus to order the preservation of the Temple.

From the Temple, the Romans quickly overran the lower city, confining the rebels to the upper city. Titus again offered terms, coming in person to speak to the leaders, who, however, rejected his advances. Forty thousand citizens who surrendered were allowed to go free.

On 26th September, 70, the Romans took Herod's palace and the upper city, killing or capturing the few surviving defenders. Several thousand Jewish captives died in gladiatorial games, while many more were sent as slaves to Rome. Most of these were later freed and joined the large Jewish population of the city.

* * *

The theory that Jews have always been persecuted is only partially true. The Roman siege of Jerusalem was a horrifying tragedy. Let us try to analyse some of the factors on the basis of history.

Firstly, the extremists who rebelled against Rome were not a majority of the Jews in Palestine. Surprisingly, many of them were Galileans or Idumaeans, people forcibly converted to Judaism, whom the Jews did not recognise as Jews by race. Their motives do not appear to have been religious, for they killed the priests and desecrated the Temple. Their motives were perhaps xenophobia, lust of power and greed. The Sadducees, the Pharisees and the eminent citizens escaped from the city as best they could.

It is probably true that peaceful communities of Jews were protected, not persecuted, by Titus and Vespasian. The treatment accorded to prisoners was brutal, but in accordance with contemporary custom. We have seen Alexander Jannaeus, the Judaean king, crucify eight hundred of his fellow Jews. When the Judaeans took Samaria, all the inhabitants had been massacred.

Secondly, it cannot accurately be said that Titus evicted the Jews from Palestine, or even from Judaea. Those professing Judaism in the world were about five times as many as the number in Palestine. There were riots by Jews in Alexandria and in Cyrenaica at the beginning of the war, but otherwise the Jews of the world were unaffected. More significant still, the privileges they enjoyed were not curtailed. Obviously the imperial government regarded these events as a rebellion in Palestine, not as a revolt of the Jews. The reason seems to have been that a large part of the Jews of the world were local converts—Italians, Spaniards, Gauls, Berbers, Greeks or Germans—who had no ties with Palestine.

The devastation wrought in Judaea and in Jerusalem cannot be called religious persecution, for many Jews helped the Romans. Two former high priests were in the Roman camp. Agrippa II, the Jewish king, with his army, took the side of Rome. This, of course, is not to say that any Jews in Palestine liked the Romans, but the educated classes realised that the rebellion must fail. The defenders of Jerusalem were mostly ignorant peasants.

* * *

We have seen how Rabbi Johanan ben Zakkai was allowed by Vespasian to open a rabbinical school in Jamnia. "It is a strange transition in Jewish history from the wild contests of the fanatic Zealots to the disputations of the learned expounders of the Law—from the bloody tribunals of Simon bar Giora, John of Gischala and Eleazar the Zealot, to the peaceful scholars at the feet of Gamaliel[10]—from the din of arms, the confusion of besieged cities, the miseries of famine, massacre and conflagration to discussions about unclean meats, new moons and the observance of Sabbaths."[11]

Canon Millman underestimates the importance of Jamnia, where spiritual Judaism rose once more above "blood and soil", ethnic groups and race hatreds, to the true brotherhood of man. "Every man who does not worship idols is a Jew," said Rabbi Johanan.

"At Jamnia," says Rabbi Raisin, "Judaism declared officially that the 'seed of Abraham' does not depend on blood and soil, but transcends all bounds of racialism and nationalism, and that whoever is hungry for the bread of life may come and eat, regardless of his ancestors' treatment of the Jews."[12]

Some rabbis still insisted on circumcision and baptism, but others made no formal rites essential. What a tragedy that these noble

[10] This was the young Gamaliel, not Paul's tutor.
[11] Henry Hart Millman, *History of the Jews*.
[12] Rabbi Raisin, *Gentile Reactions to Jewish Ideals*.

spiritual conceptions were to be again and again defeated by narrow passion and isolationism. Some rabbis saw a privilege, not a punishment, in the Dispersion. It was the duty of Israel to spread the religion of the spirit to all nations. "God did a loving kindness to Israel in scattering them among the nations."

"A proselyte was looked upon as a newly born Jewish child. He became of the seed of Abraham in the physical as well as in the spiritual sense. As such, every tie which held him to his pagan past was broken . . . His blood relations were no longer his relatives."[13]

The rabbis at Jamnia also decided that the Old Testament was not inspired verbatim by God, but written by men. The Christians, who considered themselves Jews until A.D. 70, retained the old Jewish belief that the Old Testament contained the exact words of God. The rabbis, according to Rabbi Raisin, valued the Old Testament as a source of homilies, rather than for its historicity.

The destruction of the Temple in A.D. 70 produced a spiritualising effect, as the Babylonian conquest had done, drawing all Jews together by a spiritual bond. "The school in Yavneh (Jamnia), more than any other event in history proved that the spirit is mightier than the sword."[14]

* * *

Near the end of his life, Trajan (98–117) was campaigning in Babylonia. The Jews in that country were loyal to Parthia and wrote to those of Egypt and Cyrenaica to rebel against Rome. They replied by attacking their Gentile neighbours. Hadrian, who was opposed to war, tried in vain to pacify these Jews, when he succeeded Trajan as emperor.

Eventually, losing patience, he reversed his conciliatory attitude (as Antiochus Epiphanes had done) and issued a law prohibiting circumcision. In Judaea, a man calling himself Bar Kokhba rose in rebellion. Rabbi Akiba, a teacher much respected and a famous Talmudist, hailed him as the Messiah. In 135, the revolt of Bar Kokhba was suppressed after much bloodshed, Rabbi Akiba was put to death and Jerusalem was rebuilt as a Roman city. "The way of the sword for keeping the Jews alive had failed. The second choice, the way of the spirit, was now entered upon with enthusiasm . . . The Jews were destined to be a kingdom not of this earth."[15]

[13] Rabbi Raisin, *Gentile Reactions to Jewish Ideals*.
[14] Solomon Grayzel, *A History of the Jews*, quoted by Moshe Menuhin.
[15] Moshe Menuhin, op. cit.

Not all Jews in Palestine turned to spiritual realisation. There was also a bitter xenophobic movement. Directives were drawn up in Judaea with the object of severing every contact with the world. It was forbidden to eat anything handled by non-Jews, to accept their testimony or their gifts, and even to learn their languages.

Most rabbis, however, still held that it was the duty of Israel to convert the world. In any case, these bitter reactions were confined to little Judaea. Throughout the vast empires of Rome and Parthia, co-operation with Gentiles continued, subject to conformity with the dietary laws. "All through the period under consideration" (the reign of Hadrian and after), "the ranks of Judaism were constantly being replenished with proselytes. Circumcision did not deter them nor persecution prevent them."[16]

NOTABLE DATES

Herod Agrippa I made King of Auranitis and Galilee	A.D. 37
Herod Antipas exiled to Gaul	A.D. 37
Judaea added to Agrippa's kingdom by Claudius	A.D. 40
Death of Herod Agrippa I	A.D. 44
Agrippa II King of Auranitis	A.D. 53
Defeat of Cestius Gallus	A.D. 66
Vespasian clears Galilee	A.D. 67
Operations halted on the death of Nero	A.D. 68
Escape of Johanan ben Zakkai to Jamnia	A.D. 69
Siege and Fall of Jerusalem	A.D. 70
Revolt of Bar Kokhba	A.D. 132–135

ROMAN EMPERORS

Augustus	27 B.C.–A.D. 14
Tiberius	14–31
Caligula	37–41
Claudius	41–54
Nero	54–68
Galba, Otho, Vitellius	68–69
Vespasian	69–79
Titus	79–81

[16] Rabbi Raisin, op cit.

Domitian	81–96
Nerva	86–99
Trajan	98–117
Hadrian	117–138

CONCLUSIONS

Under the Romans, Judaea broke out once again in bitter, militant isolationism which, as under the Hasmonaeans, led to a decline of spiritual religion and a rise in race hatreds. In the hour of utter disaster, however, Judaism achieved an epoch-making advance in spiritual and religious insight. In the world at large, where dwelt four Jews out of five, Judaism as a religion continued to make converts.

X

The Tragedy of Jewish - Christian Rivalry

Because on the one hand the state of affairs in the religious sphere was fixed for all time . . . in the Torah, and on the other the reins of office were held by a priestly aristocracy which was conservative and dominated by a lust for power, the growth of Yahwism was put under severe restraint and brought almost to a standstill. This meant that any sort of drastic renewal . . . had become impossible . . . This determined the attitude adopted towards the Christian community, which stood for a much more radical renewal. This latter group was felt by Judaism to constitute a plot against its own existence and was therefore rebuffed. That settled the relationship between Judaism and primitive Christianity.
    Th. C. Vriezen, *The Religion of Ancient Israel*

One great spiritual fact dominates the history of the empire: The advent of personal religion which followed on the conquest of Rome by the mysticism of the East.
    Carcopino, *Daily Life in Ancient Rome*

Judge not that ye be not judged . . . and why beholdest thou the mote that is in thy brother's eye but considerest not the beam that is in thine own eye.
    Matthew VII, 1 to 3

X

IT scarcely seems an exaggeration to say that the breach between Jews and Christians after the Crucifixion was the greatest tragedy which ever occurred in the Western world.

For several years after the Crucifixion, the Christians remained a small Jewish sect. The Pharisees had criticised some of Christ's teaching as suggesting laxity, for they "did not admit that there could be a question of gravity in a deliberate and unnecessary breaking"[1] of the Law. To break the most trivial rule was to break the whole.

Although they were the hereditary high priests, the Sadducees were primarily politicians. Like Herod, their power depended on Roman support. As long as there was no trouble, Rome left them to govern Judaea. They feared that the popularity of Jesus would lead to a rebellion, resulting in Roman intervention.

In addition, however, the Jerusalem authorities were incensed against the Christians for claiming that Christ had been the Messiah. The high priest and the council, we are told, were "enraged and wanted to kill them".[2] Peter and John were arrested, Stephen was stoned to death and "a great persecution arose against the church in Jerusalem... Saul, entering house after house, dragged off men and women and committed them to prison."[3]

Herod Antipas "laid violent hands on some who belonged to the church. He killed James, the brother of John, with the sword; and when he saw that it pleased the Jews, he proceeded to arrest Peter also."[4]

The account of Paul's missionary journeys shows how, in every town, the Jewish community tried to kill him or drive him out. Rome had granted the high priest religious jurisdiction over all the Jews in the empire. As the Christians were still classified as Jews, he could order their scourging or imprisonment wherever found.

James, the Lord's brother, was head of the community in Jerusalem. "They brought him into their midst and in the presence of the whole populace demanded a denial of his belief in Christ.

---

[1] J. Parkes, *The Conflict of the Church and the Synagogue.*
[2] Acts IV, 13 to 21, and V, 27 to 40.
[3] Acts VIII, 1 to 3.
[4] Acts XII, 1 and 2.

But when ... he showed unexpected fearlessness in the face of the enormous throng, declaring that our Saviour and Lord, Jesus, was the Son of God, they could not endure his testimony any longer, since he was universally regarded as the most righteous of men ... So they killed him."[5]

This James the Righteous is believed to have been the author of the Epistle General of James, in which he wrote, "Pure religion and undefiled is this, to visit the fatherless and widows in their affliction and to keep himself unspotted from the world."

* * *

These and similar incidents are worthy of further thought. We, alas, are familiar with religious persecution, and often fail to realise that it was virtually unknown to the ancients. If Vriezen's suggestion be true[6] that the Israelites and the Moabites were the only two groups which massacred their enemies as a sacrifice to their gods, there would seem to have been an element of violent intolerance in Israel from the days of Joshua. Since the Captivity, it is true that a new spiritual monotheism had appeared in Judaism, though periodically overlaid by narrow bigotry.

In the first century and a half after Christ, the Jews seem to have shown this persecuting mentality against the Christians, thereby releasing a chain reaction of persecutions down to our own times. It may be argued that Antiochus Epiphanes was the first religious persecutor, but the case is not parallel. It was the intrigues of rival high priests and the turbulence of the Judaeans which provoked his repressive measures, not a missionary passion to convert them to his religion.

The basic difference may be summarised by saying that ancient governments were only concerned with the *actions* of their subjects, not with their thoughts. The Jews seem to have originated religious persecution against people's *thoughts*. James the Righteous was a saintly character, but he *thought* that Jesus was the Messiah. The era, therefore, was a milestone in history. Thenceforward, not only Jews but, even more, Christians were to kill, torture and penalise people for their thoughts, no matter how innocent their lives.

Some time between A.D. 80 and 90, the rabbis, now settled in Jamnia, issued a revised form of the "eighteen Benedictions" to be read out in synagogues, which included a condemnation of the "Nazarenes".

Dr. Parkes believes that about A.D. 90, the Jewish patriarch (the

[5] Eusebius, *History of the Church*.   [6] P. 60.

high priest was abolished) "ordered the daily cursing of Christ in the synagogue". The Jews were a powerful community in the empire, entitled to religious toleration. The Christians, after their expulsion from the synagogue, lost their Jewish privileges. During the rebellion of Bar Kokhba, the Christians were actively persecuted in Judaea for refusing to recognise the rebel leader as the Messiah.

Religions are usually more bitter against their own heretics than against outsiders. Jewish leaders were incensed against Jewish converts to Christianity, more than against Gentile Christians. After 200, however, the vast majority of Christians were Gentiles. Unfortunately, the Christians had built up bitter resentment against Jews during the first century and a half of persecution. As soon as they became strong enough, they were, in a most unchristian spirit, eager for their revenge.

When considering any religion, it is always essential to differentiate between persons who belong to a religion by accident of birth, and those who really try to live by the precepts of their faith. Unfortunately even the Fathers of the Church used bitter words against Jews in the third and fourth centuries. It is worthwhile here to remind ourselves of the people whom Christ had pronounced to be blessed. They were the poor in spirit, the meek, such as hunger and thirst after righteousness, the merciful, the pure in heart, the peacemakers and the persecuted. It is impossible to reconcile these attributes with vituperation of the Jews, even if they had persecuted the early Christians.

Conversion, it may be noted, does not normally instantly change the whole character and background of a people, though it may in the case of an individual. Europe, in the second and third centuries, was largely peopled by martial barbarian races. Often a whole community was "converted" by the conversion of their king. Most of the people were illiterate, and few could find out the precepts of their new faith. If they were fired with enthusiasm for Christ, their first instinct was to fight for Him and kill His enemies. Sweeping generalisations, under such circumstances, are certain to be wrong.

Apart from such mutual vilifications, it is difficult to avoid the belief that the Jews were unwise in their use of mockery. Caricatures of Christ and comic parodies of the Crucifixion goaded Christians to fury. It has been said that Christianity is not based on a book, but on a Person. To the Christian, the personality of Christ presented a tender grace and inspired a passionate devotion little appreciated by Jews, whose religion was founded on the Law.

But probably the principal cause of hatred between Jews and

Christians was competition in the mission field. It is rarely appreciated nowadays that, before Christianity, the Jews were a powerful community, which was rapidly converting the Roman world. They were understandably indignant when the Christians, whom they considered as Jewish renegades, entered into competition with them in converting pagans.

While the surviving writings of Jews and Christians in the four centuries after Christ often show a deep and humble spirituality, both have left vitriolic denunciations of the other religion—the Christians perhaps even more than the Jews. When the Christians converted pagans, the Jews contacted the converts to assure them that the Christian teaching was untrue. Many letters from church leaders have survived, warning converts not to consort with Jews.

The fourth century produced many giants among the Christian fathers, such as John Chrysostom, Athanasius and Ambrose, Bishop of Milan. Their writings, read all over the Christian world, were of immense spiritual value, but included, here and there, forceful condemnation of the Jews. In the fourth century, reward or punishment in the next life were thought to depend, not only on quality of life, but also on belief in the correct dogma. The indignation of Church leaders would thus be roused against Jews, who endeavoured to undermine the faith of those whom they themselves had converted. But the situation was aggravated by other complications.

Firstly, decadent Roman intellectualism quickly involved the Church in hair-splitting discussions, giving rise to heresies based on the subtle mentality of the Greeks. "The Christological discussions of the fourth century were forced upon the Church, not by the inherent complications of her own faith, but by the acuteness and confusion of philosophic speculation among the Greek and Roman intellectuals."

These dogmatic intricacies, of which there is no trace in the Old Testament, enabled the Jews to brand the Christians as polytheists. Soon the Church became more hostile to its own heretics than to the Jews, a situation which was to continue for more than a thousand years.

Another factor must be noted. Reporters, as we know to our cost, like to make a story out of a murder or a riot. Thus the reports which have come down to us record the riots, the violence and the mutual burnings of churches and synagogues. But when we add up such incidents, covering five centuries, we can trace only eight, ten or twelve episodes in the whole empire. The riots in the United States alone in 1968 and 1969 seem to exceed those between Jews and Christians in five hundred years.

Moreover, here and there, we find reports of kindness and cooperation. The Jews occupied a privileged position and no imperial police officer could cross-question a Jew about his faith. After their expulsion from the synagogue in A.D. 90, however, Christians lost these immunities. They were not, thereafter, continuously persecuted, but periodic persecutions occurred, for example, under Nero (A.D. 54–68), Domitian (81–96) and Diocletian (293–313).

Cases are recorded of Jews offering sanctuary to persecuted Christians who, in a Jewish community, were safe from police interrogation. It is probable that, in everyday life, Jews and Christians lived peaceably together, though the dietary laws prevented the Jews from exchanging social amenities. These amicable relations, where they existed, were possibly due to the fact that the majority of Jews and Christians in the empire were alike local converts of the same ethnic origin.

* * *

Until the fourth century, Jews and Christians were minorities in the pagan Roman Empire. During the reign of Constantine (306–337), however, Christianity became the official religion of Rome. Two results ensued. Firstly, emperors, senators, army commanders, officials and politicians dutifully declared themselves Christians, though often indifferent to, or ignorant of, Christian ideals. Secondly, the Christians, who for three centuries had denounced Roman morals, found themselves responsible for improving them.

Despair pervaded the educated classes and the city populations. The Roman world was, in fact, decadent beyond recovery. The Christians succeeded in passing some drastic laws, but legislation cannot revive the lost spirit of sacrifice and service.

Judaism, on the other hand, remained free from political obligations. The Talmud was still being built up in Babylonia and in Palestine, where the great rabbinical school had moved from Jamnia to Tiberias. The Jews, unlike the Christians, were nowhere responsible for the morals of non-Jews. Moreover, the emphasis placed by Judaism on the sanctity of the family (an old Middle Eastern concept) had enabled Jews to avoid most of the sexual licence which had disgraced the last days of Rome.

* * *

Before embarking upon the centuries of persecution, one or two basic facts may be repeated. Firstly, the Jews seem to have been the first to punish people for their ideas. Pagan governments normally punished only actions. Sometimes a man's beliefs compelled him to break the law, but in such cases he was punished for breaking the law, not for his beliefs. The Judaeans, however, punished the Christians for thinking that Christ was the Messiah, although they had not broken the laws.

Secondly, until about the eighteenth century, it was believed that force was the only way to preserve law and order. Governments suppressed such types of persons as they believed to be a danger to the state. The Christian Roman Emperors believed two types of persons to be a danger to the state—Christian heretics and Jews. "Certainly, so far as the fourth century is concerned, it was better to be a Jew than a heretic,"[7] a situation which was to last for thirteen centuries.

It was assumed that persons who held the same beliefs as the government would be loyal. The pagan idea of suppressing communities dangerous to the state changed imperceptibly into the principle of suppressing those whose religion differed from that of the government, an idea which persisted in Europe almost until our own times.

Moreover, foreign governments might use persons of other religions as a fifth column. When the Roman Empire became Christian, Persia became suspicious of her native Christians and showed favour to her Jews. When Rome and Persia were at war, Persian Jews urged Roman Jews to rebel. As a result, Rome tended to suppress her Jews, Persia her Christians. Presented with certain incidents in history, we are horrified at the tyranny displayed. But when we analyse the process, we can see how these situations grew.

Thirdly, it is worth analysing the difference between the official attitude to heretics and Jews respectively. In dealing with heretics, we must remember the general belief that the next world was all that mattered, and that this life was necessarily short and miserable. Moreover, salvation in the next world could only be ensured if the individual in question had held the correct *intellectual* beliefs in this life. If heretics were allowed to multiply, they might undermine the faith of others, thereby depriving thousands or millions of people of eternal bliss.

Thus to exterminate heretics like rats was the only hope of saving humanity. The government, of course, assumed their own beliefs to be correct, though Greek theology was so involved that no one, in fact, understood it at all. The persecuted were no more enlightened

---

[7] J. Parkes, *The Conflict between the Church and the Synagogue.*

than their persecutors. When the victims were able to seize power, they immediately persecuted their former persecutors.

The position of Jews was entirely different from that of heretics. The Church taught that the Jews would ultimately be converted to Christianity, and that their conversion would immediately precede the Second Coming of Christ. Jews must not, therefore, be exterminated, for they were to be present at the Last Day, which, however, could not take place until they were converted. They must, accordingly, be converted, but not exterminated.

The fact that both religions advocated humility, gentleness, repentance and patience was forgotten in these communal rivalries.

* * *

Under Theodosius I (379-395), heretics were persecuted but Jews protected. Writing to the governor of the eastern provinces, the emperor said, "It is sufficiently evident that the Jewish sect is not prohibited by any law. We are therefore seriously disquieted to learn that in certain places Jewish meetings have been prohibited. Your Excellency will, on receipt of this order, restrain with suitable severity the excesses of those who, under the name of the Christian religion, are committing illegal actions, or attempting to destroy or ruin synagogues."[8]

On the death of Theodosius in 395, the empire was divided in half between his two sons. In 475, the Western Empire collapsed and was divided between various "barbarian" rulers, who, however, were already romanised and endeavoured to preserve Roman laws and institutions.

Theoderic the Ostrogoth (493-526) ruled Italy, Provence and northern Spain, and tolerated all religions. "As to the Jews," he wrote, "let the privileges they enjoy be preserved and let them retain their own judges." In a letter to the Jews of Genoa, he wrote, "We are not able to command religion, for no one is compelled unwillingly to believe."

In 590, Gregory the Great became pope. He is best known to English-speaking people for his remark that the English slave boys in Rome were not Angles but angels. In 596, he sent St. Augustine to convert Britain. A just ruler, he protected the Jews. Writing to the Bishop of Arles he says that Jewish merchants have complained to him that Jews in the bishop's diocese had been baptised by force. To another bishop, he writes disapprovingly of the use of threats. "The Jews," he adds, "are more likely to be converted by kindness."

[8] Quoted by J. Parkes, op. cit.

The possesion by Jews of Christian slaves is a constantly recurring theme right through the Middle Ages. A Gentile male slave was of little use in a Jewish house. A Jew could not even drink wine served by a Christian. It was, therefore, in the interest of his Jewish master to convert him. Girl slaves were even more frequently converted to Judaism. The Church, therefore, was anxious to prevent Jews from acquiring Christian slaves.

The slave trade, of which Jews enjoyed a virtual monopoly, also constituted a problem. Jews bought slaves in France, with the consent of the Merovingian kings, and shipped them to Naples for sale in Italy. Gregory objected to the enslavement of Christian children, but the Jews replied that they did not know their religion when they bought them.

This picture of Jewish merchants complaining to the pope and obtaining a just hearing, of Jews and Christians in business and of the protection of the Merovingian kings, conveys an impression of reasonableness and toleration.

In 507, the Visigoths, or west Goths, conquered Spain. At first they were Arians, and treated Jews and Catholics with toleration. Under King Recared (586–601), however, they became Catholics. Thereafter, they oppressed the Jews until the Arab conquest in 712.

In France, in the sixth century, a few laws were aimed at Jews, mostly to prevent Christian conversions to Judaism. A Jew who converted a Christian was liable to the confiscation of his property. Intermarriage between Jews and Christians was forbidden presumably again for fear of conversion. The constant anxiety of the Church on the subject of conversions shows that the Jews were still active proselytisers.

* * *

So much for the new barbarian kingdoms of the West. The Eastern —or Byzantine—Empire struggled on alone. Internal security could only be maintained with difficulty, and lawlessness was endemic. Every few years there was a financial crisis. The precarious emperors tended to be intolerant compared to the strong warrior rulers of the West.

Under Theodosius II (401–450) complaints were received of disorders during the Jewish feast of Purim. Jewish revellers had seized a Christian boy and lashed him to a cross in a parody of the Crucifixion, with the result that he died. This affair may have originated the medieval belief that Jews sacrificed a Christian child at the annual Passover.

A striking fact is the recrudescence of rioting in Alexandria, similar to that five hundred years before. On one occasion, some Jews having been forcibly baptised, a Jewish crowd crucified a statue of Christ amid ribald shouts. At another time, some Jews enticed Christians into the streets by shouting that the church was on fire, and attacked them as they came out of their houses. Next day, the Christians counter-attacked and looted many Jewish houses.

The Christians were as violent as the Jews. In 418, Theodosius II condemned the burning of synagogues and churches, adding, "just as we wish to make provision for the benefit of the Jews, so we consider that a warning should be addressed to them that they must not presume on their security to commit outrages against the Christian faith." The voice might be the voice of Claudius, five hundred years earlier. "There is no reason to doubt that this double rebuke was necessary."[9] The Jews do not seem to have been the patient victims of these disorders. They were ready to give as good as they got.

The Byzantines, however, were far more concerned over heretics than over Jews. They never ceased to pursue Christians, whom the Church declared to be unorthodox, a policy which was greatly to facilitate the impending Muslim conquest.

From 602-628, the Byzantines were continuously at war with Persia. In 616, the Persians were in occupation of Asia Minor, Palestine and Egypt. The Byzantine Empire seemed to be about to collapse, as had the Western Roman Empire.

The Persians tolerated all religions but tended to favour Jews, many of whom joined their advancing armies. In 614, the Jews inside Jerusalem helped the Persians to take the city, killing many Christians and demolishing their churches. In 628, peace was concluded and the Persians withdrew. The Persian occupation had increased the hostility between Jews and Christians in the Holy Land.

Outrages between the two communities would doubtless have ensued but a revolution was impending, which was to establish religious toleration in the Middle East for several centuries.

* * *

Jews, however, were by no means limited to the Roman Empire. The Jewish community in Babylonia was still the leader of world Judaism, whether in wealth and honour or in learning. The Babylonian Talmudists were probably more advanced academically than the rabbinical schools of Palestine.

[9] J. Parkes, *The Conflict between the Church and the Synagogue*.

At some time not recorded, groups of "Jews" appeared in certain oases in the northern Hejaz, notably Khaibar and Yathrib. These communities practising Judaism were probably ethnically Arabs, converted to Judaism by itinerant missionaries, before or after the time of Christ. They appear to have been indistinguishable from the surrounding native peoples, in appearance, language or customs, though more educated than they were, for Judaism always meant schools.

From A.D. 200 to 236, the Yemen was ruled by a great king called Asad abu Qarib, who is said to have conquered all Arabia up to the Euphrates. On one of his campaigns he occupied the oasis of Yathrib, where he found this Jewish community. Himself an idolater, he was as deeply impressed with Jewish monotheism as had been the pagan peoples of the Roman Empire.

On returning to the Yemen, he took with him two rabbis who converted the royal family and the ruling classes of the country to Judaism. The dynasty remained in power for three centuries after Asad, during which period the Yemen was a "Jewish" kingdom, that is to say a country in which the upper classes practised Judaism. A strong minority of Jews remained in the Yemen until, in the last twenty years, they were reported as "returning to their homeland in Palestine". It is doubtful if any of their ancestors had ever seen Palestine.

NOTABLE DATES

Capture of Jerusalem by Titus	70
Revolt of Bar Kokhba	132–135
Division of the Roman Empire into East and West	395
Collapse of the Western Empire	475
Theoderic the Ostrogoth	493–526
Visigoth conquest of Spain	507
Oppression of Jews in Spain	586–712
War between Byzantium and Persia	602–628

NOTABLE ROMAN EMPERORS

	A.D.
Nero persecuted Christians but favoured Jews	54–68
Domitian persecuted Christians	81–96
Diocletian persecuted Christians	283–313
Constantine made the Roman Empire Christian	306–337

Theodosius I (Theodosian Code protected
  Jews)   379–395

CONCLUSIONS

(1) From the Crucifixion to A.D. 135, Jews persecuted the Christians. This seems to have originated the idea of persecuting people for their beliefs, not for their actions.

(2) About A.D. 90, the rabbis introduced the cursing of Christians in the synagogue.

(3) Thereafter, Jews and Christians exchanged vilifications.

(4) The most important cause of friction was probably competition in converting the pagans.

(5) The Church forbade massacres of Jews for theological reasons, but was anxious to convert them.

(6) Even after Constantine, Jews were not persecuted, but Christians were now more numerous. There were still great numbers of Jews who were not intimidated but defiantly gave tit for tat.

(7) Riots, fights, and the burning of churches and synagogues were popular clashes, not approved by either popes or rulers. In Spain, after about 600, the Visigoths persecuted Jews.

XI

The Arab Hurricane

To the first Saracens, the call to the battlefield was like the call to a wedding feast. And these men, so terrible in battle, are eminently mild in victory. The plighted faith was rigidly kept; we hear of no indiscriminate massacres. It was no sort of disgrace to the armies of either Rome or Persia to have been discomfited by enemies like these.

FREEMAN, *History of the Saracens*

With the coming of the Arabs, a Golden Age was initiated for the Jews of Spain ... the strength of Judaism in the Peninsula became immensely reinforced. Its communities exceeded in numbers, in culture and in wealth, those of any country in the whole of the Western World.

CECIL ROTH, *A History of the Marranos*

We may as well tolerate all religions since God Himself tolerates them.

F. FÉNELON

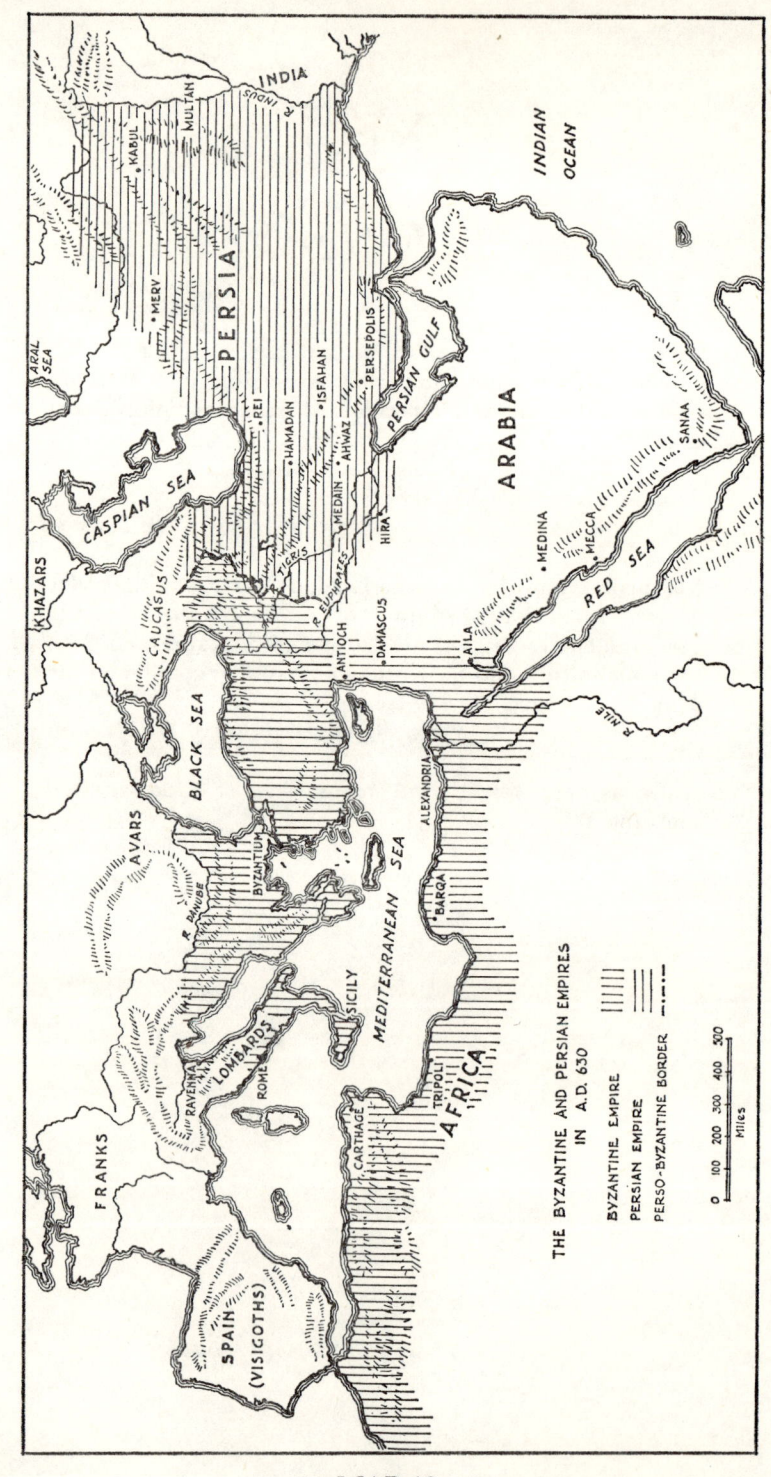

MAP 19

XI

AT the beginning of the seventh century, the civilised world (omitting distant India and China) was divided between the Byzantine and Persian Empires. The boundary between the two empires ran from Dura Europas on the Euphrates to Armenia. The peninsula of Arabia lay immediately south of the imperial frontier, and in contact with both power blocs.

The greater part of the peninsula consisted of desert, which produced sparse grazing but was without sufficient moisture for agriculture. The deserts were thinly populated by nomad tribes, which bred camels and sheep and spent much of their time fighting one another. Their wars, however, were controlled by strict rules of honour and were, to a great extent, chivalrous rivalries, in which no tribe desired either to exterminate, or even to subjugate its competitors. The nomads, though mostly illiterate, were devoted to poetry, which they spent long hours reciting, in their rolling, sonorous language.

The oasis-dwellers were also tribally organised, but earned their living by agriculture, dates being their principal crop. Many, also, were merchants, travelling with caravans laden with merchandise.

Arabia had always been of great importance to the outside world, because it constituted a barrier between the Indian Ocean and the Oriental world on one side, and the Mediterranean and the Western world on the other. Thus it lay astride the world's greatest trade route. In the seventh century, navigation was still precarious. The eastern trade was, therefore, carried by sea from India to Aden on the summer trade winds, the ships returning to India as soon as the monsoon ended. The merchandise was then transported by camel caravan to Egypt, Gaza or Damascus.

Half-way between Aden and Damascus lay Mecca, a caravan station controlled by a tribe called Quraish, many members of which were merchants. They were not camel drivers but capitalists, who bought the oriental goods landed in Aden and resold them at a profit in Egypt or Syria.

From time immemorial, there had also been a temple in Mecca, in the centre of which stood a small cube-shaped building, surrounded by a court. The building contained neither idol nor image, and could only be entered on rare occasions by the hereditary

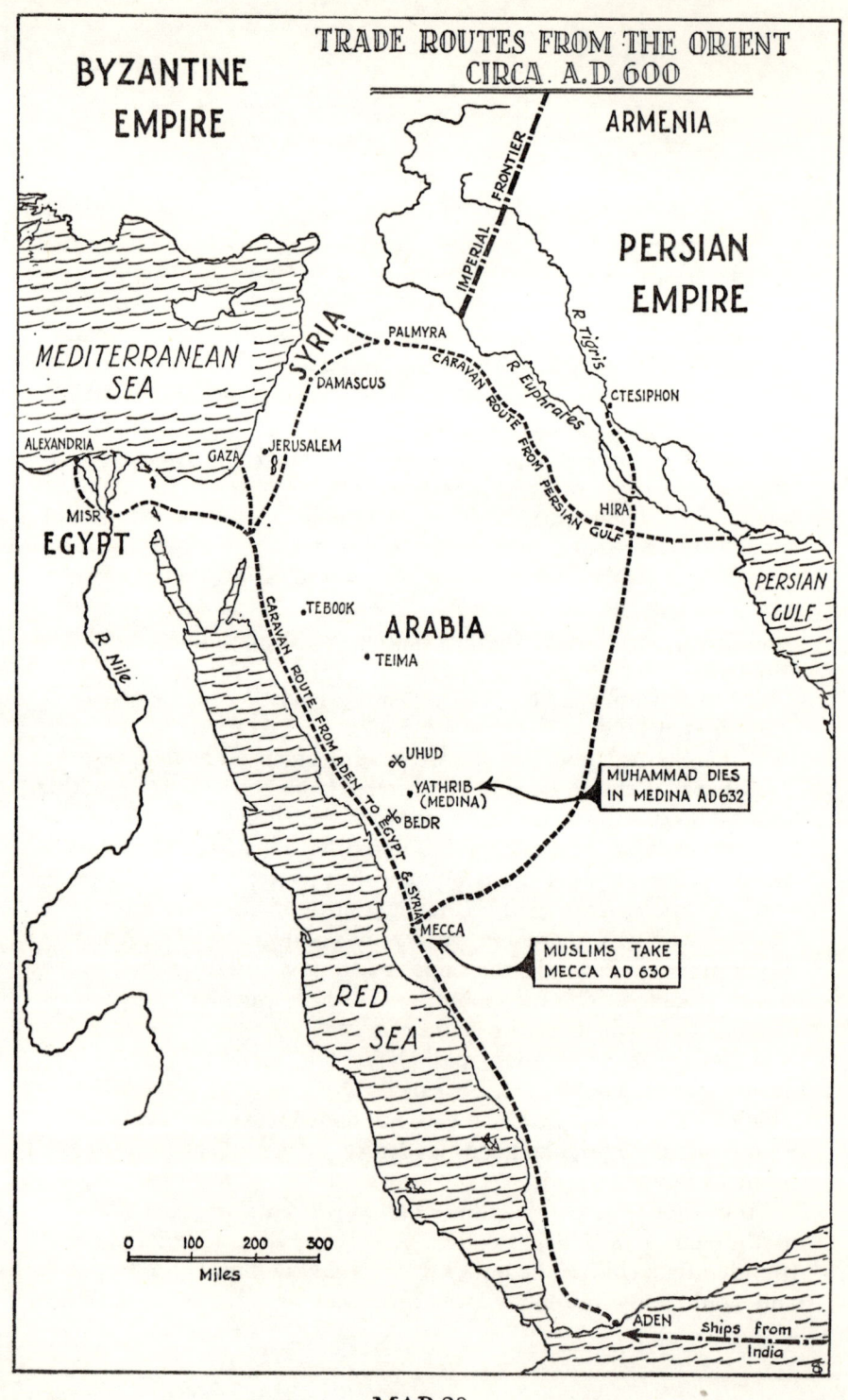

MAP 20

guardian of the shrine. The similarity of this sanctuary to the temples of Serabit al Khadim and of Jerusalem has already been mentioned. In the seventh century, the cult seems to have become debased, possibly by the importation of "idols" from Syria. The older Arabian religion appears to have recognised a single God, who was served by many spirits, some of whom dwelt in certain places near springs or in rocks. These spirits were not represented by statues made in the likeness of living things.

Although Arabia was a poor, desert land, it had lain for thousands of years between the world's most advanced cultures—Egypt, Babylonia, Greece, Persia and Rome. Although the tribes were poor, they were not unsophisticated, still less savages.

* * *

Probably in A.D. 570, a boy called Muhammad was born in the tribe of Quraish, the merchants of Mecca. His father died before Muhammad's birth, and his mother when he was six years old. Left an orphan, he was brought up for some years by his grandfather and then by his uncle. Possibly as a result of a lonely and insecure childhood, he grew up into a serious and meditative youth. To earn a living he worked in business, like all his family.

When he was twenty-five, his uncle, Abu Talib, obtained for him the job of leading a merchant caravan to Syria. The caravan belonged to a rich Meccan widow, who managed her own business affairs. Muhammad was so successful in his conduct of the caravan that the widow, on his return, suggested marriage. Khadija[1] was much older than he was, but the marriage was an unqualified success. Not only did it provide him with a loyal, sympathetic and loving partner, but the widow's money rescued him from poverty.

As the years passed, Muhammad spent more and more time in solitary meditation in the barren mountains which surrounded Mecca. One night, in 610, when he was forty years old, he was alone in a cave when he saw a vision, which called upon him to read or recite. Shattered by this profound experience, he hastened home and poured out his hopes and his fears to the ever-sympathetic Khadija.

Three years passed in doubt, after which he received the order to preach. Naturally reserved, he suffered agonies of anxiety before he began to speak in public. His first converts were Khadija, his nephew Ali, a slave boy whom he had adopted called Zaid, and a merchant of Mecca known as Abu Bekr.

[1] Pronounced Khadeeja.

QURAISH

TO SHOW THE KHALIFS AND DYNASTIES OF MUHAMMAD'S FAMILY

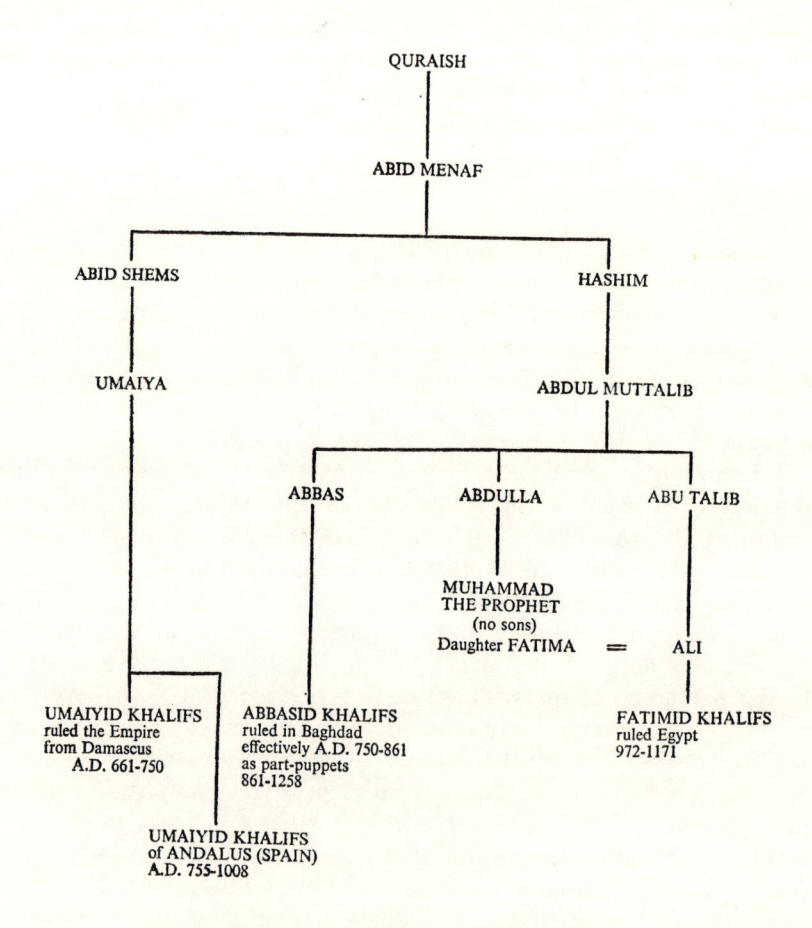

```
                          QURAISH
                             |
                        ABID MENAF
                             |
            ┌────────────────┴────────────────┐
        ABID SHEMS                         HASHIM
            |                                 |
         UMAIYA                         ABDUL MUTTALIB
            |                                 |
            |                ┌────────────────┼────────────────┐
            |              ABBAS           ABDULLA          ABU TALIB
            |                |                |                |
            |                |            MUHAMMAD             |
            |                |           THE PROPHET           |
            |                |             (no sons)           |
            |                |          Daughter FATIMA  =    ALI
            |                |                                 |
   UMAIYID KHALIFS    ABBASID KHALIFS                   FATIMID KHALIFS
   ruled the Empire   ruled in Baghdad                  ruled Egypt
   from Damascus      effectively A.D. 750-861          972-1171
   A.D. 661-750       as part-puppets
                      861-1258
            |
   UMAIYID KHALIFS
   of ANDALUS (SPAIN)
   A.D. 755-1008
```

His message was simple. There was only one God and he, Muhammad, was a messenger sent by Him. Idols must be destroyed and prayers should not be offered to spirits. One day the dead would rise, the righteous to eternal bliss, the wicked to hell-fire. There was complete religious toleration in Mecca, Christians and Jews came and went, and Muhammad had learned much from them.

Thereafter, for the rest of his life, he would periodically fall into a trance and hear a voice. When he returned to his senses, he recited the message he had received, which his followers either learned by heart or jotted down. After his death, the revelations were collated and formed the Qoran.

Muhammad's message gradually provoked opposition among the Meccan leaders. Outwardly, they objected to his refusal to recognise the "patron spirits" (rather than idols), which they believed could act as intermediaries between them and the One God. They also protested loudly against his statement that their own ancestors were suffering in hell. The leaders may also have felt that it would be impossible for them to maintain their positions, if one of the citizens continually claimed to receive direct revelations from God. Ultimately, such a man would himself have to be the leader.

In 619, the Messenger of God, as his followers called him, suffered two grievous losses. The devoted Khadija died, as also did his uncle, Abu Talib, a man of considerable influence in the town, who had hitherto protected him. After years of preaching, he had made only some seventy converts. Lonely and discouraged, Muhammad considered the possibility of leaving Mecca. He had a few friends in Yathrib, an oasis two hundred and fifty miles to the north. In the summer of 622, he slipped out of Mecca, just in time to avoid a plot to murder him.

Twelve years had passed since his first vision. Throughout this period, he had shown an extraordinary degree of patience under mockery and insult. His revelations, passionate and poetic like those of the Hebrew prophets, seemed to rise from the deep convictions of his heart. In Yathrib, however, he found himself the executive chief of the infant Muslim community. He immediately announced that the Archangel Gabriel had given leave for the Muslims to fight back against their oppressors.

As already explained, Mecca earned its living from the caravan trade between Aden, Syria and Egypt. Yathrib (later called Medina, the name which we shall use henceforward) was ideally placed as a base from which to intercept the Meccan caravans.[2] In March 624, a

[2] Map 20, p. 174.

caravan of a thousand camels was due to pass Medina, returning from Damascus. Muhammad, with three hundred and fourteen men, set out to intercept it.

The Muslims[3] missed the caravan, but at Bedr[4] encountered a force of a thousand Meccans, who had come out to protect it. Although outnumbered by three to one, the Muslims gave battle and won a complete victory. This success transformed them overnight from a small persecuted sect into a military community which began to inspire fear.

Alarmed by the threat to their caravans, on which their very lives depended, Quraish in 625 marched on Medina with three thousand men. The Muslims could only muster seven hundred. Remembering the miracle of Bedr, they nevertheless gave battle at Uhud, but were completely defeated, the Messenger of God himself being wounded. Surprisingly, however, this disaster did not put an end to the movement. Conversions continued more rapidly than before.

Two years after the Battle of Uhud, the Meccans laid siege to Medina with ten thousand men, which included many allies from the nomadic tribes. After blockading the town for three weeks, however, the attackers withdrew.

Unlike Mecca which was purely commercial, the oasis of Medina was agricultural. It contained five tribes, the two largest being polytheistic, but three smaller tribes practised Judaism. These may well have been ethnically Arabs, converted by Jewish missionaries, but nothing definite is known of their origin. Muhammad claimed that Islam was the religion of Abraham and of Moses, and had hoped that he would be supported by the Jews. Unfortunately, however, the Medina Jews mocked at his revelations and his mission.

Of the three small Jewish tribes (each seems to have had some seven hundred men) he expelled two from the oasis. The third, however, had communicated with the enemy during the siege of Medina. When the Meccans withdrew, seven hundred Jews of this tribe were put to death. The Messenger of God presumably regarded the action of these people as organised opposition to the mission with which he believed God had entrusted him. Individual Jews remained in Medina unmolested.

All through his life, Muhammad recognised a close relationship between his own preaching and the religions of Christians and Jews.

[3] Muhammad called his religion Islam, or surrender (to God). Those who practised it were Muslims.
[4] Map 20, p. 174.

He forbade his followers to use any kind of pressure to secure the conversion of Jews or Christians to Islam.

In 628, the Messenger of God concluded a truce with Quraish, much against the wishes of his supporters. In fact, however, the greater freedom of movement which followed the truce enabled Muslims and non-Muslims to mix more easily, with the result that the number of conversions to Islam increased rapidly.

In January 630, Muhammad marched on Mecca with ten thousand men and occupied the town without opposition. The images were removed from the courtyard of the temple, but the small cubical "holy of holies", the Kaaba, was pronounced to be the House of God.

The Messenger of God had now become a political power. The year 631 was surnamed "the year of deputations". From all over Arabia, delegations arrived in Medina to profess allegiance to Muhammad. He did not become the ruler of Arabia, as we would use the word, for he had no government organisation. But his influence had brought internal peace to the peninsula.

In March 632, the Messenger of God went to Mecca and re-organised the old pagan pilgrimage as a Muslim festival. He preached a farewell sermon to the pilgrims and returned to Medina. In June 632, he fell ill with headache and fever, which continued to increase until he died on the eleventh day of his illness. The symptoms seem to suggest pneumonia.

* * *

The peace which had reigned in Arabia at the end of Muhammad's life was obviously due to his personality alone. Scarcely was he dead than many of the tribes rebelled against his successor, the devoted Abu Bekr, who had been one of his first converts. The Muslims of Medina, however, were determined men, and immediately resorted to arms, but a year's hard fighting was needed to reduce the whole of Arabia to subjection.

In the summer of 633, all Arabia was at peace. But ceaseless tribal wars, battles, raids and feats of arms had been practised in the desert for thousands of years, and indeed supplied all the romance and glamour in the otherwise hard and penurious lives of the tribesmen. But Muhammad had forbidden wars between Muslims. The outcome was inevitable. If they could not fight each other, they must fight someone else.

In the spring of 633, the eastern tribes moved up to attack the

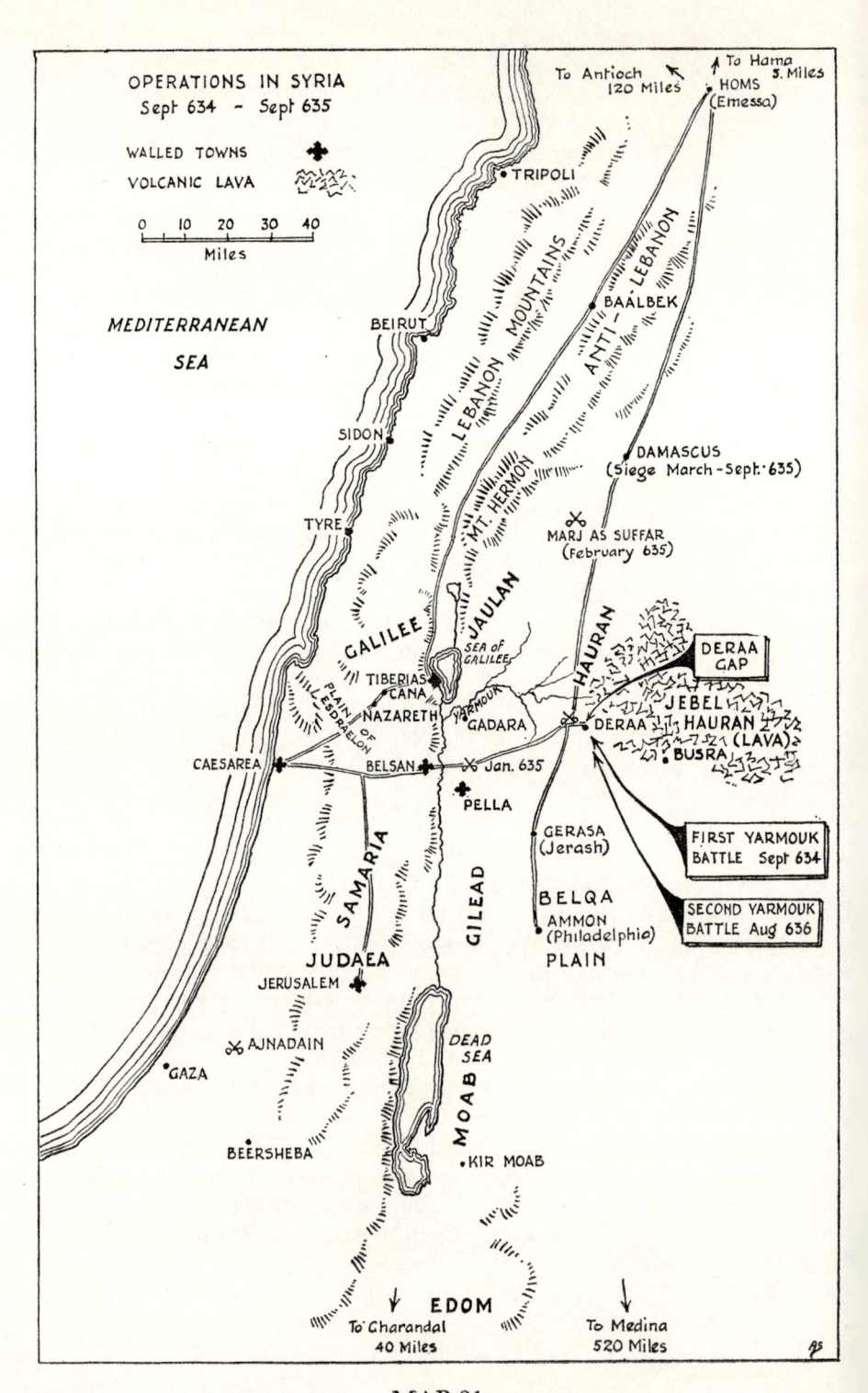

MAP 21

Persian administration along the Euphrates, capturing the two towns of Hira and Anbar. It will be remembered that the Byzantine and Persian Empires had been at war from 602 to 628. At the end of the war, Chosroes Parwiz, King of Persia, was assassinated and the whole empire fell into anarchy. In the ensuing four years, nine rival claimants seized and lost the throne. It was during this chaotic period that the Arabs advanced on the Euphrates.

Simultaneously, early in 633, three Arab columns invaded Palestine and Trans-Jordan, overrunning the whole country up to Deraa, where a narrow defile at the head of the Yarmouk Gorge enabled the Byzantines to hold a defensive position. In September 634, however, the Arabs overran the Yarmouk position and took Damascus. Early in 636, the Byzantines counter-attacked and reoccupied the Yarmouk. On 26th August, 636, the Arabs carried the Yarmouk defences for the second time and the Byzantines abandoned Syria.[5]

In February 637, on the eastern front, the Arabs completely destroyed the Persian army at Qadasiya, and, in 638, occupied the Persian capital at Medain. In 642, the Persians were again defeated at Nehawand,[6] and the Arabs split up into columns to pacify the country. By 652, they had crossed Persia to the borders of Turkistan and of India.

Meanwhile, in December 639, an Arab column of only three thousand six hundred men had invaded Egypt. Reinforced in June 640 by another twelve thousand men, they defeated the Byzantine army, the native Egyptians remaining passively neutral. In September 642, the Byzantines abandoned Egypt and sailed back to Constantinople. In ten years, the little group of sectaries in their Medina oasis had become a great empire. Of the former "Great Powers", Persia had entirely ceased to exist, while the Byzantines had been driven behind the snow-capped Taurus.

* * *

The Arab conquests had been greatly facilitated by the fact that they accorded religious toleration to all. Under the Byzantines, "heretics" had been harassed and persecuted. As most of the Egyptians and Syrians were Monophysite Christians, a denomination whom the Orthodox Byzantines condemned, they had suffered severely for their faith under their Christian rulers. As the Arabs

[5] Map 21, opposite.
[6] Map 22, p. 182.

MAP 22

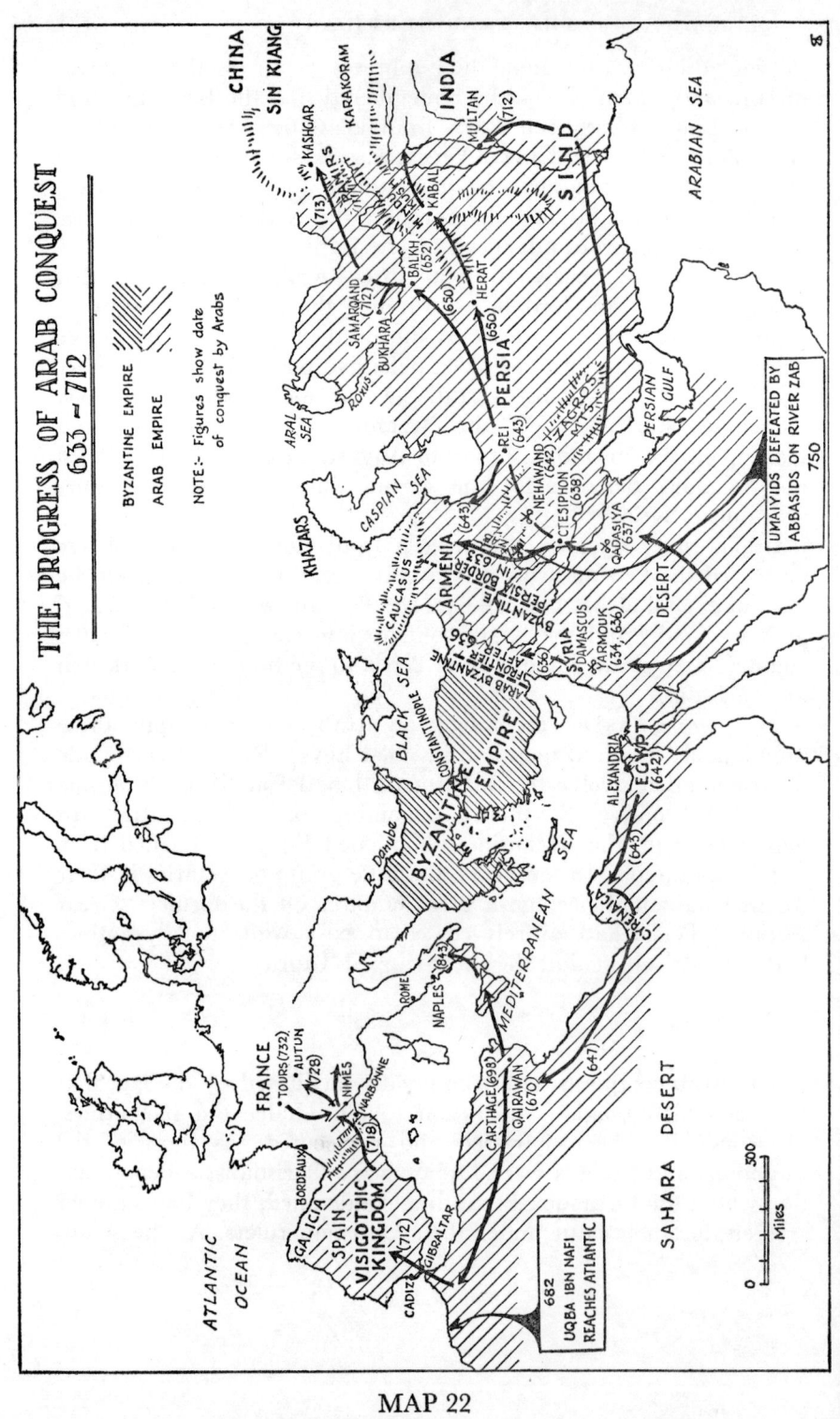

practised complete toleration, the Syrians and Egyptians preferred their rule.

The Jews had been less persecuted than Christian heretics, but under the Muslims they also received religious freedom. The Muslim position was quite clear. Rule of the conquered countries was in the hands of Muslims, but Jews and Christians were safe, as was their property. They were obliged to pay a light poll tax but, in return, were exempted from military service. No attempt was made to convert them. It was the good faith, simplicity and mildness of the Arab conquerors which often caused them to be welcomed by Jews and Christians alike. It is regrettable today to read statements that the Arabs persecuted the Syrians to make them Muslims. Such statements are incorrect.

*   *   *

As the years passed, and the men died who had received direct inspiration from Muhammad, old rivalries and jealousies reappeared. During the lifetime of the Prophet, his strongest opponents among Quraish had been the descendants of Umaiya.[7] After the surrender of Mecca, the Umaiyids had hastened to profess Islam, and had been rewarded with important appointments in the growing empire. One of them, Muawiya, was made governor of Syria while another, Othman, became Muhammad's third successor, or khalif.[8]

Othman was assassinated and was succeeded by Ali, the cousin of the Messenger of God, and hence of the family of Hashim. Muawiya refused to recognise Ali and a five-year civil war ensued. In 661, however, Ali was assassinated and Muawiya, of the Umaiyid family, became khalif. As he was at the time the governor of Syria, the capital of the Muslim Empire was moved from Medina to Damascus.

These worldly feuds had divided the rulers but, among the rank and file of the Muslims, there were still many men passionately dedicated to the teaching of the Messenger of God. No sooner was internal concord established than the frontier armies surged forward once more.

In North Africa, moving westward from Cyrenaica, the Arabs in 670 founded an advanced base at Qairawan in modern Tunisia. The Byzantines still claimed North Africa, their provincial capital being in ancient Carthage.[9]

---

[7] Genealogical Tree, p. 176.
[8] Sometimes spelt caliph.   May 22, opposite.

In 682, Uqba ibn Nafi led an Arab force right across modern Algeria and Morocco. Here tradition tells that he rode his horse into the Atlantic, exclaiming, sword in hand, "God is most great! If my course were not stopped by this sea, I would still ride on to the unknown kingdoms of the west, preaching the unity of God and putting to the sword those rebellious peoples who worship any other god but Him."

The Arab conquest of North Africa was long and arduous. In 698, Hassan ibn Naaman took and destroyed Carthage and the Byzantines were evicted. But the natives of the country, the Berbers, were of far sterner stuff. Again and again the Arabs were victorious, only to be thrown back again by a new Berber revolt. Not until 702 did the Berbers submit and adopt Islam, and North Africa was pacified as far as the Atlantic.

In 711, a force of twelve thousand men, many of them Berber converts and commanded by a Berber, Tariq ibn Zayyad, crossed the Straits and seized Gibraltar. The Rock has ever since been known by his name, Jebel Tariq, the mountain of Tariq.

The Visigoth rulers of Spain were defeated in a single battle, a few miles outside Cadiz, and almost all Spain was pacified within a year, except for a remnant of Christians in the mountains of Galicia.[10] The principal beneficiaries of the Arab conquest of Spain were the Jews who, persecuted under the later Visigoth kings,[11] were immediately granted religious freedom by the Arabs.

In 718, the Arabs broke through the eastern end of the Pyrenees and occupied Narbonne and Carcassonne in France. In 728, they took Nimes and marched up the Rhône Valley as far as Autun. In 732 they seized Bordeaux but, in October of that year, they were defeated at Tours by the Franks under Charles Martel.

*　　*　　*

While these dramatic events were occurring in the west, the Arabs had resumed their advance to the east. In 712, while their co-religionists were occupying Spain, Qutaiba ibn Muslim took Samarqand and, in the following year, crossed the Pamirs and occupied Kashgar, in the Chinese province of Sin Kiang. Again in 712, Muhammad ibn Qasim occupied Sind and took Multan.[12]

Once again, the apparently irresistible Arab advance was arrested by schisms at home. The Umaiyid branch of Quraish had ruled for eighty-nine years in Damascus as the world's greatest emperors. But

[10] Map 22, p. 182.   [11] p. 166.   [12] Map 22, p. 182.

another branch of Quraish coveted power, the Abbásids, the descendants of Abbás, the Prophet's uncle.[13] Living apparently quietly in retirement, they organised a secret network of subversion worthy of the communists of today. Rebellion broke out in Khurasan, now Afghanistan. The Messenger of God had insisted that all Muslims were equal, regardless of race, but, in fact, the Arabs, as the conquerors, could not resist the temptation to feel superior.

Persia was soon in revolt and, in 750, the Umaiyid army, already subverted by secret propaganda, was defeated on the River Zab,[14] and Umaiyid rule was at an end. The Abbásids, who assumed the dignity of khalif, built themselves a new capital at Baghdad. The Abbásid revolution effected three profound changes. It allowed men not of Arab origin to rise to the highest positions. Thereafter, the empire became Muslim, regardless of race. In the same manner, after Augustus, the Roman Empire became Mediterranean, not Italian.

Secondly, the transfer of power from the Umaiyids to the Abbásids marked the change from the military to the commercial era. We have seen the same process on a tiny scale when Solomon succeeded David in Palestine. The change from the Georgian to the Victorian age in Britain was similar.

Thirdly, the transfer of the capital from Damascus to Baghdad resulted in a marked orientalisation of Islam. Syria, before the Arab conquest in 636, had been Greek or Roman for a thousand years, as had also Palestine and Egypt. The Umaiyid Empire looked to the West. But Baghdad, which was only thirty miles from Ctesiphon,[15] the Persian capital, had been Persian for a thousand years.

*   *   *

The Roman Empire had grown rich by its maritime commerce and by the oriental trade. From the year 712 onwards, the Arab Empire extended from Spain to China[16] and also had command of the Mediterranean. "The Christians could not float a plank on the Mediterranean," wrote Ibn Khaldun. Within a few years, the wealth of Europe had vanished and her Dark Ages had begun. The cities shrank, the universities were closed, the businessmen were bankrupt. Europe became an agricultural continent, producing just

---

[13] Genealogical Tree, p. 176.
[14] The Zab was a tributary of the Tigris. Map 22, p. 182.
[15] The capital consisted of two cities, Ctesiphon and Seleucia, on opposite banks of the Tigris. The Arabs called it Medain, "the cities".
[16] Map 22, p. 182.

enough food for itself, and making its own clothing from the wool of its own sheep.

Europe was to remain more or less closely blockaded for more than seven hundred years, until Vasco da Gama discovered the way round the Cape of Good Hope in 1498. Thereafter, the tables were turned. Asia and North Africa became agricultural areas and Europe became wealthy and industrialised.

The blockade of Europe opened up an era of prosperity for the Jews. The Arab conquests had been principally at the expense of Christendom. Syria, Palestine, Egypt, North Africa, Spain, Sicily and southern Italy (conquered in 827) had all been Christian. This political accident produced the impression that the Christian and Muslim religions were the bitterest of enemies. From the religious angle, this was an error. The Messenger of God had said, "You will find the nearest to the Believers (the Muslims) in their love to be those who say, 'We are Christians'."[17]

In spite, however, of this religious affinity, power politics and war had produced ineradicable hatreds. But Judaism was the cousin of both religions. The Jews, dispersed in every country, had not fought in the wars, and they alone could live and travel in Christian and Muslim states. Not only so, but wherever Jews went, they found their co-religionists ready to help them in their business.

Jews from Christian Europe could travel to Muslim Spain, North Africa, Egypt and Syria, or, crossing the Muslim Empire, could sail on Arab ships to India and China. The blockade of Europe had made oriental goods scarce and of great value, and Jews alone were able to bring such articles to Europe.

* * *

The Abbásid era in Baghdad was one of the most brilliant in human history, though censored by authors and publishers in Europe, just as Western writings are now in Soviet Russia.

The reigns of Haroon al Rasheed (786–809) and of his son, Mamoon (813–833), marked the pinnacle of "Arab" culture, science and wealth. The Arabs had taken over the Far Eastern trade and developed it. Theirs were the largest and the best ships plying to China and Indonesia. Their merchants had reservations in Canton and on the shores of India, as Europeans had until recently in Shanghai. Under their highly developed banking system, an Arab businessman could cash a cheque in Canton on his bank in Baghdad.

[17] Qoran V, 82.

In contemporary Europe, rich men carried their money about in the form of sacks full of metal coins.

In Baghdad, everything was plastered with gold, including the pillars and ceilings of their houses, their saddles, bridles, swords and belts. In contemporary Europe, Charlemagne could not mint a gold currency, the precious metal being unobtainable. In the houses of Damascus and Baghdad, the women were covered with gold, jewels and pearls, and dressed in priceless silks. In the private apartments, fountains sparkled, the air was sweet with exotic perfumes and the ear was soothed with soft music. Conversation was intellectual and every educated person of either sex could compose and recite poetry.

But the most outstanding contribution of Muslim culture was in mathematics. They introduced to Europe our present system of numerals with the use of zero. Hitherto the cumbrous Roman way of writing numerals had blocked progress in mathematics. Armed with their new notation, the "Arabs" invented algebra (al jubber), plane and spherical trigonometry, trigonometrical ratios, sine and cosine, tangent and co-tangent, and also logarithms. They may thus be called the founders of modern science.

The first free public hospital was opened in Baghdad and Arabic medical textbooks were in use in European universities for many centuries. In the reign of Mamoon, Muslim astronomers measured the circumference of the earth with surprising accuracy, six hundred years before Europe finally admitted that it was not flat. The hatred of Christians for Muslims prevented the publication of the true source of these benefits, conferred on humanity by the Muslims.

* * *

A word of caution is needed on the use of the word "Arab". The conquerors of their vast empire were the nomads of Arabia, but their numbers were small. Some sixteen thousand Arabs conquered Egypt, with a population of more than seven millions. It has been estimated that, when the conquests were over, Arabs from Arabia constituted only one per cent of the population of the empire.

In the century following the conquest, Arabic became the lingua franca from Spain to China. Within two hundred years, most of the inhabitants had become Muslims. But the ethnic composition of the conquered countries remained virtually unaffected. Arabs did not pour into Syria and Egypt and settle there. The original populations remained unchanged, though they adopted Arabic as their language.

In the same manner, it was not normally the nomads of Arabia who were the scientists, the mathematicians, the historians or the musicians of the empire. The intellectual leaders of the Muslim Empire were Syrians, Persians or North Africans, heirs of a thousand years of Greek, Roman and Persian culture. The Arabs proper were, nevertheless, the architects of the empire. It was their courage, wisdom, common sense and chivalrous spirit which enabled them to conquer and rule such vast areas and ancient civilizations.

* * *

All this wealth, science and luxury led to inevitable collapse, as it has in every successive great nation before and since. In 861, the Khalif Mutawakkil was murdered by his slaves. Turkish mercenaries seized power. From 861 to 974, thirteen puppet khalifs were appointed by the soldiers, of whom five were murdered, three deposed and blinded, and five died a natural death. In 945, Baghdad was seized by a Persian adventurer, who assumed dictatorial powers. Most of the provinces declared their independence. In 1055, Tughril Beg captured Baghdad and founded the empire of the Seljuq Turks.

NOTABLE DATES

Birth of Muhammad	570
His first vision	610
Escape from Mecca	622
Muslim capture of Mecca	630
Death of Muhammad	632
Conquest of Syria	636
Conquest of Persia	642
Conquest of Egypt	642
Conquest of Spain	712
Conquest of Sind	712
Umaiyid Dynasty of Damascus	661–750
Abbásid Dynasty of Baghdad	750–861
Capture of Baghdad by Seljuq Turks	1055

CONCLUSIONS

(1) Muhammad lived and preached from 570 to 632. His Arab followers, in the ensuing eighty years, conquered an empire from Spain to China.

(2) The corollary of these conquests was the blockade of Europe, resulting in the Dark Ages. The Jews profited by this situation as they were the only neutrals, and could trade between Christian and Muslim countries.

(3) The Arabs tolerated Jews and Christians, and there were no forced conversions to Islam.

(4) The intellectuals of the Muslim Empire were "arabicised" members of old civilised nations. So extensive an empire, however, led to much racial intermixture.

(5) The Arabs acquired a great empire by conquest but they did not massacre civilians nor persecute other religions.

XII

The Middle Ages

Thou hast given us like sheep appointed for meat; and hast scattered us among the heathen.
Thou makest us a reproach to our neighbours, a scorn and a derision to them that are round about us.
Psalm XXXXIV, 11, 13

Christian and Jew sprang apart. As time went on, the story of the Crucifixion, told with exquisite simplicity and pathos, and becoming widely known wherever Christians met together, deepened the gulf, and the crime of a handful of priests and elders in Jerusalem was visited by the Christian Churches upon the whole Jewish race.
H. A. L. FISHER, *A History of Europe*

From the end of the 12th century the Church employed every means of persecuting and opposing heresy. It tolerated the Jews because they were outside the Church; but it could not tolerate the heretics.
HENRI PIRENNE, *A History of Europe*

If your mind is narrow, you regard your own conduct as the only normal or praiseworthy scheme of life.
ISRAEL ABRAHAMS, *Jewish Life in the Middle Ages*

XII

IN Roman times, it was possible to discuss the state of the Jews throughout the empire, the same laws being in force from Britain to Egypt. After the collapse of Rome the picture grows blurred, as Europe firstly became impoverished, and then divided into nations.

In our scientific age, we feel that we want facts, "answer yes or no", as on a government form. "Were the Jews persecuted in the Middle Ages? Answer yes or no." Human movements cannot be treated thus. Human life is infinitely complex. The immense changes produced in cultures, by the slow permeation of new ideas, are little appreciated by those who want "a straight answer".

From 712 onwards, the Jews in Muslim Spain enjoyed a long period of prosperity. There were important Jewish communities in France also, though they suffered a few minor disabilities. Despite papal protests, they continued to make large profits from the sale of Christian slaves, particularly to Muslim Spain. Jews were prosperous in the cities along the Rhine. In Italy, they were wealthy and secure.

In the Arab Empire, from Spain to India, Jews and Christians were protected, though excluded from the highest government posts. They were, however, often influential, acting as ministers, secretaries or physicians to the rulers. The Arab conquests, and the division of the Mediterranean world into two camps, proved of great commercial advantage to Jews, who were accepted by both sides as neutrals.

"By travelling from land to land until they had become intimately acquainted both with the wants and the productions of each, by practising money-lending on a large scale and with consummate skill, by keeping a constant and secret correspondence and organising a system of exchange, which was then unparalleled in Europe, the Jews succeeded in making themselves absolutely indispensable to the Christian community."[1]

It was by this means that Europe continued to receive a trickle of trade from the East, across the Muslim-Christian battle line.[2] But the Jews also brought ideas. Their tendency to seek the favour of the

[1] W. E. Lecky, quoted by I. Abrahams, *Jewish Life in the Middle Ages*.
[2] Map 23, p. 194.

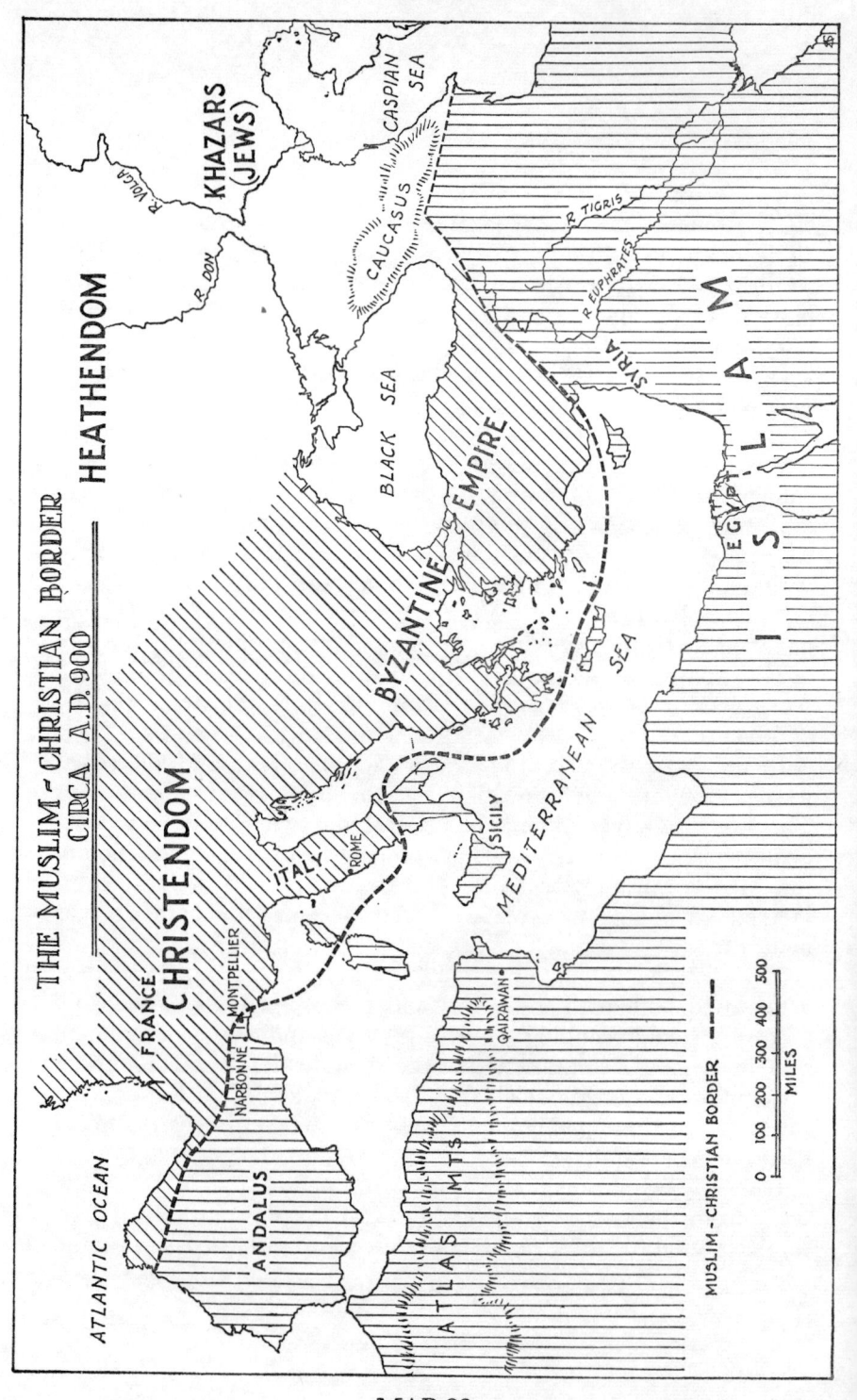

MAP 23

leading nations at any period, but to visit all countries, made the Jews unconscious bearers of ideas, like the bees who fertilise flowers by carrying the pollen unthinkingly from one bloom to the next.

To visualise the situation between Europe and the Muslim world from the eighth to the fourteenth centuries, it is enough to assume it to have been the reverse of today. Learning, science and industry were Muslim monopolies, Europe being poor, backward and ignorant. Jews who had travelled to Baghdad, Damascus or Cairo and returned to Europe, brought accounts of the marvels they had seen, producing a powerful impact on Western public opinion.

Add to this that, until about 1500, the Jews in north-western Europe everywhere had a far higher standard of education than the barbarous nations among whom they lived. Every Jewish community had a school, and almost every male Jew could read and write, at a time when scarcely anyone else could do so, except in the Church.

"There was no Christian university in Germany till the middle of the fourteenth century, but the Rhinelands had what were practically Jewish universities in the era of the first crusade" (1096).[3] As a result of these two factors—travel and education—Jews in western Europe were cultured men of the world, compared to the Christian populations.

Jews greatly assisted in the enlightenment of Europe by their translations from the standard Arabic works on philosophy, science, mathematics and medicine, which they rendered into Latin. Most of these books were of Arab origin, but some were the ancient Greek philosophers, notably Aristotle. Lost long before in Europe, they returned to the West in Latin translations from the Arabic. These works were used for centuries in the universities of Europe. The Jews were thus instrumental in conveying Arab culture to the Western world.

In common with the Arabs, whose culture they shared, the Jews were the world's leading physicians. Salerno is described by the famous Spanish Jewish writer, Rabbi Benjamin of Tudela, as "the chief medical university of Christendom". Here, "Arabic medicine was everywhere in full possession of the medical faculties."[4] Commenting on this passage, Israel Abrahams adds that Jewish and Arabic medicine was the same. Jewish writers before 1900 readily admitted the old alliance between them and the Arabs, though Zionists no longer refer to it, but often write of Arabs with contempt.

[3] Israel Abrahams, *Jewish Life in the Middle Ages*.
[4] Rashdell, *Universities of Europe in the Middle Ages*.

In medieval Europe, the Jewish doctor was as familiar a figure as the Jewish merchant. Even popes had Jewish physicians.

The spirit of enquiry which produced the Renaissance was partly roused by these translations from Arabic books. Enlightened rulers like the Emperor Frederick II (1220–1250), Charles of Anjou (1266–1282) and Alfonso X of Castile (1252–1284) employed Arabs and Jews to translate Arabic works into Latin. All these fields of active co-operation reveal the exaggeration in modern claims that the Jews have been facing genocide for two thousand years.

* * *

Jews in Muslim Spain lived in the broadminded atmosphere of Arab culture. They were consequently far ahead of Jews in France or Germany. Pope Sylvester II (999–1003), for example, received his education in the Arab University of Cordova, before becoming a Christian priest and ultimately pope. The influence of Arab culture, combined with the toleration accorded to Jews and Christians by the Muslims, penetrated also the Christian part of Spain and southern France.

The Muslims in Spain "had made Andalusia[5] the home of a civilisation, which knew no distinction of creed. The air of Spain was fresh with the breezes of perpetual intersectarian friendliness. Christian monarchs like Alfonso the Wise imitated and excelled the majestic broadminded culture of Abdul Rahman III."[6]

Writing in the twelfth century of Montpellier in the south of France,[7] Benjamin of Tudela says, "you meet there with Christian and Muslim merchants from Portugal, Lombardy, Byzantium, Egypt, Palestine, Greece, France, Spain and England." There was a prosperous Jewish colony in Montpellier, a famous rabbinical college and a Jewish university. "The Jews of this city," writes Rabbi Benjamin, "are among the wisest and the most esteemed ... Others are very rich and benevolent."

Narbonne also was in direct communication with the East, the Jewish commercial community being in touch with the Jews of southern Italy, Sicily, Qairawan and Egypt. Not without reason has it been said that, in the Middle Ages, the Jews were the greatest representatives of international commerce.

* * *

[5] The Arabs called all Spain Andalus.
Israel Abrahams, op. cit.   [7] Map 23, p. 194.

In 1158, however, the Muwahhids (Almohades), Berber fanatics from the Atlas, occupied Muslim Spain.[8] These wild tribesmen showed little respect for culture. The crisis, however, was shortlived. Within a generation, the Muwahhids adopted the culture of Muslim Spain, producing their own philosophers and men of letters. One of the victims of the Muwahhid episode was Rabbi Musa ibn Maimun (1135–1204), the famous Jewish philosopher. Under the greekised form of his name, Maimonides, he profoundly affected the thought of Western Europe, where many of his readers were unaware that he was a Jew.

Tiring of the mentality of the Berbers, he moved to Cairo, where he was received with honour and became personal physician to Sultan Saladin. Writing from Cairo, he says, "My duties to the sultan are heavy, I am obliged to visit him every day ... and when he or any of his children or any of the inmates of his haram are indisposed ... I do not return to Misr[9] until the afternoon. I find the waiting rooms filled with people, Jews and Gentiles, nobles and common people, judges and bailiffs."

* * *

Unfortunately, in 1010, the Albigensian heresy had appeared in the south of France, and was attributed, in part at least, to the influence of Arab and Jewish culture, or to certain eastern Christian sects. Israel Abrahams actually claims that the Church knew the Jews to be its instigators. Rabbi Raisin likewise claims that Jewish criticisms and sarcasms were the chief source of Christian heresies in Europe, of the scepticism of the Renaissance and ultimately of the Protestant Reformation. It is understandable, therefore, that at times the Church regarded the Jews as a fifth column in Christendom.

Hitherto, as we have seen, Jews had played an influential rôle in the south of France. In the eleventh century, for example, market day in Lyons was transferred from Saturday to Sunday to suit the Jews. Christians often made gifts to the synagogue and toleration prevailed.

There was a stir of revolt about. The famous Abélard (1079–1142) deplored those persons who claimed a monopoly of truth, "so that whomsoever they see differing from themselves in belief, they deem an alien from the mercy of God."[10] In 1209, Pope Innocent III

---

[8] Map 23, p. 194.
[9] Cairo was the area of the royal palaces, Misr the old city.
[10] H. O. Taylor, *The Mediaeval Mind*.

ordered a crusade against the Albigenses and, from 1209 to 1229, the south of France was drowned in blood. This was the origin of the Inquisition. The Albigenses were virtually exterminated. With them also was obliterated the brilliant civilisation of Provence, with its poets, its chivalry and its troubadours, borrowed from the Arabs of Spain.

Before the twelfth century, the death penalty was rarely, if ever, inflicted for religious differences. St. Augustine, St. Martin of Tours, St. Ambrose, St. John Chrysostom and St. Bernard of Clairvaux had all denounced capital punishment for religious offences. From the tenth century onwards, however, the Church made use of every form of violence in the attempt to stamp out heresy. None of these methods were employed against Jews, who were not members of the Church. Only if they professed conversion to Christianity could Jews be persecuted as heretics.

Throughout the period covered by this chapter (700–1500), Jews were, on the whole, tolerated by the Church and protected by rulers, but disliked by the mass of the people. The hatred felt by the public for the Jews was due to three causes. Firstly, because the Jews were moneylenders, and also often tax-collectors for the government; secondly, their unsociability, and their refusal to join in public festivals, or even to eat or drink with Christians. Thirdly, their real or imagined contempt for Gentiles. "The Jews were everywhere the objects of popular insult and oppression . . . though protected, it must be confessed, by laws of the Church, as well as, in general, by the temporal princes."[11]

During these centuries, there were no police or regular judiciary in Western Europe. Kings were weak, and dukes and barons fought one another. Thus rulers were often unable to maintain security or to deal with riots.

* * *

Ever since the Arab conquests in the seventh century, the Byzantine Empire, with its fortress of Constantinople, had guarded the eastern gateway to Europe. Muslim conquerors had thus been obliged to invade Europe through Spain or Sicily.

In 1055, however, the Seljuq Turks took Baghdad, and the Abbásid khalifs lost their temporal power. By 1080, the Seljuqs were outside Constantinople, and the Byzantine Emperor begged for aid from the West. On 27th November, 1095, at Clermont in France,

[11] H. Hallam, *Europe during the Middle Ages*.

Pope Urban II roused intense enthusiasm by appealing for armed help for the eastern Christians.

Several great lords began to raise armies, but a number of enthusiasts, notably Peter the Hermit, stirred up the fanaticism of the peasants of France and Lorraine. In 1096, "The People's Crusade" set out—"A herd of 200,000, the most stupid and savage refuse of the people, who mingled with their devotion a brutal license of rapine and drunkenness. The first and most easy warfare was against the Jews.

"In the trading cities of the Moselle and the Rhine, their colonies were numerous and rich, and they enjoyed, under the protection of the emperor and the bishops, the free exercise of their religion. At Verdun, Treves, Metz, Spires and Worms, many thousands of that unhappy people were pillaged and massacred... A remnant was saved by the firmness of the bishops."[12]

"During the Crusades," writes Rabbi Raisin, "the outrages against the Jews were committed mostly by outlaws and serfs... The merchants and the middle-class burghers remained as a rule friendly, and frequently afforded shelter to their Jewish neighbours in times of trouble." St. Bernard bitterly denounced the behaviour of these mobs, and risked his life to rescue the Jewish victims.

Benjamin of Tudela, who visited the Jewish communities on the Rhine seventy years after the People's Crusade, found them rich and secure. The authorities did what they could. Pope Calixtus II (1119–1124) issued a bull, stating that the Jews were under his protection. The Emperor Frederick Barbarossa (1152–1190), who himself led the third Crusade, said, "It is the duty of our imperial office... assiduously to protect the Jews." Pope Gregory IX (1127–1241) described the treatment of the Jews as "horrible and outrageous, an offence against God."

*   *   *

Jews normally served the rulers, as they had served the Ptolemies and the Caesars. In their synagogues, they prayed for the king. The latter often employed them in financial appointments, situations in which, in the absence of public accounts, they grew extremely rich.

There was no regular system of taxation in northern Europe. Rulers had few sources of income except their estates, but were expected to dispense hospitality, to raise armies and to administer justice. Consequently, they were always short of money.

[12] Edward Gibbon, *The Decline and Fall of the Roman Empire*.

> The king was in his counting house,
> Counting out his money...

The old nursery rhyme probably accurately describes the situation. He must have frequently and anxiously counted it out, poor fellow, and there never was enough. In this situation, the Jews squeezed money from the people and the king from the Jews.

These chaotic methods produced the maximum friction. The people hated the Jews for taking their money and for their social exclusiveness. In times of disorder, therefore, Jewish houses and synagogues were often attacked. But the Jews tried to pass on as little money as possible to the ruler, and there were periods of tension between the Jews and the court. Edward I was only able to expel the Jews in 1290 owing to the extension of Italian banking to England. In London, Lombard Street still recalls those days of Italian financiers.

Jews had been settled in England since Roman times and had doubtless made many pagan converts as they did elsewhere. In 1189, the year of the coronation of Richard Coeur de Lion, there were outbreaks against the Jews in London and in York, "largely due to their defaulting debtors, who murdered the lenders and burnt their books, much to the loss of the royal revenue."[13]

The Jews, however, were given special privileges by Henry II and by Richard. At the funeral of St. Hugh, Bishop of Lincoln (1186–1200), "the Jews too, weeping and wailing and declaring that he had been a mighty servant of the Lord, paid him honour by running alongside the bier and weeping." Thus in England, as elsewhere, we see the usual pattern—the Jews protected by the king and the Church, often working in partnership with Christian merchants, but hated by the poorer classes.

The position of Jews deteriorated in western Europe after 1200, as a result of the belief that they were instigators of heresy, as, indeed, both Israel Abrahams and Rabbi Raisin claim that they were.

The Jews bitterly resented the action of Pope Innocent III in 1215, directing that Jews and Muslims wear a distinctive badge. It may be noted in passing that Jews and Muslims are once again coupled together. There were, then, many Jews and Muslims living among Christians in northern Spain, the south of France and southern Italy. Jews complained that the badge exposed them in the streets to the insults of the vulgar. The badge seems to have been

[13] *Cambridge Mediaeval History.*

directed against Jewish promotion of heresy among Christians, who might imagine their interlocutors to be fellow Christians.

The promotion of heresy became more dangerous after 1200, owing to the increasing power of the Catholic Church. "Under the pontificates of Innocent III (1198–1216) and his five immediate successors, the Roman 'monarchy' seemed to have reached the pinnacle of its moral prestige, religious authority and temporal power, and this development was due in great measure to Innocent III himself."[14]

Innocent III did not show any animosity against Jews, but he was profoundly concerned about heresy. The Jewish promotion of heresy among Christians and their efforts to win converts to Judaism, alienated the Catholic Church, which had hitherto protected them, in the belief that their conversion would be the prelude to the Second Coming of Christ.

The Church could probably have exterminated the Jews of Europe as she did the Albigenses, but no such attempt was ever made. Their missionary activities and then their promotion of heresy had hitherto caused the Church to obstruct any great intimacy between Jews and Christians, but she had made no attempt to kill them.

From the twelfth century onwards, the Jews were much harassed by the treachery of their own deserters. Jewish converts to Christianity were often their most active persecutors. In 1239, Nicholas Donin, a renegade Jew, obtained a papal bull ordering the burning of all copies of the Talmud.

The practice of usury, which made the Jews unpopular, was not entirely their fault, for the establishment of trade guilds had excluded them from handicrafts. Admittance was gained through certain Christian religious rites which, whether intentionally or not, excluded Jews, who refused to perform them.

In the twelfth century, Benjamin of Tudela found Jews in the Middle East engaged in silk-weaving, goldsmiths' and silversmiths' work, embroidery with gold thread and other skilled crafts. In western Europe this was no longer possible. Yet there was still much co-operation in other directions. Jews employed Christian builders, postmen and laundrymen. In Greece, Jews worked for Christian masters.

This chapter covers six hundred years in north-western Europe, making it impossible to generalise. In many areas, Jews mixed freely with their Christian neighbours. In some places, Jews and Christians

[14] *Encyclopaedia Britannica*, "Papacy".

shared their sports and attended one another's weddings. Sometimes Jews employed Christians to light fires on the Sabbath or to milk the cows. In the Rhineland, in the fourteenth century, Jews and Christians worked together in the vineyards. The Jews borrowed the summer arbours of the Christians to celebrate the Feast of Tabernacles. Business co-operation was also active.

But while the papacy sometimes warned its legates and clergy against Jewish subversive activities, the popes protected the Jews in Italy, a country in which they were never persecuted. Rome is perhaps the only city of Europe which has preserved its Jewish community undisturbed from antiquity to the present day.

The contrast between East and West is shown by the fact that, in the twelfth century, the head of the Jewish academy in Baghdad was clothed like a king in robes embroidered with gold, and lived in a palace hung with costly tapestries. Jews continued to occupy an honoured position in Baghdad until Zionist pressure in Palestine became acute in the 1930s.

* * *

In 1347–48, Europe was devastated by the Black Death, an epidemic of bubonic plague. The mortality was staggering. It has been estimated that one quarter of the population of Europe died. Someone spread the rumour among the panic-stricken populace that the Jews had caused the disaster by poisoning the wells. From this, there developed the charge that Jews caused droughts and earthquakes in Christendom to assist their Muslim allies. The worst of such charges, circulated by a Jewish convert to Christianity according to Rabbi Raisin, was that they kidnapped and murdered a Christian child at Passover, and used its blood for the ceremony.

Public debates between Jews and Christians, a practice dating from Roman times, reappeared in the fourteenth and fifteenth centuries, usually before kings or dukes. The Christian "champion" was often a converted Jew, familiar with the Torah and Talmud. It is noticeable that the Jews spoke with extreme frankness and self-confidence, suggesting that they did not live in fear. These debates usually resulted only in increased hatreds.

The lower classes of the public jeered at passing Jews, or threw stones at them. The Jews retaliated without scruple by mercilessly fleecing them of their money, which increased the hatred of their debtors. Yet, whatever they did to them, the Jews were always richer than their neighbours. "If a historian of Philip Augustus[15] is to be believed, they possessed almost half of Paris."[16]

* * *

Yet, beneath the bitterness of factional hatreds, there were more spiritual men, who saw, beyond the strife of creeds, fellow men longing for God. Dante (1265–1321) and Thomas Aquinas (1225–1274) worked amicably with Jewish scholars. Pico della Mirandola, the Italian philosopher (1463–1494), found trusted friends in the Jewish mystics of his day.

Elias Levita, an Italian Jew, lived and studied in the house of a cardinal "for which several of the rabbis ... pronounced woe to my soul because I taught the law to a Christian. When the prince [the cardinal] heard my statement, he ... kissed me, saying, 'Blessed be the God of the Universe, who has brought thee hither.' Then we took sweet counsel together ... I imparted my spirit to him, and learned from him excellent and valuable things, which are in accordance with truth."

* * *

The synagogue was the centre of Jewish life, but there were no bishops to enforce uniformity, nor were the rabbis allowed to become arrogant.

Jews were happy in their homes. In business with Gentiles they were sometimes tricky and, feeling self-conscious, often seemed either servile or arrogant. In their homes, they were relaxed and natural. For religious reasons, they had a bath every Friday and washed their hands before meals. According to Israel Abrahams, Spanish Jews were cleaner than their co-religionists in north European countries, as a result of living among Muslims, who were cleaner than Christians in those days.

The following description is given by a fifteenth-century Christian, of a rich Jew's house in Regensburg:

"The house was a dark gray, moss-covered, hideous pile of stones ... with closely-barred windows. A passage, more than eighty feet in length, led to a dark, partly-decayed staircase. A well protected door opened ... into an apartment cheerfully decorated with flowers, with costly and splendid furniture, richly and splendidly appointed. Here, the walls panelled and decorated with

---

[15] King of France, 1165–1223.   [16] H. Hallam, *Europe during the Middle Ages.*

polished wood, with many coloured ... hangings and artistic carved work, was the owner's domestic temple ... A costly carpet ... covered the brightly scrubbed floor. The festal board, adorned with heavy silver goblets, was surrounded by high-backed, gilt-decorated chairs and cushions of shorn velvet. A silver cupboard filled with jewels, golden chains and bangles, gilt and silver vessels, rare and precious antiques, formed the rich frame which worthily embraced this picture of splendour and magnificence."[17]

One more quotation from Israel Abrahams will suffice. "A merry spirit shined on Jewish life in the Middle Ages, joyousness forming, in the Jewish conception, the coping-stone of piety." The Jewish Sabbath, he adds, was joyful. Singing, dancing and music were not forbidden. Wine and good food were the best possible, and everyone was happy. "The later, gloomy Puritan Sabbath, although copied from the Jews, showed a quite different spirit."[18]

So much for the Jews in north and west Europe from 700 to 1500. The Holy Land had enjoyed peace after the revolt of Bar Kokhba in A.D. 135 until the Persian occupation in 614 to 628, and the Arab conquest from 634 to 637. The Arabs were opposed by the Byzantines and the Palestinians took no part in the fighting, nor is there any record of massacres of civilians by the Arabs. Nevertheless, after a thousand years of Greek and Roman civilisation and two centuries of Christianity, the change to Arab and Muslim rule must at first have been uncongenial, especially to the hellenised town-dwellers. The Arabs, however, practised complete religious toleration, and soon gained the confidence of the people. Nevertheless a century and a half elapsed before the majority of the people became Muslims. No coercion was used to convert them, but Muslims enjoyed a social prestige which, over the years, was difficult to resist.

The same considerations applied to Jews as to Christians. A modern writer estimates that there were three to four hundred thousand Jews in Palestine when the Arabs came.[19] As the centuries passed, the numbers of Jews dwindled—not from massacre but from conversion to Islam. We have already noticed the extraordinary temperamental resemblance between the Palestine Arabs today and the Judaeans of Hasmonaean and early Roman times.

The long Arab peace was broken in 1071 by the arrival of the Seljuq Turks. The Seljuqs were newly converted Muslims but, like the Christians of the West, they adapted their religion to accord

---

[17] Quoted by Israel Abrahams, op. cit.
[18] Israel Abrahams, op. cit.   [19] Chaim Bermant, *Israel*.

with their desire to indulge in war. Their harder attitude to Christians provoked the Crusades, in which the Jews, in general, stood beside the Muslims against the Christians. From 1099 to 1291, the Holy Land was torn by the wars of the Crusades, but was virtually free of wars from then until the Ottoman conquest in 1516.

It is painful to realise that the Holy Land has been continuously bathed in blood whenever Jews or Christians ruled, except for the period of the Christian Roman Emperors. Otherwise, the only prolonged periods of peace have been under the rule of pagan emperors (A.D. 135 to 325) or of Muslims (627 to 1099 and 1291 to 1918). The return of Christians and Jews since 1918 has renewed the bloodbaths of ancient times.

NOTABLE DATES

Arab Conquest of Spain	712
Capture of Baghdad by the Seljuq Turks	1055
Arrival of Seljuqs on the Bosphorus	1080
People's Crusade attacks the Rhineland Jews	1096
Albigensian Heresy in France	1010–1229
End of the Crusades in Palestine	1291
Black Death in Europe	1347–1348

CONCLUSIONS

(1) The Arab Conquests (634 to 712) gave toleration to Jews in the Arab Empire.

(2) The division of the Mediterranean between Muslims and Christians brought commercial leadership to the Jews, the only neutrals.

(3) From 700 to (say) 1200, Jews were indispensable to European Christendom. Thereafter, their status deteriorated gradually owing to the advance of education in Europe, and the opening of alternative trade routes, for example, by the Crusaders.

(4) In general, the Holy Land was at peace from 637 to 1500, except for the two centuries of continuous warfare caused by the Crusaders.

XIII

Blood-soaked Centuries

One thing, however, we must always bear in mind when we read of the disabilities of the Jews during the long, dark night; all the enslaved peoples of Europe had to go through their own savage mediaeval era. They had a hopeful Renaissance but a sacrificial Reformation; a period of enlightenment but also bloody revolutions; insane, protracted religious wars, for which they paid with millions of lives.
   Moshe Menuhin, *The Decadence of Judaism in our Time*

It was in Spain that the golden age of the Jews shone with the brightest splendour... From the conquest of the Moors till the end of the tenth century, when (while Christian Europe lay in darkness) Mohammedan Cordova might be considered the centre of civilization, the Jews, under the enjoyment of equal rights and privileges, rivalled their masters in wealth, splendour and cultivation. By the perpetual intercourse kept up with their brethren in the East, their commerce was pursued with industry and success.
   Henry Hart Milman, *The History of the Jews*

Too often in the past two thousand years the worst advertisement for Christianity has been its own supporters.
   William Neil, *The Life and Teaching of Jesus*

XIII

WE must now turn to the Jews of eastern Europe, who have not hitherto been discussed.

The Khazars were a Central Asian people, first mentioned in A.D. 198, when they founded an important kingdom on the Volga and the Don.[1] They grew rich by handling the caravan trade from China and Persia, which they passed on to eastern Europe.

In 737, when the Umaiyid khalifs were at the height of their power, the Arabs conquered Khazaria. The khan of the still pagan Khazars professed Islam, in order to get rid of the Arab conquerors. But the khan's sister was married to the Byzantine Emperor, Constantine V (740–775), who pressed him to accept Christianity. Hesitating between the Byzantines and the Arabs, he decided, in about 740, to adopt Judaism, as a sign of his neutrality. He maintained religious toleration, however, and Jewish, Christian and Muslim merchants mingled in the capital, Itil.

* * *

Jews are said first to have arrived in Poland from Germany about 900. At the end of the tenth century, the Khazars were overrun by new invaders from the east. They scattered over what is now southern Russia and Poland, carrying their Judaism with them. Meanwhile, Christian missionaries from Constantinople had begun to penetrate the pagan tribes, and Judaeo-Christian missionary rivalry appeared in eastern as it had in western Europe. The Jews, however, were welcomed in Poland, where they were granted equality, religious freedom and local autonomy.

Unfortunately, in 1236–1241, however, the Mongols under Batu, grandson of Jenghis Khan, laid waste most of Poland and Hungary. In 1260, Boleslav the Pious welcomed more Jews to Poland, possibly to secure their help in the reconstruction of his country after the Mongol ravages. He guaranteed the safety and religious freedom of Jewish immigrants.

In the twelfth century, Rabbi Benjamin of Tudela had visited Constantinople and wrote that the Jews there were more harassed by the Byzantines than they were in western Europe. As a result,

[1] Map 23, p. 194.

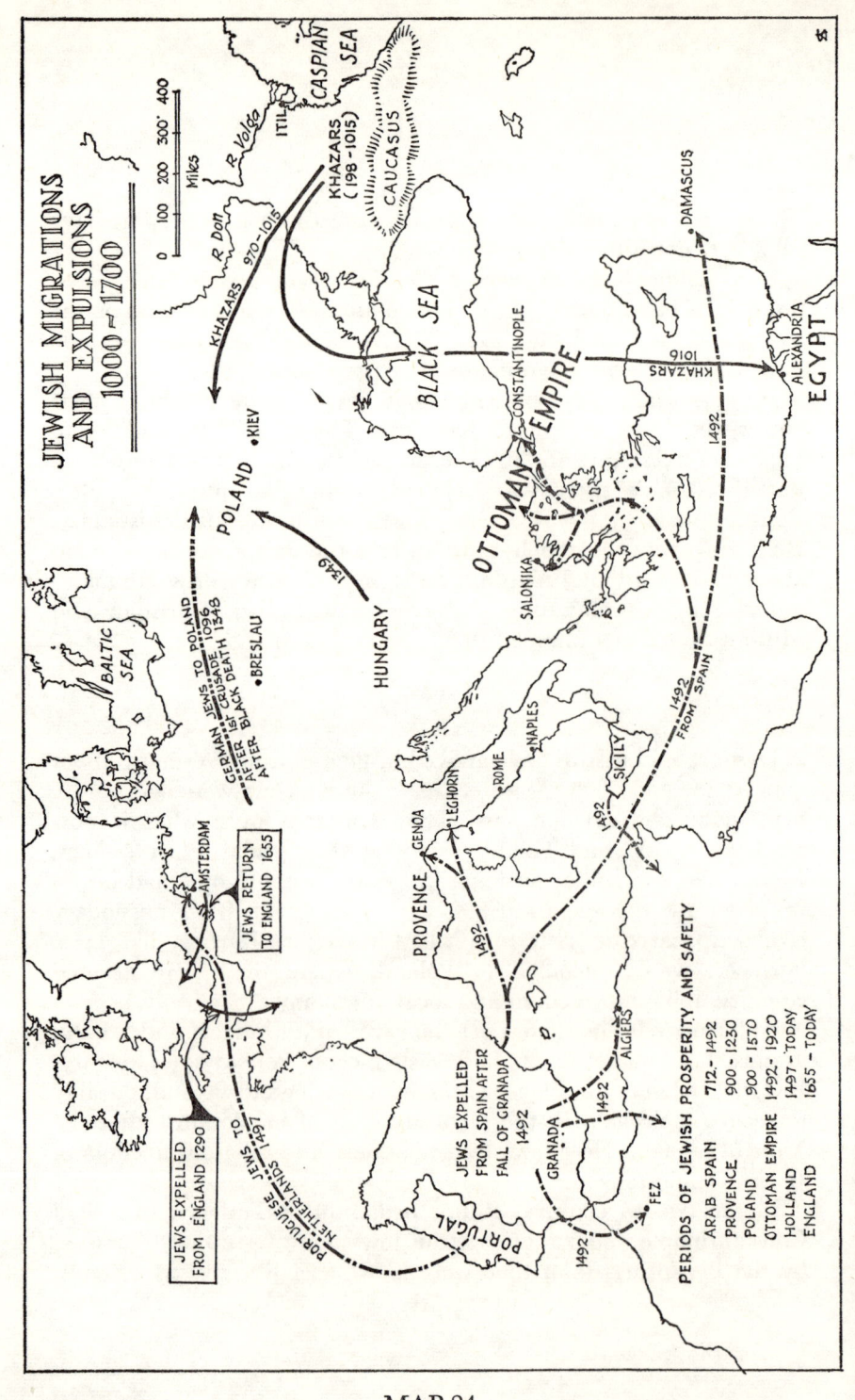

MAP 24

some moved to join the community in Poland. There were already Jews in Breslau, where they were engaged in the slave trade, exporting boys, chiefly to Muslim Spain, to serve as soldiers or eunuchs.

The best-known patron of the Jews in Poland, however, was Casimir III, the Great (1333–1370). In the fourteenth century, Jews in Germany suffered from the popular belief that the Black Death (1348) originated from the poisoning of the wells by Jews. As a result, many moved to Poland, to join the prosperous Jewish community there. In the reign of Sigismund I (1506–1548), the Jews still maintained their favoured position. The chief rabbi was confirmed in his office by the king and enjoyed wide powers of civil and criminal jurisdiction over his co-religionists.

During the Counter-Reformation, in the late sixteenth century, Jesuit missions came to Poland, to fight heresy, not Judaism. Nevertheless, the resulting intolerance indirectly injured the status of Jews also. In the interval, however, the Ottoman Turks had taken Constantinople and established religious toleration there. After six hundred years of prosperity in Poland, a number of Polish Jews moved to Constantinople.

The result of the dispersal of the Khazars and the proselytisation of heathen Slavs was to form in eastern Europe a large Jewish population with only a small proportion of Middle Eastern blood. "Some estimate," writes Rabbi Raisin, "that from sixty to seventy per cent of the Jews in southern Russia are not of Semitic descent." A Jewish friend in England recently told me that he thought that there were very few Jews in the world who did not have some Khazar blood in their veins.

*   *   *

In 1246, the Arab Kingdom of Granada became a vassal of Castile, the remainder of Spain being annexed by Christian kingdoms. In 1391, there were massacres of Jews in Christian Spain. As a result, many Jews became Christians, amounting to "the improbable figure of 200,000."[2] The rabbis ruled that a man might save his life in an emergency by any means, except murder, incest or idolatry.[3] Thus Jews were permitted to feign conversion to escape a violent death. Some were, indeed, baptised by force, but many asked for baptism voluntarily.

No sooner were they converted than a number of them rose to the highest offices, particularly in finance. Many became extremely

[2] Cecil Roth, *A History of the Marranos*.   [3] Cecil Roth, op. cit.

rich and intermarried with the aristocracy. Some, entering the Church, rose to be bishops. Rabbi Solomon la Levi, for example, assumed the name of Pablo de Santa Maria, became Bishop of Segovia and a member of the Council of Regency for Castile. As usual, the Jewish converts tended to support the king against the populace.

Again and again in history, we find that Jews, released from repression, rise so rapidly as almost to control their country of residence. Indignant at their power, the people turn against them and a new period of repression ensues. In 1449, riots occurred against the Jewish converts to Christianity, now nicknamed Marranos, especially against ex-Jewish tax farmers. The Inquisition, established in Spain by a papal bull in 1478, could only deal with heretics, not with practising Jews. But converted Jews were Christians and could thus be accused of heresy. Many, in fact, still practiced Judaism secretly. Thus the Marranos found that they had jumped from the frying pan into the fire.

On 2nd January, 1492, Granada, the last Arab kingdom in Spain, surrendered to Ferdinand and Isabella, on a pledge of religious toleration, which was immediately betrayed by the "Catholic Sovereigns", when they entered the fortress. On 30th March, 1492, in the Alhambra, they signed a decree for the expulsion of all practising Jews from Spain. The pretext offered was that the continued presence of practising Jews subverted the faith of Jewish converts to Christianity.

Religious toleration in Spain came to an end when the Arabs departed. Some two hundred thousand Jews are estimated to have left the country. As elsewhere, Jewish converts to Christianity played a leading part in denouncing them. Not content with the betrayal of their pledge at home, the "Catholic Sovereigns" insisted on the introduction of religious discrimination in Sicily and Portugal also, both countries where toleration had reigned hitherto.

In the century following the pledge of toleration given by Ferdinand and Isabella, three million Muslims are believed to have been executed or exiled from Spain. Modern Jewish writers make much of the genuine sufferings of the Jews in Spain, without mentioning that they were persecuted for being friends of the Arabs.

Until the fifteenth century, universities in southern Europe had been cosmopolitan, with Jewish, Christian and Muslim professors. Henceforward, the kindly lights of the Mediterranean world were extinguished by religious and nationalist fanaticism.

* * *

The Jews exiled from Spain made for four different destinations. Some, accompanying their Arab fellow victims, found toleration under Muslim rule in Egypt and North Africa. In the Netherlands, also, Jews were accorded religious toleration. Shiploads of Spanish and Portuguese Jews arrived in Amsterdam, where a large Jewish community has existed ever since.

Many Spanish Jews, however, took refuge in Constantinople where the Ottoman Sultan Bayezid II (1481-1512) treated them with marked favour. Writing at this time, Isaac Zafarti[4] says, "Is it not better to live under Muslims than under Christians? Here you may wear the finest stuffs ... while in Christendom you may not venture to dress your children in red or blue without exposing them to the danger of being beaten."

Another Jew, Samuel Usque, writing in 1533, says of his arrival in Turkey: "Here the gates of freedom and equality are ever open and shall never be closed against thee. Here thou mayest renew thy inner life ... and abandon the practices which, by the violence of the nations among whom thou wast a foreigner, thou wast compelled to imitate. In this realm, thou art highly favoured by the Lord, since therein He granted thee boundless liberty to begin the complete repentance of thy sins."[5]

Although Palestine was easily accessible from Constantinople, and was also part of the Ottoman Empire, few Jews went there. In Constantinople, many rose to high positions and became rich and influential. During the reign of Sulaiman the Magnificent (1520-1566), the Ottoman Empire reached the peak of its wealth and glory.

Most people in the West today believe justice and toleration to have evolved in Europe, when the Ottoman Empire was the land of tyranny, brutality and oppression. They will be surprised to hear that, when the Christians of Europe were persecuting Jews and Muslims alike, complete religious toleration existed in the Ottoman Empire, as it had under the Arabs in Spain. Such are the vicissitudes of the rise and decline of nations.

Many Jews from Spain, however, went no further than Italy. A curious paradox is presented by the pope's establishment of the Inquisition in Spain, while he protected the Jews in Italy. The explanation may lie in the fact that the papacy believed the Jews to be instigators of the Christian heresies. Where there was heresy, Jews should not be allowed to mix with Christians, but, in Italy, there were no heretics.

[4] Quoted by Rabbi Raisin, op. cit.   [5] Quoted by Rabbi Raisin, op. cit.

In Naples, also, King Ferdinand welcomed the Jewish refugees with great humanity, providing lodging and hospital accommodation. They were well received likewise in Italian commercial cities like Genoa. "A century after the Spanish expulsion, Leghorn became a veritable 'Little Jerusalem'."[6]

Some Marranos remained in Spain, worshipping publicly in Christian churches, but practising Jewish rites at home. Conversion, moreover, enabled them to travel unmolested to Holland, Constantinople or South America, reverting to Judaism on reaching their destination. The Jews in Turkey still regarded Spain as their homeland and spoke Spanish among themselves. Hearing that Marranos in South America had reverted to Judaism, the Inquisition followed them there in 1520, establishing branches in Mexico and Peru.

With the end of Arab rule in Spain, many Muslims had also become Christians. These were called Moriscoes. During eight centuries of Arab rule, the different races had intermingled and many had changed their religion. Thus many Muslims now persecuted were descendants of the Visigoths, the Romans or the Celts. After 1525, the Inquisition began to persecute the Moriscoes, for alleged religious irregularities.

These numerous conversions to Christianity presented the Church with many problems. Rabbi Raisin claims that many Marranos became Christian priests with the deliberate object of wrecking the Church from within. Others, however, were active persecutors of their former co-religionists. The notorious Torquemada was alleged to have burnt thousands of Marranos and Moriscoes. The Muslims were too numerous to be immediately evicted as the Jews had been. The screw was turned upon them more slowly but, by 1525, they were suffering cruel oppression. Not until 22nd September, 1609, was an edict issued for the final eviction of all Muslims. Their expulsion was conducted with great cruelty.[7]

Expelled from England in 1290, the Jews were re-admitted by Cromwell in 1655. In fact, a number of distinguished Jews were already living in London, where they gave valuable help in overseas trade. From the Netherlands and England, they crossed to North America.

The English Puritans were favourable to the Jews. Rabbi Raisin even calls them Christian Israelites, and says that their conduct "was modelled on the Hebrew pattern". Nahum Sokolev claims that the heroes on whom Oliver Cromwell modelled himself were

[6] Cecil Roth, *A History of the Marranos.*
[7] H. C. Lea, *The Moriscoes of Spain: Their Conversion and Expulsion.*

Joshua, Gideon and Samuel—a fact which perhaps explains the massacres of Drogheda and Wexford in 1649. The return of the Jews to England was not entirely unopposed, one of the arguments used against it being their unremitting efforts to convert Christians to Judaism.

Puritan devotion to the Old Testament is well known. "They paid to the Hebrew language," writes Lord Macaulay, "a respect which they refused to the tongue in which the discourses of Jesus and the Epistles of Paul have come down to us. They baptised their children by the names, not of Christian saints, but of Hebrew patriarchs and warriors. They sought for principles of jurisprudence in the Mosaic Law and for precedents to guide their ordinary conduct in the book of Judges or of Kings."[8]

This puritan dedication to the Old Testament in the Authorised Version profoundly affected the thought and language of England. Much of the support offered to Zionism in Britain two centuries later was due to this old puritan bias. At the end of the seventeenth century, the principal concentrations of Jews were in Poland, the Ottoman Empire, the Netherlands and England.[9]

From the Netherlands and from England, Jews spread to North America. In 1654, the first Jews landed in New York, then New Amsterdam, to receive a somewhat chilly reception. The governor, however, was equally intolerant of Lutherans and Roman Catholics. The Reformation did not immediately produce Christian toleration.

* * *

How seriously were Jews persecuted in Germany? Rabbi Raisin says that Halle was among the worst places. They suffered there, he says, from the People's Crusade in 1096, though Benjamin of Tudela found them secure and prosperous seventy years later. They were expelled in 1493, four hundred years later, and, in 1724, their newly-built synagogue was demolished by students from the university.

Three disasters in seven hundred years does not seem catastrophic to us, who experienced two world wars in thirty years. It was probably not the disaster every three hundred years which was painful, as much as the rudeness and contempt so often encountered, and the sense of belonging to an inferior caste. The Jews had a printing press in Halle, from which other printing firms were established in various German cities.

[8] T. B. Macaulay, *A History of England.*
[9] J. Parkes, *The Conflict between the Church and the Synagogue.*

In 1650, the Jews in Hamburg openly practised their religion, had a Jewish school, an officiating rabbi and an active Jewish communal life. At the time, Roman Catholic worship was forbidden in Hamburg.

Luther had at first favoured Jews, but later his ardour cooled. Frederick the Great of Prussia (1712–1786) granted them toleration, if they served the country. There was a move to make them equal citizens and, in return, many accepted Christianity.

One such, Heinrich Heine, the poet, wrote of his former co-religionists: "The Jews are of the stuff of which the gods are made; today they are trampled under foot, tomorrow they are worshipped; while some of them creep about in the filthiest mire of commerce, others ascend the highest peak of humanity... The Jews are the people of the spirit, and whenever they return to their spirit they are great. Whilst among the Jews there is every possible caricature of vulgarity, there are among them also the ideas of purest humanity."[10]

In brief, the Jews were occasionally the victims of a catastrophe, frequently they met with rudeness, but for long periods they were safe, wealthy and prosperous.

*   *   *

In 1555, a papal bull was issued by Paul IV (1555–1559) recommending for the first time the compulsory segregation of Jews. The emphasis is on the word compulsory. We have seen that centuries before Christ, the Jews of Alexandria were allotted an area of the city to live in as a special favour. Ezra had laid down that segregation from the rest of humanity was the first duty of a Jew. The rules of ritual purity, indeed, made segregation inevitable. Jewish children had for centuries always been educated in Torah schools, in intentional separation from Gentile children, from whom they remained mentally and spiritually isolated for the rest of their lives.

The medieval "Jewry", it has been said, was the inevitable expression of Jewish solidarity, established by the Jews themselves before the Christian era. Why did Paul IV wish to make segregation compulsory, for the popes protected the Jews of Italy? The year 1555 was a great turning point, at which the Catholic Counter-Reformation began to gain impetus. The Catholic Church was reformed, and Protestantism was eradicated in Italy and halted elsewhere. This was the life work of Paul IV. There seems to be no doubt that the attempt to segregate Jews was one item in the pope's struggle against heresy.

[10] G. Karpeles, *Heinrich Heine's Memoirs*, quoted by Raisin.

Most of the cities of Italy gradually complied with the bull, as did some cities in Germany. "In the rest of Europe, the formal institution never generally prevailed."[11]

Modern opinion disapproves of compulsory segregation or apartheid. It is, nevertheless, true that certain communities prefer to live together. To compel integration can be as arbitrary as to compel segregation.

Jewish quarters in cities, whether compulsory or not, enjoyed wide autonomy, with their own officials, shops, guilds, amusements and law courts. Jewish officials collected the taxes and paid them to the authorities. This high degree of independence would, of course, have been lost by integration, a fact which emphasises that segregation had advantages as well as drawbacks. Another effect of the farming of taxes by Jewish officials meant that some Jews grew rich at the expense of others.

Jewish communities passed their own ordinances, for example, to prohibit shaving, to fix a tax on meat, to limit ornaments worn by women or to decide what their families might eat.[12] Jewish communal officials were elected and normally consisted of a president, a treasurer, a council, a rabbi, two dayanim (members of the judicial court), a beadle, a school-teacher and a butcher.

"Long before residence in a restricted quarter or ghetto was compulsory," writes Israel Abrahams, "the Jews almost everywhere had concentrated in separate parts of the towns in which they lived."

Most Jewries possessed judicial powers over Jews and could sentence them to fines, corporal punishment, or sometimes even to death. They often had separate prisons, sanctioned by the government. Jews sentenced by Jewish judges could not be released by the government of the country. The most powerful weapon wielded by the Jewish authorities, however, was excommunication, or expulsion from Jewish society.

The Jewish community often owned an inn or guest house, and a public hall for dances and festivals. The Prague Judenstadt at the end of the sixteenth century had a town hall, with a bell which summoned the members of the council to meetings. It also had an official flag, awarded to the Judenstadt by the government for their patriotic services to the state. In 1492, when the Christians destroyed the last Arab kingdom in Spain, Muslims and Jews were both ordered to live in separate Moories and Jewries.

The Jewish quarter, says Israel Abrahams, was a privilege rather

[11] *Encyclopaedia Britannica.*
[12] Israel Abrahams, *Jewish Life in the Middle Ages.*

than an obligation, and was sometimes claimed by the Jews as a right. Jewish men spent their leisure at home or among relatives, to avoid ritual impurity, and, as a result, were above the average standards of sexual morality in their countries of residence.

When, therefore, in 1555, Paul IV issued his bull advocating separate Jewries, the suggestion was to make compulsory the system for which Jews used to petition, and which was almost everywhere already in existence.

The new emphasis on segregation did, however, have injurious effects. Firstly, it reduced the mixing of Jews and Christians day by day and thereby increased suspicion. Secondly, where the boundaries of Jewries were fixed, it allowed for no expansion and sometimes led to overcrowding, whereas previously Judenstadts were usually clean and spacious, with many fine buildings. Thirdly, the idea of segregation limited business activities and made many Jews poor. "The climax of Jewish impoverishment," says Israel Abrahams, "was reached at the beginning of the eighteenth century." To many people, it comes as a surprise to hear that Jews were better off in the Middle Ages than in the "Age of Enlightenment".

The decline in Jewish prosperity, however, was not solely due to segregation. The spread of education in Europe after the Renaissance terminated Jewish supremacy in this field. The disappearance of the Muslim-Christian battle front across the Mediterranean, and the discovery of the Cape of Good Hope, enabled Christian merchants to trade with the Levant and the Far East. The arrival of Christian fleets in the Indian Ocean also destroyed the trade of Muslim countries with India and China, impoverishing the Arab countries, where Jews had hitherto been prosperous.

* * *

Jews had, we have seen, enjoyed in their own communities a remarkable degree of independence, though modern propaganda has turned the word ghetto[13] into the very symbol of racial injustice. Yet, in the Middle East, separate communities were the key to freedom and toleration. Everywhere in the world, people like to live among others similar to themselves. In the Middle East, this natural trait has always been indulged. To this day, most towns have Jewish, Christian, Muslim, Persian, Armenian or European quarters, many of which have considerable local autonomy.

[13] The word "ghetto" seems originally to have been the geographical name of the Venice Jewry.

The idea of the homogeneous nation seems to have partly originated in the religious wars of Europe, which resulted in the terrible persecutions of heretics, Muslims and Jews, or of anyone not conforming to the government religion. Persecution was not solely due to religious fanaticism but to the political belief that persons professing other than the state religion might not be loyal. Today, we have ceased to persecute for religious reasons, but we still struggle to make all citizens identical, an ideal inevitably destructive of personal freedom.

How complicated are human beings who, in the West, declare segregation to be a symbol of tyranny, which in the Middle East was the embodiment of freedom. But the key to the paradox is simple—avoidance of compulsion. Those who wish to live in communities should be allowed to do so, others who desire to integrate should not be hindered. Unfortunately, some reformers are as arbitrary and as interfering with private liberty as ever was the Czar of all the Russias.

* * *

On the whole, we must appreciate that these were blood-soaked centuries. Jews in Europe suffered mentally from living constantly in an atmosphere of hatred and contempt. Their physical sufferings, however, were far less than those of Christian heretics. For example, in the massacre of St. Bartholomew in Paris, on 24th August, 1572, fifty thousand Huguenots were killed by the Catholics. No pogroms on Jews on anything approaching this scale are recorded. Hundreds of thousands of Christians were killed by other Christians in the wars of religion following the Reformation.

Yet all this butchery seemed insignificant compared with the sufferings of the peoples in the Middle East during the same period, as the next chapter will show.

NOTABLE DATES

Foundation of the Khazar Kingdom	198
Conversion of the Khazars to Judaism	740
Arrival of first Jews in Poland	900
Dispersal of the Khazars to eastern Europe	1016
Destruction of Persia by Jenghis Khan	1220–1225
Devastation of Poland by the Mongols	1236–1261
The Crusades in the Levant	1098–1291
The Black Death—German Jews move to Poland	1348

Casimir the Great welcomes Jews to Poland	1333–1370
Capture of Constantinople by the Ottomans	1453
Fall of Granada	1492
Ottoman Conquest of the Levant and Egypt	1517
Bull of Paul IV	1555

CONCLUSIONS

(1) From 700 to 1500, in spite of occasional disasters and restrictions, Jews in Europe were prosperous.

(2) The Christian conquest of Granada in 1492 was a major tragedy for the Jews of Spain, who had enjoyed prosperity and equality under the Arabs.

(3) Many escaped to Turkey, where they again found toleration under Muslim rule.

(4) The bull of Paul IV in 1555 injured the status and the prosperity of Jews.

(5) Heretics always suffered far worse persecutions than did the Jews in Europe.

XIV

Middle East Martyrdom

The nomads requiring vast areas of pasture for their flocks, the lands of sedentary cultivators seemed to them a waste of territory. The destruction of cities, villages, orchards and cultivated fields answered for them a vital necessity of their way of life.

MARCEL BRION, *Tamerlan*

The Tatars were no undisciplined horde of feckless barbarians but a force of some half a million trained light horsemen, representing an empire which in the lifetime of Jingis Khan, had been extended from Manchuria to the Caucasus at a cost of more than eighteen million lives. No empire had ever occupied so large a portion of the earth's surface or had been the cause of so much human suffering.

H. A. L. FISHER, *A History of Europe*

The Mongols ... carried the city [Nishapur] by assault and massacred every living thing (including the cats and dogs), pyramids of skulls being built as a ghastly memorial of the feat of arms. The buildings were then entirely demolished and the site was sown with barley.

P. M. SYKES, *A History of Persia*

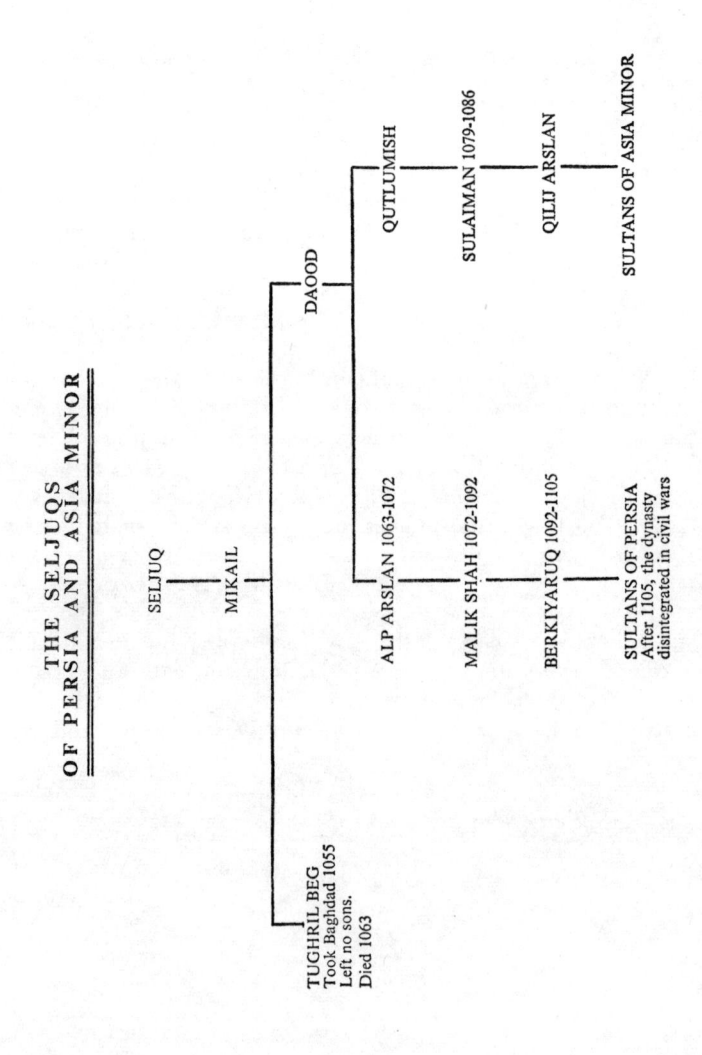

THE SELJUQS OF PERSIA AND ASIA MINOR

```
                    SELJUQ
                      |
                    MIKAIL
                      |
        ┌─────────────┴─────────────┐
    TUGHRIL BEG                   DAOOD
    Took Baghdad 1055               |
    Left no sons.          ┌────────┴────────┐
    Died 1063         ALP ARSLAN         QUTLUMISH
                      1063-1072              |
                          |              SULAIMAN 1079-1086
                      MALIK SHAH             |
                      1072-1092          QILJI ARSLAN
                          |                  |
                      BERKIYARUQ         SULTANS OF ASIA MINOR
                      1092-1105
                          |
                      SULTANS OF PERSIA
                      After 1105, the dynasty
                      disintegrated in civil wars
```

XIV

FROM 641 to 861, two hundred and twenty years, the Arab khalifate had constituted an empire of dazzling wealth, power and culture. Like Europe from 1815 to 1914, it was far ahead of every rival in every field. The Abbásid khalifs, after 833, enlisted great numbers of Turkish mercenaries from Central Asia in their armies. In 861, these Turks murdered the Khalif Mutawakkil, and set up a military dictatorship, with puppet khalifs for the sake of appearances.

In 1055, however, as already mentioned, the Seljuq chief, Tughril Beg, took Baghdad. For three generations the Seljuqs produced great sultans, whose empire extended from the frontiers of India to the Bosphorus.[1] From 1092 onwards, however, civil wars weakened the elder dynasty in Persia and Iraq. A junior branch of the family founded a state in Asia Minor, with its capital at Iconium (modern Konia). It was during this period of anarchy that the Crusaders established themselves in Palestine and Syria.

The Crusaders took Jerusalem in 1099, but the jealousies between the leaders resulted in the establishment of four states instead of one. The King of Jerusalem was accorded precedence, but was never able to secure obedience from the County of Tripoli, the Prince of Antioch or the Count of Edessa. For some fifty years, the Crusaders won every battle, largely owing to the support of the West, notably France.

The Muslim world was not only weakened by the Seljuq civil wars, but also by the establishment of an independent Fatimid dynasty in Egypt in 975. The Egyptians endeavoured to intervene against the Crusaders, but were always defeated. The Crusaders, with the crude roughness of north Europeans, relied solely on force, though the fact that the Seljuqs in Iraq and the Fatimids in Cairo rarely saw eye to eye offered them many chances for diplomacy.

In 1127, a Turkish mercenary commander called Zengi became Lord of Mosul. In 1144, by a surprise attack, Zengi took Edessa and one of the four Crusader states ceased to exist. Salah al Deen al Ayoubi (Saladin) was a Kurdish soldier of fortune in the service of the family of Zengi. In 1169, he made himself master of Egypt. In 1174, he occupied Damascus, defeated his former employers and

[1] Genealogical Tree, p. 222.

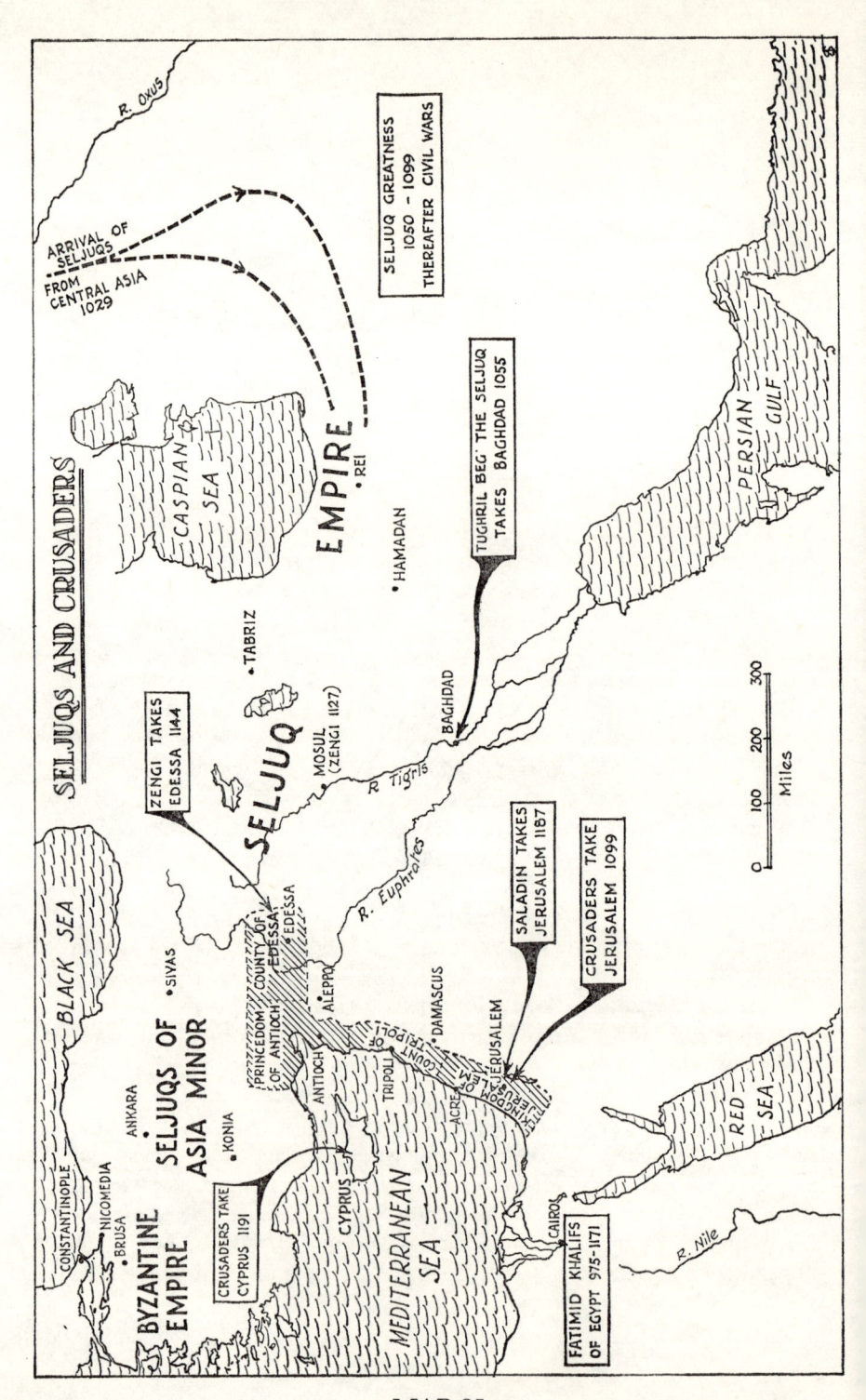

MAP 25

became Sultan of Syria and Egypt. In 1187 he defeated the Crusaders at Hattin and took Jerusalem.

The West had grown tired of receiving constant appeals for help from the Crusaders, but the fall of Jerusalem roused them to fresh efforts. In 1191, the Third Crusade landed outside Acre under Richard Coeur de Lion, King of England, and Philippe Auguste, King of France. Saladin was defeated, but Jerusalem was not retaken. Four Crusader states, however, were re-established, the "Kingdom of Jerusalem" with its capital in Acre, the County of Tripoli, the Princedom of Antioch and the Island of Cyprus.

Saladin died in 1193 but his brother ruled his empire until 1218. Thereafter his family, the Ayoubids, became weakened and divided. The Ayoubids, like the Abbásid khalifs, recruited their armies chiefly from Turkish mercenaries. In 1250, the Turkish troops murdered the last Ayoubid sultan and set up their own dictatorship.

The word Mamlook (or Mameluke) in Arabic means "owned" by somebody else. It was employed to designate slaves used as soldiers, in contrast to domestic house-slaves. These soldier-slaves of the Ayoubid family set up in Egypt one of the most extraordinary governments in history.

All Mamlooks were born in Central Asia. They were bought by slave traders as boys and brought to Egypt, where they were put through an extremely rigorous military training. As cavalry, armed with bow and arrow, sword and lance, they had no equals in the world. They were also taught deportment and the Muslim religion. Promotion from soldier-slave to ameer or even sultan was by merit alone. Having come to Egypt as slaves, they had no genealogies, no families and no influence or class feeling. Military efficiency was the sole criterion.

If they married in Egypt, their children were not eligible for enlistment in Mamlook units. Every recruit had to be born on the steppes. By these extraordinary means, they maintained for three centuries an invincible military machine.

While, however, the Mamlooks were thus establishing a Turkish slave government in Cairo, the most terrible scourge known to history emerged from Asia. The Mongol habitat was south of Lake Baikal in eastern Central Asia. In 1220–25, a Mongol army led by Jenghis Khan utterly devastated Persia, one of the oldest and most cultured nations in the world.

The Mongol technique was simple. As they marched through the countryside, they rounded up all the young men for use in labour gangs. On reaching a city, they immediately surrounded it with a

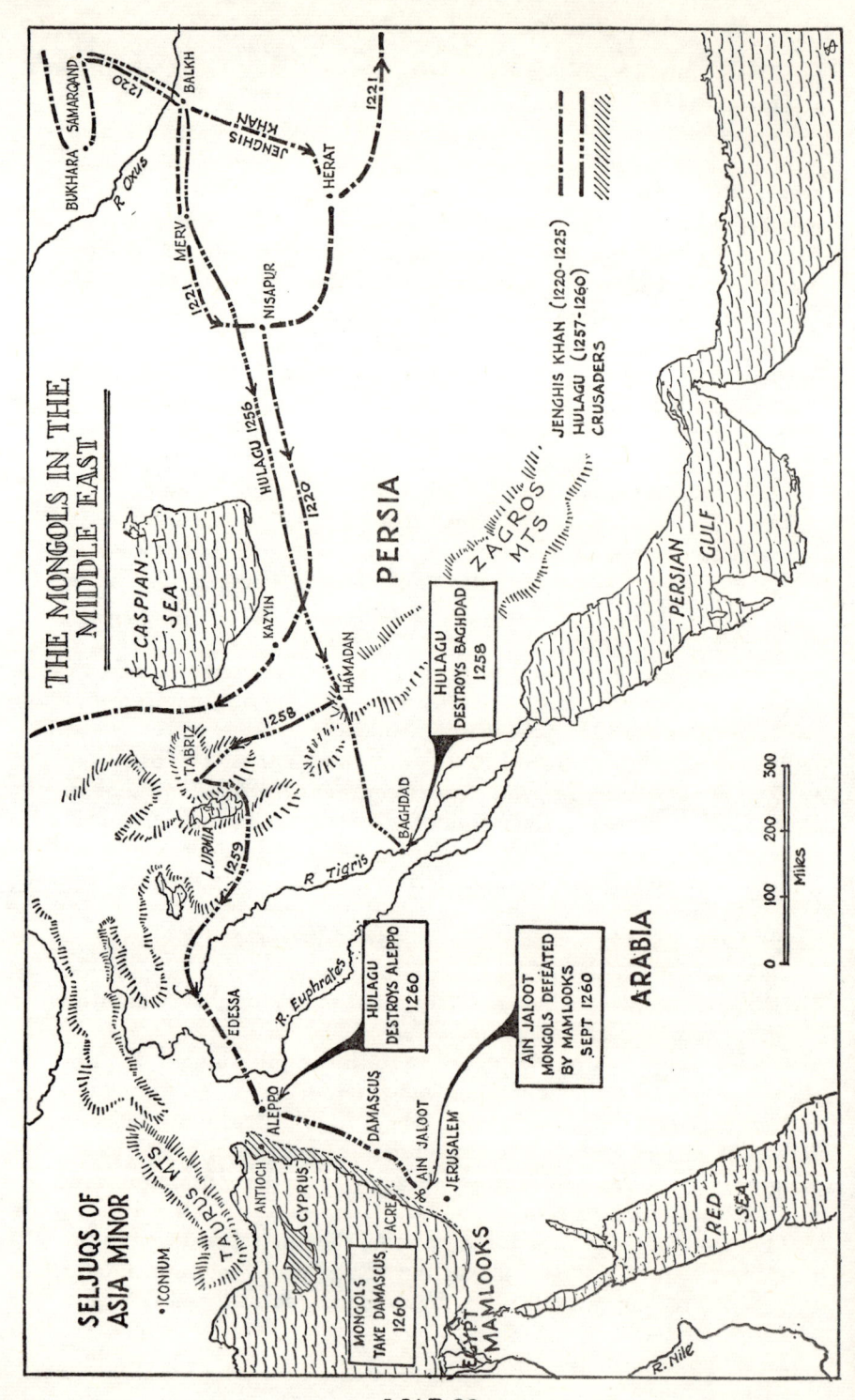

MAP 26

ditch and breastwork (as Titus had done Jerusalem), using their slave labour gangs. Then the mangonels bombarded the walls, until a breach was effected, whereupon the prisoners were driven in front of the Mongol assaulting column and suffered the heaviest losses.

When the city was taken, all the inhabitants were marshalled outside the walls in an open space. The women were raped and then the whole population was massacred, regardless of age or sex. Finally, the city was looted and burned to the ground.

Jenghis Khan died on 18th August, 1227. From that date to 1241, the Mongols invaded eastern Europe, destroying Moscow, Kiev, Cracow and Breslau, among major cities, and approaching to within a few miles of Vienna. Everywhere the population was tortured, raped and massacred. Poland and Hungary were virtually depopulated. In 1254, Hulagu, a grandson of Jenghis Khan, set out to conquer the Middle East.

On 13th February, 1258, the Mongols captured Baghdad. The Abbásid Khalif Mustasim and his sons were sewn up in sacks and trampled to death beneath the horses of the Mongol cavalry. The city of Baghdad in 1258 was little more than the ghost of the capital of Haroon al Rasheed, which, four hundred years before, had been the wealthiest and most cultured city in the world. Yet it was still a city of libraries, colleges and mosques, with a university believed to be the most up-to-date in the world. The destruction of Baghdad required seven days, during which eight hundred thousand people were massacred. When Hulagu moved on, mounds of rubble and an unbearable stench of decaying human flesh alone marked the site of what had once been the world's greatest city.

Hulagu wintered in Tabriz. Early in 1259, he marched through Nisibin, Harran and Edessa. On 20th January, 1260, Aleppo was carried by assault and the inhabitants exterminated, except for a hundred thousand women and girls who were driven off to amuse the soldiers. When all Syria and Egypt seemed about to meet the fate of Iraq and Persia, Hulagu was recalled to Mongolia by the death of the Great Khan. A Mongol army nevertheless went on and occupied Damascus and Palestine.

It will be remembered that, in 1250, the Mamlooks, the Turkish slave soldiers of Egypt, had murdered the last sultan of Saladin's family and had set up a military régime. The Turks, however, once the terror of the Middle East, seemed powerless against the Mongols. When, however, Hulagu returned to Mongolia, Qutuz, the Mamlook Sultan, decided to fight. On 3rd September, 1260, at Ain Jaloot—the Spring of Goliath—Qutuz completely defeated the Mongols, who evacuated Syria. The Mamlooks annexed all Syria, Lebanon and Palestine, constituting a considerable empire.

A weak remnant of the Crusader states had been the impotent observers of the fighting between the Mamlooks and the Mongols. When, however, the Mongols withdrew beyond the Euphrates, the Mamlooks turned upon the surviving Christian states. On 18th May, 1291, the Mamlooks took Acre, the capital of the Kingdom of Jerusalem. Every living person in the town was massacred. There were no more Crusader states, except for the Lusignan dynasty which ruled Cyprus.

The Mongols then fell out among themselves, and civil wars at home hampered further conquests. The descendants of Hulagu became rulers of Persia with the title of Il Khan. Their régime was one of extreme barbarism and Persia, for thousands of years one of the world's leading nations, was reduced to a sparsely populated semi-desert. The remnant of the Seljuq dynasty of Asia Minor paid tribute to the Mongol Great Khan. The Mongols periodically invaded Syria, but, after heavy fighting, were repulsed by the Mamlooks.

The Mamlooks created a great empire in the Middle East. Their system of promotion by military merit alone produced leaders who had fought their ways from slave to sultan by sheer personality and courage. Their rule was harsh, particularly in Egypt, where the agricultural labourers were little more than slaves. The Egyptian cultivators suffered from the Mamlooks as much as the Jews did from the Christians in Europe. No Syrians, Palestinians or Egyptians were recruited in the army, though Arab desert nomads were employed as auxiliaries. But the single-minded Mamlook dedication to soldiering produced a secondary benefit. They willingly left the administrative services, education, religion and law, to the natives, and Syrians and Egyptians rose to high rank in these occupations and were received at court. The Mamlooks did not condescend to learn Arabic and Turkish was their official language.

They wisely encouraged trade, and their empire became extremely wealthy. Mamlooks went clad in silk, satin and cloth of gold and their weapons and saddles were plastered with the precious metal. The priceless oriental trade came up the Red Sea, was taken overland to Alexandria and re-shipped to Europe. Jews were scattered far and wide over the Middle East but concentrated their efforts on trade and eschewed politics. As one community in a mixed population, they attracted no great attention.

* * *

When Jenghis Khan was devastating Persia in 1220–1225, a small group of pagan Turkman[2] nomads moved west from Persia into the Turkish Seljuq Sultanate of Asia Minor. The sultan settled them at Suqut, on his border with the Byzantine Empire. Ertoghul, the leader of this Turkman community of some four hundred families, died in 1288 and was succeeded by his son, Othman, who was converted to Islam.

With the enthusiasm of a new convert, Othman began to encroach on the neighbouring Byzantine Christians, probably the object with which the Seljuq sultan had settled the Turkmans on his border. The disappearance of the Seljuqs of Asia Minor between 1285 and 1300, left the whole area a chaos of petty ameerates, among them that of Othman. When he died, about 1326, he left a tiny state, including the two towns of Brusa and Nicomedia.[3] His followers were henceforth known as Othmanlis, later corrupted in Europe to Ottomans. While this rapid Ottoman expansion was in progress, the Mamlooks were at the pinnacle of their wealth and power under Malik al Nasir Muhammad (1303–1341).

Othman's son, Orkhan, further enlarged his territory, adding a large part of Thrace across the Dardanelles. The Byzantine Empire was utterly decadent. Murad (1359–1389), the grandson of Othman, having conquered Thrace, Bulgaria and Macedonia, was killed at Kossovo in modern Yugoslavia. Meanwhile, he had established his capital at Adrianople in Europe.

The Othmanlis now held a great empire, almost entirely in Europe. Bayazid I (1389–1402) the son of Murad, turned back to Asia Minor, conquered all the little states which had succeeded the Seljuqs, and established his eastern frontier at Sivas.[4]

* * *

On 8th April, 1336, was born at Kish in Trans-Oxiana a boy by the name of Timur, of an obscure Turkish tribe. The Il Khanate, the empire of Hulagu, had collapsed two years earlier and Persia was in anarchy. When some twenty-three years old, Timur received an arrow wound in the leg, which lamed him for life. He was nicknamed Timur i Lenk, or Timur the Lame, corrupted in Europe to Tamerlane.

In forty years spent entirely in wars, Tamerlane conquered all

---

[2] There is no exact line to be drawn between Turks and Turkmans at this time. In general, the word Turkman was applied to tented Turkish nomads.
[3] Map 25, p. 224.   [4] Map 25, p. 224.

Persia, the steppes of southern Russia, modern Afghanistan, and invaded northern India, destroying Delhi. Wherever he went, he imitated Jenghis Khan, razing every city to the ground and killing all the inhabitants. Tamerlane made no attempt to administer his conquests. He tortured and massacred the people, burned the cities and marched away.

Tamerlane was confronted on the west by two military empires, the Othmanlis and the Mamlooks. It may be noted that both he and they were all Turks. In August 1400, Tamerlane took Sivas, a city belonging to Bayazid. In October, he took Aleppo and Hama, which belonged to the Mamlooks. All men and children were butchered, but thousands of women were rounded up, even in the mosques, stripped naked and given over to the troops.[5] At the end of February 1401, Damascus was taken, the now decadent Mamlooks being unable to defend it. The usual butchery began. All women were collected, stripped and raped publicly. The inhabitants were torn limb from limb, flayed or burned alive. The raping, killing and torturing lasted for nineteen days. Finally Tamerlane set fire to the city and marched away on 19th March, 1401, leaving Damascus a furnace of smoke and flames.

In July 1401, he laid siege to Baghdad, which offered a desperate resistance. When the city was finally taken, the inhabitants as usual were exterminated after the customary orgies.

Having now terrorised the Mamlooks and all possible rivals in the east, Tamerlane decided to cross swords with the Othmanlis. On 20th July, 1402, the two mighty Turkish empires met at Anqara, the capital of the Turkish Republic today. After desperate fighting all day long, the Othmanlis were defeated and Bayazid taken prisoner. Tamerlane's army then carried massacre, fire and sword over Asia Minor.

Returning to his capital in Samarqand the old warrior, though he was now sixty-nine, decided to conquer China, but died in his tent on 18th February, 1405. His empire broke up as soon as he was dead. Only devastated countrysides, mounds of charred rubble and human bones whitening in the sun marked where Tamerlane had passed.

The incredible sufferings endured by the peoples of Western Asia from Jenghis Khan (1220–1227) to Tamerlane (1359–1405) are probably unequalled in the history of the world. Certainly the sufferings of Christian heretics or Jews in Europe were but a drop in the ocean compared to the agonies of the Middle East from 1220 to 1405.

* * *

[5] Ibn Taghri Birdi, *Al Nujoom al Zahira*.

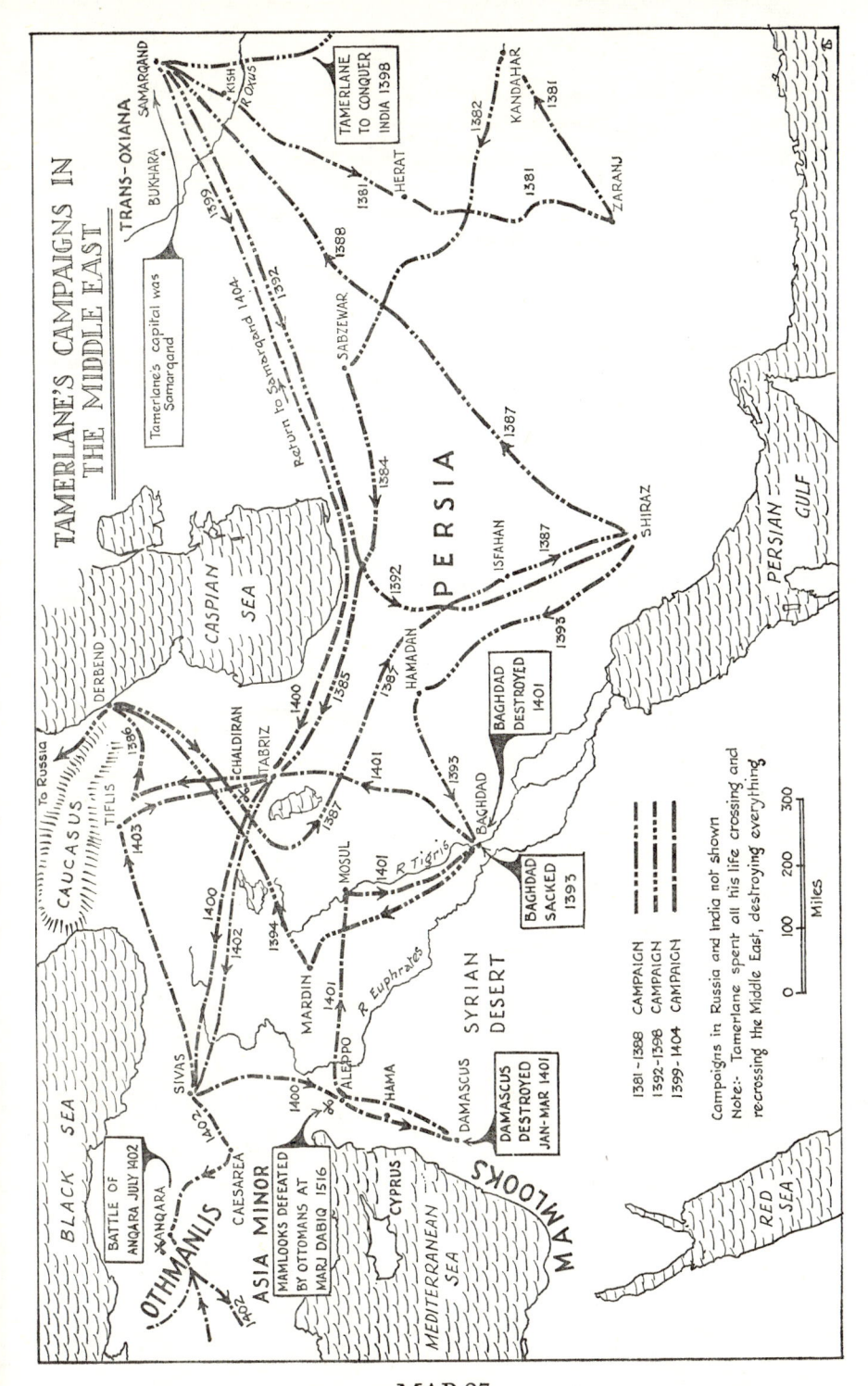

MAP 27

The Ottoman Empire appeared irrevocably shattered by the Battle of Anqara in 1402, but there was no rival in the field to give it the coup de grâce. After 1413, it slowly began to recover. In 1453, under Sultan Muhammad II the Conqueror, the Othmanlis took Constantinople, and, after a thousand years, the last traces of the Byzantine Empire vanished from the map.

The Mamlook Empire also revived. The sultans were now mostly Circassians from the Caucasus, not Turks. They were less efficient than the Turks as soldiers, and the discipline of the army deteriorated. In Persia, a national revival was beginning after the endless miseries suffered under Mongol and Turkish conquerors.

In 1512, Saleem I, the Grim, became Ottoman Sultan. He inaugurated his reign by defeating the Persian ruler, Ismail Shah, at Chaldiran, near Lake Urmia.[6] The Ottomans, now recovered from their defeat, were the most powerful state in the world. Their army was better trained and disciplined, and armed with more modern weapons than any in Europe. They were well ahead of all rivals in the use of firearms, both artillery and hand-guns. The Persians at Chaldiran had no firearms at all.

After defeating Shah Ismail, Sultan Saleem turned back to Syria. The Mamlook army consisted entirely of cavalry. They refused to use firearms in battle, regarding them as dishonourable.

The two empires, both Turkish, met at Marj Dabiq, north of Aleppo on 24th August, 1516. The Mamlook cavalry with sword and lance charged again and again with desperate gallantry, but were mown down by the Ottoman firearms and almost exterminated. The Othmanlis occupied Syria and Palestine without further fighting. In January 1517, they took Cairo.

The Ottomans, after their capture of Constantinople in 1453, offer one more example of the absurdity of popular ethnology. The Turks who emerged from Central Asia were small men of sallow complexion with sparse beards. The typical Turk, pictured in Victorian times, was a big man with fair skin and long moustaches. The original Othmanlis were a group of Turkish nomads a few hundred strong, who conquered the Balkans, modern Yugoslavia, Hungary, Albania, Bulgaria and Greece, and remained in these countries for four or five hundred years, integrating with the local peoples. There were, however, Turks and other Asians in Asia Minor, since the Seljuq conquest of the area about 1075. Before that, Asia Minor had been Greek for thirteen hundred years, but the "Greeks" were of course, mixed with many early races, such as Hittites, Gauls,

[6] Map 27, p. 231.

Armenians and Persians. Suffice it, therefore, to say that the population of the Ottoman Empire included only a small proportion of Central Asian Turkish stock, the remainder being a mixture of a dozen or more European and Middle Eastern strains, with the European possibly slightly the more numerous.

One other characteristic of the Ottomans must be appreciated. It will be remembered that the Seljuq Sultan of Asia Minor settled the original nomadic group at Suqut on the Byzantine border. Wild fighting men, the sultan thought that they would be more than a match for the Christian Byzantines. Othman, with the enthusiasm of the convert, enlarged his borders at the expense of his Christian neighbours. The pattern was to endure for centuries. The Ottomans always regarded themselves as the champions of Islam, fighting against Christendom. Their self-imposed rôle of "Muslim Crusaders" resulted in the devotion of most of their strength to wars in Europe. This policy, ironically enough, was disastrous to their fellow Muslims in Asia and North Africa, whose welfare they completely neglected.

* * *

The Ottoman conquest of Syria and Egypt in 1516 and 1517 resulted in the rapid deterioration of the administration and the prosperity of these countries. The Mamlooks, it is true, had been barbarian soldier-slaves, but at least they lived in Cairo, with a viceroy in Damascus. Moreover, the Mamlooks, although themselves purely soldiers, had the common sense to realise that their interests coincided with the welfare of Syria and Egypt. Non-military government positions were held by natives of these countries, and the authorities encouraged merchants and commerce.

The Ottomans, by contrast, were absentee landlords. Engrossed in their European wars, they scarcely spared a thought for their Asian territories. Moreover, the Ottomans were essentially military and tended to despise commerce, as the Spaniards did after the eviction of the Jews and the Muslims from the peninsula. We have seen how the Jews exiled from Spain were welcomed and grew rich in the Ottoman dominions. This was due to the fact that the Muslim Ottomans looked upon themselves as soldiers, and were not jealous of foreign merchants.

* * *

Though Saleem I, the Grim, had devoted several years to defeating the Persians and the Mamlooks, his son, Sulaiman the Magnificent (1520–1566), returned to the traditional Ottoman policy of expansion in Europe. In 1526, he completely defeated the Hungarians at Mohaç and annexed Hungary. The Ottomans were to remain in control of most of the country for a hundred and seventy-four years. Europe in the sixteenth century was torn with religious persecution between Catholics and Protestants; only in the areas held by the Turks did religious toleration prevail.

The Ottomans, like the Russians today, realised that naval command of the Mediterranean was essential to the conquest of Europe. In 1565, they laid siege to Malta. They already controlled the eastern half of the Mediterranean, and hoped, with a naval base in Malta, to dominate the western Mediterranean also. The siege failed owing to the heroic defence by the Knights of St. John of Jerusalem. The abortive siege of Malta proved to be the turning point in the Ottoman conquest of Europe.

* * *

The Ottoman army, from 1450 to perhaps 1650 had been the finest in the world, but the Ottomans gave little thought to Syria, Palestine or Egypt. In 1534, however, Sulaiman the Magnificent took time off for an eastern campaign, during which he captured Baghdad, which at the time was held by Persia. Thereafter the Ottomans endeavoured to maintain large garrisons in Mosul and Baghdad but the remainder of what is today Iraq was not administered or controlled.

Ever since prehistoric times, Egypt, Syria and Palestine had been in the centre of the world's leading civilisations. Only after 1516 did they fall rapidly behind. One reason for this cannot be imputed to Ottoman neglect. The wealth of the Middle East had been largely due to the transit trade from the Orient which crossed Egypt and Syria. But when Vasco da Gama discovered the way to the Indian Ocean round the Cape of Good Hope, Europe rapidly built up great fleets which brought her the wealth of the East without crossing Muslim territory. From being the very hub of world trade, Egypt and Syria suddenly found themselves in a backwater.

* * *

Although, in the sixteenth century, Ottoman administration in the European provinces was just, tolerant and efficient, it was of a low standard in Syria and Palestine. Ottoman governors of Syria secured their appointment by bribery in Constantinople (which we will henceforward call Istanbul), and their first preoccupation was to recoup their expenses. (The same system had been followed in the Roman Empire.)

In the Middle East, however, personal ties are of supreme importance and everything depends on good relationships between the rulers and the public. But Ottoman governors were changed so often that they contracted no personal attachments. In the first one hundred and eighty years of Ottoman rule, Damascus suffered no less than one hundred and thirty-three governors.

The general pattern of Ottoman administration in Syria and Palestine can be briefly defined. Large garrisons were maintained in the principal cities, such as Aleppo and Damascus. Taxes were collected and justice enforced in an area extending a few miles outside these major government centres. Beyond that, government control became increasingly precarious, until, in tribal areas, it vanished without trace.

In agricultural areas, some distance from the great cities, administrative officials, assisted by a few gendarmes, asserted a precarious influence by alternately fraternising with the people or threatening them with the vengeance of the sultan. Every few years, some tribe or other would exceed the permissible degree of lawlessness. Then a large military force would move out, the villages would be burnt, the flocks driven off, and a few people killed. The tribe would then make its submission, for a year or two some taxes would be paid and then the process would recommence.

The Ottomans had the advantage of being of the same religion as the majority of the population in Syria and Palestine. Racialism was not a subject of controversy. Everybody, including the tribes, paid lip-service to the sultan. The lawlessness did not, as a result, lead to hatred or fanaticism. Compared with the bitter feuds which rend our world today, Arab rebelliousness against the Ottomans was little more than a rough sport.

The Lebanese mountains being difficult for military punitive columns, the sensible Ottomans made the area semi-autonomous, from 1517 to 1697 under the Mani Ameers, from 1697 to 1840 under the Shihabis. The attempt to administer Trans-Jordan was early abandoned and for three hundred years the area was ruled by Arab chiefs.

Palestine was always one of the most peaceful Ottoman provinces. The people were of mixed ethnic origin and of different religions.

Lacking in military traditions, few Palestinians served in the Ottoman armies.

* * *

When Saleem the Grim left Egypt in 1517 to return to Istanbul, he left behind an Ottoman governor and five thousand troops. But the Mamlooks constituted the whole ruling class, who soon began to reassert themselves, whittling away the authority of the Ottomans, who could not afford a military reconquest of Egypt. By 1700, the country was once more, except in name, under the control of the Mamlook aristocracy.

* * *

The relatively peaceful stagnation of the Middle East was rudely shattered on 1st July, 1798, by the landing of Napoleon Bonaparte in Egypt. His penetrating intellect had grasped the fact that possession of Egypt and naval command of the Mediterranean were the keys to the domination of Europe.

Having occupied Egypt, he marched into Palestine and besieged Acre, which was defended by a magnificent bandit, Ahmad Pasha al Jazzàr (the Butcher). Ahmad had been a Bosnian slave boy who, like Joseph, was sold into Egypt. In a number of years spent in intrigue, violence and civil war, he had made himself virtual ruler of Syria. The Sublime Porte,[7] unable to eject him, appointed him governor with the rank of pasha.

Assisted by the British fleet, the Butcher successfully defended Acre. Meanwhile, on 1st August, 1798, the French fleet had been destroyed by Nelson in the mouth of the Nile. Napoleon abandoned his enterprise and returned to France. The emperor always claimed that the failure of this campaign had changed his destiny. Had he been able to hold a French base in Egypt and naval command of the Mediterranean, he might have established an empire of united Europe.

His irruption into the Middle East ended the age of peaceful stagnation and opened the door to further European intervention.

---

[7] The diplomatic name for the Ottoman government.

NOTABLE DATES

Loss of the power of Abbásid Khalifs	861
Seljuq seizure of Baghdad	1055
The Crusades	1099–1291
Persia devastated by Jenghis Khan	1220–1225
Destruction of Baghdad by Hulagu	1258
Mamlook rule in Egypt	1250–1517
Ottoman conquest of Syria and Palestine	1517
Napoleon's Middle East campaign	1798

CONCLUSIONS

(1) Visitors to the Middle East sometimes refuse to believe that these countries led the world for untold centuries. Their present state is largely explained by the incredible savagery of Mongols and Turks from 1220 to 1405.

(2) The Roman Empire was destroyed by barbarians from northern Europe, but they were civilised compared to the savage hordes of Central Asia.

(3) In the whole history of mankind, no such sufferings are recorded as those of western Asia in this period. Religious wars or Jewish persecutions in Europe were parlour games in comparison. Middle East history, however, has never been taught in the West, while the disasters of Europe have received full and continuing publicity.

XV

The Consequences of Contempt

And the men of Israel answered . . . and said . . . "Why then did ye despise us?"
II Samuel XIX, 43

Thou makest us a reproach to our neighbours, a scorn and a derision to them that are round about us . . . My confusion is continually before me, and the shame of my face hath covered me.
Psalm XXXXIV, 13, 15

What God has cleansed, that call not thou common.
Acts X, 15

XV

In regard to persecution, twelve points seem to emerge from the previous chapters:

(1) Since the days of Joshua, Yahweh worshippers showed an intolerance towards other religions which was otherwise unknown in antiquity, except perhaps among the Moabites.

(2) The Assyrian and Babylonian captivities were not religious persecutions of Jews. These cruel empires used deportation as an instrument of policy. Elamites, Medes, Persians, Syrians and others were similarly treated.

(3) There were no persecutions under the ancient Persians (538–332 B.C.).

(4) There were no disasters or persecutions under the Ptolemies or the Seleucids, until Antiochus Epiphanes (175–163 B.C.). The conflict with Epiphanes resulted from the violence of rivalries for the office of high priest, but it degenerated into religious persecution in Judaea.

(5) The rebellions in Judaea at the time of Titus, from A.D. 67 to 70, and under Bar Kokhba (A.D. 133–135) were political risings against Rome. Meanwhile, however, the great majority of Jews were already living in the Roman or Persian Empires, where they enjoyed privileges rather than disabilities.

(6) With the conversion of the Roman Empire to Christianity under Constantine (306–337), the Jews gradually lost their privileges, and even suffered certain disabilities, but without physical persecution. With the collapse of the western Empire in A.D. 475, their fate varied in different countries. It was worst in Visigothic Spain from 586 to the Muslim conquest in 712. In the Eastern or Byzantine Empire, they were harassed rather than persecuted.

(7) The Arab conquests everywhere introduced improved conditions and religious toleration for Jews, though it is true that Muhammad himself fell foul of them in Arabia. In some countries, notably Muslim Spain, the seven centuries of Arab rule were a golden age for Jews. They were never persecuted in Italy.

(8) The worst persecution suffered by Jews in France and Germany was at the hands of the fanatical and chaotic People's Crusade in 1096. From 1348 onwards, they suffered severely in Germany, as a result of the charge that they had caused the Black

Death. Many migrated from Germany to Poland, where most of the Jews were local converts.

(9) Jews, ever since Ezra, have always preferred to live together, owing to their laws concerning diet and ritual purity. This aloofness aroused resentment, hundreds of years before the time of Christ.

(10) During the five or six centuries of Muslim-Christian hostility (say from A.D. 650 to 1250), the Jews enjoyed wide opportunities for trade, being the only people who could travel between Europe, Asia and Africa. Their presence was thus essential to the economy of western Europe and many Jews became extremely rich. In most cities, the Jewry was a well-built quarter, with handsome edifices. They were normally protected by rulers and by the Church, but disliked by the people.

The fall of Granada in 1492 was disastrous for the Jews of Spain, who were obliged to go into exile. The Marranos, or Jewish converts to Christianity, suffered terribly from the Inquisition. Their Muslim colleagues endured the same sufferings. Jewish exiles from Spain went to Holland, Italy or the Ottoman Empire.

(11) The Papal Bull of 1555 injured the Jews, though they were nearly all living in separate communities already. The reason for the bull seems to have been the fact that they were proselytisers, and also instigators of heresy.

(12) The horrors and sufferings of Western Asia from the Turks and the Mongols were far worse than any persecutions suffered by heretics or Jews in Europe. In general, massacres of Jews were rare in Europe. Their worst sufferings were probably due to the sneers and sarcasms of the common people, which produced in Jews a profound psychological effect.

* * *

Our modern contempt for the Middle Ages makes it surprising to us to read in Jewish writers that the year 1700 marked the lowest point of their fortunes. With the spread of education in the West, the Jews lost their former advantage in this field, while anti-Jewish writing gained volume. In 1505, a converted Jew called Pfefferkorn, under the auspicies of the Dominicans, collected passages in the Talmud offensive to Christianity. Published in Germany in 1507, under the title of the *Judenspiegel* (the Jewish Mirror), it caused much controversy.

At the end of the seventeenth century, a Protestant professor, J. A. Eisenmenger, wrote an attack on Judaism, which was published in

Königsberg in 1711. Such writings may have increased Judaeo-Christian resentments.

In the nineteenth century, France produced a number of anti-Jewish publications, such as Toussenel's *Les Juifs, Rois de l'Epoque*, and Abbé Lemann's, *L'Entrée des Israelites dans la Société Française*. As so often occurred, Abbé Lemann was a converted Jew. The nineteenth century in Germany also saw an increase in writings against Judaism. An alleged Jewish plot directed against the whole world was embodied in the famous *Protocols of the Elders of Zion*, which purported to be a plan to undermine Christian Society in order to establish Jewish World Dominion.

The Greeks, before the birth of Christ, had accused the Jews of being "enemies of the human race". The Emperor Claudius had warned the Jews of Alexandria against making a plague in the whole world. It is extraordinary how such phrases recur. Perhaps Jewish solidarity in face of the Gentile world gave rise to the belief in their hatred of the whole of humanity.

* * *

In order to be completely objective, let us consider the arguments put forward by those who claim that modern Jews are an ethnic group.

(1) The principal argument brought forward is that there is a facial resemblance between them—large nose, sallow complexion, and black hair. The answer to this question seems to me to be, firstly, that they do not all have these distinguishing features but those who do not are often not recognised as Jews. Secondly that these are Middle Eastern rather than Jewish peculiarities. The large nose, we have seen, was Hittite, not Israelite. This physiognomy is frequently encountered among Armenians and Syrians. As we have seen, Jews in England originally came largely from Spain and Portugal, where they had mostly established themselves with their Arab friends from the Middle East, at the time of the Arab conquests.

Russian Jews, however, who today form the majority of the ruling class in Israel, have considerably less Middle Eastern blood, consisting largely of pagan Slav proselytes or of Khazar Turks. Many east European Jews have fair hair and blue eyes.

(2) The second argument lies in the resemblance in conduct between Jews in Egypt and Rome, before the time of Christ, and their tactics and way of life down to our own times. Does not this

suggest an ethnic connection? This factor can be accounted for by the principle rigidly enforced since pre-Christian times, that converts to Judaism must abandon their families and homes, and come to live in a Jewish community. Add to this that Jews always had schools attended by all Jewish children. They never passed through a period of ignorance, as did the peoples of Europe during the Dark Ages. Thus Jewish mentality, Jewish tradition, and the Jewish attitude to the rest of the human race has been passed down without a break from generation to generation.

* * *

The middle of the eighteenth century produced the first breath of liberalism in Europe. A group of emancipated Jews, led by Moses Mendelssohn (1729–1786), appeared in Berlin and won much support. Christian sympathisers wrote books, depicting the Jews as wise and virtuous as they had previously been said to be evil and malevolent. George Eliot's novel, *Daniel Deronda*, was in the same vein.

By advising Jews to abandon the "ghetto mentality" and to join in the life of their native countries, Mendelssohn gave a new direction to Jewish thought. He became a famous philosopher, even suggesting that different persons might require various religions to suit their differing personalities. He claimed that religious Jews could also be loyal citizens of their native countries.

Mendelssohn's ideas divided the Jews, some of whom wished to become ordinary citizens while others feared the assimilation of Jews into other cultures, and the loss of their distinctive Jewish qualities. Zionism was to be one aspect of this conservative fear of absorption. When the end of the ghetto was in sight, some Jews discovered that they would prefer to continue living in separate communities.

During the second half of the eighteenth century, liberalism continued to grow. In October 1781, Joseph II, Emperor of Austria, opened the doors of universities and academies to Jews, reminding the Austrian people that Jews were fellow men and equal citizens. Finally, in 1789, came the French Revolution, abolishing all religious disabilities.

At the end of the eighteenth century, a movement grew in England also for the removal of religious disabilities. Speaking in the House of Commons, in favour of the motion, Lord Macaulay said, "Let us not, mistaking her (Christianity's) character and her interests, fight the battles of truth with the weapons of error, and endeavour to support by oppression that religion which first taught the human race the great lesson of human charity."

* * *

At the time of his Middle East campaign in 1798, Napoleon Bonaparte issued an appeal for the support of all Jews in Africa and Asia. It elicited no response whatever.

In Syria, the Jews had influential positions under the Ottomans. Saul Farhi, and his son Haim, were chief secretaries to Ahmad Jazzár, the governor. Indeed, the key post of chief secretary was almost a hereditary possession of this Jewish family. In the defence of Acre against Napoleon, Haim Farhi was Ahmad Jazzár's right hand man.

There were, in 1798, a thousand Jews in Jerusalem to nine thousand Muslims and Christians. The Jews voluntarily joined other communities in digging trenches when a Napoleonic attack was feared. All Middle East Jews were loyally devoted to the Ottomans.

There were Jewish communities in Acre, Tiberias, Safed and Hebron in Palestine. Damascus had a community of five thousand Jews and Aleppo six thousand. Many of these Jews were poor, especially in Jerusalem, where they formed a religious, not a commercial community.

In the larger cities, however, were wealthy Jewish merchants, who controlled important business enterprises, trading with Egypt and India, and who were influential and respected citizens. The Farhis, father and son, drafted the despatches from the Pasha of Damascus to the Sublime Porte. Jazzár once said that "Farhi's notes to the Porte have the wonderful quality of being polite as well as expressive."[1]

The Rev. John Wilson, in his book *Land of the Bible*, gives an account of his visit to Damascus in 1843. In it he writes, "We visited one of the princely mansions of the Farhis, the richest bankers and merchants of Damascus." In his *Report on Syria*, Sir John Bowring (1792-1872) writes, "As a class, the Jewish foreign merchants of Damascus are the most wealthy ... The two most opulent are believed to be Mourad Farhi and Raphael Nessim Farhi, whose wealth in trade exceeds one and a half millions each."[2] Mr. Graham, a companion of Sir John, doubted if the style of living of Britain's Royal Family equalled that of these Jewish merchant princes.

In recent years, Zionist writers allude to the terrible conditions

[1] Nahum Sokolow, *A History of Zionism*.   [2] Nahum Sokolow, op. cit.

under which Jews formerly lived in Arab countries. The quotations given suffice to dispel these illusions. The peoples of western Europe, frequently reminded of the cruelties practised by their own ancestors, readily believe that Jews in the Middle East endured even worse sufferings, but, in fact, this was not the case.

* * *

In 1807, under Napoleon, a Grand Sanhedrin assembled in Paris, and the Jews of France became strong supporters of the emperor. The influence of Moses Mendelssohn was obvious in the attitude of French Jews.

In the nineteenth century, also, the so-called "higher criticism" resulted in attacks on Christianity, which were taken up by some Jews, a number of whom published Lives of Christ. This literature served only to increase antagonism. A little silence, (alas, in our times, unobtainable) would have allowed such resentments to cool.

Throughout the nineteenth century, liberal tendencies continued in the West. The year of revolutions, 1848, further improved the status of Jews. In 1849, the full equality of Jews and Christians was ratified in Denmark. In 1859, the new Italy was united under Victor Emmanuel II, the Jews obtaining complete citizens' rights. Since then, many Jews have rendered devoted service to Italy.

Jews early obtained political rights in the United States, and have served there as senators, in Congress, in the armed forces, and in commerce and finance. By the end of the nineteenth century, Jews had won equality in almost every country. The principal exception was Russia.

* * *

Even when the Russian Empire was born under Peter the Great (1672–1725) Jews were already disliked. Peter himself is alleged to have said, "I would rather see in our midst nations professing Muhammadanism and paganism than Jews, who are all rogues and cheats."

His widow, Catherine I, and Catherine II, the Great (1762–1796), almost purged Russia of Jews. In 1796, however, a large Jewish population was transferred to Russia by the partition of Poland, one of the most unfortunate events in Jewish history.

The idealistic Czar Alexander I (1801–1825) forbade the persecution of Jews, but under Nicholas I (1825–1855) their forcible conversion was resumed. With the coronation of Alexander II

(1855–1881) the laws against Jews were again abolished. In Russia, says Rabbi Raisin, as in many other countries, the worst persecutors of Jews were Jewish converts to Christianity.

Unfortunately Alexander II was assassinated in 1881, a number of Jews being involved in the plot, with the result that his successor, Alexander III, returned to the policy of repression. Jews were severely harassed, and a number of pogroms occurred in 1881 and 1882. Many Jews consequently accepted baptism and disappeared into the population. Ethnically the majority of them were Europeans in any case. Jews who accepted Christianity out of fear were doubtless an unhappy class but their descendants, brought up in their new religion, often lost this feeling. Such, indeed, can be the only object of forced conversion, which obviously can rarely be sincere.

* * *

Puritan devotion to the Old Testament continued to influence Britain, the possible "return" of the Jews to Palestine being considered as a fulfilment of prophecy. In fact, most of the verses quoted, even if taken literally, were written before the return from Babylon, which could be considered as having fulfilled the prophecy.

Most of this early nineteenth-century writing was ill-informed. The Jews were thought to have been living in Palestine until evicted by Titus, whereas we have seen that five Jews out of six were living out of Palestine centuries earlier. Titus, moreover, did not evict those living there, except for prisoners-of-war. The centuries of intense Jewish proselytisation were also not known, and Jews in the nineteenth century were thought to be descended from those in Palestine at the time of Christ.

The Old Testament was believed to be the exact words of God, and the speeches attributed to the patriarchs to be verbatim reports. Above all, the public did not know that Yahweh was the tribal god of Israel, and that the name had only been changed to "the Lord" less than three centuries before Christ.

In 1805, the Palestine Society was founded in London. In 1865, the Palestine Exploration Fund was constituted, both societies being basically religious and intended to throw more light on the Bible. Several distinguished officers of the Royal Engineers were lent for the survey of Palestine, including Captain, later Lord, Kitchener. Colonel C. R. Conder (1848–1910) devoted his life to Palestine studies.

Some Jewish advocates of a "return" to Palestine indulged in

MAP TO ILLUSTRATE ARTICLE
IN DER ORIENT, 1840

AREA SETTLED BY ISRAELITES 1200-724 BC
AREA CLAIMED IN DER ORIENT 1840 "THE INHERITANCE OF OUR FATHERS"

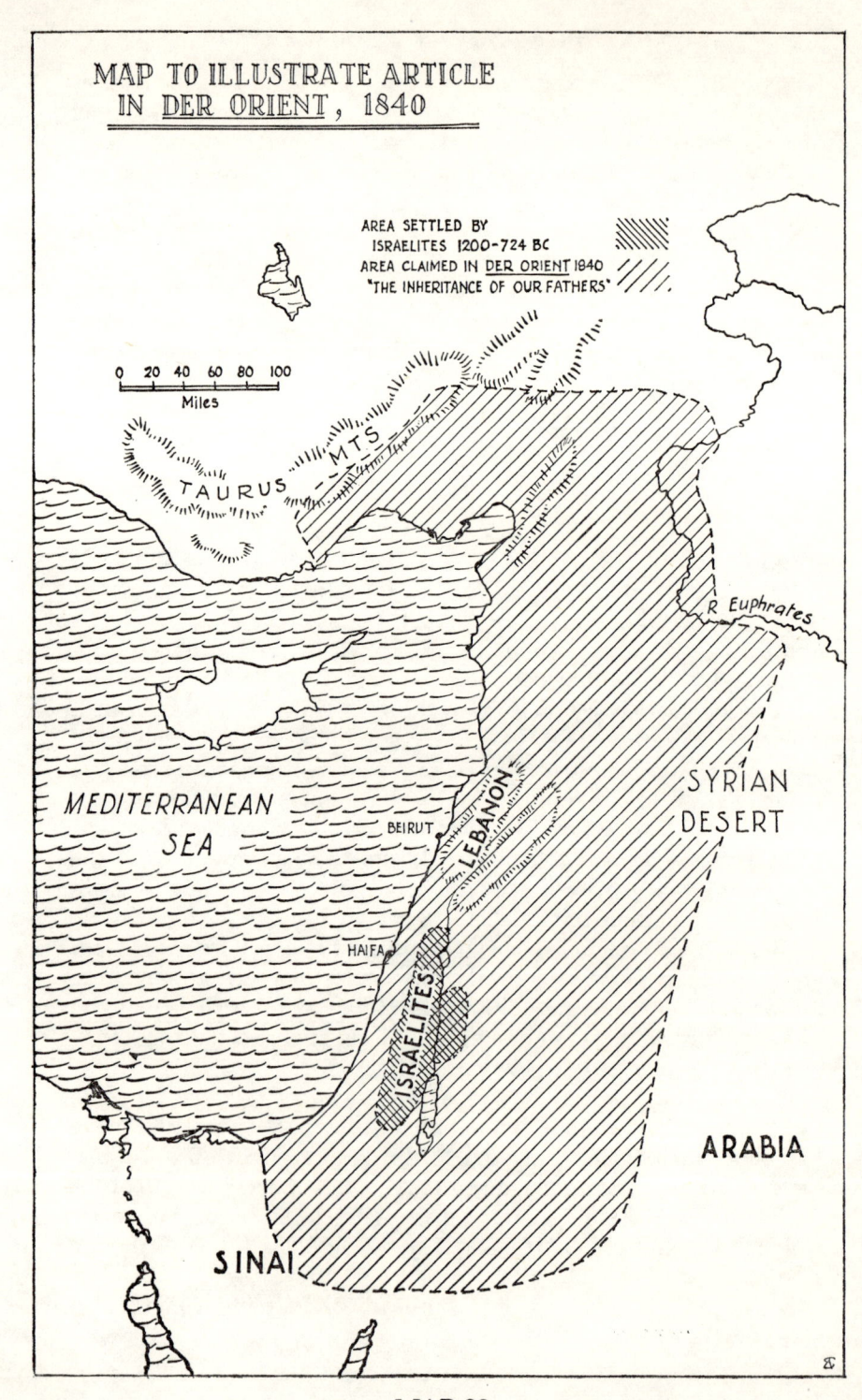

MAP 28

somewhat fanciful dreams. On 24th December, 1840, the London *Times* published an extract from *Der Orient*, which read as follows:

"We, the Jews, have a country, the inheritance of our fathers, finer, more fruitful, better situated for commerce, than many of the most celebrated portions of the globe. Environed by the deep-delled Taurus, the lovely shores of the Euphrates, the lofty steppes of Arabia and of rocky Sinai, our country extends along the shores of the Mediterranean crowned by the towering cedars of Lebanon, the source of a hundred rivulets and brooks, which spread fruitfulness over shady dales."

The area claimed in this romantic passage is shown on the map opposite.

The reader will remember that the only area occupied by the ancient Israelites was the mountain range of Judaea, Samaria, and Galilee, two thousand five hundred years ago. Ten out of the twelve tribes disappeared soon afterwards and cannot be traced. Judah alone survived as an imperial province until nearly two thousand years ago. Moreover, the Jews of today are not the lineal descendants of the Judaeans, but a mixture of innumerable ethnic stocks from Europe, Asia and Africa. In brief, this inspiring passage is almost pure fantasy.

* * *

The chaos produced in Egypt by Napoleon's invasion of 1798 led to the rise of an Albanian officer, Muhammad Ali, who became dictator of the country. Between 1831 and 1839, he annexed Palestine, Lebanon and Syria also. In 1840, however, Britain, Austria, Russia and Prussia compelled Muhammad Ali to withdraw, France alone supporting him.

"Public opinion had for a long time laboured under the impression that the intricacy of the Eastern Question was due much more to the conflicting interests of the Powers engaged in its solution than to any insurmountable barrier."[3] If the date were changed to 1970, this sage remark would remain equally true today. *Plus ça change, plus c'est la même chose.*[4]

During a rebellion in Syria against Muhammad Ali in 1840, a number of Jews were arrested in Damascus, and claimed to have been beaten by the police. At about the same time, Sir Moses Montefiore (1784–1885), a man much respected in England, paid a

[3] Nahum Sokolow, *A History of Zionism*.
[4] The more things change, the more they remain the same.

visit to Palestine. He hoped to buy land in Palestine and settle Jews upon it.

Writing in his diary at Safed in Galilee, on 24th May, 1839, Sir Moses says "the land in this neighbourhood seems to be particularly favourable for agricultural speculation. There are groves of olive trees, I should think, more than five hundred years old, vineyards, much pasture, plenty of wells and abundance of excellent water; also fig trees, walnuts, almonds, mulberries etc., and rich fields of wheat, barley and lentils." Later the diary continues, "many Jews now emigrate to New South Wales, Canada etc., but here they will find wells already dug, olives and vines already planted and a land so rich as to require little manure."[5]

This passage, written by an eminent Jewish philanthropist, is of interest today because Zionist propaganda has claimed in recent years that Palestine was a desert of rocks and sand before the establishment of the state of Israel.

Sir Moses visited Lord Palmerston to protest against the alleged police brutality in Damascus. His lordship replied that the Christians had suffered more than the Jews in these disturbances. Nevertheless, in 1841, Palmerston instructed British consular agents in the Levant "to afford their protection to all Jews" who were oppressed. The British Ambassador in Istanbul was also instructed to make representations to the Porte on behalf of Jews complaining of oppression.

To this day, Zionists protest forcibly in all Western capitals and secure the intervention of the Powers on behalf of their co-religionists, although no Western government pays any attention to the sufferings of Middle Eastern Christians.

Under the Treaty of London, in July 1841, Muhammad Ali evacuated Syria and Palestine in return for the recognition of his heirs as the hereditary rulers of Egypt.

The greatest British philanthropist of the time, Lord Shaftesbury, a devout Christian, was a warm supporter of Jewish settlement in Palestine. Indeed, correspondence in the press at the time was marked by the highest idealism, chiefly on the part of Christians, who regarded it as a fulfilment of prophecy. It never occurred to anyone that Jews might ever persecute anyone else. On the contrary, as themselves the victims of persecution they enjoyed the warmest humanitarian sympathy. No one spoke of the possibility of using force. All the land acquired for Jewish settlement was to be bought.

* * *

[5] Quoted by Nahum Solokow, op. cit.

Familiar patterns of international rivalry appeared in the second half of the nineteenth century. Ever since its emergence, the Russian Empire had cherished the ambition to acquire a naval base in the Mediterranean. In 1852, Russia claimed a protectorate over eleven million Orthodox Christians in the Ottoman Empire, a pretext for the destruction of the Ottomans. But the Western Powers were determined to keep the Russians out of the Mediterranean. The Crimean War resulted, and the Russian threat to Europe was averted for a hundred years.

In 1860, in Lebanon, the Druzes[6] attacked the Christians. On 9th July, riots broke out in Damascus, the Muslims killing a large number of Christians. The Ottoman Empire was increasingly decadent but was bolstered up by the Western Powers in order to keep the Russians out of the Mediterranean. In August 1860, a French force landed in Beirut, remaining until June 1861. The Ottoman governor of Syria was sentenced to death in connection with the Damascus riots.

By the Organic Statute of 6th September, 1864, negotiated between the Western European Powers and Turkey, Lebanon was made an autonomous state under a Christian governor, with direct access to the Sublime Porte, and not subject to Syria. The statute remained in force from 1864 to 1914.

* * *

The Disraeli family left Spain in the sixteenth century to escape the Inquisition and settled at Ferrara in Italy. About 1750, Benjamin Disraeli moved to England. His grandson, another Benjamin, was born in London in 1804, and was converted to Christianity at the age of thirteen.

In November, 1869, the Suez Canal, largely a French enterprise, was opened by the Empress Eugénie, the wife of Napoleon III. In 1875, however, when Disraeli was Prime Minister, the Khedive of Egypt, threatened with bankruptcy, sold his Suez Canal shares. Disraeli immediately borrowed four million pounds from the Rothschilds and bought the shares without parliamentary sanction. This stroke, so profitable for Britain, was carried out with remarkable initiative by two assimilated British Jews, without the knowledge of the British people. In 1882, owing to the breakdown of the Khedive's government, Britain intervened in Egypt. On 13th

[6] The Druze Community professes a secret pseudo-Muslim faith. They enjoyed a considerable reputation as fighters in their own mountains.

September, 1882, a British force under Sir Garnet Wolseley defeated the Egyptian army at Tel al Kabir, and occupied Cairo. Major Baring, later Lord Cromer, was appointed British Consul General. An unprecedented period of peace and prosperity followed for Egypt.

* * *

Baron Edmond de Rothschild was the first person to give financial support for Jewish agricultural colonies in Palestine. By 1897, there were some thirteen villages of Jews in Palestine, most of the colonists being from Russia or Roumania.

But coming events were already casting their shadows before. Ahad Ha-'Am,[7] the famous Jewish writer, already foresaw the end. "In 1861, Ahad Ha-'Am laid his finger on the ... fundamental though neglected problem of Zionism in Palestine—the Arab problem. He pointed out that there was little untilled soil in Palestine. He warned that the Jewish settlers must under no circumstances arouse the wrath of the natives by ugly actions, but must meet them rather in the friendly spirit of respect. 'Yet what do our brethren do in Palestine?' he asked. 'Just the very opposite! Serfs they were in the lands of the Diaspora and suddenly they find themselves in freedom, and this change has awakened in them an inclination to despotism. They treat the Arabs with hostility and cruelty, deprive them of their rights, offend them without cause and even boast of these deeds; and nobody among us opposes this despicable and dangerous inclination. We think that the Arabs are all savages, who live like animals and do not understand what is happening around. This is, however, a great error.' "[8]

These prophetic words were written by a great Jew in 1861. He penetrated the heart of the problem of Israel today, which lies in the psychological fact that those who have been treated with contempt by others, subconsciously lose confidence in themselves. They may attempt to conceal their inner doubts from outsiders by an assumption of arrogance, but their secret lack of confidence in themselves remains. It is for this reason that, when they find other people weaker than themselves, they practise upon them the same contempt and the same cruelties as they themselves have previously endured.

People often say to me, "How can those who have suffered so much inflict the same cruelties on others?" The reason is, I believe,

---

[7] This was a pen name. His real name was Asher Ginzberg.
[8] Dr. Hans Kohn, quoted by Moshe Menuhin, op. cit.

that many Israelis are subconsciously satisfying themselves that they are as good men as their former oppressors. A parallel instance is that of a workman who has been dismissed by his employer and who goes home and beats his wife. He does not know why he lost his temper with her that day, but the fact is that he is unconsciously trying to prove to himself that he is a big man too. This psychological reaction is common to the whole human race and not in any sense peculiar to Jews. Given the same background and experience, we should have behaved in the same way.

Ironically enough, the Egyptians suffer from the same disease as the Israelis. The strategic importance of their country has led to its occupation by every great empire since the Assyrians, two thousand five hundred years ago. This situation has resulted in many sarcastic and contemptuous remarks at their expense all down the centuries, producing in them subconscious or conscious feelings of inferiority and doubt—just as occurred with the Jews. The bellicose threats of the Egyptians and the arrogant ruthlessness of the Israelis are thus due to the same cause—the rudeness and contempt which they have suffered from others.

NOTABLE DATES

End of Arab Rule in Spain	1492
Discovery of the Cape Route by Vasco da Gama	1497
Papal Bull on Jewish Segregation	1515
Moses Mendelssohn	1729–1786
The French Revolution	1789
The Partition of Poland	1796
Napoleon's Invasion of Egypt	1798
Crimean War	1854–1856
French Landing in Lebanon	1860
Opening of the Suez Canal	1869
British purchase of Canal Shares	1875
Assassination of the liberal Alexander II	1881
British Occupation of Egypt	1882

CONCLUSIONS

(1) The sufferings inflicted on the Middle East peoples by Turks and Mongols from 1055 to 1517 were far greater than

any borne by Jews or heretics in the West, but have not been publicised in anything like the same way.

(2) Massacres of Jews in Western Europe were rare, but psychologically to live in an atmosphere of contempt was more injurious.

(3) Moses Mendelssohn (1729–1786) was one of the earliest thinkers who urged his fellow Jews to leave the ghetto and live like normal citizens. His writings divided Jews once again into internationalists and isolationists.

(4) The Partition of Poland in 1796 transferred large numbers of Polish Jews to Russia.

(5) Under the Ottomans, Jews in the Middle East were often rich and influential.

(6) Napoleon's invasion of Egypt in 1798 drew the attention of the Great Powers to the strategic importance of the Middle East. Russia, particularly, was determined to get a fleet into the Mediterranean.

(7) The establishment of Jewish agricultural colonies in Palestine was commenced in the middle of the nineteenth century. According to the famous Jewish writer, Ahad Ha-'Am, the colonists began immediately to act in a cruel and contemptuous manner towards the native Palestinians.

(8) Today, Israeli aggressiveness and Egyptian threats have the same cause; they are subconscious attempts to recover their self-respect by people who have often met with contempt.

XVI

The Coming of Zionism

Jewish influence in the Christian world reached its climax in the first quarter of the twentieth century... Meanwhile Jewish nationalists began to express the fear that if the Jews as a whole mingled with the Gentiles and became assimilated to them the entire community would eventually lose the Jewish individuality which it had hitherto preserved by segregation... They began, therefore, to dream of establishing a territorial centre for the Jews and so transforming Jewry... into a community kept together by nationalism.
Nevill Barbour, Nisi Dominus

The word *race* scientifically is meaningless, no less with Jews than with other sections of humanity.
Cecil Roth, A History of the Marranos

Disdain reservations and subterfuges, sharp practices and, evasions. Woe to him who builds his house thereon.
Maimonides, the Jewish Philosopher

All of our misfortunes come from the fact that the Jews want to climb too high. We have too much brains... All of the hatred against us stems from this.
Baron de Hirsch, the Jewish millionaire

XVI

NOW that we are entering the sphere of modern politics, may I, firstly, repeat my request to the reader to make a determined effort to free his mind of preconceived ideas. We are about to discuss an extremely complicated problem, which requires careful thought to evaluate the factors involved.

Secondly, there is no hero and no villain in this drama. Every situation "builds up" step by step. Every hasty action or rash statement provokes an even stronger response. Moreover, these actions and pronouncements grow out of experiences and inherited emotions thousands of years old, of which the present-day actors are not even aware.

Thirdly, having been intimately (though most unwillingly) involved in this problem for some thirty-five years, I constantly find myself confronted, by both sides, with bitter recriminations *concerning the past*. If I ask a Palestinian why the Mufti of Jerusalem allegedly caused his rivals to be assassinated, I receive the heated counter-question, "Why did the Jews blow up the King David Hotel?" Or conversely, if a Jew be asked why Israel used force in 1948 to conquer more territory, the angry reply is "Why did Nasser threaten to throw Israel into the sea?"

This endless exchange of mutual recriminations concerning the past serves only to intensify hatred. The only constructive way to approach the Middle East chaos of today is to let bygones be bygones, and to seek a solution. It is, of course, necessary to consider the "build-up" of the present situation by the actions and counter-actions of the persons involved, but not in a spirit of recrimination.

*   *   *

In the last chapter, we saw that Jews had obtained virtual equality with non-Jews all over the world in the second half of the nineteenth century, excepting in Russia. (Poland, of course, no longer existed.) In 1881, the liberal Czar Alexander II was assassinated, and Jews were found to have been involved. The crime led to a reaction against liberalism in Russia in general and against Jews in Russia in particular. There were anti-Jewish riots in 1881 and 1882, in which the actual casualties were not heavy, but in which repression was intensified.

As a result of this anti-Jewish violence, an organisation called "The Lovers of Zion" came into being in Russia, its first headquarters being in Odessa. It evoked little interest in the West, where Jews were already free and contented.

The interest of Western Jews was largely roused by Theodor Herzl (1860–1904), an Austrian Jew and a native of Vienna, who had previously been assimilated into Austrian life and culture. In his diaries, Herzl has left us a detailed description of his work. The first impression which the reader receives is one of an extraordinary proliferation of ideas, some broad, vague and romantic, others petty, trivial, even ridiculous—but always new ideas. A journalist and an author, he lived at one moment in a world of dreams, at the next in a maze of trivialities. Yet there must have been something more in him also. "Suddenly a compelling force had arisen, and he dominated us with his extraordinary personality, with his gestures, manner of speech, his ardour and vision."[1]

"I understand what anti-Semitism is about," wrote Herzl. "We Jews have maintained ourselves, even if through no fault of our own, as a foreign body among the different nations. In the ghetto, we have taken on a number of anti-social characteristics... Anti-Semitism is a consequence of the emancipation of the Jews. The peoples about us who lack a historical understanding... do not see us as a historical product... When we came out of the ghetto, we were... 'ghetto Jews'. We should have been allowed time to accustom ourselves to freedom." There is much food for thought in passages such as this.

Other entries seem trivial or quaint. "Circenses[2] as soon as possible. German theatre, international theater, opera, musical comedy, circus, café concert, Café Champs Elysées." (Herzl was in Paris as a reporter for the *Neue Freie Presse*.) "Moses made the mistake of leaving the fleshpots in Egypt. We shall take ours with us." "The High Priests will wear impressive robes; our cuirassiers, yellow trousers and white tunics; the officers, silver breastplates." It is impossible entirely to acquit Herzl of a certain megalomania. "In the Tuileries, before Gambetta's statue. I hope the Jews put up a more artistic one of me."

Herzl's principal activity consisted of visits to great people, to win them for his dream of a Jewish state. Kaiser Wilhelm II, Sultan

---
[1] Rabbi Mordecai Braude.
[2] The Roman word for public games.

Abdul Hamid of Turkey, Joseph Chamberlain, Pope Pius X, and the King of Italy were all on his visiting list. While visiting the great ones, he was acutely conscious of his own dramatic, almost Messianic, rôle. He was also passionately anxious to be correct. The cut of his grey frock-coat caused him anxiety. When received by the Kaiser, he notes that he forgot to remove the glove from his right hand—a breach of etiquette. The first Zionist Congress was held at Basle, in Switzerland, on 29th August, 1897. At the same period, an increasing number of Russian Jews began to emigrate to western Europe and North America, where they formed the principal advocates of the new Zionist movement. The Basle Congress declared the objects of Zionism to be twofold. Firstly, the promotion of Jewish "colonisation" in Palestine. Secondly, the binding together of world Jewry and the fostering of Jewish national sentiment and consciousness.

The first objective has received more publicity than the second, which, however, gives us a wider insight. The twentieth century has witnessed attempts all over the world to revive small "nations" and to recover their ancient languages. In Britain itself, the Irish, the Scots and the Welsh provide examples; in Europe, Czechs, Slovaks, Croats, Slovenes, Serbs; in the Middle East, the Kurds, and many more, which had previously been submerged in great empires.

To some extent, the objective of fostering "Jewish national sentiment" was part of this worldwide tendency, but in some ways it differed from them. The small "nations" mentioned were mostly of reasonably homogeneous ethnic origin and occupied a limited geographic area. Jews, as we have seen, are not of uniform ethnic origin, but the policy of isolationism which they have followed for two thousand five hundred years has created a similarity in their way of life, whether they be Slavs, Germans, Poles or Turks by racial origin.

Whereas, however, other small nationalities had limited geographical areas where they were in a majority, the Jews had not. The greatest concentrations of Jews for two thousand five hundred years have been in great commercial cities in other countries—Alexandria, Rome, Amsterdam, London, New York. On the analogy of other small nations, the Jews might claim that if they possessed a geographical area, they could retain their identity.

Here, however, a vital point of difference arises. The Czechs, the Serbs, the Basques or the Irish do not attempt to retain the political allegiance of their people who emigrate, and who soon become British, Americans, Australians or South Africans. The Zionists, on the other hand, claim that every Jew in the world is automatically a citizen of Israel, and owes his first loyalty to her and not to the country of his residence. This action tends to produce, in the places where Jews live, a feeling that they are not ordinary loyal subjects of their countries. Such a feeling is then denounced as anti-Jewish discrimination. Without attempting to praise or blame anyone, it will be seen that these attitudes do present a very real dilemma.

* * *

To return to the Zionist Congress in 1897, Nahum Sokolow[3] adds to his account a note that the "re-gaining"[4] of Palestine was not to be "by brute force or political adventure, and not by an act against the government or the population of the country."

As, however, he admits that there was a population, some explanation seems to be necessary as to how the Zionists were to take the country without using force. We shall see, however, that Mr. Sokolow's colleague, Dr. Weizmann, was a believer in progress by stages. The use of force was not appropriate in the early stages.

A notable feature of Mr. Sokolow's plans is their vagueness. "Palestine (and gradually the thinly populated neighbouring districts) can become a great outlet for Jewish population. Palestine can again be made to blossom like a rose, and be capable of supporting a great population as in the glorious days of David and Solomon. Vast tracts of the so-called Syrian desert are only regions deforested and wherever the hum of men comes peacefully, the arid soil bursts into life. The plains of the Hauran, the villages of the Jordan and the land of Gilead would form one of the richest and largest food-producing areas in the world."[5]

This poetic outburst is entirely devoid of facts. The Syrian desert, for example, is not de-forested, but the rainfall is inadequate for trees. The casual reader might not notice that, in an airy manner, Mr. Sokolow has included most of Jordan and Syria as available for Jewish settlement.

Referring to Palestine, Dr. George Adam Smith wrote in 1894, three years before the first Zionist Congress, "The idea that it [Palestine] can ever belong to one nation, even though this were the

---

[3] Nahum Sokolow, *A History of Zionism*.
[4] It is interesting to note how often the whole question is prejudged by the use of small words. "Re-gain" suggests that Jews once owned all Palestine, which is not correct.
[5] Nahum Solokow, *A History of Zionism*.

Jews, is contrary both to Nature and to Scripture."[6] We have already seen that the whole of Palestine never did belong to the Israelites, and indeed it is doubtful if they ever constituted a majority of the population. Yet Sokolow assumes that all Palestine "belongs to the Jews", and quietly annexes "vast tracts" of Syria and Jordan also.

Yet he also writes, "Zionism is not a source of conflict but a source of peace and unity . . . Zionism has never desired to use its influence to the disadvantage of non-Jews in Palestine." He also denounces the "manifest absurdity" of the idea that Zionism could be incompatible with the loyalty of a Jew to his country of residence—a dilemma which was to arise with increasing force.

Britain was still ready to help Jews from a humanitarian angle, especially as further anti-Jewish outbreaks occurred in Russia in 1903. In August 1903, Britain offered a large area of Uganda for Jewish settlement, but the offer was refused.

It is noticeable that Britain intended a humanitarian gesture, but neither the Zionists nor the British gave a moment's thought to the Ugandans. It is essential to remember that Zionism was conceived in the age of imperialism, when all Europe thought on these lines. Jews, who were ethnically largely Europeans, made their plans in complete disregard of the "natives" of the Middle East. Zionism and the Union of South Africa alone retain this colonialist mentality today.

In the British General Election of 1900, the English Zionist Federation sent a letter to all candidates, asking for a public expression of sympathy with Zionism, an early example of pressurisation on politicians in other countries.

* * *

The man who, more than any other, transformed Zionist dreams into action was Chaim Weizmann. Born near Pinsk in southern Russia, he went to Germany as a student at the age of eighteen. At the Berlin Polytechnic, he writes, "was an enormous Russian-Jewish student colony".[7] The anti-Jewish attitude of the Russian government produced a great migration of Jews to western Europe and the United States. There was little contact in Berlin between the Russian and German Jews, "most of whom were assimilationists", comments Weizmann bitterly.

[6] George Adam Smith, *The Historical Geography of the Holy Land.*
[7] Chaim Weizmann, *Trial and Error.*

In 1898, he moved to Freiburg. In neighbouring Switzerland, he met many Russian revolutionaries, Lenin and Plekhanov being there. The revolutionaries, he notes, accused Zionists of double loyalties. A Russian revolutionary, they said, could not simultaneously serve another cause. The Russian attitude seems to be unchanged today—no prejudice against Jews, but you cannot be simultaneously a loyal Russian and a Zionist. Weizmann also opposed Herzl and the Western Zionists, whom he criticised as being bourgeois. In 1904, Dr. Weizmann moved to Manchester, where he worked on chemistry.

Meanwhile, in Russia, tens of thousands of young Jews were joining the revolutionaries, where the *Bund* was a Jewish revolutionary organisation. Thousands of Jews were imprisoned, not as Jews but as revolutionaries. In 1903, there was a pogrom at Kishinev, the first since 1881. Forty-five Jews were killed, out of five million Jews in Russia.

In the 1906 British election, Arthur Balfour was a candidate in Manchester. Weizmann obtained an interview with him and half an hour's conversation. "It is curious," Mr. Balfour is alleged to have said, "but the Jews I meet are quite different." "Mr. Balfour, you meet the wrong kind of Jews," Weizmann says that he replied. Mr. Balfour's Jewish friends were assimilated and looked upon themselves as loyal British subjects. Dr. Weizmann represented the Russian Jews, the sworn foes of assimilation, whose bitter isolationism had been intensified by persecution.

The continuous migration of Russian Jews to England began to tip the balance. "The old English-Jewish families might just as well have belonged to another world," writes Chaim Weizmann. At the eighth Zionist Congress in The Hague in 1907, the "Western" president, Dr. Wolffsohn, was ousted. Weizmann had been one of the principal speakers. The same year, he paid his first visit to Palestine.

After the outbreak of war in 1914, Weizmann met C. P. Scott, the editor of the *Manchester Guardian*, and, in December 1914, he saw Mr. Lloyd George, in company with C. P. Scott and Mr. Herbert Samuel. The latter then submitted a memorandum to the Prime Minister, Mr. Asquith, suggesting that Britain annex Palestine after the war, and "plant" in it three or four thousand Jews. "I confess that I am not attracted to this proposed addition to our responsibilities," noted Asquith in his diary on 28th January, 1915. Later he added that "curiously enough, the only other partisan of this proposal is Lloyd George, who does not care a damn for the Jews or their past or their future". Meanwhile, another group of Zionists opened an office in Denmark. They believed in a German victory, and opposed any contacts with Britain.

Dr. Weizmann's autobiography impresses the Gentile reader with the extreme readiness of the Zionists to change their country. Born in Russia, he had lived in Germany, Switzerland and England. A few years before 1914, he nearly returned to Germany. His associates led similar lives, their loyalty being to Jewry alone. The only exceptions which he mentions were the British Jews, who regarded themselves as British citizens whose religion was Judaism. Dr. Weizmann regarded them as "assimilationists", his bitterest enemies.

Our task is not to blame the Zionists or the assimilationists, who regarded themselves as sincere French, British or American citizens of the Jewish religion. Our only task is to diagnose the problem. The stream of Russian Jews who have arrived in the West in the last fifty years, and the apparent triumphs of Israel, have today resulted in the majority of Jews in Britain, America and France being of the type praised by Weizmann, Jews first and only loyal to their countries of residence to a much smaller degree.

Yet as citizens of these Western nations, these new immigrants from eastern Europe can, and often do, achieve high positions in the governments, the newspapers, the politics, the banks, or the industries of their countries of residence. A very reasonable Hungarian recently said to me, "Our country, I am glad to say, is now almost free of Jews. Many of them were extremely capable and valuable men, but one knew that their loyalty was not to Hungary but to world Jewry. In the interests of Jewry, they would, if necessary, betray Hungary. This gave us an uncomfortable feeling, while they were in our midst."

The Zionists largely agreed, and indeed used such statements as an argument. Jews, they said, are a peculiar people. Only when they have a country of their own will they become like anyone else. The fallacy in this argument is that Palestine today holds only two and a half million Jews, of an estimated sixteen million in the world. But Israel is not willing to allow Jews in other countries to be assimilated, as are Greeks, Italians, Irish or English emigrants to America.

We therefore face a predicament. Either the great majority of Jews must live in Israel, necessitating the conquest of all Syria, Palestine, Lebanon and Jordan, and the liquidation of their inhabitants. Or alternatively, a continuance of the present situation in which many of the most powerful citizens in the West are Jews, some of whom may feel only a secondary loyalty to the countries in which they live.

There is an interesting diatribe in Weizmann's autobiography. "The Jews of Germany," he says, "had captured the German stage, press, commerce and universities and were putting into their pockets, only a hundred years after emancipation, everything the Germans had built up in centuries." The Germans resented "having to receive so much moral and material culture at the hands of the Jews", who, says Weizmann, had been largely responsible for the German chemical industry and for progress in every branch of science. "The crux of the Jewish problem was that those Jews, who were giving their energy and their brains to the Germans, were doing it in their capacity as Germans, and were enriching Germany and not Jewry."

In this revealing quotation, Dr. Weizmann disapproves of those Jews who give devoted service to their native countries. Yet his assistant, Dr. Sokolow, denounces as a "manifest absurdity" the idea that Zionism could conflict with the devotion of a Jew to his country of residence.

The unhappy dilemma of Jewry is plain. Segregation, voluntary or imposed, made them a peculiar people. They complained of their treatment until the Western nations removed all their disabilities, whereupon they began to transform themselves into ordinary French, British or American citizens. Dr. Sokolow stated that Zionism had two objectives, to occupy Palestine and to revitalise Jewish "national" sentiment, an objective which involved making Jews, in other countries, Jews first and French, British, Americans or South Africans second. Many small ethnic groups, as we have seen, have tried to revitalise their ancient languages and traditions, but none have claimed the political loyalty of their emigrants, who have become citizens of other states.

Isolation—or the ghetto—made the Jews a peculiar people, and with the end of the ghetto, they tend to become ordinary citizens. But the Zionists do not want this either. In Israel, it may be argued, they have made a larger and a better ghetto, where they can remain isolated, a peculiar people, segregated from the rest of mankind.

* * *

In 1916, Weizmann moved to London and obtained employment on chemical work under the Admiralty. He was now the leader of the Zionists in Britain, and made himself intimate with many leading politicians. Palestine, Syria, Lebanon and Iraq were behind the Turkish lines, and their peoples could not be consulted. Egypt had, at that time, no interest in the Arab countries east of Sinai. The

Zionists, accordingly, had no opponents in Britain, except the old Anglo-Jewish families.

In 1915, a Turko-German force crossed Sinai to the Suez Canal, but was repulsed. The British advanced slowly across Sinai to Gaza, but the operations dragged. No more troops could be spared from the Western Front. Local help was needed. From Cairo, the British High Commissioner, Sir Henry MacMahon, corresponded with Sharif[8] Husain in Mecca. Sharif Husain asked for a British pledge of independence after the war for the Arabs east of Sinai.

In subsequent correspondence, Lebanon was excluded. The sharif was told of an Anglo-French proposal to share economic and administrative benefits. No formal agreement was signed, but the Arabs trusted British good faith and rebelled against the Turks in June 1916. The subsequent military assistance received from the Arabs materially assisted the allied cause in the Middle East.

On 16th May, 1916, Britain and France signed the Sykes-Picot Agreement dividing the economic benefits in the proposed Arab State. The sharif had been told of this, even if, perhaps, in rather vague terms. There was no suggestion of concessions to the Jews in Palestine, for Asquith was still Prime Minister.

In December 1916, however, Lloyd George, whom Weizmann had already cultivated as a friend, became Prime Minister. On 17th February, 1917, a Zionist Conference was held in London, attended by Sir Mark Sykes on the instructions of Lloyd George. The memorandum submitted to the British government, embodied two points: firstly, that Jews in Palestine should be recognised as "the Jewish nation", a phrase meant to suggest that all Jews were a single ethnic stock, which we have seen is not the case. For two thousand five hundred years, the bond uniting Jews had been religion, but religion did not constitute a claim to land. The Zionists also attached importance to the phrase, "the land of our fathers", which conveyed the impression of a single ethnic stock, without actually telling a lie.

Secondly, the memorandum insisted that the Suzerain (already visualised as Britain) would grant free immigration to Jews from all over the world. Aware that Palestine was already populated by natives, they required outside protection until they could bring in enough Jews to form a majority. Thereafter, either by a demand for free elections or by the use of force, they would be able to form a Jewish state. Meanwhile, however, the armed protection of an outside Power would be necessary to repress any resistance by the Palestinians.

[8] Pronounced shareef.

Sir Mark Sykes warned the meeting of the rising nationalist feeling among the Arabs, who, he said, "had intelligence, vitality, and linguistic unity. But he believed the Arabs would come to terms with us—*particularly if they received Jewish support in other matters.*"[9]

Addressing this same meeting, Weizmann claims that he said that to set up a Jewish republic immediately would be premature. "The way to achieve it is through a series of intermediary stages." This was a candid admission of the policy of "little by little". Yet, for many years, the Zionists were indignantly to deny any ambition to form a Jewish state.

"I need hardly say," he added, "that we Jews will be meticulously and scrupulously careful to respect the sentiments of any religious group or sect in Palestine."[10]

Dr. Weizmann notes that Jewish capitalists in the United States were strongly opposed to Zionism. The American Jewish Year Book for 1918 stated, "The American Zionists represent, according to the most recent statistics available, only a small proportion of the Jews living in this country, 150,000 out of 3,500,000." The total world Zionist membership in 1917 was 250,000 out of 12,000,000 Jews.

Immediately after the Russian revolution in 1917, all religious disabilities were abolished. Russian Jews celebrated it with enthusiasm, many of them having played a leading part in bringing it about.

* * *

In May 1917, the Board of Deputies of British Jews and the Anglo-Jewish Association published a joint manifesto in *The Times*, which stated, "Zionist theory regards all the Jewish communities of the world as constituting one homeless nationality incapable of complete social and political identification with the nations among whom they dwell and it is argued that for this homeless nationality a political centre and an always available homeland in Palestine are necessary. Against this theory, the conjoint committee strongly and earnestly protest. Emancipated Jews in this country regard themselves primarily as a religious community, and they have always based their claims to political equality with their fellow citizens of other creeds on this assumption—that they have no separate aspirations in a political sense.

"The second point in the Zionist programme which has aroused

---

[9] Chaim Weizmann, *Trial and Error*. The italics are his.
[10] Chaim Weizmann, op. cit.

the misgivings of the conjoint committee is the proposal to invest the Jewish settlers in Palestine with certain special rights in excess of those enjoyed by the rest of the population ... Any such action would prove a veritable calamity for the whole Jewish people. In all the countries in which they live the principle of equal rights for all religious denominations is vital for them."

Dr. Weizmann, when replying to this manifesto, said in a letter to *The Times*: "The Zionists are not demanding in Palestine monopolies or exclusive privileges ... It always was and remains a cardinal principle of Zionism as a democratic movement that all races and sects in Palestine should enjoy full justice and liberty."

Yet the mandate was to give the Jews in Palestine exactly that special position. Although in 1919, Mr. Sokolow was to deny indignantly that a Jewish State formed any part of the Zionist programme, Lord Rothschild wrote in 1917, "We Zionists cannot see how the establishment of an autonomous Jewish State ... can be considered for a moment to be in any way subversive ..."

On 1st October, 1917, the *Manchester Guardian* wrote, "How can we, as champions of the cause of nationality, refuse our sympathy to the attempt to end the age-long exile of the Jewish people from their political home in Palestine?" As champions of the cause of nationality, the *Manchester Guardian* failed to consider that Palestine was already occupied by another nation.

The Balfour Declaration was issued on 2nd November, 1917, in the form of a letter from Mr. Balfour to Lord Rothschild.

It read as follows:

"His Majesty's Government view with favour the establishment in Palestine of a National Home for the Jewish people, and will use their best endeavours to facilitate the achievement of this object, it being clearly understood that nothing shall be done which may prejudice the civil and religious rights of the existing non-Jewish communities in Palestine, or the rights and political status enjoyed by Jews in any other country."

Mr. Sokolow hailed the declaration by saying: "Our ancient home has again arisen for civilisation. For nineteen centuries it has been made a desert," the usual rhapsodic generalisation of which we have already seen the falsity. Judaea under the Hasmonaeans and the Herods was not particularly civilised. Under the Roman, Byzantine and Arab empires, however, it progressed very considerably.

Since the Ottoman conquest in 1517, it had fallen behind the industrial nations of the West, but so had all of Asia and Africa. Considerable progress in education had been made in recent years and the country, largely agricultural, was quiet and reasonably prosperous. Jaffa oranges, grown by Palestinians, were world famous before the First World War.

Some of the British press commentaries make wry reading:

"A large and thriving Jewish settlement in the Holy Land ... would make for peace and progress in the Near East" (*Spectator*).[11] "To make Palestine once more prosperous and populous, with a population attached to the British Empire, there is only one hopeful way, and that is to effect a Zionist restoration" (*New Statesman*).[11]

Nobody foresaw that, twenty-five years later, Zionists in Palestine would be loading Britain with violent abuse and blowing up and murdering British officials, soldiers and police. No one suspected that Zionist settlement in the Holy Land would make for endless war and ruin in the Near East. Yet, in reality, this outcome was already obvious, for it was even then evident that the Zionists planned to seize Palestine and dispose of its inhabitants.

On 2nd December, 1917, a great demonstration was held in the Albert Hall in London, under the presidency of Lord Rothschild.

On this occasion, Lord Robert Cecil made a speech which included the following sentiments: "The keynote of our meeting this afternoon is liberation. We welcome among us not only the many thousands of Jews that I see, but also representatives of the Arabian and Armenian races, who are also in this great struggle, struggling to be free. Our wish is that Arabian countries be for the Arabs, Armenia for the Armenians and Judaea[12] for the Jews.

"There are two great foundations upon which the policy of this country has always been based. I believe that they are often desscribed by the two words, 'Liberty and Justice'. We hear a great deal of a new word 'Self Determination'. One of the great steps we have taken in carrying out this principle is the recognition of Zionism." Lord Robert Cecil was an idealist. Perhaps the explanation of this eloquent speech is that he believed Palestine to be an empty desert, a statement frequently made by Zionists. Unfortunately Palestine was already populated and Britain had already promised "self-determination" to the Palestinians.

His peroration, however, was truer than he suspected. "I don't like to prophesy what ultimate results that great event (the establishment of the Jewish home in Palestine) may have, but for myself I believe it will have a far-reaching influence on the history of the

---

[11] Quoted by Solokow, op. cit.

[12] Judaea was of course only a small area in Palestine, but idealists rarely study maps.

world, and consequences which none can foresee on the future history of the human race."

The only strong opposition to the Balfour Declaration in the British cabinet was that of Edwin Montagu, an "assimilated" British Jew. He was, doubtless, aware that one of the principal aims of Zionism was to make "assimilation" impossible.

NOTABLE DATES

Assassination of Alexander II	1881
Action against Jews in Russia	1881 and 1882
First Zionist Congress in Basle	1897
British offer of Uganda	1903
Kishinev "pogrom"	1903
Weizmann comes to Manchester	1904
Pledge of self-determination to Arabs east of Sinai	1916
Dr. Weizmann moves to London	1916
Balfour Declaration	1917

CONCLUSIONS

(1) By 1881, Jews had won equality in almost every country. In that year, as a result of the murder of Alexander II, repression of Jews was resumed in Russia.
(2) Consequently Jews from Russia migrated to the West. These east European Jews had never tasted liberation and equality, and were bitter and isolationist. It was they who ultimately overcame the assimilated Jews of France, Britain and America and carried through the Zionist programme. Western Jews were originally strongly opposed to isolationism and regarded Judaism as a religion.
(3) It was principally Chaim Weizmann who made himself intimate with British politicians and persuaded them to issue the Balfour Declaration.

XVII

The Mandate

The Allied Powers ... have entrusted to my country a Mandate to watch over the interests of Palestine, and to ensure to your country that peaceful and prosperous development which has so long been denied to you.
You are well aware that the ... Powers have decided that measures be adopted to secure ... a National Home for the Jewish People.
I realise profoundly the solemnity of the trust involved in the government of a country which is sacred alike to Christians, Muhammedans and Jews, and I will watch with deep interest and warm sympathy the future progress and development of a state whose history has been of such tremendous import to the world.

*Message from His Majesty King George V
to the People of Palestine, 7th July, 1920*

And now a word to the Jews in Palestine. I have no doubt that they are going about it the wrong way. The Palestine of the Biblical conception is not a geographical tract. It is in their hearts. But if they must look to Palestine as their national home, it is wrong to enter it under the shadow of the British gun ... They can settle in Palestine only by the goodwill of the Arabs.

MAHATMA GANDHI (1917)

XVII

ON 8th January, 1918, President Woodrow Wilson delivered an address to Congress in which he stated his famous fourteen points. Point Twelve read as follows:
"The Turkish portions of the present Ottoman Empire should be assured a secure sovereignty, but the other nationalities which are now under Turkish rule should be assured an undoubted security of life and an absolutely unmolested opportunity of autonomous development."

This paragraph reaffirms the basis of the discussions between Sir Henry MacMahon and Sharif Husain in 1915 and 1916 to the effect that the Arabic-speaking countries east of Sinai would be given self-determination after the war. It cannot be a pledge of support to the Zionists, who had never been under Turkish rule. The future Israelis were, in 1918, still Russians, Poles and Germans. But President Woodrow Wilson also expressed support for Zionism. The president, like Lord Robert Cecil, was an idealist, and, also like him, had omitted to study the facts.

As we have seen, only two hundred and fifty thousand out of an estimated twelve million Jews were Zionists. Even Dr. Weizmann admitted that "the Jews were against us". The issue of the Balfour Declaration was an extraordinary tribute to the skill of Dr. Weizmann and his little group in London, who, by their cultivation of the intimate friendship of men like Lloyd George and Balfour, persuaded them to support their plans.

Applying his little-by-little technique, Weizmann, though clearly envisaging the final objective of the seizure of all Palestine, always asked for small concessions, moderately worded. Once this concession was won, he immediately started to demand another.

The Zionists, moreover, already followed the policy of harassment, which they have since developed extensively, constantly bringing pressure to bear on those whom they wish to influence. Consequently, waverers agree to their demands, if only for a quiet life, and opponents remain silent to escape constant attack.

* * *

In 1919, Dr. Sokolow summarised Zionist demands as follows:

(1) The Homeland of the Jewish people must be in Palestine.

(2) Palestine must be made capable of fulfilling this function by patient colonisation.

(3) Recognition must be accorded to the rightful claim of the Jewish people to regenerate Palestine.

This summary is full of phrases, quietly assumed to be true, though in reality false. "The Homeland of the Jewish people must be in Palestine." If the modern Jews were descendants of the Judaeans, they might perhaps claim Judaea. But they are not. The "Arabs" of Palestine are probably more closely related to the Judaeans than are modern Russian or German Jews. If the claim were to Judaea, "in Palestine" would be correct, but in his next sentence Dr. Sokolow includes all Palestine.

"The *rightful* claim of the Jewish people to *regenerate* Palestine." It is difficult to see what rightful claim modern world Jewry has to seize Palestine. The controversial phrase "the Jewish people" suggests, without actually stating, that Jews are the ethnic descendants of the ancient Judaeans. What is meant by regenerate? Zionists sometimes point to motorways or concrete flats and say that, in Turkish times, there were only horses or donkeys. But this "regeneration" has occurred all over the world, in Beirut, Amman, Damascus—even in London and Washington.

If moral regeneration be intended, a peaceful agricultural province has, with its neighbours, been endlessly soaked in blood. To say such things today is to be denounced as anti-Semitic, a hater of Jews. But it may be pointed out that, when Dr. Sokolow wrote, ninety-eight per cent of Jews were not Zionists. Even today, it is possible to feel a deep sympathy with Jews and their dilemma, and yet to think that their attempted conquest of Palestine by force is a mistake.

"But," continues Sokolow, "it has been said and is still being obstinately repeated by anti-Zionists again and again, that Zionism aims at the creation of an independent 'Jewish state'. But this is wholly fallacious. The Jewish state was never a part of the Zionist programme." Yet Theodor Herzl, the founder of Zionism, wrote a book called *The Jewish State*.

Mr. Sokolow and Dr. M. Gaster were Dr. Weizmann's closest colleagues. At the Albert Hall meeting referred to in the previous chapter, Dr. Gaster said, "What they wished to obtain in Palestine was not merely a right to establish colonies... They wanted to establish in Palestine an autonomous Jewish Commonwealth in the fullest sense of the word." The key to all this double talk seems to be that the Zionists knew perfectly well what they wanted, but that Dr. Weizmann preferred to advance little by little, concealing the ultimate objective.

Nahum Sokolow also mentions, as a further objective, the rebirth of Jewish culture and civilisation. The meaning is not explained. The age of David, we have seen, was a blood-soaked tribalism, typical of primitive races. Is he referring to the culture of the Hasmonaeans or the Herodians? The Israelites and Judaeans were primitive mountain tribes, always less cultured than their neighbours the Egyptians, the Philistines or the Tyrians. Jews today, admittedly, are in many cases extremely cultured, but their culture is that of Europe and North America.

"Jews are not anxious to acquire military power," adds Mr. Sokolow. "They reject and condemn the idea of subjugating any other people. They want to be united in an organic community, to feel entirely at home.

"Zionists," he adds, "are Jews, idealists, the People of the Book; all they seek for is life in peace."

* * *

The opinion of a Jew, who wrote in the early days of Zionism, may here be quoted. "The superficial appearance of a national entity," writes Israel Abrahams, "has, I fear, originated the movement now popular with some modern Jews in favour of creating a Jewish state, politically independent and perhaps religiously homogeneous. I speak regretfully because one does not like to see enthusiasm wasted over a conception which has no roots in the past and no fruits to offer for the future.

"The idealised love of Zion which grew up in the Middle Ages had no connection whatever with this process of nationalisation through which Judaism has passed... National aspirations are nursed by persecution, but the medieval longing for the Holy Land grew up, not in persecution, but in the sunshine of literature. The Spanish-Jewish poet... came to Jerusalem as the medieval troubadour loved his lady, and the love grew with the days. Jehuda Halevi uses the very language of medieval love in this passionate address to his woe-begone darling:

> Oh! Who will lead me on to seek
> The spots where in far-distant years,
> The angels in their glory dawned upon
> Thy messengers and seers?

> Oh! Who will give me wings
> That I may fly away,
> And there, at rest from all my wanderings,
> The ruins of my heart among thy ruins lay?

"The same Jehuda Halevi[1] who sings thus declared that Israel was to the nations as the heart to the body—not a nation of the nations but a vitalising element to them all."[2]

* * *

On 5th March, 1919, thirty prominent American Jews submitted a protest to President Woodrow Wilson, saying in part:

"We raise our voices in warning and protest against the demand of the Zionists for the reorganisation of the Jews as a national unit to whom, now or in the future, territorial sovereignty in Palestine shall be committed ... For the very reason that the new era upon which the world is entering aims to establish government everywhere on principles of true democracy, we reject the Zionist project of a 'National Home' for the Jewish people in Palestine."

* * *

On 8th March, 1918, a Zionist commission, led by Dr. Weizmann, left London for Palestine. The war was going badly. The German offensive on the Western Front opened on 21st March, and many British troops in Palestine were being withdrawn to France.

When the British army entered Palestine from Gaza in November 1917, it found a country inhabited by a peaceful, friendly population, who offered their co-operation. The army knew nothing of the busy political intrigues in London, and felt little enthusiasm for the Zionist Commission, which claimed that they were going to take over the country. The orthodox Jews in Palestine were even more resentful. Themselves completely arabicised, they had nothing in common with these Russian politicians. Dr. Weizmann was no less impatient with the army. Knowing himself the personal friend of Lloyd George, Balfour and the leading London politicians, he could not but regard colonels and generals as rather small fry.

---

[1] Jehuda Halevi (1086–1145) was born in Toledo, Spain. "His love of Zion was a purely sublimated, religious spiritual attachment to the Holy Land with no political implications." Moshe Menuhin, op. cit.

[2] Israel Abrahams, *Jewish Life in the Middle Ages*.

Speaking in Palestine on 27th April, 1918, Dr. Weizmann said that "all fears expressed openly or secretly by the Arabs that they are to be ousted from their present position are due either to a fundamental misconception of Zionist aims or to the malicious activities of our common enemies."[3]

In June 1918, Dr. Weizmann visited the Ameer Feisal, who was commanding the Arab army on the right of the British line. He himself tells how he "stressed the fact that there was a great deal of room in the country if intensive development were applied, and that the lot of the Arabs would be greatly improved through our work there." At about the same time, but before a different audience, he said that he wished "to make Palestine as Jewish as England is English".

When British and American leaders had been won over by Dr. Weizmann's soothing syrup, how was the simple Feisal to see through the warm and friendly assurances which he received?

Meanwhile, to other audiences, Dr. Weizmann asserted that "the Jews possess an inalienable right to the possession of Palestine". Modern publicity experts allege that the public believes anything which is repeated sufficiently often. The idea becomes familiar, and the mind absorbs it unconsciously, without pausing to examine its veracity.

A curious commentary on the inalienable right to possess Palestine is provided by the question: What is a Jew? "The question is less simple than it seems. In Jewish Law, a person is a Jew if he is the child of a Jewish mother or has been converted by a recognised rabbinical court. The Minister of the Interior, Israel Bar Yehuda, has ruled that 'Jewish nationality' could, for purposes of registration, be applied to anyone who declared himself a Jew and did not profess any other faith."[4] Yet it scarcely seems reasonable that anyone who declares himself a Jew should thereby acquire an inalienable right to the ownership of Palestine, and that, to make room for him, the native Palestinians must be evicted.

It is to be noted also, that this definition of a Jew is purely religious. Yet, only a few months ago, when I was discussing this problem with a German Jew, he assured me that ninety-eight per cent of modern Israelis are atheists—an exaggeration no doubt. The qualification necessary, as attributed by Mr. Bermant to the Minister of the Interior, is that the applicant should not profess any other religion. Atheists are, therefore, permissible, but no Christian, Muslim or Hindu can presumably qualify.

* * *

[3] Quoted by Nevill Barbour, *Nisi Dominus*.   [4] Chaim Bermant, *Israel*.

On 23rd February, 1919, the Council of Ten at the Peace Conference of Versailles, heard the Zionist delegation. Dr. Sokolow put forward "the historic claim of the Jewish people to Palestine". Dr. Weizmann followed, stating that "the Jewish problem revolved fundamentally round the homelessness of the Jewish people". But we have just seen that religion is the only basis on which a man may claim to be a Jew. "The homelessness of the Jewish people", therefore, means the homelessness of people who claim to practise Judaism or who profess no religion. I am not aware of any other claim to the sole ownership of a country based on religion or atheism alone.

The last speaker for the Zionists was Mr. Sylvain Levi, a French Jew, who began by praising the work of the Rothschild Jewish colonies in Palestine. He then, however, raised certain doubts.

Firstly, that Palestine was a poor country, that the Jews had a higher standard of living than the Arabs, and would tend to dispossess them.

Secondly, that the Jews who would go to Palestine would be mainly Russian Jews, who had explosive tendencies.

Thirdly, that a Jewish National Home in Palestine would place Jews living in other countries in the embarrassing situation of having double loyalties.

The Zionist delegation was extremely angry, but Mr. Lansing, the United States Secretary of State, eased the tension by asking Dr. Weizmann, "What do you mean by a Jewish National Home?" Dr. Weizmann, in answer, "defined the Jewish National Home to mean the creation of an administration which would arise out of the natural conditions of the country—always safeguarding the interests of non-Jews".[5] According to Dr. Weizmann, Mr. Lansing commented that this was quite clear. It is open to doubt whether the reader will agree with him.

Dr. Weizmann also came to an agreement with the Ameer Feisal, who was at Versailles to represent his father, Sharif (then King) Husain. Feisal, however, inserted in the text a note stating that such an agreement would depend on the fulfilment of the allied pledges to the Arabs and would otherwise be void. The allied pledges were never fulfilled.

As Palestine had been promised self-determination, King Husain had been alarmed by the Balfour Declaration. The British government quieted his anxieties with the following message: "So far as Palestine is concerned, we are determined that no people shall be subjected to another but in view of the fact, (a) that there are in

[5] Chaim Weizmann, *Trial and Error*.

Palestine ... Holy Places ... of interest to vast masses of people ... there must be a special régime to deal with such places approved by the world.[6] (b) That as regards the Mosque of Omar [*sic*], it shall be considered as a Muslim concern alone, and shall not be subjected directly or indirectly to any non-Muslim authority.[7] That since the Jewish opinion of the world is in favour[8] of a return of the Jews to Palestine, and inasmuch as His Majesty's Government view with favour the realisation of this aspiration, His Majesty's Government are determined that, *in so far as is compatible with the freedom of existing populations, both economic and political*,[9] no obstacle should be put in the way of the realisation of this ideal."

It will be seen that the Zionists were not the only people who indulged in meaningless double-talk.

* * *

Article 22 of the League of Nations Covenant defined a mandate, stating that "peoples not yet able to stand by themselves under the strenuous conditions of the modern world (should be entrusted as) a sacred trust of civilisation to advanced nations ... Certain communities formerly belonging to the Turkish Empire have reached a stage of development where their existence as independent nations can be provisionally recognised ... The wishes of these communities must be a principal consideration in the selection of the Mandatory."[10] In fact no attempt was made to follow the wishes of the Palestinians, ninety-three per cent of whom were "Arabs". Of the seven per cent who were Jews, some four per cent were Arabicised Orthodox Jews, who, Dr. Weizmann alleges, were opposed to Zionism.

The Mandate for Palestine as passed by the League of Nations mentions the words Jew or Zionist twelve times. There is only one reference to "other sections of the population", although they formed ninety-three per cent of the inhabitants.

The full text is too long to quote, but the following extracts are of interest. "The Mandatory shall be responsible for placing the country under such ... conditions as will secure the establishment of the Jewish National Home ... and also for safeguarding the civil

---

[6] At the time of writing, 1970, all the Holy Places are held by Israel. The United Nations have repeatedly protested in vain.

[7] It is now held by Israel.

[8] This does not appear to have been true. Dr. Weizmann repeatedly complains that the Jews were against him.

[9] The italics are mine.

[10] See also Nevill Barbour, op. cit.

and religious rights of all the inhabitants of Palestine." "A Jewish Agency shall be recognised for ... the establishment of the Jewish National Home, and the interests of the Jewish population of Palestine." "The Zionist Organisation shall be recognised." "The Administration of Palestine ... shall facilitate Jewish immigration ... and shall encourage close settlement by Jews on the land," and so on.

Nobody could possibly guess, on reading this document, that ninety-three per cent of the Palestine population were non-Jews. The Mandate was "fixed" in New York, the city with the greatest Jewish population in the world. It has been described as a charter for the Zionist invasion and conquest of Palestine, utterly regardless of the "natives".

On 27th March, 1923, Lord Grey of Falloden made a speech in the House of Lords from which the following passages are an extract:

"I seriously suggest to the government that the best way of clearing our honour is officially to publish the whole of the engagements ... which we entered into during the war ... I think ... that we should state frankly that, in the urgency of war, engagements were entered into which were not entirely consistent.

"I am sure that we cannot redeem our honour by ... pretending that there is no inconsistency. The Balfour Declaration ... promised a Zionist home without prejudice to the civil and religious rights of the population of Palestine. A Zionist home, my Lords, undoubtedly means or implies a Zionist government, and as ninety-three per cent of the population are Arabs, I do not see how you can establish other than an Arab Government without prejudice to their civil rights ...

"I should like to say very seriously to the government that, unless they can ... prevent this question from drifting till there really is a hostile population ... they may find themselves in the impossible position of either having to abandon the commitment ... or to uphold it ... by a use of force of which they would find the country is not prepared to approve."[11] The whole course of events which led to ultimate disaster was thus foreseen in 1923.

The Zionists wished Britain to remain in Palestine and to protect them from the resentment of the native population until, by immigration, they attained a majority. They would then demand a democratic constitution, and the end of "British imperialism" (which they themselves had brought about).

* * *

[11] Hansard, vol. 53, 27th March, 1923.

From 1918 onwards, the Zionists behaved as if Palestine belonged to them. General Bols, the first military administrator of the country, reported as follows in connection with a disturbance in Jerusalem in 1920, in which six Jews were killed (Dr. Weizmann calls it a pogrom). "When the strain came, the Zionist Commission did not loyally accept the orders of the administration, but from the commencement, adopted a hostile, critical and abusive attitude... They seek... that in every question in which a Jew is interested discrimination in his favour shall be shown."

In December 1927, Dr. Weizmann made a speech at Czernowitz, in which he said: "We Jews got the Balfour Declaration quite unexpectedly, or, in other words, we are the greatest war profiteers. We never dreamt of the Balfour Declaration; to be quite frank it came to us overnight... The Balfour Declaration of 1913 was built on air... I trembled lest the British Government would call me to ask, 'Tell us, what is this Zionist Organisation? Where are they, your Zionists?' For these people think in terms different from ours. The Jews, they knew, were against us; we stood alone on a little island, a tiny group of Jews with a foreign past."[12]

The persuasive picture of world Jewry longing to return to Zion is here contradicted by Dr. Weizmann himself.

"Why," asks he in his autobiography, "was it later an almost universal rule that such British administrators as came out to Palestine favourably inclined to the Jews turned against them in a few months?" The answer is simple. In London, as in New York and Washington, the Zionists commanded the ear of the government and of the public, and there was no one to state the Palestinian case. It was only on his arrival in Palestine that the official discovered that the country was inhabited by a pleasant and intelligent people, whom it was the intention of the Zionists to evict.

So much propaganda has been circulated, claiming that Palestine was a desert of sand and rocks, that the report submitted by Sir John Hope Simpson in 1930, on an enquiry into agriculture in Palestine, is worth quoting. "The fellah[13] is neither lazy nor unintelligent. He is a competent and capable agriculturist, and there is little doubt that, were he to be given the chance of learning better methods and the capital which is a necessary preliminary to their employment, he would rapidly improve his position... The fellah is tremendously anxious for education."

Nevertheless, the Mandate seemed for a time as if it might succeed.

[12] *Chaim Weizmann*, edited by P. Goodman, quoted by Nevill Barbour, *Nisi Dominus*.
[13] A farmer or agriculturist.

The figures for Jewish legal immigration from 1920 to 1936 were as follows:

1920	5,514	1929	5,249
1921	9,149	1930	4,944
1922	7,844	1931	4,075
1923	7,421	1932	9,553
1924	12,856	1933	30,327
1925	33,801	1934	42,359
1926	13,081	1935	61,844
1927	2,713	1936	29,727
1928	2,178		

It will be seen that, after large influxes in 1924, 1925 and 1926, the figures petered out in 1927 and 1928. In one year, more Jews left Palestine than arrived. There appeared to be a reasonable chance that the hundred thousand Jewish immigrants who had arrived could be absorbed. Then the Nazis came to power and the persecution of Jews began in Germany. From 1932 onwards, the immigration figures shot upwards. It was obvious that Palestine could not hold so many people. On 25th April, 1936, the "Arab Higher Committee" in Jerusalem proclaimed a strike against Jewish immigration and the agricultural population revolted against Zionist acquisition of land.

On 5th November, 1936, a Royal Commission arrived in Palestine to investigate. In comparison with the Zionists, who were first-class international publicists and politicians, the Palestinians were children. Unfamiliar with the Western world, they made mistakes verging on suicide. One of these was their disastrous habit of boycotting political enquiries. The Zionists strained every nerve to put their case in a favourable light, but the Palestinians refused to give evidence.

The Palestine leaders were convinced that the British government was entirely pro-Zionist, and that the Royal Commission would be ordered to report in favour of the Jews. The Palestinians did not seem to realise that the hearings would be reported in the press and that the report of the commission would be published. The commission consequently spent three months listening to Zionist evidence and to government officials. Only during the last five days did a few Arabs relent.

The commission reported six months later. It recommended the partition of Palestine into two states, Arab and Jewish, Jerusalem being an international area, the most practical solution ever suggested. The proposed Jewish and Arab states were compact and

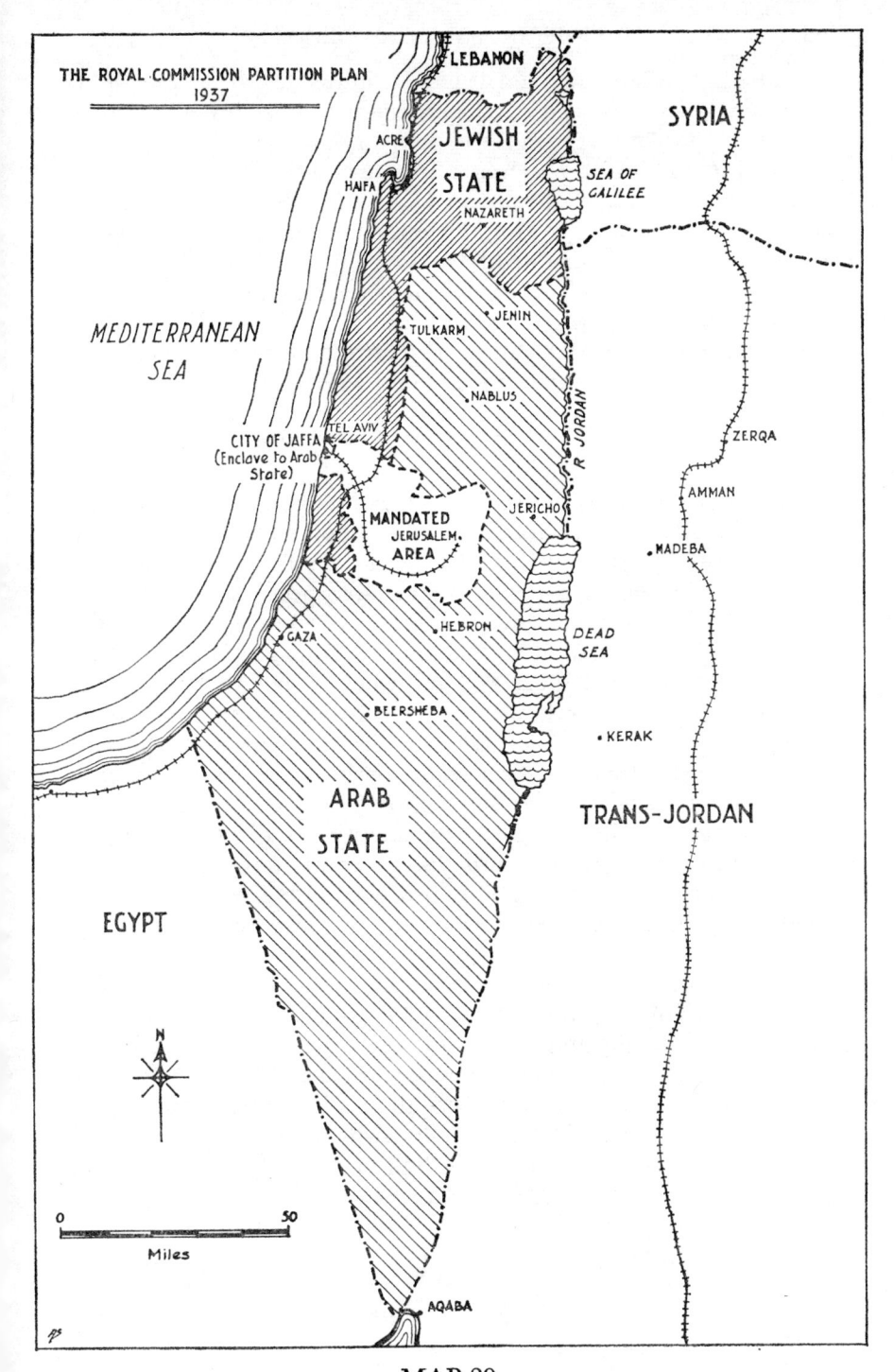

MAP 29

separated. The retention of a British or international force in Jerusalem might have averted a war between the two states. The Ameer Abdulla of Jordan expressed his approval. Events, in the long run, usually proved him right, as was to happen in the present case.

The plan envisaged the union of "Arab" Palestine to Jordan, which left no rôle for the Mufti of Jerusalem and the "Arab Higher Committee", who consequently rejected it. In Palestine the Jews acquiesced with a bad grace, for they wanted the principle of a Jewish state. In August 1937, however, the twentieth Zionist Congress in Zurich rejected partition. The British government vacillated until the outbreak of the Second World War in 1939.

* * *

Innumerable books, newspaper articles, pamphlets and speeches have analysed and paraphrased every detail of the Palestine struggle from November 1917 onwards. The general public, overwhelmed by a flood of propaganda, speeches and counter speeches, promises and denials, have mostly forgotten the origin of the dispute. It is the object of this work to omit both detail and propaganda and to hold firmly to the original sources of the trouble—not for purposes of recrimination but because without a clear diagnosis it is impossible to cure the disease. The basic sources of the trouble were as follows:

(1) Since five hundred years before Christ, there has always been a party in Jewry advocating isolationism from the rest of the world. This attitude was made rigid by the adoption of dietary and ritual laws, which made Jewish-Gentile integration impossible.

(2) This apparent unsociability provoked public resentment, but their high standards of education and financial skill made Jews valuable to governments.

(3) Jews were enthusiastic proselytisers at the same time as being isolationists. This paradox was overcome by insistence that proselytes abandon their family and friends, and come and live in an all-Jewish community. Thus, although Jewry soon included an integration of innumerable ethnic stocks, they were all in spirit a single community.

(4) Jews had already been living for two thousand years in voluntary isolationism before the Papal Bull of 1555 advised their compulsory isolation. The Bull seems to have been largely caused by alleged Jewish fomentation of heresy among Christians.

(5) In the nineteenth century, Jews were accorded "emancipation" and equality almost all over the world, except Russia. In the West, many Jews rose rapidly to wealth and power. Intermixture

with non-Jews, however, made social isolation more difficult and led to integration into the life of their respective countries.

(6) This provoked a reaction lest the characteristics of Jewish life be lost. The resulting movement was also influenced by similar movements in many Western countries to revive small communities and their languages.

(7) The continued repression of Jews in Russia until 1916, caused great numbers to emigrate to the West. Their recent humiliations produced in Russian Jews a fiery and embittered isolationism, which had evaporated in the West after a century of freedom and equality.

(8) Asian Jews, who had lived among Muslims since the seventh century, were integrated into Arab or Persian life.

(9) During the First World War, a small group of capable Russian Jews in London, led by Dr. Weizmann, persuaded the British government to support Jewish colonisation in Palestine, and subsequently won support in the League of Nations. Only a small percentage of world Jewry supported them.

(10) From the first, Zionists envisaged the establishment of a Jewish State and the liquidation of the population of Palestine. Dr. Weizmann, however, insisted on gradual expansion and strongly denied the real objectives.

(11) In Palestine, however, the Zionists, having once obtained a foothold, continued energetically to widen it, largely by constant pressure, prevarication and harassment of any critics in the capitals of the Western Powers.

(12) In many respects, we are obliged to sympathise with the Jews of the world in the agonising dilemma which confronts them, as to whether they should or should not assimilate with the remainder of the human race. But we are, I submit, at the same time, free to criticise their policy of conquest, coercion and eviction in the Middle East. Not only is military conquest, and racial and religious discrimination opposed to modern ideas, but these methods sow hatred, render counter-violence sooner or later inevitable, and are not in the long-term interests of Israel herself.

XVIII

The Slide to Anarchy

The almost inevitable result of . . . the intensification of nationalist propaganda was an increase of terrorist activities on the part of extremist elements in the Jewish community. In a speech on March 20, 1943 . . . Mr. Ben Gurion exhorted Jewish youth to prepare themselves for the fighting which would fall to their lot at the end of the war.
Royal Institute of International Affairs,
Great Britain and Palestine

The partitioning of Palestine was the first and only major issue on which the U.S. and the U.S.S.R. had worked together in the closest harmony . . . The U.S. government demonstrated . . . once more a complete lack of comprehension of Communist tactics . . . Soviet Russia had pressed the United Nations for the earliest possible withdrawal of the Mandatory Power, and for obvious reason: the earlier the evacuation, the sooner the collapse of law and authority; and the greater the chaos, the better the chances for Communist scheming in the area.
ALFRED M. LILIENTHAL, *What Price Israel?*

These twists in American policy were to a large extent due to the division of responsibility between the White House and the Department of State. While the latter was concerned with the Middle East as a whole, the former tended to treat the Zionist problem . . . as a factor of domestic politics.
DR. GEORGE LENCZOWSKI,
The Middle East in World Affairs

I thought it a most disastrous and regrettable fact that the foreign policy of this country was determined by the contributions a particular bloc of special interests might make to the party funds.
JAMES FORRESTAL, U.S. Secretary of Defence, in
The Forrestal Diaries

XVIII

WHEN the Second World War broke out, disturbances in Palestine ceased, as if all were stunned by horror. Both Jews and Palestinians enlisted in the British Army. Trans-Jordan placed all its resources at the disposal of Britain. Later, the Jordan government, on its own initiative, declared war on Germany. When local politicians attempted to dissuade the Ameer Abdulla from this step, as Germany seemed to be winning, he replied, "The British are our friends. Arabs do not abandon their friends just because they are in trouble."

Of all the mandates allotted by the League of Nations, that of Trans-Jordan was about the only successful one. The friendship between Trans-Jordan and Britain was genuine and spontaneous and permeated all classes. In the spring of 1940, soon after the fall of France, Mr. Anthony Eden, Secretary of State for War, and General Wavell, commander-in-chief in the Middle East, arrived in Amman by air to ask if Trans-Jordan could raise more troops, the British forces in the Middle East being quite inadequate. The Jordan government agreed to strain every nerve to help. In April 1941, after a military coup d'état in Baghdad, Iraq declared war on Britain. The Jordan army (the Arab Legion) accompanied an improvised British column from Palestine. Baghdad was retaken and the legitimate government re-established.[1]

In June 1941, the Arab Legion joined in the British invasion of Syria, which had been placed under Italo-German control since the fall of France. The Germans had occupied Greece and Crete and it was feared that they might invade Syria.

The Jews in Palestine, many of whom were actually fugitives from the Nazis, were deeply apprehensive, and co-operated readily with the British army. Some received military training, others were taught underground resistance, in case the Germans should occupy Palestine. When the Nazis invaded Russia and later, when Rommel was defeated at Alamein, these fears were relaxed, and the attitude of Jews in Palestine became less friendly.

In May 1942, Menachem Begin arrived in Palestine. Himself a native of Poland, he had escaped from that country by joining that Polish army which, by way of the Caspian and Baghdad, had joined

[1] J. B. Glubb, *The Story of the Arab Legion*.

the British forces in Palestine. He was not without experience of suffering in Russian prison camps.

Begin's philosophy, as expounded in his book, *The Revolt,* was simple. The whole of Palestine and Trans-Jordan was "the land of Israel". But there was a British army there. The latter were, therefore, brutal imperialists, trying to make Israel, his "homeland", into a British colony. An educated man, he was familiar with the history of the Zionist movement and of the fact that it was the Zionists themselves who had principally engineered the British mandate.

Nor was he concerned with the fact that non-Jews had always lived in Palestine. In a footnote, he says that the Land of Israel, the motherland of the Children of Israel, "has always comprised" Palestine on both sides of the Jordan.

The British, in those days at least, had the reputation in the Middle East of being clever, although, in fact, their successive governments were always bewildered, vacillating and confused. The "Arab" States believed that Britain had brought the Jews to Palestine in order to make Arab unity impossible. Mr. Begin claimed that the British had made Zionism a pretext in order to secure the Palestine mandate, after which they proposed to abandon the Jews.

He quotes with approval a speech by another Jewish Palestine leader at the time. The latter described the British mandatory government as "a régime of the gallows—that is the régime you want to establish in this country . . . In your stupid wickedness, you assume that, by this means, you will succeed in breaking the spirit of our people . . . You will learn that what you have come up against is steel—love of the Homeland and freedom, hatred for the oppressor and invader . . . How blind you are, British tyrants."

This is the feeling, says Mr. Begin, which infused the Irgun Zvai Leumi, the principal Jewish terrorist organisation, which called the Jews in Palestine to revolt against Britain in January 1944. In its manifesto, the Irgun stated, "The British régime has sealed its shameful betrayal of the Jewish people and there is no moral basis whatsoever for its presence in the Land of Israel. There is no longer any armistice between the Jewish people and the British administration in the Land of Israel . . . Our people is at war with this régime— war to the end."

The ordinary British voter was often mildly favourable to Zionism, because a "return" of the Jews was "in the Bible", and because the poor Jews had suffered so much. Few British voters would have recognised themselves as the bloodthirsty tyrants of the Irgun manifesto. As an illustration of the vicissitudes of this imperfect world, it is interesting to recall the ardent assurances of the Zionists in London in 1917 that it would be a great asset to Britain in the Middle East to have a Jewish population in Palestine, which could always be trusted to be friendly. It is scarcely necessary to emphasise that, from 1918 to 1940, the Jewish immigrants had only succeeded in landing in Palestine because British troops had protected them from the resentment of the native Palestinians. "Throughout all the years of our uprising," writes Menachem Begin, "we hit at the British government's prestige, deliberately, tirelessly, unceasingly."

Space does not allow a detailed account of the actions of Zionist terrorists. Their most frequent attacks were against British soldiers and police. In August 1944, an attempt was made to assassinate the British High Commissioner in Palestine and, on 6th November, 1944, Lord Moyne, a British cabinet minister, was murdered by Zionist terrorists in Cairo.

A short time before this event, a few British officers serving the Jordan government had drawn up a memorandum, which I sent with a personal letter to Lord Moyne. We gave our opinion that hatred and anarchy in Palestine had reached such a pitch that partition seemed to be the only solution, but that *it would be essential to maintain sufficient troops in the country until the partition had been peacefully implemented*. Otherwise only endless bloodshed would result. I received a personal letter from Lord Moyne in reply, agreeing with our views, and promising to support them. A few days later, he was assassinated. I still believe that this was our last chance of a peaceful solution, but the U.S.A., Russia, the Jews and the Palestinians clamoured for an immediate British withdrawal.

* * *

Other actions by the Zionist terrorists included the blowing up of railways and bridges and the organised theft of arms from British forces. In August, September and December, 1943, trials took place in Jerusalem of individuals concerned in a series of thefts of arms from military installations. The trials revealed the existence of a large and wealthy organisation for the systematic theft of arms and explosives from the British army, not only in Palestine but throughout the Middle East. The convicted men were Jews and British deserters.[2]

The Irgun's most famous exploit, however, was the blowing-up

[2] Hansard, October 12, 1943, quoted in Royal Institute of International Affairs, *Great Britain and Palestine*.

of the King David Hotel in July 1946. The hotel housed the secretariat and headquarters of the mandatory government. The officials and office employees, men and women, British, Jews and Palestinians, were buried beneath the rubble.

* * *

In the century before the Nazi rise to power, Jews had found equality in almost all the world, Russia being one of the few exceptions. In Germany, Jews had risen to wealth and influence in almost every profession. There was still the possibility of repression in Russia, but even there the situation had improved after the revolution.

Their despair can be imagined when persecution broke out in Germany, the heart of cultured Europe. Moreover, the Nazi persecution was the worst that Jews had ever experienced, worse than that of the Black Death in Germany in 1348, or that of the Inquisition in Spain after 1492.

A panic-stricken flight from eastern Europe began. But the world was at war, transport was unobtainable, and there were no ships owing to the Atlantic submarine campaign. The Zionists everywhere urged all Jews to come to Palestine. The British were pledged to protect the civil and religious rights of the Palestinians. Some Jews were temporarily sent to Cyprus, some to Mauritius. Great numbers, however, reached Palestine illegally, landing at night on lonely beaches. As some of them, like Mr. Begin, started to shoot British soldiers, the mandatory government was perhaps not enthusiastic to receive more.

The Palestinians, farmers and villagers with a few politicians and lawyers in the towns, were completely unable to deal with this flood of Poles and Russians. The British government now faced the situation foretold by Lord Grey in 1923. The alternatives were dishonourably to abandon the task they had undertaken, or the inauguration of military operations which the people of Britain were unwilling to support. Britain had, alone, saved the world from Nazi rule, but she had been maimed in the struggle.

If only there had been time, something could perhaps have been worked out, but, in a world of unrestrained savagery and fanaticism, no time was available.

* * *

The Jews have always been sensitive to impending changes of

power. Having served the Pharaohs for two hundred years, they went over to Alexander in time to earn his gratitude. After serving the Ptolemies for three centuries, they switched to Julius Caesar just in time, and won special privileges from the Romans.

Towards the end of the Second World War, it became evident that Britain was exhausted and that the United States would be the Great Power when peace came. Extremist Zionist propaganda, therefore, devoted itself to the vilification of Britain in the United States, where much ill-feeling was roused, even while the war was still in progress.

The Balfour Declaration had guaranteed the civil and religious rights of the native Palestinians, though these rights had already been prejudiced. Now the Zionists were demanding the complete abrogation of these rights, and the establishment of an independent Jewish state, although Jews still constituted only about one third of the population.

The British government sought to gain time by sending another commission of enquiry. To reduce American hostility, the United States was invited to name half the members, although she would not be responsible for the implementation of the Commission's recommendations. Before the appointment of the committee, President Truman had requested the British to admit a further hundred thousand Jewish immigrants. His predecessor, President Roosevelt, had previously assured the Ameer Abdulla and Ibn Saud that the United States would take no action which would be inimical to the Arabs in Palestine.[3] British officials and the armed forces were aware that Arab friendship was vital,[4] but politicians were influenced by Jewish political pressure. Even Soviet Russia began to wonder if support for the Jews in Palestine might not assist her by providing bases for her expansion into the Mediterranean, a two-hundred-year-old ambition of the Russian Empire. The Russians, at the same time, however, expressed sympathy for Arab aspirations. In 1945, Russia applied for a mandate for Libya, a further warning of her determination to intervene in the Mediterranean by whatever means came to hand.[5]

During the course of the war, American oil companies had started to develop the oil resources of Saudi Arabia on a large scale. For strategic purposes, the United States had also built up a considerable fleet in the Mediterranean. Whether, therefore, for oil or for strategy, the Americans had also become interested in the Middle East.

[3] Nevill Barbour, *Nisi Dominus*.   [4] See also Chapter XXI below.
[5] Nevill Barbour, *Nisi Dominus*.

The Russian ambitions, however, were still in the stage of long distance planning. There were no Russians in the Middle East and no Soviet ships in the Mediterranean. Britain and America were supreme on the site. *If only they had co-operated the Palestine problem could have been settled once and for all.* Unfortunately, the policy of the United States government seems to have been guided by the desire to win the imminent presidential election. As a result, the whole weight of the United States was used to support the Zionists, regardless, it would appear, of either justice or long term American interests.

The report of the Anglo-American Committee of Enquiry was published in May 1946. Today it makes sorry reading. It recommended the issue of immigration permits to a further hundred thousand Jewish immigrants, a sop to President Truman. It stated that neither a Jewish nor an Arab state should be permitted. For the present, the mandate should continue with the object of setting up a Palestinian state, in which Muslims, Jews and Christians should have equal rights—incidentally an interesting phrase, showing that the committee regarded the protagonists as religious groups. The Zionists, of course, were determined to represent the Jews as a "race" or a "nation", not as a religion. The committee, however, stated that a Palestine state should not be set up until Jewish-Arab hostility had disappeared. Meanwhile, the use of violence by either side should be suppressed. In other words, the solution recommended was that all concerned should behave nicely.

In fact, the Zionists were already determined to land sufficient Jews in Palestine to enable them to drive out the native Palestinians, and to conquer the country for themselves. Even the question of the number of permits to be issued for Jewish immigrants was scarcely more than academic, since the Zionists had developed their technique for illegal immigration.

The Palestinians were completely unaware of realities. They had no shadow government ready to take over, no leader, no weapons, no armed forces. The Zionists were, on the contrary, well organised and well armed. Great numbers of weapons had been smuggled in, or stolen from the British during the war, and small factories were making armoured cars, mortars and bombs. Before the Anglo-American Committee, the British General D'Arcy stated that, if British troops withdrew, the Jews would occupy the whole of Palestine within twenty-four hours.

In Palestine, both Jews and Palestinians demanded that Britain withdraw. In the United Nations, Russia and the United States,

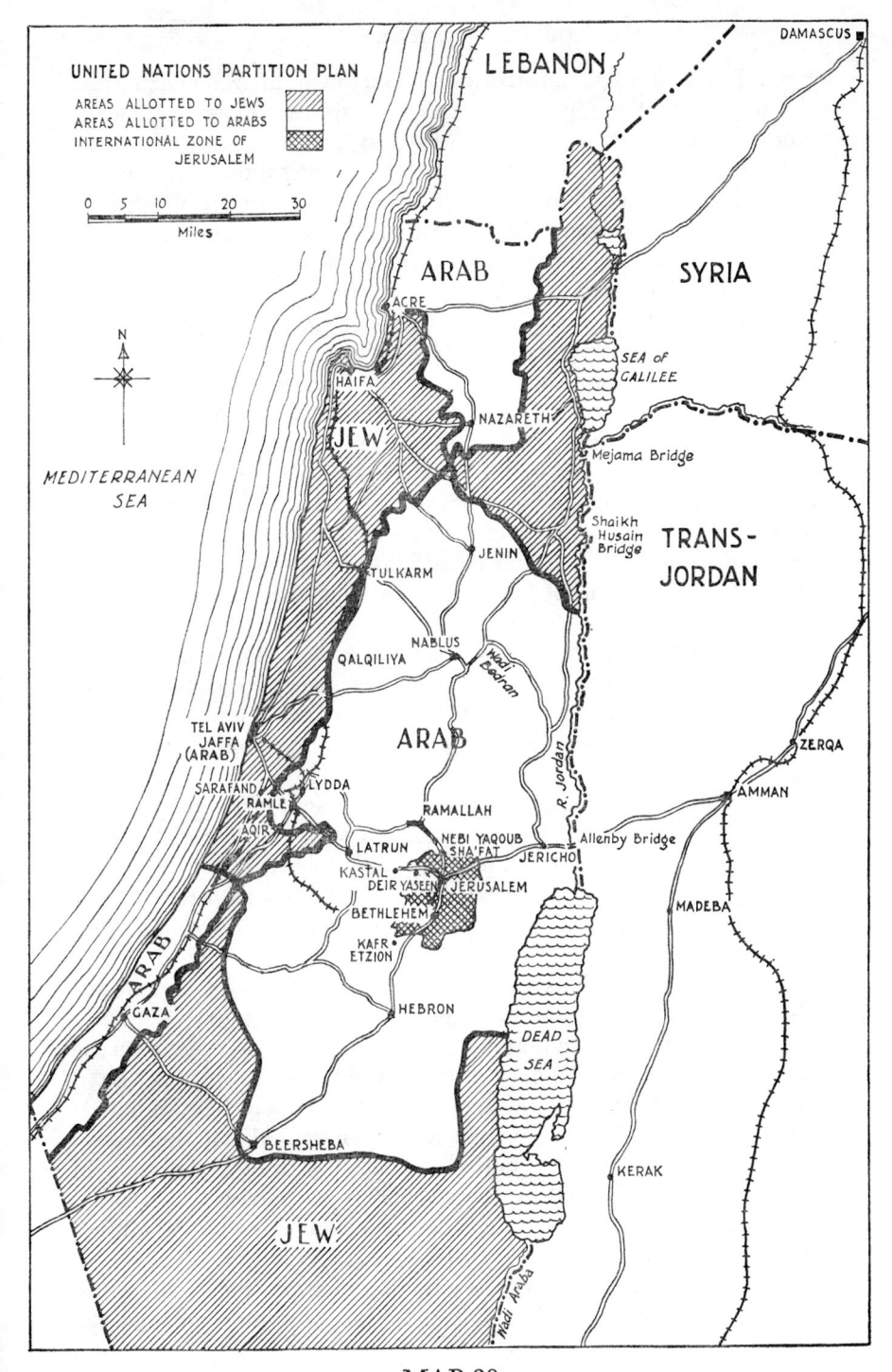

MAP 30

agreeing almost word for word, insisted on a British evacuation. Britain notified the United Nations that she would surrender the mandate and withdraw on 15th May, 1948.

Another committee of enquiry arrived in Palestine, this time on behalf of the United Nations. On 31st August, 1947, it submitted a majority report recommending partition. Seven members supported the recommendation, but four opposed it.

By twenty-five votes to eighteen, with eleven abstentions, a committee appointed by the General Assembly defeated a proposal by certain Arab governments to submit the legality of the Balfour Declaration to the International Court of Justice at The Hague. By only twenty-one votes to twenty, the committee dismissed the question whether the United Nations was entitled to enforce partition without the consent of the people of Palestine.

These were important basic questions. *Does* the United Nations possess the legal power to hand over a country, or part of a country, to another community? What should we say if the United Nations ordered the separation of Scotland from England, or the partition of the United States along the Mason-Dixon line?

The Zionist reply to this comparison is that the cases are not parallel. The United States and Britain are sovereign nations, whereas Palestine was a mandated territory, but this is a lawyers' answer. "Colonialism" is one of the forms of activity most frequently denounced in the United Nations—that is to say, the imposition of foreign rule on a people, without their consent. The partition of Palestine by the United Nations was just such an action, for two-thirds of the people in Palestine were still "Arabs". Never before or since, to my knowledge, has the United Nations attempted to deprive a people of their country, or to impose foreign rulers upon them.

In the United Nations debate on partition in 1947 the native Palestinians, who were to be deprived of their country, were not represented. It is a fundamental rule of justice that no man be sentenced without being heard. But it was not justice which actuated the United Nations, but power politics and political bargaining. It is true that "Arab" governments were represented but these were sovereign states, differing entirely from one another, except in language. If the United Nations decided to partition Australia, would it be sufficient if the latter's case were presented by the United States, on the grounds that they both spoke English?

An indefensible injustice in the partition plan was the award of the area from Beersheba to the Gulf of Aqaba (commonly called the

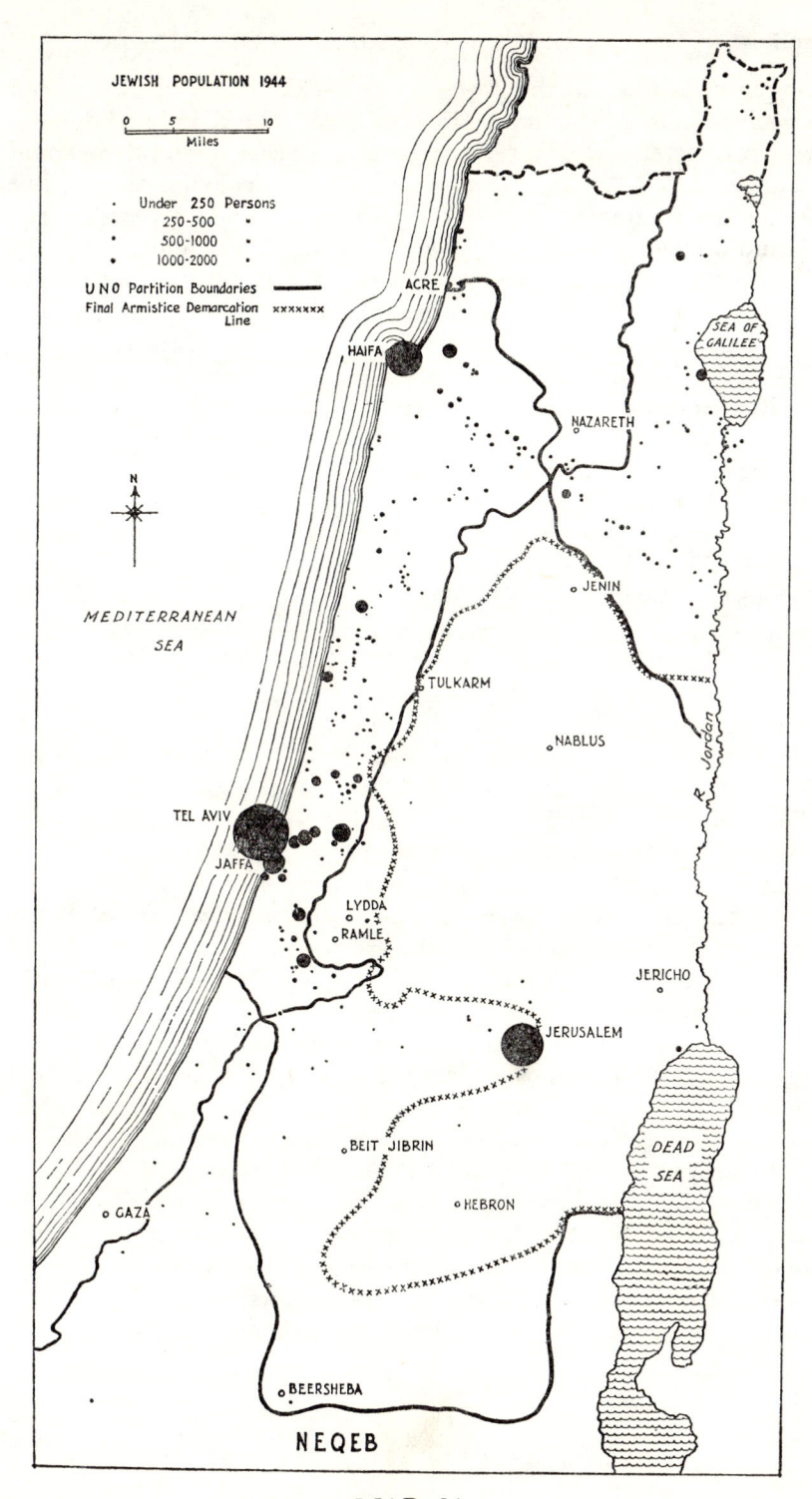

MAP 31

Neqeb or Negev) to the Jewish state.[6] This area had never been Israelite, from Abraham until 1948. Under the name of Edom, it was conquered by David three thousand years ago and Solomon made a port at Aqaba and mined copper as a colonial project. But Alexander conquered the Middle East seven hundred years later—should we then give the Middle East to Greece? The allotment of the Neqeb to Israel was pure imperialism—she wanted a port on the Red Sea. It also cut off Arabia, and the eastern Arab countries from Egypt and blocked one of the world's oldest trade routes.

In New York, the Zionists engaged in frenzied lobbying. The United States and Russia worked hand-in-hand, firstly, to decry Britain, and, secondly, to support the Zionists. In this unexpected partnership, the White House had its eye on the forthcoming presidential elections, the Russians on that fleet in the Mediterranean with which they hoped to wrest control of the area from the United States.

The Pakistani Foreign Minister uttered a prophetic warning to the Western Powers. "Remember," he said, "that you may need friends tomorrow, that you may need allies in the Middle East. I beg of you not to ruin and blast your credit in those lands." On 29th November, 1947, the General Assembly, urged on by the United States and Russia, accepted the partition plan drawn up by the special committee. It is worthy of note that all states in Asia and Africa, except the Philippines, South Africa and Liberia, voted against the motion. The United States and Europe, including Russia, forced Israel upon the Asians and Africans against their total opposition.

Six per cent of the land of Palestine belonged to Jews, but the partition plan gave fifty-four per cent of the land to the Jewish State. In effect, forty-nine per cent of the area of Palestine was transferred from the Palestine "Arabs" to the Jews, by a stroke of the pen in New York.

While Jews only owned six per cent of the land in 1948, the Palestinians did not legally own ninety-four per cent, because some land belonged to the government. This was a relic of Ottoman times, when all land belonged to the state, and farmers were technically government tenants, though they bought, sold and inherited their landed property. Most of the land had been surveyed by the British and registered in the names of private owners, but, when the mandate ended, considerable areas were still unregistered. But all unregistered land was settled by Arabs. Jews never bought land without registering it. The argument that some of the land given to

[6] See map of distribution of the Jewish population in 1944, p. 297 and Map 33, p. 311 for the Neqeb.

or seized by the Jews was government land, and did not belong to the natives is deceptive. All such land was in use by "Arabs".

* * *

The Zionist claim that, at the end of the mandate, the "Arabs" invaded Israel has been accepted by the Western world. The facts are more complicated. The term Israel in this chapter is used to describe the part of Palestine allotted by the United Nations to the Jewish State. (Menachem Begin, as we have seen, meant all Palestine and Trans-Jordan when he used the word, Israel.)

A careful examination of dates, however, shows that it was Israel who attacked first. "In the months preceding, the Arab invasion," writes Menachem Begin, ". . . we continued to make sallies into the Arab area. In the early days of 1948, we were explaining to our officers and men, however, that this was not enough . . . It was clear to us that even the most daring sallies carried out by partisan troops would never be able to decide the issue. Our hope lay in gaining control of territory. At the end of January 1948, at a meeting of the Command of the Irgun in which the planning section participated, we outlined four strategic objectives: (1) Jerusalem, (2) Jaffa, (3) the Lydda-Ramleh plain, (4) the Triangle (the towns of Nablus, Jenin and Tulkarm), comprising the bulk of the non-desert area west of Jordan."[7]

This passage seems to prove that, four months before the "Arab Invasion", but two months after the publication of the U.N. Partition Plan, a Zionist conquest of the whole of Palestine, in defiance of the United Nations, was already being planned. Implementation of the "Zionist Invasion" began early in April 1948, five or six weeks before the "Arab Invasion".

Jerusalem had been allotted by the United Nations to an International Area. At the beginning of April, the Hagana, the official Jewish army, attacked and occupied Katamon, an area occupied by well-to-do Arab families.

I have told elsewhere,[8] how, in December 1947, two British officers and a Jewish official in the mandatory government were discussing the newly published U.N. partition plan over an evening drink. One of the British officers asked the Jewish official whether the Jewish state would not have a great deal of trouble, in view of

[7] Menachem Begin, *The Revolt*. Mr. Begin was a member of the Israeli cabinet until the summer of 1970.
[8] J. B. Glubb, *A Soldier with the Arabs*.

the fact that there would be as many Arabs in it as Jews. "Oh, no!" replied the Jewish officer. "A few calculated massacres will soon get rid of them." This was five months before the "Arab Invasion".

Early in April 1948, a month before the "Arab Invasion", the Irgun entered the Arab village of Deir Yaseen, just west of Jerusalem, and massacred every living soul, nearly all of them women and children, for the men were away at work. The massacre was "calculated", for the village was notorious for its good relations with the Jews. Police subsequently recovered two hundred and fifty dead bodies, which had been thrown down the village well. Mr. Begin claims that Deir Yaseen was taken with the approval of the Hagana, the official Jewish army. "None of the barbarities the Arabs have committed . . . can excuse this foul thing done by Jews," comments a Jewish writer then in Jerusalem.[9]

Later in April 1948, the Hagana attacked the Arab working-class quarter in Haifa. "The Jewish forces proceeded to advance through Haifa like a knife through butter. The Arabs began fleeing in panic, shouting 'Deir Yaseen'."[10] This passage seems to illustrate how the Deir Yaseen massacre acted to get the Palestinians moving out. The poorer classes of Arabs fled from Haifa. The Israelis have since alleged that they did so "on orders from their leaders". No such leaders or orders have ever been discovered.

From 25th to 28th April, three weeks before the "Arab Invasion", the Irgun launched an attack on the all-Arab town of Jaffa, allotted by the United Nations to the Arab state. For three days the town was mercilessly bombarded, chiefly by mortars. "British sources reported numerous Arab casualties", remarks Mr. Begin. The inhabitants of Jaffa, after four days of bombardment, panicked and fled, some to the Arab area further east, some to Trans-Jordan, where they formed the first refugees. The Israelis subsequently claimed that they "left voluntarily". Mostly unarmed civilians, women and children, they fled to escape being killed.

In 1939, millions of French people abandoned their homes and fled before the advancing German armies. Presumably they too "left voluntarily". But when the war was over, they were allowed to return to their homes. The Palestinians, who fled under similar circumstances, have never been allowed to return.

It was most unfortunate that the British lost control in Palestine before the end of the mandate. In fact, it often seemed that they had

---

[9] Harry Levin, *Jerusalem Embattled*. Mr. Levin had been Middle East correspondent of the *Daily Herald*.
[10] Menachem Begin, *The Revolt*.

given up trying. Abused alike by Russians and Americans, Jews and Arabs, their attitude seemed to be, "All right, if you don't want us, you can sort yourselves out." As a result, everything was in chaos. Bands of guerrillas arrived from Syria, while every Palestinian tried to buy a rifle. The difference between the two sides was that the Zionists had a well thought out plan to conquer the Arab state, while the Palestinians, as individuals or in groups, fought back without any plan, trying to save their homes.

* * *

In early 1948, a delegation under Taufiq Pasha, Prime Minister of Jordan, went to London to secure certain changes in the Anglo-Jordan treaty. After these discussions, Taufiq Pasha took me with him to interpret at a private interview with the Foreign Secretary, Mr. Ernest Bevin.

Taufiq Pasha explained that the Zionists had a government, a police force and an army ready to take control when the mandate ended, but that the Palestinians had nothing at all. Consequently, many Palestinian deputations had begged King Abdulla to allow the Jordan army—the Arab Legion—to defend the area allotted to the "Arab" state. If this were not done, the Jews would occupy all Palestine in a few hours, regardless of the United Nations boundaries.

Mr. Bevin replied, "It seems the obvious thing for you to do, but do not invade the areas allotted by the United Nations to the Jews." In saying this, Mr. Bevin was not trying to assist the Jews, but was warning us that we might get into trouble. On this basis, the Arab Legion crossed into the "Arab" area of Palestine on 15th May, 1948. Far from invading Israel, it everywhere met Israeli forces invading the Arab state.

* * *

The Hagana was unable to conquer the whole of Jerusalem before the end of the mandate owing to the presence of British troops in the city. Within minutes of the British departure, however, the Hagana launched their attack on the Arab half of the city. Mr. Harry Levin gives an interesting description of the city on 15th May, when the British had left.[11]

"Nearby a loudspeaker burst out in Arabic. Hagana broadcasting to civilian Arabs, urging them to leave the district before 5.15 a.m.

[11] Harry Levin, *Jerusalem Embattled*.

'Take pity on your wives and children and get out of this bloodbath,' it said. 'Surrender to us with your arms. No harm will come to you. Or get out by the Jericho road, that is still open to you. If you stay, you invite disaster.' The commander [of the Jewish forces] was glad to see us go; he even smiled. 'Come back when we've captured the rest of Jerusalem and I'll tell you all about it,' he said."

Meanwhile, the Jordan government ordered the Arab Legion *not* to enter Jerusalem, out of respect for the United Nations. From 15th to 19th May, the Israelis conquered most of the city, opposed only by miscellaneous parties of Arabs, trying to defend the Arab quarters. Only on 19th May did the Arab Legion, despairing of the United Nations, enter Jerusalem and defend what it could of the Arab city.

NOTABLE DATES

The Jordan army (the Arab Legion) marches with the British army to retake Baghdad and to invade Syria	May to July 1941
Declaration of the Irgun revolt against Britain	January 1944
Report of the Anglo-American committee on Palestine	May 1946
Massacre of Deir Yaseen	8th April, 1948
Seizure of Katamon quarter of Jerusalem by Hagana	April 1948
Capture of Jaffa by Irgun	April 1948
End of the mandate	15th May, 1948
Entry of the Arab Legion into "Arab" Jerusalem	19th May, 1948

CONCLUSIONS

(1) The exchange of bitter recriminations regarding past events makes the Palestine problem insoluble. Only by burying the past and looking to the future can peace be secured.

(2) There are no heroes or villains in this tragedy. The reactions of all concerned are the result of deep prejudices and emotions, many of them subconscious, and reaching back for centuries into the past. It is not our task to blame the British, Americans, Russians, Jews, Arabs, Egyptians or Palestinians, but to seek constructive and unemotional

ways of bringing them together. We have no right to criticise them, because we have not experienced the peculiar past influences which have subconsciously moulded their present emotional make-up.

(3) "When disaster strikes the world in the form of... wars, it is impossible for you to pinpoint the origin of the disorder. Be willing to accept the mysterious solidarity of men... but always keep in mind the fact that for every sin which appears in the world, somewhere a new suffering makes itself felt... When, out of love for others, you enlist in the struggle against suffering, you can be sure that you are entering into the plan of God."[12]

---

[12] Michel Quoist, *The Christian Response*.

XIX

The Psychology of Suffering

The pattern of war was old, tried and tested. Not the mature Jehovah of Amos, Isaiah and Hillel was to be followed, but the primitive, immature, minor, junior, angry, revengeful, eye-for-an-eye (no, ten-eyes-for-one-eye) Jehovah of Joshua and of Menachem Begin and Ben Gurion.
  Moshe Menuhin, *The Decadence of Judaism in our Time*

Thou shalt not kill has been ingrained in us since Mount Sinai. It was inconceivable ten years ago that the Jews should break this commandment. Unfortunately they are breaking it today ... I hang my head in shame when I have to speak of this fact.
  Chaim Weizmann, to the United Nations Committee on Palestine

We've played the power game too long, and the time has come when we must face up to what it means to be human. Jesus said: "All who take the sword shall die by the sword..." He was rejecting all the aggressive, bullying, power-based tactics men employ ... for there's no future in it ... We have to make up our minds whether we want to live ... with the basic attitudes of cave men.
  Rev. William Magee, *Thought for the Day* on B.B.C.

Magnanimity in politics is not seldom the truest wisdom.
  Edmund Burke

XIX

ONE of the most productive propaganda lines developed by Israel has been the David and Goliath story. It alleges that less than a million Israelis defeated a hundred million Arabs. The latter figure is obtained by adding up the total populations of all the Arab-speaking countries from Morocco to the Persian border. Scarcely any of these countries participated, or have since taken any part whatever. An alternative version claimed that the Israeli army had defeated eleven armies. In fact, no such armies took part or have taken any part ever since. Egypt and Jordan were the only two countries which were drawn into serious fighting.

The forces actually in the field on the "Arab" side in May 1948, were approximately as follows:

Egypt	10,000
Jordan (Arab Legion)	4,500
Iraq	3,000
	17,500

Israeli strength is not easy to reckon, because it involved many categories.

Palmach (regulars, fully trained)	3,500
Hagana	55,000
Irgun	4,000
	62,500

Such figures are unreliable but they, at any rate, reveal the absurdity of the David and Goliath story. The Israelis, moreover, had interior lines, which they used with great skill. All their settlements were fortified with minefields, barbed wire and concrete, sufficient to delay the advance of any attacker. This gave them freedom to constitute a central mobile force, which they could move rapidly from one front to another. Their enemies came from several hundred miles away, their communications radiating in different directions.

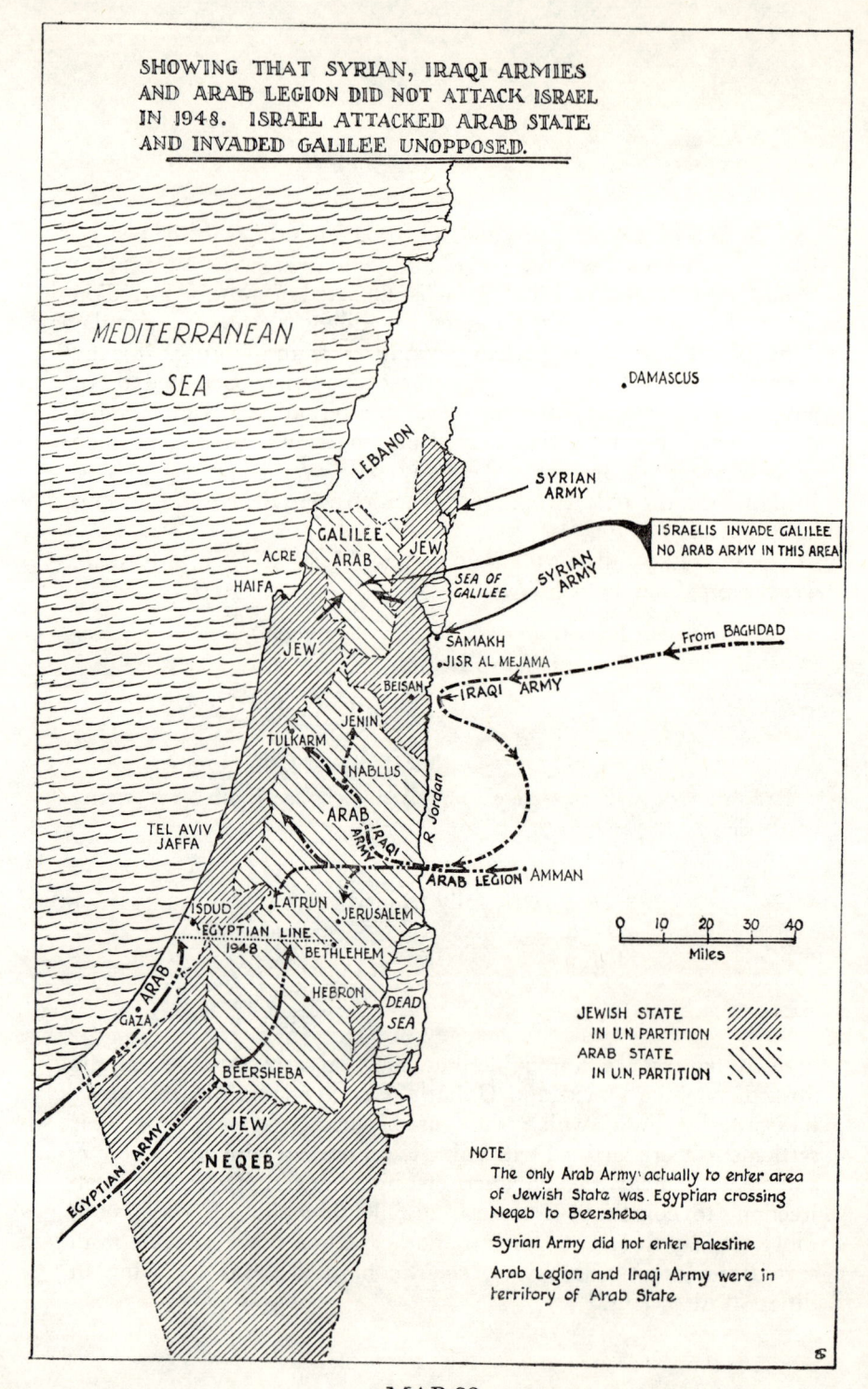

MAP 32

Israel gained immense prestige from the David and Goliath story. Millions of people, Jews and Gentiles, in the West were deeply stirred by the heroism of "brave little Israel", battling against the millions of Asia. In cold fact, the picture is incorrect. The Israelis always outnumbered their enemies on the ground.

* * *

The claim that, on 15th May, 1948, the Arab states attacked Israel has already been disproved. We have seen that the Zionists attacked the area allotted by the U.N. to the proposed Arab state several weeks before the "Arab Invasion". Apart, however, from the time factor, no Arab army attacked Israel, except the Egyptian, which crossed from Sinai into an area allotted to the Jewish state in the partition plan.

The Jordanians only entered the Arab state, which they found had already been invaded by the Israelis. All the battles fought between the Arab Legion and the Israeli army took place on the territory of the Arab state or in the Jerusalem international area, both of which had been attacked by the Israelis before the Arab Legion arrived. Jordan never, on any occasion, attacked Israel.

Of the other Arab states, Lebanon took no part in 1948. Syria fought one border action at Samakh and then withdrew. She did not invade Israel. The Iraqi army sent a token force of three thousand men, which engaged the Israelis across the Jordan at Jisr al Mejama. It then withdrew through Amman and joined the Arab Legion in defending the Arab state in the Nablus—Jenin—Tulkarm triangle. When holding Jenin, it was attacked by an Israeli force which tried to seize Jenin (a town allotted to the Arab state) but was repulsed. The Iraqis, throughout all the fighting, remained on the defensive inside the Arab state. They also did not attack Israel.[1]

* * *

The Israeli qualities which deserve unstinted admiration, then and since, are not so much military heroism as organisation, and financial and diplomatic skill. Weizmann's persuasive diplomacy was almost miraculous. The manner in which the United States itself was persuaded to lobby for the Zionists to pass the partition plan is amazing. The vast sums of money collected all over the world

[1] Map 32, opposite.

for Israel indicate an organisational and financial skill unequalled anywhere in the world.

While, moreover, the Israeli armed forces always outnumbered their enemies, to place such a high proportion of the population in the field required an organizational skill and an enthusiasm which no Middle East country could approach. All this depended on high standards of education and on administrative experience gained in Europe.

On the technological side, Israel enjoys the same advantages. Her people are on the technological level of Europe and the United States. The vast majority of Jordanians and Egyptians work in agriculture. I have some personal experience of this problem, having been obliged for seventeen years to train an army of farmers and shepherds to use the same equipment as the British army. Technology can only achieve a high level in industrialised communities. At least a hundred years, possibly more, are needed to transform an agricultural into a technological society.

Meanwhile, today, those who enjoy this technological superiority can obliterate communities which lag behind. Such a process partakes more of bullying than of battle.

* * *

In 1948, Jews constituted about thirty-three per cent of the population of Palestine. The United Nations, however, allotted about fifty-four per cent of the country to the "Jewish State". In the course of the subsequent fighting, Israel seized a further twenty-five per cent of the land. As a result, thirty-three per cent of the people obtained possession of about eighty per cent of the country. Ironically, the only area left to the Palestinians was the area held by Israel in Old Testament times.[2]

The Israelis were allowed to retain the whole area which they had occupied, because their publicity organisation convinced the Western world that it was "the Arabs" who had attacked and who, therefore, deserved all they got. We have seen, however, that this was incorrect—the Israelis attacked the "Arab state" before the Arab armies arrived. In any case, Egypt was the only country whose army entered an area allotted to the "Jewish state". The Lebanon took no part in the fighting, yet, under cover of the cloud of propaganda about Arab attacks, Israel was able to invade and annex Galilee, where there were no Arab armies, only a few guerrillas.

[2] Compare Map 33 opposite and Map 34, p. 313, with Map 5, p. 58.

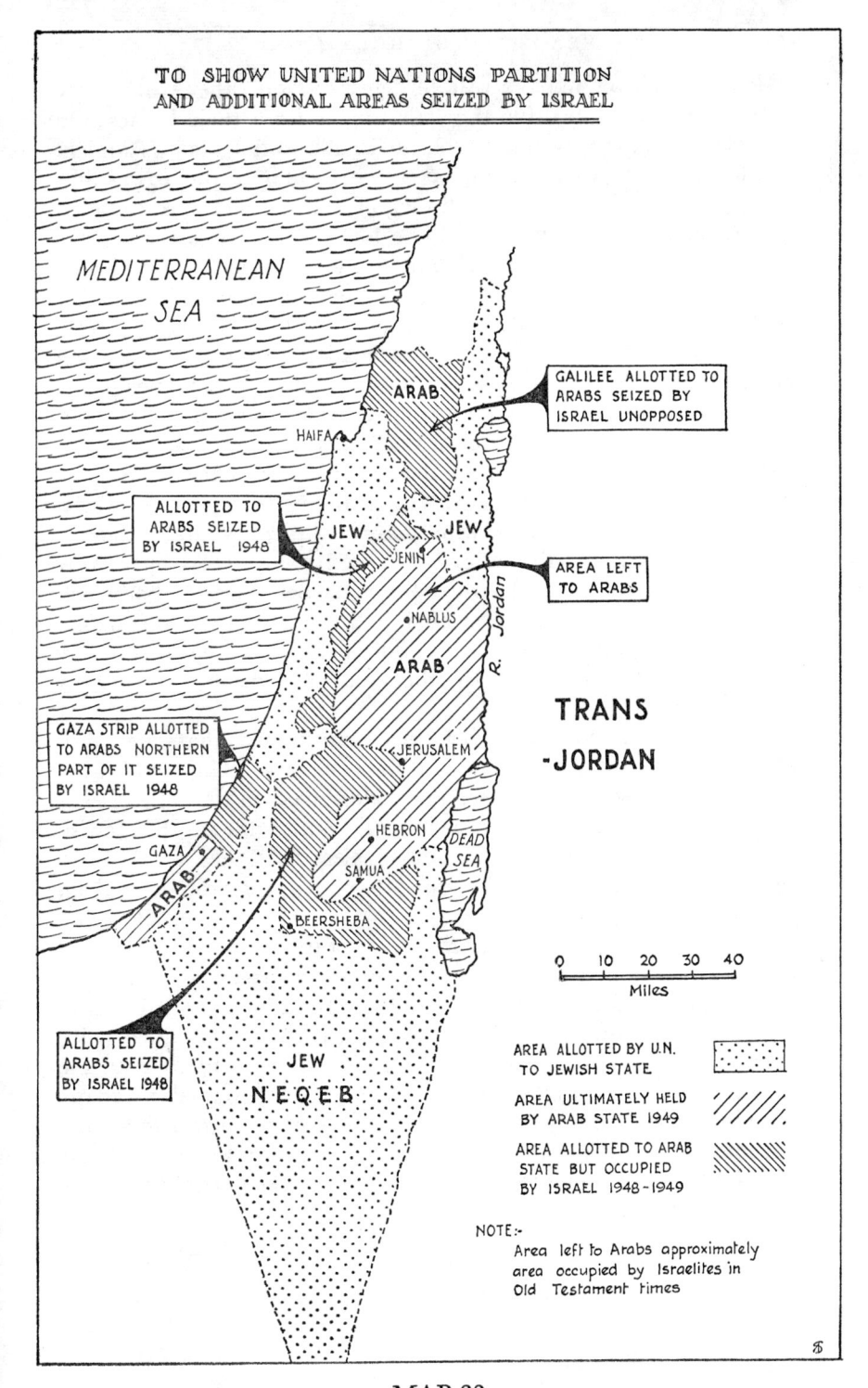

MAP 33

Having thus pinned the title of aggressors on "the Arabs", the Israelis were able to drive the Palestinians from their homes. On the occasion of the Israeli attack on Lydda and Ramle (Ramleh, Ramla) in July 1948, loudspeaker vans entered the towns immediately behind the troops. All men of military age were rounded up and driven away in trucks. The loudspeaker vans then drove through the streets ordering everyone, men, women and children, to leave the town within half an hour—the same technique as Harry Levin described in Jerusalem.

Israeli soldiers broke into and searched the houses, the women receiving a good deal of unceremonious handling to emphasise the point that it would be better to leave. "Perhaps thirty thousand people or more, almost entirely women and children, snatched up what they could and fled from their homes across the fields. The Israeli forces ... commandeered all means of transport. It was a blazing day in July in the coastal plains—the temperature about a hundred degrees in the shade. It was ten miles across open hilly country ... to the nearest Arab village at Beit Sira. Nobody will ever know how many children died."[3] Some exhausted and panic-stricken women abandoned their children, which were subsequently picked up by the Red Cross. In other smaller towns and villages the same procedure was followed.

Israeli propaganda has ever since maintained that the Arab refugees left voluntarily, and quoted the instances of Haifa and Jaffa, before the end of the mandate. The Palestinians in these two towns fled, as we have seen, as a result of bombardments by Jewish mortars. The Israelis can, therefore, assert that they did not *tell* them to go. But as soon as the mandate ended, they did evict them by force.

This situation, however, was the result of the previous sequence of events. Israel hoped to occupy all Palestine in 1948, as Mr. Begin states, and would have done so if the Egyptian army and the Arab Legion had not intervened. But Palestine, in 1948, contained twice as many Arabs as there were Jews. Even the area allotted to the "Jewish State" in the U.N. Partition plan contained as many Palestinians as it did Jews. Having already gone so far, therefore, it seemed to the Zionists that the Jewish state would never be safe and viable unless they could get rid of the greater part of the native inhabitants.

* * *

[3] J. B. Glubb, *A Soldier with the Arabs*.

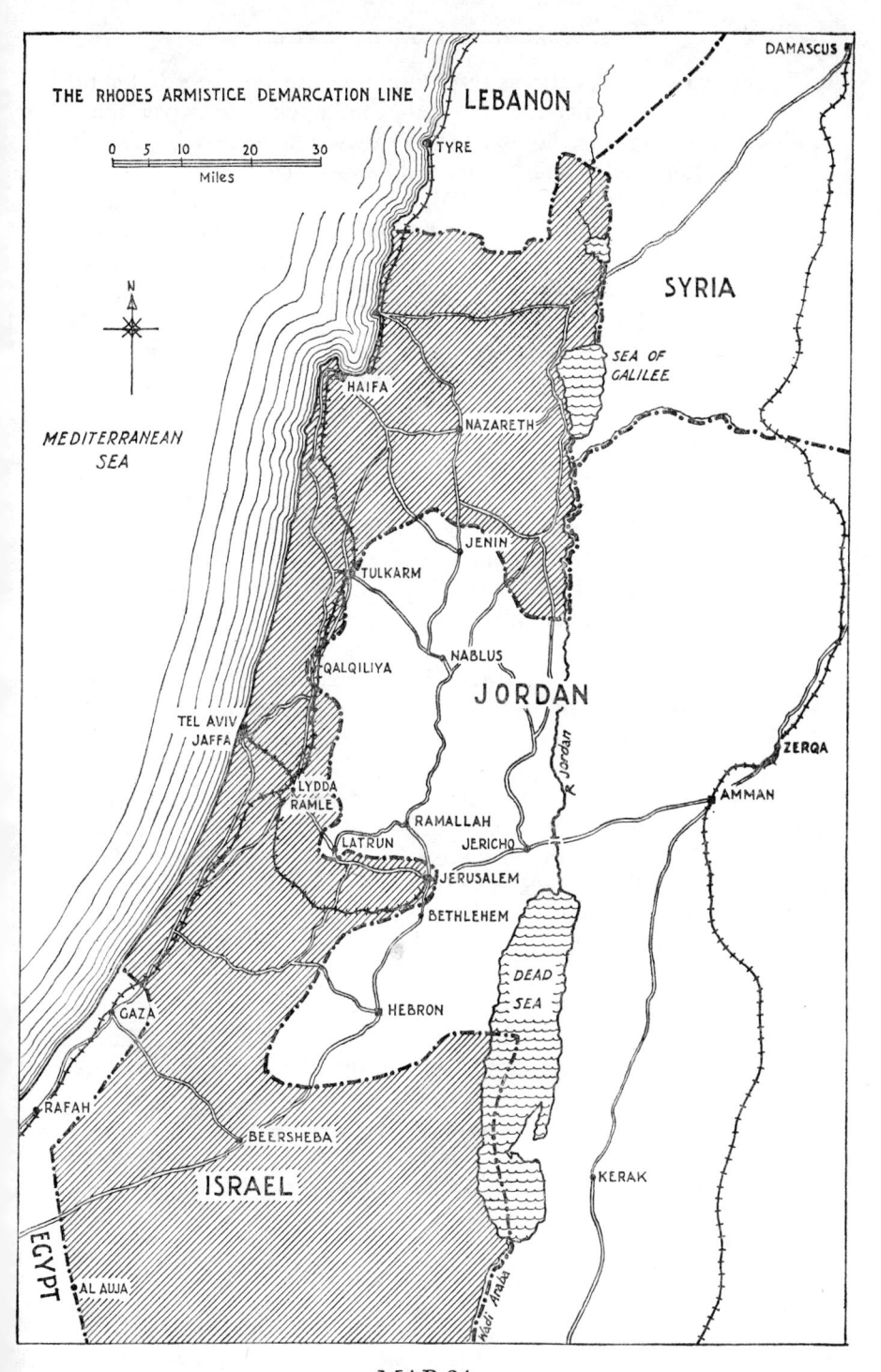

MAP 34

From 1948 to 1956, I was responsible on the Jordan side for the security of the armistice line. In 1948, the Israelis had driven many Palestinians from their homes. Most of these refugees were collected in camps along the hills of Judaea and Samaria (to use Bible names), by the United Nations. Nearly all, when driven out, had left their valuables in their homes, money, stock-in-trade, animals, fruit trees, grain. When the fighting ended, many went back at night to see what could be rescued. Those caught by the Israelis were shot.

Thereafter, such persons went armed, but as private individuals, not as organised guerrillas. Thus a sub-war developed increasingly at night along the armistice line. The Jordan government disapproved. Many refugees were killed and no injury was done to Israel, who complained loudly of "Arab aggression". I personally, through the U.N. Truce Committee, suggested that Israeli and Jordan police posts be connected by direct telephones across the armistice line. Jordan even proposed joint police patrols, and submitted a draft "Local Commanders' agreement", for border co-operation. The Israelis rejected all proposals for co-operation.

For a time, our police officer in Jenin was a friend of the Israeli police officer across the line, having worked with him in mandate days. No incidents ever occurred in their sector. Then the Israelis replaced their man by another officer, and incidents were soon frequent. We concluded that police co-operation could prevent incidents.

We never knew why the Israelis rejected co-operation. Some surmised that night incidents, reported as "Arab raids", maintained the flow of financial aid from the West on the grounds that Israel was in danger. Others thought that the Israelis regarded themselves as European conquerors, who would demean themselves by co-operating with the "natives". They preferred simply to "punish" those who displeased them.

On 13th October, 1953, for example, they complained to the Truce Committee that three infiltrators had thrown a bomb into a window in Tirat Yahuda and killed a woman and two children. We offered to allow Israeli police to cross the line to search, and our own police offered a reward and searched refugee camps.

Two nights later, an Israeli military force broke into Qibya, a village a mile and a half inside Jordan. Sixty-six civilians were killed, mostly women and children. Every house in the village was blown down. Israeli reprisals were based on the principle that, if one Israeli was killed, twenty Palestinians must die.

In March and April, 1956, I and all the British officers and technicians in Jordan were dismissed. Inevitably the professional standard of the Arab Legion deteriorated, for the Jordanians, who were splendid material, had not had time to acquire technological skills. The most important aspect of the change, however, attracted no public attention. In 1948, the Arab Legion everywhere repulsed the attacks of the invading Israelis. Since then, however, Israel had admitted many immigrants and had imported large numbers of aircraft, tanks and weapons, until she was fifteen or twenty times stronger than Jordan.

I calculated that, in the event of future operations, Jordan could resist Israel for three days but no longer. Egyptian resistance I estimated at forty-eight hours. Jordan's only hope of survival lay in the fact that she had a military alliance with Britain. British troops could not reach Jordan in three days, but the R.A.F. could. I therefore obtained approval for R.A.F. intervention, should Israel attack Jordan. Soon after my departure, Jordan denounced her military alliance with Britain, leaving herself at the mercy of an ever more heavily armed and aggressive Israel.

* * *

On 20th July, 1956, the United States cancelled the loan which she had virtually promised for the Aswan Dam, and the Russians took up the commitment. This was a milestone on the road to the extinction of Western influence. French and British landed at Suez but the United States obliged them to withdraw. The West was in chaos. The Soviet Union had nothing to do but sit still and rake in her winnings. President Eisenhower compelled the Israelis to evacuate Sinai, which they had occupied. The president's career had culminated in victory in Europe in 1945. He was not obliged to worry about the Jewish vote.

After the Israeli withdrawal, United Nations troops occupied Gaza, the Sinai border and Sharm al Shaikh,[4] on the Egyptian side. Israel would not allow them on soil held by her. Paradoxically, Israel has frequently shown her dislike of the U.N., although a resolution of that organisation was her only title to existence.

* * *

We have seen how Moses Mendelssohn and his successors wished to draw Russian Jews to the freedom of the West. Some Jewish

[4] Map 35, p. 331.

writers, wishing to persuade Jews to leave Russia, published bitter comments on Jewish life in that country. Frishman, a Jewish author, wrote that Jewish life in Russia was "a dog's life that evokes disgust". Brenner described Russian Jews as "gypsies, filthy dogs". These writers were trying to persuade Jews to emigrate from Russia to the West.[5] The Zionists later used such passages to convince the world that Jews could never find freedom and dignity except in a Jewish state.

Ever since 1791, world Jewry has been intensely divided, whether to accept equality and emancipation, retaining Judaism as a religion, or whether to remain aloof, separated, a holy nation, a chosen people, mixing with the human race only in the course of business. "To be rooted is perhaps the most important . . . need of the human soul."[6] Was a Jew to be an American, or a Frenchman of the Jewish faith, or was he to remain everywhere an alien? The choice henceforward rested with the Jews themselves.

Ashkenazi Jews, the Germans and Russians, lived for many centuries in extreme isolation from their neighbours and developed a bitter, inward-looking mentality, determined to avoid Gentile contamination. The liberal Jewish millionaire, Baron de Hirsch, spent his fortune trying to move Jews out of Russia into the West. He wanted them to abandon their "ghetto-mindedness", as he put it. After 1881, indeed, increasing numbers of Jews did migrate to the West, but they brought their "ghetto-mindedness" with them. "It was in this climate that 'Jewish' political nationalism—neurotic, paranoid nationalism—was conceived by some of the spiritually maimed ghetto intelligentsia."[7]

During the First World War, as we have seen, Chaim Weizmann and a group of Russian Jews, captured the ear of the British government. British and American Jews were strongly opposed to what they considered the reactionary idea of a Jewish nation living in Palestine. To them, Jews were literally the salt of the earth, exerting their intellectual and spiritual influence among all nations.

A small group of British politicians, Lloyd George, Balfour and Ormsby Gore, gave the victory, in this inter-Jewish struggle, to the isolationists, thereby creating history's biggest and most inward-looking ghetto. This analysis is necessary in order to understand the impossibility of a bi-national state in Palestine. Jews, whether

---

[5] Michael Selzer, *The Arianization of the Jewish State*.
[6] Simone Weil, *The Need for Roots*.
[7] Moshe Menuhin, op. cit.

consciously or subconsciously, have gone to Palestine to create a completely Jewish community, isolated from and uncontaminated by the rest of humanity. It is this attitude which accounts for the forcible eviction of the Palestinians from their country. The Israelis wish to create an all-Jewish community which, like the old Ashkenazi ghettos, will be inhabited exclusively by Jews.

The only statesmanlike way to achieve this ideal would have been that intended by the original Zionists like the Rothschilds, to buy the land gradually, giving a good price to such Palestinians as agreed to sell. This method was abandoned for various causes. Firstly, it was slow, and dreamers and idealists are always in a hurry. Violence, therefore, is irresistibly tempting to them.

Secondly, as Mr. Sylvain Levi had remarked at Versailles, "Russian Jews are of explosive tendencies." Moreover, the east European Jews who came to Palestine had been hardened and embittered by ill-treatment in Russia and by the Nazi persecution. Inured to violence, torture, police brutality, terrorism, and concentration camps, it was inevitable that they should apply some or all of these methods, with which they were so familiar, in their dealings with the Palestinians. Moreover, the great majority of those from eastern Europe were not practising Jews. Many were overt atheists.

Thirdly, the Nazi persecution supervened and made the situation more emotional and passionate.

Fourthly, when the German and Russian Jews arrived in Palestine, they realised how vulnerable the Palestinians, and how unprepared all the peoples of the Middle East would be, if exposed to ruthless military action, such as they had witnessed on the part of the Nazis and the Russian revolutionaries.

Fifthly, we may remember that the blue-print of the Zionist movement was drawn up from 1897 to 1900, at the height and in the spirit of European imperialism. European public opinion has since undergone a complete change of heart in its outlook. Only Israel and South Africa still maintain the contempt for the "natives", which was common in the West seventy years ago. Many South African Nationalists "saw the success of the Jews against the Arabs as a victory of white over non-white. Malan himself... voiced with much fervour a highly emotional people-of-the-book enthusiasm for the restoration of the Jews to their ancient homeland in accordance with Biblical prophecy."[8]

[8] Dr. Richard P. Stevens, *Zionism, South Africa and Apartheid*. Dr. Stevens is a professor at Lincoln University, Pennsylvania.

This passage, incidentally, refers to one of the many paradoxes connected with modern Israel. If the Israelis are white, conquering the non-white natives, how can Palestine be their homeland? The whiteness of European Jews is, of course, due to the fact that they are ethnically Europeans. A further paradox lies in the fact that many "liberals" in the West are passionately hostile to South African apartheid, but supporters of Zionism.

While Zionists, therefore, were the conquering imperialists in the Middle East, the funds which made their survival possible were sent to Israel from the West, on humanitarian grounds. There, Israel was depicted as the underdog, the poor, persecuted Jew, formerly massacred by the Nazis and the Russians, now once again exposed to extermination at the hands of a hundred million Jew-hating Arabs.

How was Israel to play the double part of the haughty conqueror in the Middle East, while retaining in the West the "image" of the down-trodden and persecuted Jew? It was here that President Nasser came to her rescue.

* * *

Most persons with experience of the Middle East are aware of Egyptian loquacity, and discount it. The Egyptians have the oldest civilisation in the world. Upper-class Egyptians are cultured, courteous and charming, the less educated are cheerful and humorous. But they have never been successful as soldiers. Such is the strategic importance of Egypt that, since 331 B.C., it has always been held by foreign conquerors, who defended it with foreign armies. Perhaps, also, overcrowding and a hot climate sapped the initiative of its down-trodden people.

Most of Egypt's foreign masters did not hesitate to express their contempt for the military inadequacy of the Egyptians and this scorn bit deeply into their souls. Somewhat ironically, Israeli aggressiveness was also produced by the contempt of other peoples. Thus Israeli military aggressiveness and Egyptian threats may both be traced back to the same cause—an inferiority complex produced by the arrogance of others.

President Nasser had a persuasive personality and, like Mussolini, he was a born demagogue. He employed his eloquence and his threats and fulminations against Israel to win the support of the simple-minded masses. But this political technique, aimed at his own people, enabled Israel to claim that she was threatened with extermination, and to acquire masses of modern weapons, maintain the flow of financial aid and yet, in the eyes of the West, remain the persecuted underdog. As long ago as 1957, I wrote that Egypt would not be able to resist an Israeli attack for more than forty-eight hours, yet, in the Western democracies, Israel was believed to be daily threatened with extermination.

Another Israeli stroke of genius was to attribute everything said by Nasser to "the Arabs". Until after the Second World War, Egypt had never associated herself with "the Arabs", whom she affected to despise. Moreover, there is very little Arab blood in the Egyptian's ethnic composition. There were some fourteen "Arab" States, not including the small ones, of whom only Egypt, Jordan and, to a minor extent, Iraq and Syria, had been in any way involved. The boastings and threats had been limited to Egypt and, occasionally, to Syria. Nevertheless, by attributing Nasser's menaces to "the Arabs", it was possible to add up all those countries from Morocco to Persia and to claim that a hundred million Arabs had vowed to exterminate Israel, although, in fact, she was twenty or thirty times stronger than Egypt and Jordan, the only states militarily involved.

Under cover of the general belief that her own extermination might well be imminent, Israel was able to act towards the Palestinians with extreme ruthlessness, beating and torturing them, driving them from their homes, or ruling the survivors by military law, while complaining plaintively that the "Arabs" were so aggressive.

The exchange of recriminations does more harm than good, yet some reference to the present situation is necessary. In May 1969, for example, five thousand Palestinians were estimated to be in Israeli "Detention Centres", held under military law, and not under Israeli civil law. It is alleged that none of these persons had been tried, nor had any charges been brought against them. They were said to be under constant interrogation, and subjected to humiliation and ill-treatment. Neither the International Red Cross, nor the United Nations nor Amnesty International have been allowed to visit these Detention Centres, nor can their relatives contact the prisoners. These methods were in use under the Nazis and in Russia.

In June 1967,[9] three "Arab" villages, Amwas, Yalu and Beit Nuba, were completely bulldozed out of existence. The total number of inhabitants was 9,150. The villagers were not given time to collect their belongings, and furniture, clothing, carpets and books were bulldozed into the rubble.[10] Apart from these three villages, some

[9] The six-day war is discussed in the next chapter.
[10] John Carter, *An Eyewitness in Jerusalem, Spring 1969*.

3,392 Arab homes had been bulldozed down by April 1969 and the residents left homeless. So little notice is given that a case is quoted of an old woman who was bulldozed into the ruins of her house, because she failed to get out in time. This type of destruction of property is contrary to the Geneva Convention, ratified by Israel on 12th August, 1949.[11]

The economic life of those Palestinians who still remain in territory under Israeli military occupation is increasingly precarious. The Israeli government, for example, controls all imports by licence, and can, if it wishes, put any Palestinian trader out of business. The Israeli government also controls all hotel accommodation for tourists, and is accused of injustice in filling Jewish hotels and leaving "Arab" hotels empty. There are so many economic means by which Palestinians can be reduced to penury that proof is impossible. It is claimed that the Israelis hope to hold all Palestine as a Jewish state in which there will be virtually no non-Jews. These various forms of pressure are believed by the Palestinians to be intended to compel them to abandon their country.

In April 1970, Amnesty International published a report on the treatment of prisoners in Israel. The report stated that, according to information available, Israeli military authorities detain some eighty "Arabs" each week under military law.

Amnesty International alleges that they pressed the Israeli government for twelve months to allow a commission of enquiry into charges of torture in military Detention Centres, but without success. Some of the items mentioned in the report published by Amnesty are horrifying.[12]

In the 1950s, I myself on one occasion met a party of Palestinians evicted from Israel. Several bore long, still-open wounds across their backs, the result of flogging. Some had broken teeth, which they alleged were from blows with rifle butts. One man had had his finger nails torn out, a painful torture used by the Nazis—doubtless on the Jews.

* * *

People have often said to me, "How *could* Jews, who have suffered so much, inflict similar persecutions on others?" This question raises an extremely interesting psychological problem, of which something

---
[11] John Carter, op. cit.
[12] *Report on the Treatment of Certain Prisoners under Interrogation in Israel.* Published by Amnesty International, Turnagain Lane, Farringdon Street, London, E.C.4.

on the following lines seems to me to be the most probable explanation.

When a man or a community suffers persecution or humiliation at the hands of another group, he may bear it humbly and patiently, or he may react outwardly with an arrogant defiance. But if the humiliation continues for long, he feels a haunting fear that he and his relatives really are of an inferior type. He bitterly envies his haughty and contemptuous military persecutors. But that which most undermines his character is his loss of confidence in himself.

Then, by a turn of fortune's wheel, he finds himself in a position to inflict the same sufferings on someone else. If this potential victim were the same person who had previously tortured him, then his action might be attributed to revenge. But what if the victim is a complete stranger, why should he wish to torture him?

I suggest that the answer lies in the fact that the motivation is the subconscious desire to recover confidence in himself. To prove that he is as good as his former persecutors, he imitates them closely and behaves towards his victims as his former tormentors behaved to himself. He blossoms out as an exact imitation of the strutting military bully whom he formerly so much feared, envied and admired. Himself now dressed as an officer, he wields on his cowering victim the same horsewhip beneath the lash of which he himself formerly cringed. At last, his ego gains satisfaction, he has become a big he-man wielding power over lesser breeds.

It is even sometimes a pleasure to be unjust. Merely to enforce the law is dull, ordinary, bourgeois. But to be manifestly unjust gives a sense of power. "I do this just because I feel that way—can anyone prevent me?"

*   *   *

Many people are surprised to hear of colour prejudices in Israel. There are, of course, Jews of many different colours and races. We have seen that Jews were, for centuries, the world's greatest international traders and that, from A.D. 650 to 1498, they enjoyed the immense advantage of being able to travel from Europe to the Muslim countries and on to India and China. Where they established trading stations, they doubtless required servants. But non-Jewish servants were useless in Jewish households, owing to the laws governing diet and ritual purity. Doubtless for this reason, or for the purpose of proselytism in general, such Jewish trading posts converted many of the local natives.

A news item in a recent daily paper told how a party of Indian Jews had moved to Palestine. In appearance, the report said, these Jews were indistinguishable from their Indian neighbours. The headline above this item, however, read "The Call of the Homeland". There are Jews in China and Africa, also, presumably converted by Jewish merchants long ago.

Michael Selzer was a Jew born in India, but educated at an English public school and at Balliol College, Oxford, moving from there to Israel. "In Jerusalem's prosperous Bet Hakerem suburb," he writes, "there is what is known as an Anglo-Saxon housing project where, despite this name, Central and East-European Jews live together with English-speaking settlers. Not all of the former can even speak English. Yet they are all counted as Anglo-Saxons of a kind. On the other hand, a Jew from India who spoke English as his mother tongue would not be admitted into this co-operative because (as we are told by some of the residents there) "we would never admit a black!"[13]

"What the Jews from Eastern Europe really dislike about their fellow Jews from the Orient is the fact that the latter tend to remind them of the social and cultural conditions prevailing only a few decades ago in their now rejected ghettos in Russia and Poland. It is this uncommon eagerness on the part of most East European Jews to forget and disown their own past, their own selves almost, which has led, on the one hand, to their present rejection of the "Sephardo[14] Orientals" and, on the other, to the dangerous drift away from their own true traditions and culture ... Indeed, one cannot help thinking that the constant current talk about the "cultural gap" dividing Israel's two communities fills a veritable psychological need."[15]

These psychological analyses, all written by Jews, are of great interest. The Eastern European Jew, it is suggested, is still, consciously or subconsciously, ashamed of his own past. To satisfy himself that he is now a conquering white race, he is under an urgent necessity to show contempt for races whose beliefs and customs resemble uncomfortably those of his own grandfather. He feels a compelling urge to be scornful of Eastern Jews and Arabs, in order to satisfy his own pride. Perhaps this also accounts for the allegedly numerous atheists among East European Jews in Israel. For ortho-

[13] Michael Selzer, *The Arianization of the Jewish State*.
[14] Sephardi Jews were originally those in Spain, who were evicted in 1492. The term is now often incorrectly used to mean Oriental Jews in general.
[15] "Israel's Community Controversy", *Midstream*, June 1964, quoted by Michael Selzer.

dox Judaism suggests the poor, suppressed Jew of Russia, the very image which the German, Russian and Polish Jews wish to forget. Yet to become Christians or Muslims would exclude them from Israel, where the strongest religious discrimination is practised. There is, therefore, no alternative for an Israeli who wishes to expunge the past but to become an atheist.

I lived in Iraq from 1920 to 1930. One of my first recollections on reaching Baghdad is of the Jews parading down the main street on Saturdays in all their finery. Jewish ladies wore cloaks made of a peculiar type of shot silk which was really beautiful. Young British officers vied with one another to buy these cloaks and send them to their lady friends in England. The Jewesses also wore heavy gold bracelets, bangles and other jewellery, which was visible to the passer-by. There was certainly no attempt to conceal the fact that they were the richest people in Baghdad. When parliamentary government was introduced in Iraq, the minister of finance was, as a matter of course, a Jew.

More remarkable, perhaps, was a wealthy Jew who lived in a small town on the Middle Euphrates in a tribal area which, in those days, was only partly under government control. He was a money-lender, or perhaps an agricultural bank, to the tribes in the area. His was the best house in the district and the chiefs of the surrounding tribes stayed with him when they came to town.

I remember once riding into the place across tribal country and overtaking his son Elias, riding alone and unarmed, his cloth saddle-bags stuffed with money, which he had been collecting from tribal debtors. I was accompanied by two armed men, but the young Jew rode alone.

I knew an Englishwoman who, since the Second World War, had worked for a refugee organisation, principally among refugees from behind the Iron Curtain. Then her organisation sent her to Baghdad, to facilitate the escape of Jewish refugees to Israel. On arrival, she visited one of the leaders of the Jewish community and, in the deepest secrecy, informed him that she had come to rescue them. "Go to Israel", he exclaimed to her in amazement, "most certainly not. Here in Iraq the people treat us as equals, but in Israel we would be looked down upon as 'coloured'." Since the 1967 war, however, the Iraqi attitude to Jews has deteriorated. When I sometimes see propaganda references to the terrible conditions in "the Baghdad ghetto" I cannot but remember those happy days in the 1920s.

*　　*　　*

It is neither right nor expedient for us, who have not undergone these trials, to express disapproval or indignation. But while we may attribute the arrogance of the ruling class in Israel to natural psychological causes, it does not mean that we should help them to continue to use these methods. For in my opinion, for what it is worth, the ruthlessness of the Israeli government is not a crime but a mistake.

Their professed contempt for the other peoples of the Middle East, their reliance on force alone, their reference to "punishing" those who resist them, cannot fail to rouse bitter hatreds, which will produce the same psychological stresses and complexes, as those by which Jews themselves are tormented. Many Jews, inside and outside Israel, are doubtful of the wisdom of the policy of more force, more and more bombings, and burnings[16] and torturings. We, too, may sympathise with past Jewish sufferings, but we should nevertheless, I submit, prevent them from continuing to use these suicidal methods, and persuade or, if inevitable, coerce them to come to terms with their neighbours and to live in peace. For, looking further ahead, it is only by such means that they themselves can permanently survive.

---

[16] By dropping napalm from the air.

XX

By Force Alone

Those who have been once intoxicated with power, and have derived any kind of emolument from it, even though but for one year, can never willingly abandon it.
>EDMUND BURKE

O my people, your rulers mislead you and destroy the road you walk on. Yahweh rises from his judgement seat, he stands up to arraign his people. Yahweh calls to judgement the elders and the princes of his people: "You are the ones who destroy the vineyard and conceal what you have stolen from the poor. By what right do you ... grind the faces of the poor?"
>*Isaiah III, 12 to 15* Jerusalem Bible

Force is all-conquering, but its victories are shortlived.
>ABRAHAM LINCOLN

War settles nothing, and after all the destruction and bloodshed are over, reason must resume its task of solving the controversy according to the principles of right and justice.
>JANE ADDAMS (1931 Nobel Peace Prize Winner)

To the Israelis I say that you ... should drop the attitude of the conqueror and the conviction that force and a policy of retaliatory killings is the only policy that your neighbours will understand. You should make your deeds correspond to your frequent utterance of the desire for peace. To the Arabs I say you should accept this state of Israel as an accomplished fact.
>HENRY A. BYROADE, Assistant Secretary of State, U.S.A. 1954, in *The Middle East*, Department of State publication, May 1954

XX

AFTER the 1956 crises, the situation seemed to be growing calmer. Israel, however, continued to increase her forces until she was so strong that only a few hours would be needed for her to conquer all her neighbours. Nearly all her increase in strength depended on the United States. Egypt, however, by her violent speeches and broadcasts, enabled Israel still to pose as the underdog.

On 4th November, 1966, Egypt and Syria signed a joint defence agreement, though the two governments, in fact, were mutually suspicious. Nasser was growing more cautious, though the Syrian government consisted of impetuous young army officers. Jordan, aware of her own weakness, was in favour of peace. No other "Arab" governments were involved.

The unhappy Palestinians were impatient. Nasser had promised to liberate Palestine and had done nothing. To quiet such critics, Nasser appointed Ahmed Shukairi as President of the Palestine Liberation Organisation, which began to raise an "army". The movement had, for Nasser, the additional advantage that it could make trouble for King Husain, under whose government most of the Palestinians lived. King Husain refused to admit Shukairi or his army, but the Syrians received him. Soon, however, young Palestinians realised that Shukairi was only a talker, and founded an organisation which would act. They called it Al Fateh, the Victory.

The Arab governments at this period were trying to avoid trouble. At a meeting attended by their chiefs-of-staff, they decided that they were too weak to fight Israel and agreed not to offer provocation. The young Palestinians alone wanted to fight, because they had lost their country.

Levi Eshkol was Prime Minister of Israel. He and many of the new immigrants did not want a war. Abba Eban, an English Jew and a Cambridge graduate, replaced the more activist Golda Meir as Foreign Minister. The Arabs in Galilee inside Israel, who had been under military rule since 1948, were promised a civil administration.

Mr. Ben Gurion, however, the former advocate of massive reprisals, with his supporters Dayan and Peres, accused the Eshkol cabinet of weakness, and opposed counsels of moderation. A few minor raids by Al Fateh gave the activists an excuse to demand old-style massive reprisals. On 13th November, 1966, a mine exploded on the Israel side of the line, west of Hebron. Eshkol was hustled into agreeing to a reprisal and the village of Samua,[1] east of the line, was attacked by a force of infantry, tanks and jets. The village was completely destroyed, eighteen Jordanians were killed and a hundred and thirty-four injured.

Violent riots took place west of the Jordan, fanned by Shukairi's Liberation Organisation. The Jordan government was accused of connivance with Israel. But Nasser was also blamed for not intervening.

* * *

The Syrian-Israeli Armistice agreement of 1949 established a demilitarised zone on the border, in which the Arab civilian inhabitants were to be allowed to continue to live and to cultivate their lands. Israel later refused to respect this agreement, drove out the cultivators and blew up the village of Tawafik, inhabited by Syrians. The Israelis then began to cultivate certain Arab lands in the demilitarised zone, in spite of repeated warnings by the U.N. Truce Commission.

General Van Horn, Chief of the U.N. Truce Supervision organisation from 1959 to 1963, reported that "the Jews developed a habit of irrigating and ploughing in stretches of Arab land." At ploughing and harvest, when the Israelis worked the land, the Syrians fired on them. "It is unlikely," wrote the general, "that the Syrian guns overlooking the demilitarised zone would ever have come into action had it not been for Israeli provocation."[2] In the Western press, which normally took the Israeli view, these incidents were reported as Syrians firing on Israeli farmers.

In January 1967, the usual incidents occurred when the Israelis began to plough the Arab land in the demilitarised zone. In Israel, the activists accused Mr. Eshkol of weakness. The Syrians, they said, must be taught a lesson. In April 1967, further incidents occurred, and exchanges of fire resulted. As a reprisal, Israeli aircraft raided the suburbs of Damascus, shooting down six Syrian aircraft. Further bitterness was provoked by arrogant Israeli comments that the Syrians had been "punished", or "had had a warning". Eshkol was

[1] Map 33, p. 311.
[2] General Carl Van Horn, *Soldiering for Peace*.

being pushed by the Israeli army into further reprisals. On 12th May, General Rabin, Chief-of-Staff of the Israeli army, declared that there could be no peace until the government in Damascus had been overthrown.[3] The Syrians replied defiantly.

President Nasser was uneasy. He had been severely criticised for not intervening in the Israeli attack on Samua in Jordan, or in Israeli provocation in the Syrian demilitarised area. Early in May 1967, reports of Israeli military activity on the Syrian border were received from Syria and Lebanon. Worst of all, the Soviets warned Nasser of aggressive Israeli intentions against Syria. If Israel attacked Syria and he did nothing, his career would be over.

Many theories have been held as to causes of the 1967 war. Firstly, some believe that Israel stirred up the trouble, by aggressive public statements and by artificial radio messages, intended to be picked up by ships in the Mediterranean, and by Syrian and Egyptian listening posts. The Israelis are masters of secrecy, and would not have allowed their plans to leak out unintentionally. Moreover, no "preparations" were needed if they wished to attack Syria for their plans for secret mobilisation are highly efficient. It is possible that the army broadcast these messages unknown to Mr. Eshkol.

Secondly, the Russians have been blamed for engineering the war, in order to achieve their ambition to pass a fleet into the Mediterranean. The Western press, indifferent to strategy and emotionally influenced by Israel, neglected this possibility. Every soldier with any knowledge of the Middle East knew that Egypt could scarcely resist Israel for a few hours. As early as 1957, I had estimated her resistance at forty-eight hours, and Jordan's at three days. The Pentagon seems to have thought the same. Ever since, in 1956, the United States cancelled her loan for the Aswan Dam, there had been many Russians in Egypt. It is inconceivable that the Soviets can have thought that Egypt would win.

Egypt depended on Russia for arms and for the Aswan Dam. During the weeks of rising tension preceding June 1967, Russia could have restrained Egypt and the latter could scarcely have resisted such pressure especially as no Arab country wished for war. Yet the Russians did not act to ease the tension.

That Russia for two hundred years had wished for a naval base in the Mediterranean is incontrovertible. Yet throughout this time, the Western Powers were determined not to allow her to obtain one, and maintained strong fleets to prevent it. For two hundred years,

[3] Maxime Rodinson, *Israel and the Arabs*.

1967 was the first chance the Russians had to enter the Mediterranean without risking a major war. Ever since 1798, Britain had shown her determination to retain naval command of the Mediterranean. In the 1950s, however, she had evacuated Egypt. In the 1960s, perhaps for the first time since Charles II, she had lost her realisation of the fact that her survival depended on a strong navy. The Royal Navy was drastically reduced and the Mediterranean virtually abandoned.

At the same time, the United States was deeply involved in Vietnam, and pacifist feeling in the country was growing. Perhaps never again would conditions be so favourable for Russia.

Another factor supporting the charge that the Soviet wanted the war lies in the fact that, when Nasser later closed the Straits of Tiran, Russia supported his action and informed Turkey that she was sending a fleet through the Bosphorus. The Soviet government is always cautious and deliberate. Unlike the Western democracies, it does not take hasty and ill-considered action on the basis of outbursts of popular emotion. To send a battle fleet into strange waters at a period of tension requires thought and preparation. That the Russians were able to do this, suggests that it had been planned well ahead.

The one theory which seems obviously wrong is the one still generally believed in the West, namely that Nasser decided to risk another war. Two factors must be remembered. Firstly, that the nature of Egyptians is to threaten but not to act. (No other Arabic-speaking people has this characteristic, except, perhaps, to a lesser degree the Syrians.) Secondly, President Nasser was essentially a politician. His rise to fame was due to his claim that he could defeat Israel. Since then, he had barely maintained his position by bold speeches, though aware that he was powerless to act.

President Nasser believed that Israel would attack Syria, and that, if he did nothing, his career would be over. His position was precarious, and his only course was to try bluff. On 15th May, 1967, columns of Egyptian troops passed ostentatiously through Cairo, heading for Sinai.

On the same day, 15th May, Israel held a military parade in Jerusalem, in defiance of the United Nations, who still claimed that Jerusalem was an international zone. Nasser was defying Israel, Israel was defying the United Nations. On 16th May, Egypt requested the withdrawal of the U.N. troops on the Sinai border, for Nasser's critics had sneered that he was hiding behind them.

Syria and Jordan were unaware of the president's intentions.

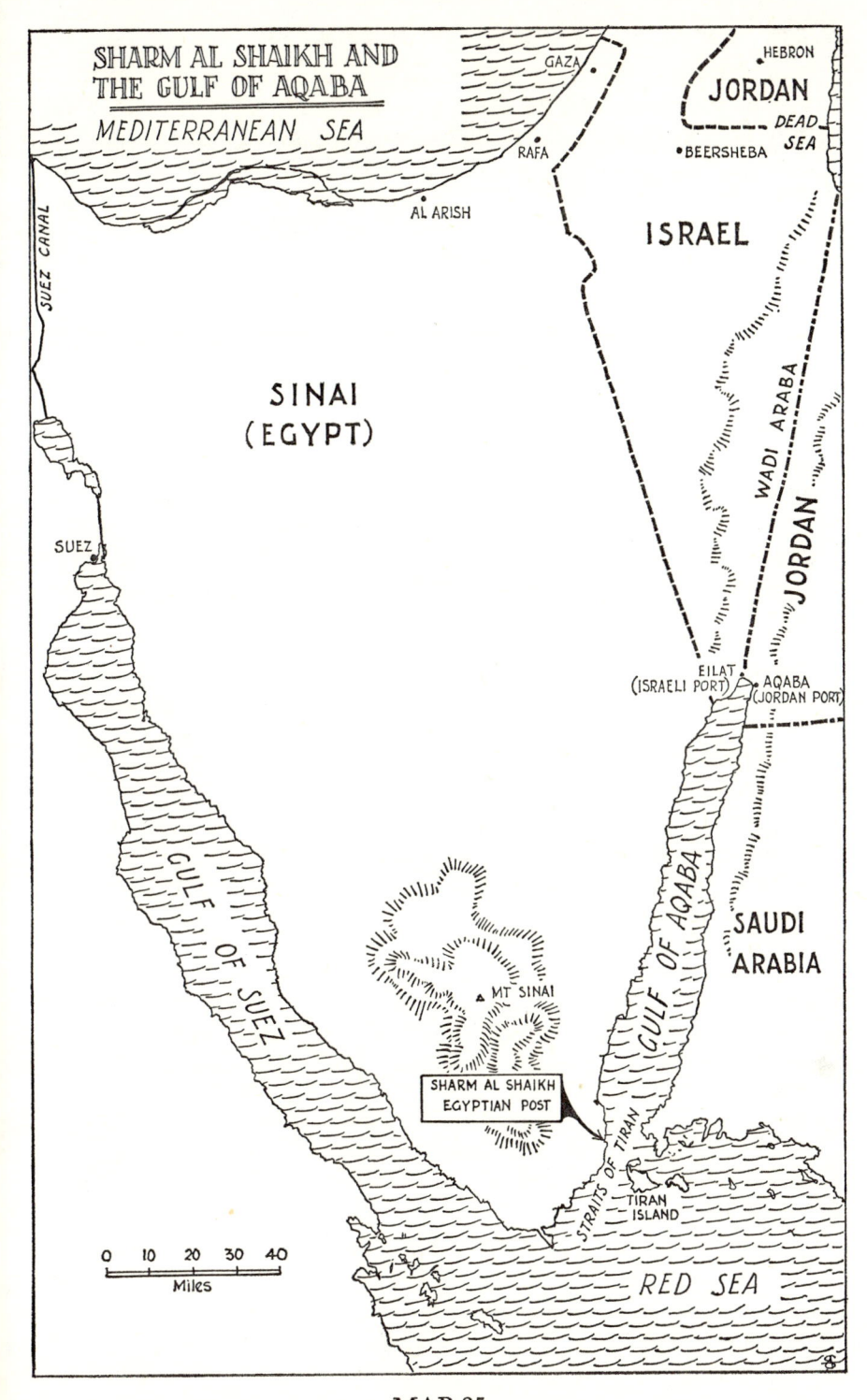

MAP 35

The Egyptian radio, at this moment, was engaged in a violent campaign urging the Jordanians to dethrone King Husain. The Egyptians may be unpractical but surely, if they had been preparing for war, they would first have come to terms with their "allies". In addition, a large part of the Egyptian army was far away in the Yemen. It is scarcely believable that most of these troops would not have been recalled, if Nasser really meant to fight.

The United Nations had evacuated Sharm al Shaikh, on Egyptian territory, and, on 21st May, it was occupied by an Egyptian post. The Egyptian commander-in-chief said that the straits would not be closed but, on 23rd May, Nasser announced their closure to Israeli shipping. The Western press proclaimed in startling headlines that Israeli's life-line was cut. In fact, only five per cent of Israel's trade passed through the straits, but she did import most of her oil that way, chiefly in neutral tankers.[4]

The arguments regarding Egypt's alleged right to close the straits are complicated. No two nations interpret maritime law alike. The closure, for a considerable time, would have had little effect on Israel's trade or food supply, though oil might have been awkward until supply could be arranged to Haifa.

On 23rd May, Nasser had closed the straits to Israeli ships and to oil tankers, but not to Israeli trade in neutral ships. On the same day, U Thant, Secretary General of the U.N., arrived in Cairo and conferred with the president. It was agreed that the United Nations would seek a compromise with Israel. Meanwhile, Nasser agreed not to increase the tension. In connection with Nasser's activities, it may be surmised that he wanted to make so much fuss that Israel would abandon her attack on Syria, but he did not wish to involve himself in war.

The Israeli activists seized on the closing of the straits to push Mr. Eshkol into war. But the most disastrous effect was in the United States, where President Johnson immediately stated that the straits must be reopened. Senator Robert Kennedy demanded that the United States navy reopen them by force. On 24th May, Mr. Harold Wilson, the British Prime Minister, said that Britain would be willing to assist in international action to reopen them. These reckless statements were to change the world balance of power in favour of Russia, for, if they had not been made, the Russian plan would not have succeeded.

Suddenly the United States was as bellicose as Egypt or Israel. There was no mention of negotiation or arbitration, or even of the

[4] Maxime Rodinson, *Israel and the Arabs*.

United Nations. This rash and biased attitude was not based on statesmanship, thought, knowledge, or even patriotism, but on party politics in the United States, who, by showing that she was not guided by reason or justice, destroyed her own chance of influencing events.

Nasser's rash move had also unleashed the enthusiasm of the mob. The ill-starred Ahmed Shukairi made a wild, demagogic speech, calling for the extermination of Israel, man, woman and child, which was widely publicised and roused great enthusiasm for Israel in the West. It also materially assisted the Israeli war party, who demanded instant action to save Israel from extermination, though they were well aware that they could defeat Egypt in a few hours. The usual technique was used, claiming that "the Arabs" were threatening Israel, and had moved "their armies" forward. In fact, President Nasser alone was involved, not because he wanted trouble, but owing to the precarious political situation in which he found himself.

Although Nasser's speeches were highly inflammatory, yet his every pronouncement seemed carefully to leave a door open for compromise. Normally, the conciliatory parts were not reported in the Western press. On 26th May, for example, he declared that, "*If Israel attacked Syria or Egypt*, the war would be total. The objective would be the destruction of Israel,"[5] a statement which could have been interpreted as trying to deter Israel from attacking Syria. The majority of Western newspapers omitted the phrase which made the threat conditional on an Israeli attack, and reported only that the war would be total with the object of destroying Israel.

The Soviet government had hitherto encouraged the increasing tension and had done nothing to restrain President Nasser, because they hoped to achieve their ambition of a fleet in the Mediterranean, but, at 3.30 a.m. on 27th May, an official from the Soviet Embassy woke President Nasser with a message from Mr. Kosygin, urging him not to attack, which he had never intended to do.

Had the Soviet government suddenly given way to panic, or was this much publicised visit before dawn a part of Russia's inscrutable game of chess? Perhaps it could be attributed to two causes. Firstly, the cautious Russians were determined not to clash with the United States and this move might convey the impression that they were anxious for peace.

The second possible cause requires a little explanation. The success of the Russian plan depended on two requirements. Firstly,

[5] Maxime Rodinson, *Israel and the Arabs*. The italics are his.

that the United States make a statement supporting Israel, thereby rendering it impossible for her to act any more in a judicial capacity restraining both sides. This President Johnson had obligingly done. The second requirement for Russian success was that Egypt be defeated.

The Egyptians wanted to be powerful and independent, not Russian satellites. But if Egypt suffered a shattering defeat (the United States having already aligned herself with Israel), the Egyptians would be obliged to throw themselves unreservedly into the arms of Russia. The only danger here lay in the possibility that the Egyptians might see through the Russian plot, by which the Russians had manœuvred her into war, and then failed to rescue her. It was, therefore, advisable at this stage to convey the impression to the Egyptians that Russia was afraid that Egypt might get involved in war.

On 29th May, an American representative arrived in Cairo, and discussed with Nasser a number of compromises, leaving room for further negotiation. The American envoy, Mr. Charles Yost, stayed five extremely critical days in Cairo, only leaving on 3rd June, "having given an assurance that Israel would not attack as long as diplomatic activity was maintained."[6] Nasser must have heaved a sigh of relief.

On 30th May, 1967, King Husain flew to Cairo, although the Syrian and Egyptian radios were still vilifying him in terms as violent as they used against Israel. The King believed that he had no alternative. If war came, Jordan remained neutral and Egypt were defeated, all the blame for everything would be heaped on the "treachery" of Jordan. For many years, Egypt and Syria had been fomenting revolution in Jordan. Her refusal to co-operate against Israel might enable them at last to liquidate her.

On 1st June, the Israeli war party compelled Mr. Eshkol to accept Moshe Dayan as Minister of Defence. The absurd demagogues of Cairo and Damascus had united Israel for war. On the same day, the Israeli government seems to have decided to attack. When, on 3rd June, Mr. Charles Yost assured Nasser that Israel would not attack, the Israeli divisional commanders already had their operation orders. The United States government, according to Rodinson, had "not thought it necessary to inform the Israelis of Yost's negotiations, nor of the Egyptian concessions."[7]

It is impossible to lay all the blame for the 1967 war on one villain, for such situations always build up. It is possible that the Israeli

---

[6] Maxime Rodinson, op. cit.   [7] Maxime Rodinson, op. cit.

army, though not the government, first worked for war. The Russians quickly realised how much they might gain and, thereafter, both worked with the object of provoking one. In the last century, somebody said that the Jews were the cleverest people in the world but the least wise. Unequalled at organisation and planning, they work out every detail, provide for every contingency, foresee every eventuality—but in the end it appears that the whole operation was unwise.

The Israeli army knew that it could win in a few hours, after which it expected the abject surrender of all its neighbour states. This proved to be an error. But the Russians, unlike the Israelis, achieved all their objectives.

* * *

To this day, the public in the West believes that "the Arabs", in June 1967, "attacked Israel." This belief is erroneous. At 7 a.m. on 5th June, 1967, the Israeli air force took off and completely destroyed the Egyptian and Jordanian air forces on the ground. Egypt had a considerable number of aircraft, but Jordan had only twenty-four obsolete jets. The Egyptians seem to have been completely unprepared and were not expecting operations.

When, it would appear, the Egyptian army was already defeated, Nasser spoke directly to King Husain, telling him that the Israelis were in flight and asking for the Jordan army to intervene from the direction of Hebron. The king in person led his little armoured column along narrow roads in mountainous country, without air support or anti-aircraft weapons. The column was exterminated from the air by the Israeli jets using napalm. Doctors who treated survivors reported that they saw no bullet wounds, but only burns. One report read, "The Mobile Field Hospital, containing 350 patients, was incinerated with all its patients and staff by napalm."

One of the drawbacks of air warfare is that the attackers do not see the effect of their action. We shudder with horror at the thought of the Inquisition, which burned heretics alive. Yet the United States and Israel burn alive great numbers of people with napalm, without anyone giving the matter a thought, because the American public does not see their agonies.

When the Israeli army reached the Suez Canal, the Soviet fleet arrived in Port Said and Alexandria and received a popular ovation as the saviours of the country. This was a truly brilliant, if unscrupulous, example of combined diplomacy and strategy. The

Russians in a week achieved an ambition more than two hundred years old without firing a shot.

A Western newspaperman recently reported that an Israeli said to him, "What do the Russians want with us? If they wish to destroy Israel, they will have to kill every one of us first." Small countries often imagine that the Great Powers are anxious to fight *them*. This, however, is rarely the case. The Super Powers are concerned with one another. The Russian objective is to dominate the Mediterranean and Western Europe and to force the United States out of Europe to isolation beyond the Atlantic. The Russian bases in Egypt are directed solely against the Western democracies. Israel, Egypt, Syria and Jordan are but tiny pawns in Russia's world power politics.

* * *

In this chapter, I have departed from my resolution not to go into detail, because the events of 1967 still dominate the situation, and reveal the characteristics of the disputants, but are still little understood in the West. Yet concentration on detail tends to obscure the original cause of the problem. The endless arguments regarding the villanies of Nasser, the bravery (or the cruelty) of Israel, or the unscrupulous conduct of Russia have indeed caused us to forget how it all began. This is not basically a war between Israel and Egypt, or a jockeying for strategic positions between the United States and Russia or an alliance of Asia and Africa against the West. All these evils are subsidiary and grow from one original act of injustice. The origin of all these mischiefs was the fact that the Palestinians, a pleasant, unwarlike people, were driven destitute from their homes and their country by military force.

Opposition to so-called "colonialism" is one of the strongest sentiments among the public in the Western democracies today. The Palestinians, Syrians, Jordanians and Egyptians were conquered by the Ottoman Turks in 1517. As a result, they fell behind the material wealth of the West, which has developed since the Industrial Revolution. Say, if you wish, that they were backward. But so were all the peoples of Asia and Africa which became European colonies in the nineteenth century, but who have since received their independence. No one claims that the coloured peoples in South Africa or Rhodesia are as efficient as the white population, yet the whole world seems to be bitterly critical of apartheid. The curious factor is that only in the case of Israel is "backwardness" held to justify the eviction of a whole people from their country.

Yet the Israeli conquest of Palestine is more brutal than European colonialism, which indeed involved a war at the commencement. But, when victory was won, nineteenth-century colonialism did not involve the liquidation of the native population, or their forcible eviction from their country and its resettlement by an alien race and culture. Normally, a small staff of Europeans were left to administer the country, junior officials, police and soldiers being from the native population. Usually a period of development ensued, roads were constructed, schools were opened, wealth increased, law and order were established. But, in modern opinion, none of these material advantages are thought to compensate for the imposition of alien rule. I cannot recollect any instance, at least for four hundred years past, when a colonising power liquidated the native population as Israel has done.

President Nasser may have been a demagogue, but he was the head of an independent state. Whatever crimes he may or may not have committed, they do not justify the ruthlessness of Israel towards the poor people of Palestine.

In 1967, Israel had a wonderful opportunity to win a lasting peace. After so shattering a victory, a generous gesture might have saved all. But the Israeli government was not big enough to be statesman-like. When her enemies did not surrender, she resumed her hard line, driving her victims from their homes, bulldozing down whole villages, bombing the refugee camps and the towns and villages of the neighbouring countries. Force can do much, but too much force can defeat its own ends. Men and women who have nothing more to lose may well become dangerous. To drive an enemy to complete and utter despair may be unwise.

* * *

It is a common device of Israeli propaganda to denounce as anti-Semitic, Jew-hater, or Nazi anyone who criticises the Israeli government in office at any particular time. These accusations are not justifiable. Israel claims to be a bastion of democracy, yet democracy, as understood in the West, permits criticism of the government. I do not believe that the majority of Jews in the world approve of Israel as a ruthless, colonising, military state. Many are doubtful or disapproving but cannot speak out, for the key propaganda posts are in the hands of Zionists. Others have been misled by Israeli propaganda, or believe that "the Arabs" are aggressive and anti-Semitic, and that Israel is still in danger of extermination.

I personally believe that the continual use of force alone is a lack of political judgement. The continued use of violence raises up more violence against itself. Peace can only be gained and made secure and enduring by the adoption of a just, reasonable and sympathetic approach to the other party. Israel, it seems to me, missed a great opportunity after her victory in 1967. Her neighbours were shattered and would probably have accepted a generous final settlement. But Israel was too exhilarated by her triumph and expected unconditional surrender. This Egypt and Jordan were not prepared to offer and, as time passed and they recovered from their shock, they became less ready to submit. Moreover, the presence of the Russians in Egypt has now changed the situation. Egypt did not want to lose her independence to Russia, but a Soviet garrison was at least preferable to an Israeli occupation.

Two new developments ensued. Firstly, the Israelis resumed their hard line, chiefly in the form of bombing and dropping napalm on Egypt and Jordan. As time went on, this air action became increasingly indiscriminate, for neither Egypt nor Jordan possessed operational air forces. As it proved, intensified Israeli bombing of the Egyptian delta played the Soviet game, for it provided an excuse for the strengthening of the Russian build-up in Egypt, including the despatch of ground-to-air missiles and of Soviet pilots. The usual vicious circle continued. The United States supplied more bombers to Israel, who stepped up her air attacks on Egypt. The Russians were thus given a pretext to increase their strength in Egypt, with a view to its ultimate use, not against Israel, but against the Western allies.

The second result of the Arab débâcle of 1967 was a marked increase of activity on the part of the Palestine guerrillas. Regular armies having failed, the refugees decided to act for themselves. Reports of their exploits roused great enthusiasm all over the Arabic-speaking, and even the whole Muslim, world, and funds and weapons poured in to support them. Unfortunately, some of the guerrillas became arrogant and behaved in an increasingly high-handed manner towards the governments, particularly Lebanon and Jordan.

In June 1970, the United States government put forward proposals for a cease-fire to allow of negotiations. These proposals were accepted by Egypt and Jordan and, later on, somewhat hesitatingly, by Israel. Shortly afterwards, however, Israel withdrew from the negotiations, on the grounds that Egypt had taken advantage of the cease-fire to move forward certain Russian missile sites. This may or may not have been true, but Israel also had profited by the truce to improve her defences. In any case, fixed anti-aircraft missile sites are defensive, not offensive, installations.

As has already been emphasised, the origin of the fighting in the Middle East was the eviction of the native population of Palestine from their homes. The American proposals treated the problem as a war between Israel, Egypt and Jordan, which could be ended by negotiations between the three governments. The Palestine refugees, the heart of the problem, were scarcely mentioned.

The guerrillas cannot defeat the Israeli army but they can prevent the establishment of peace until their very real grievances have been redressed. The Jordan government had agreed to negotiate, with the result that fighting broke out in Jordan on 17th September, 1970, between the guerrillas and the Jordan army. It is futile to argue which side was responsible. The existence of two armies, following different policies, in one city was a situation which could not last.

The clash, however, was not solely due to refugee opposition to the Egyptian and Jordanian acceptance of negotiations. The long procrastinations on the part of the Great Powers had led to the increasingly rapid diffusion of extreme political views among refugee leaders, some of whom were confessed Marxists or Maoists. For such, Jordan as a pro-West monarchy was an obvious target. There had also been an undercurrent of jealousy between Syria and Jordan since 1945, especially as the former country, in 1970, had a left-wing government in office. Syrian tanks crossed the border to assist the guerrillas to overthrow the Jordan government but were sharply repulsed by the Jordan army.

Ultimately, the guerrillas were evicted from Amman, but clung to a number of points in the north-west corner of Jordan. The fighting, however, left a legacy of hatred between Jordan and many Palestinians. To the historian, it is impossible to escape the resemblance between this vicious gang warfare in the very presence of a powerful outside enemy, and the similar feuds between John of Gischala, Simon bar Giora and Eleazar the Zealot, while the Romans were besieging Jerusalem. These peculiar psychological attitudes are so unlike the mentality of the Arabs in other areas, that some explanation seems necessary. Can it be that the so-called Arabs of Palestine today are to a considerable degree the descendants of the defenders of Jerusalem against Titus, converted first to Christianity and then, after A.D. 650, to Islam?

*   *   *

On 5th February, 1971, the cease-fire which had been due to end on that day was extended until 6th March. The Egyptian government, however, emphasised its unwillingness to continue prolonging the cease-fire indefinitely, while Israel consolidated her hold on the territories she had occupied. The negotiations had been conducted in secrecy and the likelihood of a peaceful outcome was difficult to assess.

The possibility of achieving peace seems to me to depend on the United States government. A reasonable solution seems to be not impossible, if the United States were to support it. But if America supports Israel alone, regardless of right or justice, a solution will not be found. It is possible that the Israeli government might wish for an Egyptian refusal to renew the cease-fire, which would enable her once again to lay the blame for the renewal of hostilities on the "Arabs", and would thus provide her with a pretext to conquer more territory. A book is said to have been recently published in Hebrew in Israel, under the title of *A Great Land For a Great Nation*, advocating the conquest of Iraq and Kuwait.[8] Perhaps the neighbours of Israel need security more than she does.

---

[8] *Middle East Perspective*, New York, 1970.

XXI

The Middle East— Key to World Power

Italy was at the mercy of any man who once got control of Egypt, for the province is the key to both sea and land.
Tacitus

Egypt is the most important country in the world.
Napoleon Bonaparte

In fifty years' time armies will no longer have much significance. We shall have undermined our enemies to such an extent before war breaks out that it will be impossible to set the war machine in motion in the hour of need.
Lenin (in 1920)

XXI

HISTORY in the Middle East goes back for five or six thousand years. Almost all the world's great empires during this period have been involved in that area. In the West at least, the only exception has been the Spanish Empire in America.

The Middle East produced the Pharaohs, the Assyrians, the Babylonians and the ancient Persians. These were followed by the Greeks after Alexander, the Romans, the Byzantines, the Arabs, the Ottomans and the British. Each of these, in its time, was the world's greatest empire and every one of them at the height of its power controlled the Middle East and most particularly Egypt. It is an exaggeration, but not a very great exaggeration, to say that, for five thousand years, the Power which controlled Egypt was the greatest Power of the time.

A cursory glance at the map supplies the explanation. Firstly, it will be noted, Egypt is almost at the centre of the Old World, the three continents of Europe, Asia and Africa. Indeed, if China be omitted, Egypt is the exact centre. Secondly, the arrangements of deserts and mountains are such that transport between east and west is forced through a defile leading up the Red Sea to Egypt.

Thirdly the basin of the Indian Ocean, from East Africa to India and Indonesia has always exported many commodities which cannot be produced in Europe. Consequently, for thousands of years, the passage way from the Indian Ocean to the Mediterranean and vice versa, was the world's most important trade route.

Fourthly, from a strategic point of view, any Power with a base in Egypt, can move into Africa, Asia or Europe at will. This was illustrated in the Second World War, when Britain, from her base in Egypt, moved her armies into North Africa, Greece, Abyssinia, Iraq and Syria. Conversely, of course, the Power which holds Egypt can prevent its enemies moving their forces from any one of these continents to another.

Fifthly, Egypt has harbours on two seas, the Mediterranean and the Red Sea, leading to the Indian Ocean. Thus a naval Power based on Egypt can pass its fleet from the Mediterranean into the Indian Ocean and back at will, while its enemies are obliged to go round the Cape of Good Hope and back through the Straits of Gibraltar.

The immense strategic importance of Egypt has been appreciated

THE MIDDLE EAST — KEY TO WORLD POWER

AN EGYPTIAN BASE PERMITS:
1. MOVEMENT AT WILL INTO EUROPE, ASIA OR AFRICA
2. DENY SUCH MOVEMENT TO ENEMIES
3. NAVAL BASES ON MEDITERRANEAN AND RED SEA
4. ABILITY TO SWITCH SAME FLEET BACKWARDS AND FORWARDS FROM MEDITERRANEAN TO INDIAN OCEAN
5. CONTROL OF GREAT EAST-WEST TRADE ROUTE
6. AIR BASE DOMINATING EUROPE, NORTH AFRICA AND WEST ASIA

SEA LANES
VASCO DA GAMA
EGYPTIAN BASE

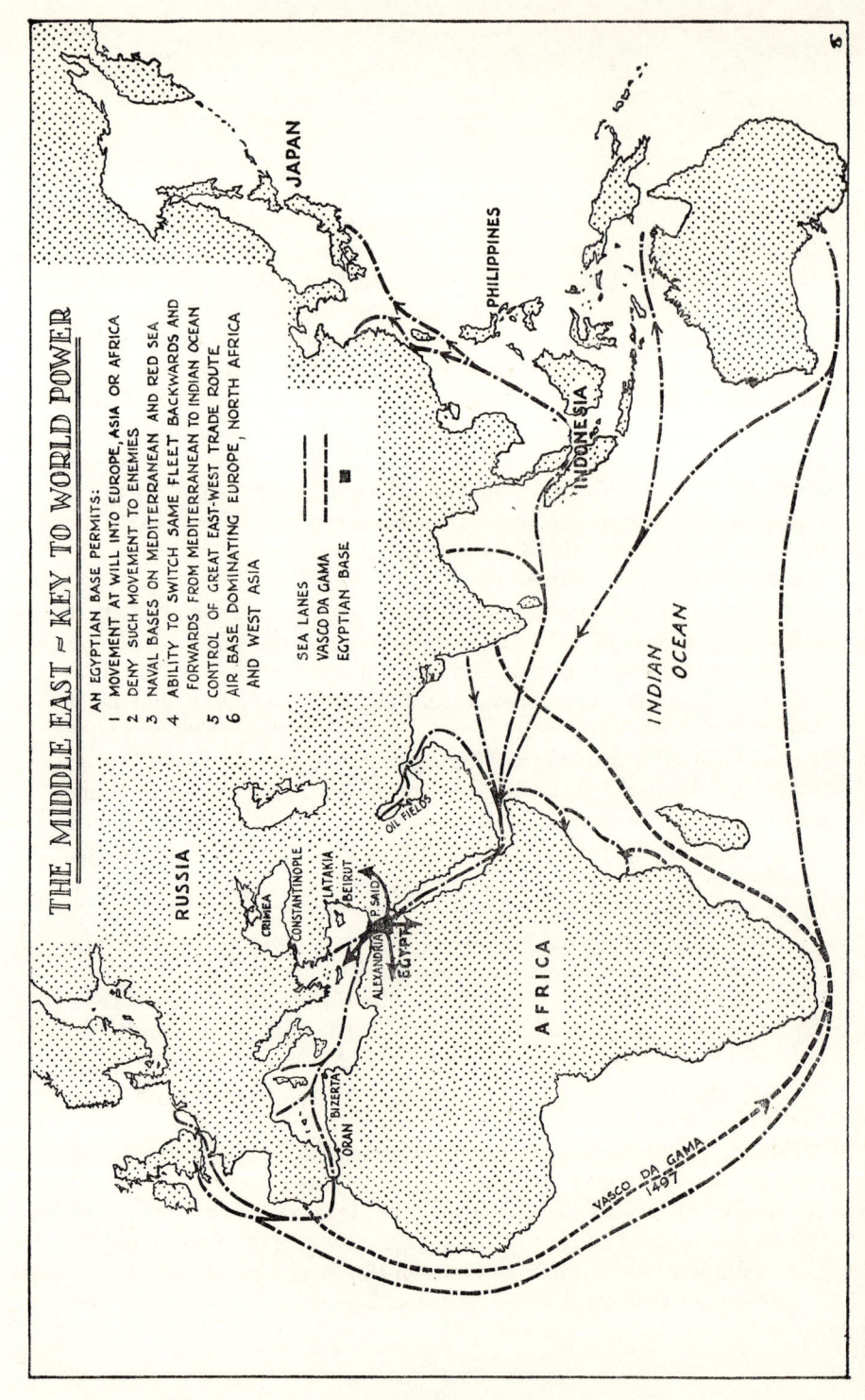

MAP 36

since the earliest times. The Assyrians, the Babylonians and the Persians occupied the country. When Alexander the Great set out to destroy the Persian Empire, he defeated the Persian army at Issus in northern Syria. But he did not pursue the defeated enemy back to Persia, as might have seemed tactically desirable. He marched down the east shore of the Mediterranean and made sure of Egypt. Only then did he return to conquer Persia.

When Rome replaced the Greeks, she too seized Egypt. The Roman Emperors thought the country so important that they personally appointed the governors. They would not permit the Senate to appoint a politician, as it did to most other provinces.

We have already seen how the Arab conquest of Egypt in A.D. 642 quickly reduced Europe to a primitive agricultural community—the Dark Ages. Europe remained blockaded by the Muslim world for eight hundred and fifty years. The turning point came at the end of the fifteenth century. In 1492, Columbus discovered America, and in 1497, Vasco da Gama sailed round the Cape of Good Hope.

The Portuguese quickly turned the tables on the Muslims. From the Indian Ocean, they sailed up the Red Sea and the Persian Gulf and blockaded the Arabs in turn. The trade of the Indian Ocean was carried to Europe round the Cape. This change in the control of the trade route to the East reversed the balance of power of the world. Hitherto, the Muslim nations had been the most powerful, the most enlightened, the most industrialised and the richest in the world. After 1497, the Muslims slipped into *their* Dark Ages and Europe forged rapidly ahead.

The Muslims, however, the Mamlooks in Egypt and later the Ottomans, still possessed formidable land armies. The seizure of Egypt was beyond the strength of Europe. But they neutralised her by their ships in the Indian Ocean—the Portuguese, then the Dutch, then the British—and carried away the riches of the East by sailing round Africa.

The next milestone in our brief history of the Middle East occurred in 1798, three hundred years after Vasco da Gama. Revolutionary France was at war with the whole of Europe, and Napoleon Bonaparte was beginning his military career. He did not do so by setting out to destroy his European enemies. He embarked his army on the Mediterranean and landed in Egypt. His penetrating mind had grasped the fact that Egypt was the key to world power.

Napoleon's plan was to establish a French military base in Egypt and naval command of the Mediterranean. Thence he would have built a French fleet on the Red Sea, and seized naval command of the

Indian Ocean from the British, whose ships and armies had to be maintained round the Cape of Good Hope. This grand strategic plan was frustrated by Nelson's destruction of the French fleet in the mouth of the Nile on 1st August, 1798. Having lost naval command of the Mediterranean, the base in Egypt could not be maintained.

Napoleon returned to France and spent the next fourteen years defeating the Great Powers of Europe again and again. Yet his loss of Egypt and naval command of the Mediterranean prevented his achieving a final victory. The failure of his Middle East plan, he said, had changed his destiny. Shortly before his death, when discussing the balance of power with Sir Hudson Lowe, the governor of St. Helena, the emperor is reported to have said, that it was essential "always to remember that Egypt is the most important country in the world".

Russia was a latecomer among the Great Powers. It was not until the 1750s that she aspired to compete with France, Britain or the Empire. As soon as she did so, she appreciated that naval command of the Mediterranean was the key to the domination of Europe. She hoped to achieve this end by the annexation of Constantinople, the capital of the Ottomans, which possessed also a historical and religious attraction, for the Czars claimed to be the heirs of the Byzantine Emperors, and the Russian Church the successor of the Greek Orthodox.

In a period of one hundred and sixty years, from 1754 to 1914, Russia attacked the Turks some ten times, that is, a war on an average every fifteen years, always against the same enemy. The Ottoman empire was decadent. In the sixteenth century it had been the most powerful and efficient in Europe, but in the nineteenth it was collapsing. The Western Powers, however, were fully alive to Russia's ambitions and were determined not to allow her to obtain a naval base in the Mediterranean.

Whenever the Ottoman Empire was in danger from the Russians, the Western Powers came to her aid. The Crimean War was fought by France, Britain and Piedmont (soon to become the Kingdom of Italy) to prevent the Russian fleet emerging into the Mediterranean. On other occasions Austria, Prussia and other European governments joined in supporting the Ottomans.

In 1914, the annexation of Constantinople was again one of the principal Russian war aims, but in 1916 the revolution placed Russia *hors de combat*. The Soviets, however, retained the policy of the Czars in their ambition to place a Russian fleet in the Mediterranean.

Meanwhile, in 1869, the Suez Canal had been opened, largely

through the efforts of the Khedive of Egypt, Ismail Pasha. But the latter, in his passion for modernisation, had borrowed large sums in Europe, which he could not repay. In 1875, he put off the evil day by selling his shares in the Suez Canal, which were snapped up on his own initiative by Britain's great Prime Minister, Benjamin Disraeli. Nevertheless, in 1876, Egypt was virtually bankrupt, and an Anglo-French commission took charge of the country's finances.

In 1882, disorders broke out all over the country and, in May, the British and French fleets were sent to Alexandria, where a massacre of European residents occurred on 11th June, 1882. The British government invited France and Italy to join her in landing troops but both declined. As a result, the British landed alone and, on 13th September, 1882, the Egyptian army was completely defeated at Tel al Kabir by Sir Garnet Wolseley. The Khedive's government remained in power but was obliged henceforward to accept the advice of the British Consul General. A period of prosperity ensued, the administration was modernised, forced labour abolished and the irrigation system was brought up to date.

From 1882 to 1914, therefore, Egypt, the most important country in the world, was under British control and Europe's lifeline to the East was secure. The exclusion of Russia was further secured by Britain's traditional policy of support for the Ottomans.

We have already seen that this traditional policy was shattered in 1914, when Turkey joined Germany in the First World War. Britain conceived the wise and far-seeing policy of replacing the Ottoman Empire by an Arab Empire or confederation, east of Sinai. This long-sighted plan was wrecked by the French seizure of Syria in July 1920, and by the Balfour Declaration promising help for a National Home for the Jewish people in Palestine. Concessions were made to Egyptian aspirations, but a British garrison remained in Egypt and a British fleet in Alexandria.

In 1940, Britain found herself in the same position as France had been in 1798—at war with Europe and imminently threatened with invasion. Yet, at this supreme crisis, Mr. Winston Churchill denuded the home defences and sent a British army by sea round the Cape with orders, whatever happened, to hold on to Egypt. The fact that Napoleon Bonaparte and Winston Churchill, the greatest strategists in the world in the past two hundred years, both risked the safety of their countries in order to maintain a base in Egypt, is of profound significance.

If Britain had not retained Egypt and naval command of the Mediterranean, Hitler would probably have won the Second World

War. It is also worthy of note that the first counter attack against Nazi Germany started from the north coast of Africa against what Winston Churchill called "the soft underbelly of Europe".

In 1945, Britain still hankered after her traditional "Ottoman" policy, an allied and powerful Arab bloc in the Middle East. As a result, it was she who, during the Second World War, was instrumental in bringing together Arab governments to form the Arab League. The Arab League Charter was signed on 22nd March, 1945. It embodied a new feature—Egypt identified herself with the Arabs, which she had never done before. Not only so, but the headquarters of the Arab League were sited in Cairo, which virtually gave the leadership to Egypt. No sooner was the Charter signed than Britain hoped to conclude a comprehensive alliance with the League. The object of her policy was not "colonialism" but to find an ally in the Middle East, who would help to keep the Russians out, as the Ottomans had done in the past.

Unfortunately, however, the massive Jewish immigration into Palestine so alarmed the Arab neighbours of that country that the Arab League rapidly became hostile to the Western Powers. The collapse of the Mandate and the fighting of 1948 finally resulted in a rapprochement between the Arab League and Russia.

Britain still made one more effort to keep the Russians out. The neighbours of Israel—with the exception of Jordan—having ceased to co-operate with the West, a new league was built up, consisting of Muslim states, Turkey, Persia, Iraq and Pakistan, to prevent Russia's southward expansion. This group, which was associated with Britain, was called the Baghdad Pact. In 1958, however, a military revolution took place in Iraq and a republican régime, largely dominated by army officers, was installed. As a result, Iraq withdrew from the Baghdad Pact, which was thereafter known as Cento.

Shortly after the Second World War, a friend of mine was talking to a distinguished German diplomat who expressed the opinion that Germany lost both the world wars because she never obtained possession of Egypt. "But," he added, "I can assure you, my friend, that the Russians fully understand this fact. They will play their hand very carefully until they have seized Egypt." These words were spoken fifteen years before the six-day war which enabled the Russians to achieve their ambition.

Since the Second World War, public attention in the West, particularly in the United States and Britain, has been largely focused on the past relations between European empires and their colonial territories. It has often been assumed by the general public that the object of European powers in stationing garrisons overseas was to "exploit" the native inhabitants. In fact, this consideration often played no part. The rival powers of Europe were afraid of one another. The most obvious example was the chain of British naval bases from Gibraltar, to Malta, Cyprus, Egypt, Aden and Singapore, all of which were intended to enable Britain to protect her sea-borne trade from European rivals. Both the Arab League and the Baghdad Pact had the same object as the Crimean War, and the bases in the Mediterranean—to prevent Russia from dominating sea-borne trade to the East.

The six-day war, however, virtually destroyed Cento. With a Russian fleet in the Eastern Mediterranean, and Russian influence strong in Syria and Egypt, Turkey found herself surrounded. The British government, meanwhile, announced its withdrawal from the Persian Gulf, the Indian Ocean and countries east of Suez, leaving Persia and Pakistan unsupported. Realising that Western supremacy was, for the time being, at an end, these nations felt that they had no alternative but to turn to Moscow.

The basis of world power is the sea. The wealth of nations depends on their overseas trade and, in the event of war, their ability to continue the import of food and strategic materials from other continents. It was the realisation of this essential fact which enabled Britain, a small European nation, to be the greatest Power in the world for more than a hundred years.

The conquest and development of colonial territories is entirely distinct from this vital question of sea power. Perhaps Britain's colonial empire was acquired, as is said, in a fit of absence of mind, but her sea power was not. Her rulers were fully aware that everything depended on the Royal Navy, an axiom only forgotten in the 1960s. It would have been possible to grant independence to all colonial territories, but still to maintain a large measure of control of the oceans of the world—complete command of them with the assistance of the United States.

All this, for the present, seems to have been thrown away, though much of it might still be recovered. The claim that Britain still has a navy to defend her own shores is scarcely relevant. She can be starved into surrender by fleets far away in the Atlantic and the Indian Ocean.

If the Russian establishment in Egypt after the six-day war has jeopardised the future of Britain as an independent country, it has also placed all Western Europe in peril. As we have seen, it was naval command of the Mediterranean which defeated Napoleon, Kaiser Wilhelm and Hitler. If the power to strangle Europe were to pass completely into the hands of Russia, the future would be dark indeed. Today, however, there are still fleets in the western Mediterranean.

In so far as aid from America is concerned, it should also be remembered that submarines in the Atlantic nearly caused the defeat of the Allies in both world wars. Russia now has many times more submarines than Hitler had. Thus, in so far as conventional weapons are concerned, if Russia obtained complete command of the Mediterranean she would be in a position to blockade Europe.

It is scarcely believable now that, twenty-five years ago, the United States and Britain were the only Powers which completely dominated the Mediterranean, the Indian Ocean, the Atlantic and the Pacific. There was scarcely a Russian to be seen anywhere, outside the borders of the Soviet Union. Now, for a time at least, Russia seems to be on the way to dominate the world. It would be an exaggeration to say that the establishment of Israel has been the sole cause of the reversal of the balance of power, but it has undoubtedly been a major factor.

It is not an exaggeration to say that the friendship, or at least the neutrality, of the Arabic-speaking countries from Morocco to Syria is essential to the defence of Europe. Not, of course, that these countries have great fleets, armies or air forces which would make them powerful friends or dangerous enemies. All of them are weak and backward. But three thousand five hundred miles of coast, on the southern and eastern shores of the Mediterranean, belong to them. Israel has one hundred and thirty miles of coast.

The "Arab" countries concerned have some of the finest naval bases in the world, Latakia in Syria, Beirut in Lebanon, Port Said and Alexandria in Egypt, Bizerta in Tunis and Oran in Algeria.[1] All these great bases were built by France or Britain, and have near them aerodromes available for shore-based aircraft. Israel has only the inferior port of Haifa. If all these bases and airfields were controlled by a hostile power, the defence of Europe would become extremely difficult. Moreover the whole Muslim world feels deeply for the Palestinians and increasingly resents the apparent injustice of American policy. The corollary of this growing hatred of the United States all over Asia is a steady rapprochement with Russia.

Britain has ties with Asia and the Muslim world dating back some two hundred and fifty years. Many of these ties still exist or could be

[1] Map 36, p. 344.

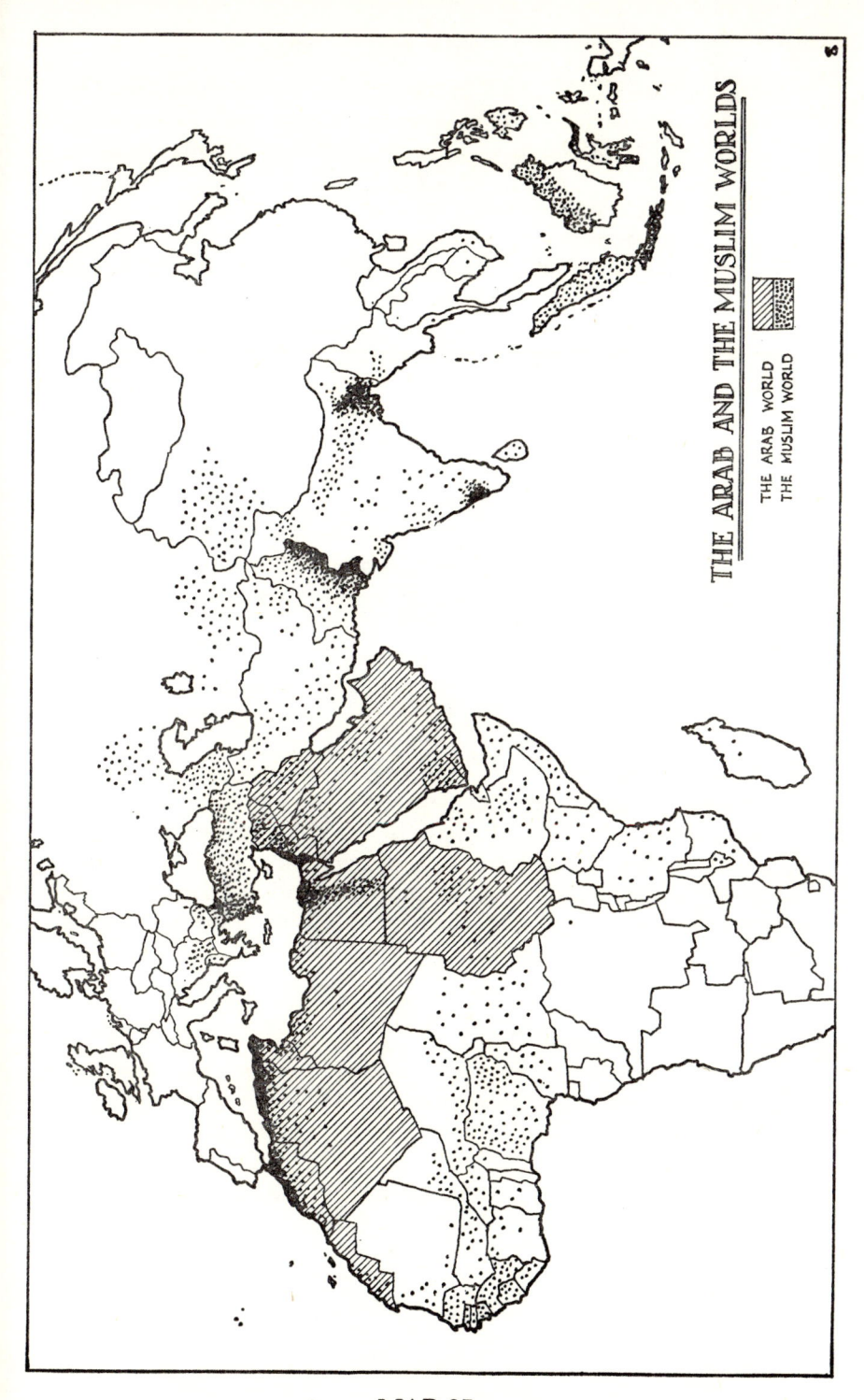

MAP 37

revived, especially in the field of trade, culture and friendship. The British emotional reaction against empire has tended to convey the impression in the public mind that we are hated in those countries which formerly were our dependencies. This is far from the case. Deep ties of friendship and culture still exist. Britain cannot live without the Muslim and Indian worlds.

Two factors have eroded these old partnerships. Firstly, Britain's announcement of withdrawal from east of Suez, which is interpreted by many Asians as British indifference to their fate. We fail to realise that these people do not wish to be ruled by us, but do need the aid of a modern industrialised Power. In view of our apparent indifference to their interests they turn for help to Russia.

The second cause of our loss of friends in Asia is the belief that Britain is now an American satellite. The United States has no ancient emotional and cultural ties with Asia, and is hated for her continual use of violence, in Israel even more than in Vietnam.

It is not, of course, a foregone conclusion that Russia will consolidate and maintain the position of the world's greatest Power. Twenty-five years ago, the United States seemed to be in an even more dominating position. The United States and Britain were together the unchallenged mistresses of the world. Perhaps Russia too will weaken.

One of the principal problems involved is that the Soviet government does not have to think of the next election. As a result, it can plan many years ahead in complete secrecy, for it does not have to explain its actions to the electorate. In the West, governments often think more of the next election than of the future of their countries. They are, consequently, at the mercy of emotional swings of uninformed public opinion, over which many outside influences exercise sway.

CONCLUSIONS

(1) The geographic situation of Egypt makes it the most important country in the world, a fact which has been realised by the Great Powers of every age from 3000 B.C. to today.

(2) Alexander the Great, Napoleon Bonaparte and Winston Churchill, when engaged in major wars elsewhere, all risked defeat in other theatres in order to make sure of securing a base in Egypt.

(3) World dominion depends on sea power. A base in

Egypt and naval command of the Mediterranean and the Indian Ocean gives domination of Europe, Asia and Africa.
(4) Russia has grasped these basic principles and seized the opportunity of the six-day war to put them into practice.
(5) A tragic vicious circle has made everything easy for the Soviet Union. Zionist pressure on the United States leads to the sale of more American weapons to Israel, whose neighbours are alarmed and seek help from Russia. The latter is thereby enabled further to strengthen her bases in Egypt and the Mediterranean, intending to use them to destroy—not Israel—but the United States and her allies. Such an increase in Russian strength causes Israel to demand yet more weapons, whereupon the Russians have yet another pretext for increasing their strength. The extreme cleverness but lack of wisdom in Israeli policy is resulting in the elimination of American influence from Asia and Africa—yet America is Israel's only friend.
(6) A further source of anxiety today is the possibility that Russia may seek an agreement with Malta to enable the Russian fleet to use the magnificently equipped former British naval base on the island. The withdrawal of the British fleet and garrison from Malta has left the island's economy in a precarious condition. As La Rochefoucauld remarked, "We all have strength enough to endure the misfortunes of others." The United States government is willing to endure the dangers which threaten her European allies. Western politicians seem often too ready to denounce the iniquities of the Soviet government, without taking adequate steps to secure the means of defence. It might be wiser to look more carefully to our defences, while behaving with more politeness and restraint towards the Russians. Malta is an island long connected with Britain and stood manfully by the Western Allies in the Second World War.

XXII

An Outline Solution

Agree with God and be at peace; thereby good will come to you ... For God abases the proud but he saves the lowly. He delivers the innocent man; you will be delivered through the cleanness of your hands.
Job XXII, 21, 29-30. Revised Standard Version

O pray for the peace of Jerusalem;
They shall prosper that love thee.
Psalm CXXII, 6

I prefer the most unfair peace to the most righteous war.
CICERO

Peace rules the day, where reason rules the mind.
WILLIAM COLLINS, *Eclogues*

It must be a peace without victory. Only a peace between equals can last; only a peace the very principle of which is equality, and a common participation in a common benefit.
PRESIDENT WOODROW WILSON
22nd January, 1917

Israeli colonialism since the establishment of the state is one of the two blackest cases in the whole history of colonialism in the modern age ... If it is true that an unbroken series of victorious wars makes a nation dangerous to the rest of the world and itself, the United States and Israel must be today the two most dangerous of the one hundred and twenty-five sovereign states.
ARNOLD TOYNBEE, *Experiences*

XXII

BEFORE suggesting a cure, it may be permissible to summarise our historical analysis of how the present situation arose. The conflict in Palestine is rooted in four thousand years of history. To discuss the problem on the basis of events since 1948, or even since 1917, is to misread almost all that has happened.

CHRISTIANITY AND JUDAISM

First, however, let me state the opinion that sincere Christians cannot possibly feel hatred or repulsion for Judaism or for those who profess it. Judaism was the religion of John the Baptist and of Joseph and Mary. Christ Himself was brought up as a Jew, and Christianity is saturated with Jewish religion. To read about the history of the Jews is to conceive for them a considerable degree of sympathy, and, in some cases, of admiration. The problem perplexing us is that raised by the exploitation of religious feelings and of human sympathies to further the policy of ruthless military conquest, as pursued by the present Israeli government.

THE HISTORICAL ANALYSIS

(a) The tribes which took Jericho about 1200 B.C. are believed to have been some fifteen thousand strong. On entering Palestine, they rapidly integrated with the much more numerous people of the land. The subjects of David were not by any means the pure descendants of the captors of Jericho.

(b) Ten of the twelve tribes were carried off captive to Assyria in 724 B.C. and were lost. Other populations were planted in Palestine in their place.

(c) The Dispersion began in 587 B.C. with the Babylonian conquest of Judah. By the time of Titus, A.D. 70, some four Jews out of five were living outside Palestine. Titus did not evict the Jews from Palestine.

(d) Between 300 B.C. and A.D. 200, Judaism was a monotheism in a pagan world, and converted great numbers of "heathen".

(e) From about A.D. 200 onwards, intense rivalry developed in the mission field between Judaism and Christianity. Had it not been for the appearance of Christianity at this time, the whole Roman Empire might well have been converted to Judaism.

(f) After the appearance of Islam, Jews were the allies of the Muslims against the Christians for nearly a thousand years.

(g) Jews never faced genocide in Europe, unless it were under the Nazis, but for many centuries they met with rudeness and contempt, sufficient to distort their psychology. The discrimination was on a religious basis, for their ethnic origins were very mixed.

(h) In the nineteenth century, equality and emancipation were achieved almost all over the world with the exception of Russia. In Western countries, Jews were mostly assimilated, and regarded their Judaism as a religion, not a nationality.

(i) Between 1881 and 1914, large numbers of Russian Jews moved into Western Europe and the United States. They were still bitter and isolationist, as a result of their repression in Russia. They formed the core of the Zionist movement.

(j) They wished to escape from all Gentiles and live in a country solely populated by Jews. Under the leadership of Dr. Weizmann, the ultimate objective was at first concealed, and the movement appeared to be purely humanitarian. The basic objective of Zionism —a state inhabited solely by Jews—renders plans for a bi-national State of Palestine impossible to realise.

(k) Under the stress of Nazi persecution, the Zionists determined to conquer Palestine by force and evict the native population, who were themselves partly descended from the ancient Israelites. The modern Israeli leaders were probably predominantly of north European ethnic origin.

(l) Zionism was born in the 1890s, in the age of European domination. The movement has retained the supercilious attitude towards Asians and Africans, which the Western democracies have meanwhile abandoned.

(m) Owing to her high level of technology, the outside financial support she has received and the supply of weapons by the U.S.A., Israel has been able to defeat all her Asian and African neighbours. She now completely dominates the Middle East, although her propaganda continues to depict her as threatened with genocide. Financial contributions from outside might well decrease, if Israel's complete military dominance over her neighbours were understood in the West.

(n) The skill and cleverness, diplomatic, financial and military, which have enabled Israel to establish herself, are astounding. It is, nevertheless, doubtful if her policy is wise. She undisguisedly relies solely upon force, by which, at the moment, she completely dominates all her neighbours. The use of her military predominance to drive most of the native Palestinians from their country has built up against her a great intensity of hatred, which might last for centuries if no steps are taken to reduce it.

(o) The unilateral support of Israel by the United States has obliged the greater part of the Arabic-speaking world to appeal to Russia, and has thereby enabled the latter to maintain a fleet in the Mediterranean and to increase her naval presence in the Indian Ocean. The world balance of power has swung sharply in favour of Russia, as a result of America's unilateral support of Israel. The manifest injustice of her policy has destroyed the prestige of the United States in Asia.

(p) In the long run, the policy of the present Israeli government in its reliance on force alone may well prove suicidal. It has already made the Soviets the dominant Middle East power. It is suggested that Israel would be wiser to modify her hard line, and work towards peace with her neighbours, while she is still strong.

(q) Some of the proposals which follow are already familiar. Two new suggestions, believed of vital importance, do not seem to have been as yet sufficiently emphasised. Firstly, the necessity of stationing neutral troops between the two sides during the period of negotiation and implementation. Secondly, the vital importance of the resettlement of the refugees on the West Bank or in Jordan, at the expense of the Great Powers.

A TENTATIVE SOLUTION

The word tentative is used of the following proposals, because it is not intended that the Great Powers should impose a detailed solution, which must obviously be worked out in consultation between all concerned. It is suggested that the United Nations or the Great Powers should prepare proposals on the basis of the following points, discuss them with the parties concerned, and, if necessary, bring some form of political or economic pressure on such as refuse to give a reasonable amount of co-operation.

The governments of Egypt, Israel and Jordan are specifically mentioned, because it is they who have agreed to negotiate. It would be extremely valuable to secure the co-operation of Syria also and, of course, of any other Middle East governments, but a settlement should not be delayed until all the "Arab" governments agree.

THE SOLUTION

1. *Israeli Withdrawal*

ISRAEL should withdraw to her pre-1967 border. This withdrawal

MAP 38: AN OUTLINE SOLUTION

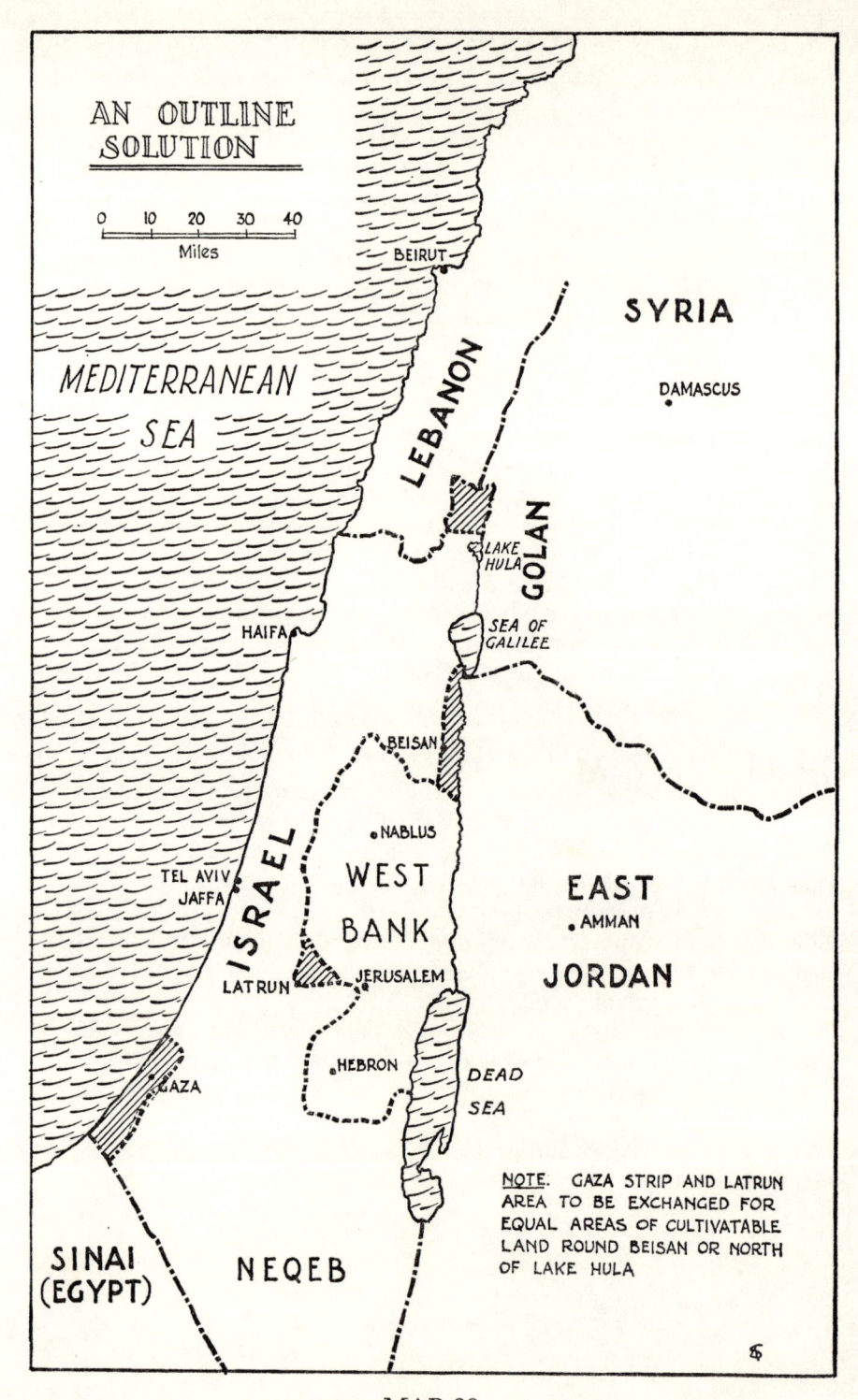

NOTE. GAZA STRIP AND LATRUN AREA TO BE EXCHANGED FOR EQUAL AREAS OF CULTIVATABLE LAND ROUND BEISAN OR NORTH OF LAKE HULA should be accompanied by an Egypto-Jordanian declaration recognising the existence of Israel, and promising free navigation of the Suez Canal and the Straits of Tiran.

This withdrawal is the only obligation incumbent on Israel.

2. *Occupation by Neutral Troops*
As soon as Israel withdraws, the area between the Jordan River and the Israeli border (hereafter referred to as the West Bank) should immediately be occupied by neutral troops. Smaller detachments could also be placed at Al Arish and Sharm al Shaikh. (Map 35, p. 331).

The Jordan government could provide civil servants and police for the West Bank, but the Jordan army should remain east of the Jordan River.

3. *Resettlement of the Refugees*
The heart of the problem does not lie in making peace between Israel, Egypt and Jordan but in the resettlement of the native population of Palestine, who have been forcibly evicted from their country.

4. *Constructive Projects*
When Israel has withdrawn to the pre-1967 line, one-fifth of the area of Palestine will be freed to accommodate the population which previously occupied the whole country.

A consortium of Great Powers, presumably under the auspices of the United Nations, should then undertake to develop this area to enable it to carry a larger population. The Palestinians are good farmers but, of course, have no capital. Nor have they the technical knowledge to undertake major projects. Considerable agricultural development and a certain amount of industrialisation are possible in this area.

5. *Provision of Capital and Technical Control*
The Powers concerned will have to supply the technical control and the necessary capital. It is useless to say that Israel should pay compensation. Israel is not herself viable, but lives on funds collected from abroad.

It is likewise useless to pay compensation to individual refugees. The only solution is for the Powers to execute major development projects, and then to offer the refugees homes, land and employment.

6. Reconstruction of Jordan

Funds should also be provided for the reconstruction and development of Jordan east of the river. The Jordan economy has been wrecked, largely because of Israeli bombing. (Israel has suffered no damage of this kind for none of her neighbours have operational air forces.)

It will be essential to revitalise the East Jordan economy, because it is unlikely that the West Bank will accommodate all the refugees. Some, who so wish, should be able to find work and a permanent livelihood in East Jordan.

7. Time Required for Implementation

This settlement, involving the necessary surveys, drawing-up of projects and the execution of the work, will probably occupy between five and ten years. Neutral troops should remain in the area until the work is completed and all is quiet.

8. Political Future of the West Bank

At some period, after five or ten years or when the settlement is complete, the Palestinians established on the West Bank should be allowed to decide, by plebiscite or other means, on their own political future.

9. Exchange of Territory

The Gaza Strip should be annexed to Israel and an equivalent area of cultivatable soil west of the Jordan be surrendered by her in return. If Israel wishes to retain the Amwas-Latrun area, an equal area of cultivatable land west of the Jordan should be given in exchange.

The following could be suitable areas:

(1) The area between Beisan and the Jordan.
(2) The Israeli colonies south of the Sea of Galilee.
(3) The Israeli colonies north of Lake Hula.

Israel should evacuate the Golan Heights.

The basis on which border exchanges should be arranged should be to provide land to resettle the refugees, not to bow to Israel's demands for strategic positions. The only ultimate and permanent security for Israel lies in amicable relations with her neighbours, not in piling up armaments and in expansion to secure "strategic frontiers".

APPENDIX I

COPY of a memorandum issued by Bertrand Russell a few hours before his death. (By permission of the Estate of Bertrand Russell.)

The development of the crisis in the Middle East is both dangerous and instructive. For over 20 years Israel has expanded by force of arms. After every stage in this expansion Israel has appealed to "reason" and has suggested "negotiations". This is the traditional rôle of the imperial power, because it wishes to consolidate with the least difficulty what it has already taken by violence. Every new conquest becomes the new basis of the proposed negotiation from strength, which ignores the injustice of the previous suggestion. The aggression committed by Israel must be condemned, not only because no state has the right to annex foreign territory, but because every expansion is also an experiment to discover how much more aggression the world will tolerate.

The refugees who surround Palestine in their hundreds of thousands were described recently by the Washington journalist I. F. Stone as "the moral millstone around the neck of the world Jewry". Many of the refugees are now well into the third decade of their precarious existence in temporary settlements. The tragedy of the people of Palestine is that their country was "given" by a foreign Power to another people for the creation of a new State. The result was that many hundreds of thousands of innocent people were made permanently homeless. With every new conflict their numbers have increased. How much longer is the world willing to endure this spectacle of wanton cruelty? It is abundantly clear that the refugees have every right to the homeland from which they were driven, and the denial of this right is at the heart of the continuing conflict. No people anywhere in the world would accept being expelled en masse from their own country; how can anyone require the people of Palestine to accept a punishment which nobody else would tolerate? A permanent just settlement of the refugees in their homelands is an essential ingredient of any genuine settlement in the Middle East.

We are frequently told that we must sympathise with Israel because of the suffering of the Jews in Europe at the hands of the Nazis. I see in this suggestion no reason to perpetuate any suffering. What Israel is doing today cannot be condoned, and to invoke the horrors of the past to justify those of the present is gross hypocrisy. Not only does Israel condemn a vast number of refugees to misery; not only are many Arabs under occupation condemned to military rule; but also Israel condemns the Arab nations, only recently emerging from colonial status, to continuing impoverishment as military demands take precedence over national development.

All who want to see an end to bloodshed in the Middle East must ensure that any settlement does not contain the seeds of future conflict. Justice requires that the first step towards a settlement must be an Israeli withdrawal from all the territories occupied in June 1967. A new world campaign is needed to help bring justice to the long-suffering people of the Middle East.

Bertrand Russell,
January 31, 1970.

APPENDIX II

AMERICA'S VERY SPECIAL RELATIONSHIP WITH ISRAEL

An article from *The Times*, 5th February, 1971. (Reproduced from *The Times* by permission.)

The White House invitation and reception recently accorded Israel's Defence Minister, Moshe Dayan, is illustrative of the very special relationship the United States has developed with his country over the past twenty-two years. It is doubtful whether a Nato or Seato defence chief would have been granted such high protocol treatment. Most would have had to be satisfied with meeting the Defence Secretary, Mr. Melvin Laird, or in exceptional cases, the Secretary of State, Mr. Rogers, or the Vice-President.

When President Truman said in October 1948: "We are pledged to a state of Israel, large enough, free enough and strong enough to make its people self-supporting and secure", the stage was set for the gradual establishment of an association between the United States and another country unique in American history. Today, that association is far closer in all areas—defence, economic collaboration, intelligence exchange, common citizenship, and mutual diplomatic support than enjoyed, for example, between the United States and Great Britain.

Unique also is Israel's almost total immunity from criticism in the United States—a situation hardly paralleled by any of our European or Asian allies, many of whose faults and frailties are daily aired in our communications media and by our legislative representatives. Perhaps as James Reston of the *New York Times* suggested a short while ago, ". . . you can put it down as a general rule that any criticism of Israel's policies, will be attacked as antisemitism". And so it goes in reverse, with Israel's image as a small, democratic, courageous little country struggling to survive in a sea of uncivilised, bloodthirsty, pro-communist Arabs, representing—rightly or wrongly—the view of most Americans . . .

In dollars and cents, America's assistance to Israel through the years, both governmental and private, has been prodigious. During the 20-year period between 1948–1968, the United States government economic aid totalled $11,000m., while dollar transfers from private sources amounted to $25,000m., a total of $36,000m., or $1,400 per capita on a current population of 2,500,000. This greatly exceeds on a per capita basis, United States assistance to any ally and compares to $35 per capita to the peoples of 13 neighbouring states. Since 1968, American assistance to Israel has greatly increased. Dollar transfers in 1970 reached $800m. and in 1971 will approximate $1·5 billion.

Until 1967, we assured Israel a continuing supply of modern military equipment directed through West Germany and France and we were thus able to avoid Arab hostility. However, with the conclusion of German "reparations" and de Gaulle's change in Middle East policy, America has since 1967 become the exclusive purveyor of arms to Israel. Of greater significance is the fact that qualitatively, America has provided aircraft, missiles, and electronic systems of greater sophistication and greater strike capability than those furnished our Nato and Seato allies . . . A few weeks ago, the House of Representatives passed an amendment to the Defence Procurement Bill giving the President open-ended authority to transfer military equipment to Israel without total cost limitation . . . Great Britain at the height of its struggle with Hitler, never received such a "blank cheque". Nor, in more recent times, has South Vietnam. The Senate on 15th December, by a 60 to 20 vote, killed the Williams' Amendment to the Defence Appropriations Bill which would have restricted the President from sending United States troops into Israel without Congressional permission . . .

There has been significance also in Washington's reaction to the Soviet action in putting an anti-aircraft missile defence system in Egypt which began before and was apparently completed after the cease-fire arrangements undertaken at the Secretary of State Mr. Rogers's initiative last summer. The concern has greatly exceeded that generated by reports of air-to-ground Soviet missiles and nuclear submarines in Cuba today in defiance of the 1961 Kennedy-Khrushchev understanding.

In the area of nuclear weapons, the United States has also pursued an exceptional position vis-à-vis Israel. During the years when we were pressing over 100 nations in the world community with whatever diplomatic, economic and military leverage we might have to adhere to the Nuclear Non-Proliferation Treaty, Israel alone was exempted from strong representations. In fact we may have encouraged Israel to refrain from assuming the obligations set forth in this international undertaking. Through a study prepared at White House request by the Rand Corporation of California, we provided Israel with the most advanced technical and political data on the effective use of nuclear weapons in the Middle East. *The Jewish Press* in December summarised the nuclear situation: "The experts who before the Six Day War felt that India would become the next member of the nuclear club now believe that the next member will be Israel." This, in fact, has already occurred. The nuclear reactors at Dimona and Nahal Sorek have been reported for several years to be producing plutonium sufficient for ten 25-kiloton bombs a year. The widely-read *Nuclear War and Nuclear Peace* recently published by the former head of Israel Army Intelligence, General Y. Harakabi, is the current authority on the use of nuclear weapons in the Middle East conflict. In contrast to our intense opposition to France's nuclear development, the United States has supported Israel in virtually an identical policy.

In the exchange of intelligence, American co-operation with Israel is unprecedented and goes far beyond the special nuclear arrangements with Great Britain based on the McMahon Act. During the months before the June 1967 hostilities, the military intelligence requirements required by Washington from American embassies, the Central Intelligence Agency and military intelligence staffs in the Middle East were very largely based on Israeli needs, not on American interests. The effectiveness of the Israel air strikes on 5th June 1967, was assured at least in part, by information on Egyptian airfields and aircraft disposition provided through American sources ... When the American Naval Intelligence ship *Liberty* was attacked by Israeli air and sea units in June 1967—with the loss of 34 dead and 71 injured—the incident resulted in minimum official reaction. It boggles the imagination to speculate as to the reaction were the attackers to have been British or French, much less Egyptian, as initially assumed.

Israel also enjoys an exceptional position on the question of dual citizenship. Under long-standing citizenship laws an American voting in the elections or serving in the armed forces or government of a foreign country loses his citizenship. By a recent Supreme Court interpretation, Americans may serve in Israel in this manner without loss of citizenship.

Under the Israel Law of Return, an American Jew entering Israel is automatically given Israeli nationality.

Since the war in June 1967, and particularly during the past year, American commitments to Israel have been greatly expanded. Before 1967 the United States was committed to Israel's territorial integrity within the 1948 armistice lines and to her economic viability. Tangentially, Washington favoured a military balance in the Middle East. In the United Nations Resolution of November 1967, America, in effect, opposed Israel's retention of the territories conquered by force the previous June. This fundamental position has now changed very radically.

Last summer, in a series of statements from the San Clemente "White House", the Nixon Administration would appear to have extended the territorial integrity commitment to include until a final peace settlement, the occupied territories; to have moved from assuring a military balance, to guaranteeing Israel a "military superiority capable of launching a rapid knock-out blow" against her neighbours and to have supported Israel's continued "racial exclusiveness" thereby negating our 18 years of support for the United Nations Palestine refugee formula of "repatriation or compensation". When asked during his 10th December press conference whether America still adhered to its position on Israeli withdrawal from the "occupied territories", President Nixon, for the first time, evaded the issue by saying that it was a matter for negotiation.

Finally, the assignment and advancement of personnel in the Department of State to the top positions relating to Middle East policy, have traditionally been subject to prior approval by the American Zionist leadership. As an example in reverse, the firing of the United Nations Ambassador, Mr. Charles W. Yost, was demanded by "the pro-Israel lobby", as recently reported by the columnists, Evans and Novak...

Only history can provide the total explanation for this very special American-Israeli relationship. It has now reached a point where Israel's security and welfare is considered vital to American welfare, but our reaction to any threats against Israel is more intense than with any of our Nato or Seato allies. One State Department humorist has said: "Were Israel's survival to be seriously threatened, we would be in the Third World War in two minutes—with Berlin, it might take several days!"

David Nes

Mr. Nes spent 26 years in the United States foreign service. He was Chargé d'Affaires in Cairo immediately before and during the 1967 war.

A SHORT BIBLIOGRAPHY

Abel, Le Père *Histoire de la Palestine*
Abrahams, I. *Jewish Life in the Middle Ages*
Antonius, G. *The Arab Awakening*
Barbour, N. *Nisi Dominus*
Begin, M. *The Revolt*
Bell, H. I. *Jews and Christians in Egypt*
Benjamin of Tudela *Travels*
Bentwich, N. *The Jews*
Berger, E. *The Jewish Dilemma*
Bermant, C. H. *Israel*
Bible, The Holy, King James Authorised Version
—— Revised Standard Version
—— The Jerusalem Bible
—— Monsignor Ronald Knox
—— The New English Bible
Bright, J. *A History of Israel*
Butler, A. J. *The Arab Conquest of Egypt*
Carcopino, J. *Daily Life in Ancient Rome*
Cambridge Ancient History
Carmichael, J. *The Shaping of the Arabs*
Cattan, H. *Palestine, the Arabs and Israel*
Chiha, M. *Palestine*
Clements, R. E. *Abraham and David*
—— *Prophecy and Covenant*
Davis, J. H. *The Evasive Peace*
Davis, S. *Race Relations in Ancient Egypt*
Dearden, A. *Jordan*
Dozy, R. *The Moslems in Spain*
Eusebius *History of the Church*
Fisher, H. A. L. *A History of Europe*
Gilbert, M. *Jewish History Atlas*
Glover, T. R. *The Ancient World*
Glubb, J. B. *A Soldier with the Arabs*
—— *The Great Arab Conquests*
—— *The Empire of the Arabs*
—— *The Course of Empire*
—— *The Lost Centuries*

Glubb, J. B. *A Short History of the Arab Peoples*
Guillaume, A. *Islam*
Hallam, H. *The Middle Ages*
Herzl, T. *The Jewish State*
Hitti, P. *A History of the Arabs*
Horn, C. Von *Soldiering for Peace*
Hutchison, E. H. *The Violent Truce*
Institute for Palestine Studies *Israel and the Geneva Conventions*
Josephus *Antiquities of the Jews*
—— *Wars of the Jews*
Juster, J. *Les Juifs sous l'Empire Romain*
Keller, W. *The Bible as History*
Khadduri, M. *The Arab-Israeli Impasse*
Khouri, F. J. *The Arab-Israeli Dilemma*
Kirk, G. E. *A Short History of the Middle East*
Kishtainy, K. *Verdict in Absentia*
Kittel, R. *The Scientific Study of the Old Testament*
Lea, H. C. *The Moriscoes in Spain*
—— *A History of the Inquisition*
Levin, H. *Jerusalem Embattled*
Lilienthal, A. M. *What Price Israel?*
Litvinoff, B. *A Peculiar People*
Lowenthal, M. *The Diaries of Theodor Herzl*
Margoliouth, D. S. *Relations between Arabs and Israelites before Islam*
Menuhin, M. *The Decadence of Judaism in our time*
Millman, H. H. *The History of the Jews*
Moscati, S. *Ancient Semitic Civilizations*
Neil, W. *One Volume Bible Commentary*
Parkes, J. A. *The Conflict of the Church and the Synagogue*
—— *A History of the Jewish People*
—— *A History of Palestine*
Perowne, S. *The Life and Times of Herod the Great*
—— *The Later Herods*
Petrie, F. *Palestine and Israel*
Pfeiffer, C. F. *Egypt and the Exodus*
Philips, J. B. *Four Prophets*
Pirenne, H. *A History of Europe*
Raisin, J. S. *Gentile Reactions to Jewish Ideals*
Randall, R. *Jordan and the Holy Land*
Renan *Life of Jesus*
—— *St. Paul*
Robnett, G. W. *Conquest through Immigration*

Rodinson, M. *Israel and the Arabs*
Roth, C. *A History of the Marranos*
Royal Institute of International Affairs *Great Britain and Palestine 1915–1945*
Schurer, E. *History of the Jewish People*
Selzer, M. *The Arianization of the Jewish State*
Smith, G. A. *The Historical Geography of the Holy Land*
Sokolow, N. *History of Zionism*
Stevens, R. P. *Zionism, South Africa and Apartheid*
—— *American Zionism and U.S. Foreign Policy*
Suetonius *Lives of the Caesars*
Tacitus *Annals*
—— *Histories*
Taylor, H. O. *The Mediaeval Mind*
Thubron, C. *Mirror to Damascus*
Weizmann, Ch. *Trial and Error*
Wright, G. E. *The Old Testament against its Environment*
Wright, G. E. and Fuller, R. *The Book of the Acts of God*

INDEX

Aaron, 33
Abbásids, 185–88, 198, 223, 225, 237
Abdul Hamid, Sultan, 259
Abdulla, King (Trans-Jordan), 135, 284, 289, 293, 301
Abdul Rahman III, 196
Abel, F. M., *Histoire de la Palestine*, 138 *fn.*
Abélard, 197
Abner, Commander (Israel), 62
Abraham, 21–24, 26, 29, 36, 39, 62, 178
Abrahams, I., *Jewish Life in the Middle Ages*, 193, 195–96, 200, 204, 217–18, 275–76
Absalom (s.o. David), 65–66
Abu Bekr, 175, 179
Abu Talib, 175, 177
Abyssinia (Ethiopia), 113, 341
Achish, King (Gath), 62
Acre, 225, 228, 236, 245
Aden, 134, 173, 177, 349
Administration, 235, 309–10, 335
Adonai, 45, 110–11, 117, 120
Adonijah (s.o. David), 66
Adrianople, 229
Aegean, 48, 57
Afek, 57, 59
Afghanistan (Khurasan), 185, 230
Africa, general, 242, 245, 267, 298, 336, 343, 345, 353
Agag, King (Amalekite), 59
Agriculture, Israelite, 38, 42, 46, 50–52, 60, 76, 77; Arab, 173, 178; European, 185–186; Palestinian, 252, 254, 268, 274, 278, 281, 310
Agrippa I, *see* Herod Agrippa I
Agrippa II, *see* Herod Agrippa II
Ahab, King (Israel), 74, 76–77
Ahad Ha-'Am (Ginzberg, Asher), 252, 254
Ahaz, King (Judah), 80
Ahimelech (Hittite), 65
Ahmad Pasha al Jazzàr, 236
Ain Jaloot, 227
Ain Qudeis, *see* Kadesh Barnea
Air power, 315, 328, 335, 350
Akiba, Rabbi, 119, 153
Al Arish, 361
Albania, 232, 249
Albigensian Heresy, 197–98, 201, 205
Aleppo, 227, 230, 232, 235, 245
Alexander I (Russia), 246

Alexander II (Russia), 247, 257
Alexander III, 247
Alexander the Great (Macedon), 92, 95, 104, 109–10, 120, 293, 298, 343, 345, 352
Alexander Jannaeus, *see* Jannaeus
Al Fateh, 327—28. *See also* Palestine guerrillas
Alfonso X (Castile), 196
Alfonso the Wise, 196
Algeria, 184, 350
Ali (nephew of Muhammad), 175–76
Almohades, *see* Muwahhids
Al Shaddai (mountain god), 22
Amalekites, 59, 117
Ambrose, St. (Bishop of Milan), 162, 198
America, *see* United States of *and* South
Ammon (Philadelphia; mod. Amman), 98–99, 309, 339
Ammonites, 41, 59–60, 64, 76, 85, 89, 99
Amnesty International, 319–20
Amnon (s.o. David), 65
Amorites, 41, 46, 50, 52–53, 66
Amwas, 319, 362
Ananus, high priest, 145
Andalusia, *see* Spain
Anglo-American Committee of Enquiry, 293–94, 302
Anglo-Jewish Association, 266
Anglo-Jordan Treaty, 301
Anjou, Charles of, 196
Anqara (mod. Ankara), 230, 232
Anti-British propaganda, 290–91
Antioch, 95, 98, 129, 135, 223, 225
Antiochus III, the Great, 95, 98
Antiochus IV, Epiphanes, 97–99, 101, 103–105, 116, 129, 153, 160, 241
Antiochus V, Eupator, 101
Antipater I, 127
Antipater II, 127–31
Antipatris, 144
Anti-Semitism, 166, 198–202, 212, 215, 219, 241–43, 246–47, 258, 261–62, 274, 337
Apartheid, 217, 261, 317–18, 336
Aqaba, Gulf of, 67, 296, 298, 315, 330–32
Aquinas, Thomas, 203
Arab Conquest, 177–81, 223, 345
Arabia, 24, 35–36, 42, 173, 175, 179, 241, 298
Arabic language, 187, 195–96, 228, 273, 301, 350

INDEX

Arab League, 348–49
Arab Legion, 289, 301–2, 307, 309, 312, 315
Arab refugees (Palestinian), 300, 314, 320, 338–39, 363
Arabs, religion, 35–36; Nabataeans, 103; Jewish communities among, 113–14; characteristics of Arabian Arabs, 135; Empire, 166, 173–89, 193–98; decline of empire, 204–14, 217–18, 220; Mamlook army, 228; anti-Ottoman, 235; tolerance of Jews, 241, 243; Palestinian Arabs, 252–53; Balfour Declaration and Palestine mandate, 265–74, 277–84; World War II, 289–90; U.N. Truce supervision, 293–315; Israeli aggression, 319–20, 327–28, 333, 363. *See also* Abbásids; Muhammad; Umaiyids
Aramaeans (Syria), 64
Aramaic language, 110
Arbela, 95
Archaeology, 19–20, 35, 59–60
Archelaus (Herodian), 138
Arians (Arius of Alexandria), 166
Aristobulus (Judah), 125, 127, 129
Aristotle, 195
Ark, 29, 53, 57, 64
Armenians, 20, 113, 173, 218, 233, 243, 268
Army, *see* Military affairs
Arnon, river, 41
Artaxerxes I, 92
Asad abu Qarib, 168
Asher, 50
Ashkenazi Jews, 316–17
Ashurbanipal, King, 84
Asia, general, 186, 230, 233, 237, 242–43, 245, 267, 285, 298, 336, 343, 350, 352–353. *See also* Central Asia
Asia Minor, 61 *fn*., 67, 80, 90, 95, 113, 125, 135, 167, 223, 229–33
Asquith, H. H., 262, 265
Asshur-nasir-pal II, 76
Assimilationists, 261–66, 269. *See also* Integration
Assyrians, 76–78, 80–84, 89, 109, 113, 241, 253, 343, 345, 357
Astronomy, 187
Aswan Dam, 315, 329
Ataroth, 60
Athanasius, St., 162
Atheism (Israel), 317, 322–23
Atlantic Ocean, 349–50
Augustine, St., 198
Augustus, Emperor (Octavius), 114, 131–135, 138, 185
Auranitis (mod. Hauran), 135, 138, 154

Australia, 250, 259
Austria, 244, 249, 346
Ayoubids (Kurds), *see* Saladin

Baal, 65, 68, 74, 77
Baasha, King (Israel), 76
Babylonians, 21, 38–39, 64–65, 80, 82–85, 89–90, 94–95, 109, 113–14, 116–18, 120–121, 125, 139, 153, 160, 163, 167, 175, 241, 247, 343, 345, 357
Baghdad, 185–88, 195, 198, 202, 205, 219, 223, 227, 230, 234, 237, 289, 302, 323
Baghdad Pact, 348–49
Balaam, 41
Balas, Alexander, 101
Balearics, 113
Balfour, A. J., 262, 267, 273, 276, 316
Balfour Declaration, 267–69, 273, 278–81, 293, 296, 347
Balkans, 232
Banking, 186, 200, 245
Baptism, 152
Barbarians, 165, 168
Barbarossa, Emperor Frederick, 199
Barbour, Nevill, *Nisi Dominus*, 277, 279, 281, 293
Bar Giora, Simon, 148, 150, 152, 339
Bar Hebraeus, 114
Bar Kokhba, 153–54, 161, 168, 204, 241
Bar Yehuda, Israel, 277
Basra, 51
Bathsheba (Hittite), 64–65
Bayazid I, Sultan, 229
Bayazid II, Sultan, 213
Bedr, 178
Beeroth, 64
Beersheba, 24, 28, 38–39, 50
Begin, Menachem, *The Revolt*, 289–92, 299–300, 312
Beirut, 143, 148, 251, 350
Beisan, 362
Beit Nuba, 319
Beit Sira, 312
Ben Gurion, assistant to Ananus, 145
Ben Gurion, David, 327
Benjamin of Tudela, *Travels*, 195–96, 199, 201, 209, 215
Ben Zakkai, Johanan, 147, 152, 154
Berbers, 184, 197
Bermant, Chaim H., *Israel*, 204, 277
Bernard, of Clervaux, St., 198
Bethel (mod. Beitin), 48, 50, 53, 64
Beth Horon (mod. Beit Aur), 48, 50, 53, 67, 101, 144
Bevin, Ernest, 301
Bizerta (Tunisia), 350

INDEX

Black Death, 202, 205, 211, 220, 241–42, 292
Boleslav the Pius (Poland), 209
Bols, General, 281
Bosphorus, 205, 223, 330
Bowring, Sir John, *Report on Syria*, 245
Braude, Rabbi Bordecai, 258 *fn.*
Brenner, 316
Breslau, 227
Bright, J. A., *History of Israel*, 23, 50, 80–81, 89–90
Brion, Marcel, *Tamerlan*, 221
Britain, 115, 165, 185, 196, 200, 214–15, 225, 236, 243–44, 247–53, 259, 261–68, 273, 277, 280–81, 285, 289–301, 314–16, 330, 343–52
Brusa, 229
Bulgaria, 229, 232
"Bund" (Russian Jews), 262
Burning Bush, 26, 30, 33, 42
Byzantines, 166–68, 173, 181–84, 196, 198, 204, 209, 229, 232–33, 241, 267, 343, 346

Cadiz, 184
Caesarea, 134, 138, 143–44, 147–48
Cairo, 195, 197, 232–33, 252, 265, 291, 330, 332, 334, 348
Calebites, 39, 50
Calixtus II, Pope, 199
Cambridge Ancient History, 98–99, 104, 125, 127
Cambridge Mediaeval History, 200
Canaan, 23, 35, 38, 46, 50, 52–53, 61, 65, 74, 76
Canada, 250
Cape of Good Hope, 186, 218, 234, 253, 343, 345–47
Caravan routes, *see* Trade
Carchemish, 84
Carmel, 66
Carter, J., *An Eyewitness in Jerusalem*, 319–320
Carthage, 76, 183–84
Casimir III, the Great (Poland), 211
Caspian Sea, 82, 289
Cassius, Proconsul (Syria), 131
Castile (Spain), 196, 211–12
Catherine I (Russia), 246
Catherine II, the Great, 246
Catholicism, 216, 234. *See also* Inquisition
Cecil, Lord Robert, 268–69, 273
Celts, 214
Cento, 348–49
Central Asia, 61 *fn.*, 209, 223–27, 230–33, 237

Chaldiran (Lake Urmia), 232
Chamberlain, Joseph, 259
Chariots, *see* Military affairs
Charlemagne, 187
Chasidim, *see* Pharisees
Chemosh, 38, 60
Cherethites (Philistines), 65
Chilperic, 115
China and Far East, 173, 184–88, 209, 218, 230, 343
"Chosen People", 47–48, 52, 61, 68, 73–74, 79, 85, 92, 94, 105, 111, 118, 316
Christian Israelites, 214
Christian-Jewish rivalry, 157–69, 209
Christianity, 34, 45–47, 61, 73, 89, 93–94, 110, 113–15, 125, 145, 153, 159–65, 178–79, 185–87, 193, 197, 201, 204, 211, 214, 218, 230, 233, 241–42, 245–46, 250–51, 357, 358
Chrysostom, St. John, 162, 198
Churchill, Winston S., 347–48, 352
Cicero, 111
Circassians (Caucasus), 232
Circumcision, 36, 99, 113, 125, 152–54
Citizenship (Jewish), 259
Claudius, Emperor, 114–15, 143, 145
Cleanliness, *see* Ritual Laws
Clements, R. E., *Abraham and David*, 23, 24
Cleopatra, 132, 134
Colonialism, 336–37, 348–49
Colonisation of Palestine, 259, 274
Colour prejudice, 321
Columbus, Christopher, 343
Commerce, 66–67, 76–77, 134, 185–86, 193, 196, 205, 218, 233, 242, 245–46, 320
Conder, Col. C. R., 247
Constantine, Emperor, 163, 168, 241
Constantine V (Byzantium), 209
Constantinople (Istanbul), 181, 198, 209–211, 213–14, 220, 232, 235–36, 250, 346
Conversion (proselytism): to Christianity, 114, 161–65, 198, 201, 211–12, 214–16, 242–43, 246–47, 251; to Islam, 177–79, 183–84, 189, 201, 204, 211–12, 244, 247, 251, 321; to Judaism, 103, 110–13, 115, 117–20, 125–29, 139, 147, 151–55, 160–63, 166, 169, 184, 201, 211, 242–44, 284, 321
Cordova, Arab University, 196
Corinth, 147
Counter-Reformation, 211, 216
Cracow, 227
Crete, 48, 57, 289
Crimean War, 251, 253, 346, 349
Cromer, Lord, 30, 252
Cromwell, Oliver, 214

Crusades, 198–99, 205, 219, 223–25, 228, 237
Crusader States, 228, 237
Ctesiphon and Seleucia (Medain), 181, 185
Culture, 227, 275, 322
Cyprus, 66–67, 95, 225, 228, 292, 349
Cyrenaica, 113, 152–53, 183
Cyrus the Persian, 89–90

Da Gama, Vasco, 186, 218, 234, 253, 345
Dagon, 57, 60
Dalmatia, 113
Damascus, 41, 64–65, 67, 76, 78, 80, 129, 135, 173, 178, 181, 183–85, 187–88, 195, 223, 227, 230, 233, 235, 245, 249–51, 328–29, 334
Daniel, Book of, 101
Dante, 203
Danube, 148
D'Arcy, General, 294
Dardanelles, 229
Darius III (Persia), 95
Dark Ages (Europe), 185–86, 189, 345
David, House of, 74, 81–82, 89
David, King, 23, 62–69, 73–74, 78–80, 94, 125, 185, 260, 285, 298, 307, 309, 357
Davis, S., *Race Relations in Ancient Egypt*, 110, 114
Dayan, Moshe, 327, 334
Debates, public (Jew-Christian), 202
Decapolis, The (Trans-Jordan), 98, 145
de Hirsch, Baron, 316
Deir Yaseen, 300, 302
Demetrius I, 98, 101
Demetrius II, 101, 103
Denmark, 246, 263
Deraa, *see* Edrei
Der Orient, 249
Detention Centres (Israeli), 319–20
Deuteronomy, Book of, 84
Diaspora, *see* Dispersion
Dibon (mod. Dhiban), 59–60
Dietary laws, 113, 154, 163, 166, 198, 242, 284
Diplomacy, 223, 309
Dispersion, 89, 105, 109, 111, 117, 121, 153, 252, 357
Disraeli, Benjamin, 251, 347
Doeg (Edomite), 65
Domitian, Emperor, 154, 168
Donin, Nicholas, 201
Donkey bedouin, 21, 23, 26, 29
Dorians, 48
Druze community, 251

"E" Narrative, 76

Eastern Question, 249
Eban, Abba, 327
Ecclesiasticus, 116
Economic controls, 320
Eden, Anthony, 289
Edessa, County of, 223, 227
Edom (mod. Neqeb), 39, 41, 64–65, 67, 76, 80, 298
Edrai (mod. Deraa), 41, 67, 181
Education and learning, 185, 195–96, 203, 205, 212, 218, 242, 267, 284, 310. *See also* Schools; Universities
Eglon, 48
Egypt, 21, 24–30, 38–39, 65–68, 74, 80, 82–85, 89–90, 95, 99, 104–5, 109–14, 129, 132–34, 148–50, 167, 173–75, 181, 197, 223–34, 236–37, 243, 249, 264, 307–312, 315, 318–19, 327–37, 340, 343–53, 359, 361
Eisenhower, President Dwight D., 315
Eisenmenger, J. A., 242–43
Elah, King (Israel), 76
Elamites, 241
Eleazar (Zealot), 150, 152, 339
El Elyon, 64
Eliakim (Alcimus), 101
Elijah, 77
Eliot, George, *Daniel Deronda*, 244
Elisha, 77
Emancipation of Jews, 258, 264, 266
Emmaeus, 147–48
Encyclopaedia Britannica (Papacy), 201, 217
English Zionist Federation, 261
Ephraim, tribe of, 50, 79
Epiphanes, Ptolemy V, 95, 104
Ertoghul (Turkman), 229
Eshkol, Levi, 327–29, 332, 334
Esdraelon, Plain of, 57, 67, 78
Ethiopia, *see* Abyssinia
Ethnarchs, 129
Ethnology, Levant, 20, 90–92, 98, 103, 110–11, 118, 135, 139, 152, 163, 187, 232, 235, 243, 249, 259, 265, 274. *See also* Integration
Euphrates, 41, 46, 51, 84, 98, 168, 173, 181, 228
Europe, 184–87, 189, 193–95, 217–19, 227–29, 233–34, 236, 242, 259, 261, 298, 317–18, 336–37, 343, 346, 349, 353
Eusebius, *History of the Church*, 160
Exodus, 26, 28–29, 35–42, 48–51, 53
Ezekias, 131
Ezra, 92–94, 104–5, 116, 216, 242

Family, sanctity of, 163
Far East, *see* China

INDEX

Farhi family, Damascus, 245
Fatimid Dynasty (Egypt), 223
Feisal, Ameer, 277-78
Female rulers, 127
Fertility rites, 46
Finance, 67, 110, 114-15, 119, 198-200, 211, 246, 284, 309-10
Florus (Procurator, Judaea), 144
Fortresses, military, 67
France, 113, 165-66, 184, 193, 196-200, 205, 223-25, 236, 241, 243-46, 249, 251, 253, 258, 265, 278, 289, 315-16, 345-47, 350
Frederick the Great (Prussia), 216
Frischman, 316
Frederick II, Emperor, 196

Gadara (mod. Umm Qeis), 98, 125
Galba, Emperor, 147
Galicia (Spain), 184
Galilee, 19, 78, 119, 125, 129, 131-32, 138-39, 143, 145-48, 151, 154, 249, 310, 327, 362
Gallus, Cestius (Syria), 144-45, 154
Gaster, Dr. M., 274
Gath, 57, 62
Gaul, 65, 115, 135, 138, 143, 147, 154, 232
Gaulonitis (mod. Golan), 125, 138
Gaza (Tel al Ajjul), 35, 95, 98, 125, 173, 265, 276, 315, 362
Geba, 59
Geneva Convention, 320
Gentiles, 111, 113, 117-20, 125, 144-45, 153-54, 161, 166, 197-98, 216, 243, 263, 316, 358
Geography, Levant, 19
Gerasa (mod. Jerash), 98, 127
Germany, 113, 115, 135, 148, 193-96, 199, 202-5, 209, 211, 215-20, 241-44, 249, 258-59, 262-63, 273, 282, 289, 292, 346-348, 350. *See also* Nazi persecution
Gezer, 50, 67
Ghettos, *see* Jewries
Ghetto mentality, 244, 316
Gibbon, Edward, *The Decline and Fall of the Roman Empire*, 199
Gibeon (mod. Al Jib), 48
Gibeonites (Amorites), 48, 64, 66
Gibraltar, 184, 341, 349
Gideon, 215
Gilboa, Mount, 62
Gilead, 19, 41, 77, 260
Ginzberg, Asher, *see* Ahad Ha-'Am
Gischala, John of, 145, 148-50, 152, 339
Glubb, J. B., *The Lost Centuries*, 46; *The Story of the Arab Legion*, 289; *A Soldier with the Arabs*, 299, 312
God of the Universe, 46, 52, 110, 117, 121. *See also* Yahweh *and* Lord.
"God-fearers", 113-14, 120
Golan Heights, 362
Gontran, 115
Goodman, P., *Chaim Weizmann*, 281
Gore, W. D. Ormsby, 316
Graeco-Jewish riots, 114-15, 144
Granada (Spain), 211-12, 220, 242
Gray, J., *The Desert Sojourn of the Hebrews*, 34
Grayzel, Solomon, *A History of the Jews*, 153
Great Land for a Great Nation, A, 340
Greece, 61 *fn.*, 66, 92, 94-99, 103-4, 109-115, 120-21, 125-27, 131, 144, 162, 164, 175, 185, 188, 196, 201, 204, 232, 243, 289, 298, 343, 345
Greek cities, 98, 103, 110, 129, 145
Greek language, 45, 110, 119, 195
Greek Orthodox Church, 346
Gregory the Great, Pope, 165-66
Gregory IX, Pope, 199
Grey of Falloden, Lord, 280, 292
Guerrillas, 310, 339

Hadrian, Emperor, 153, 155
Hagana (Israeli army), 299-302, 307, 328-329
Haifa, 65, 300, 312, 332, 350
Halevi, Jehuda, 275-76
Hallam, H., *Europe during the Middle Ages*, 198, 203 *fn.*
Hamath (mod. Hama), 76, 230
Handicrafts, 201
Haroon al Rasheed, 186, 227
Harran, 227
Hashim family, 183
Hasmonaeans, 99-105, 111, 115, 119, 125-135, 138-39, 147, 151, 155, 204, 267, 275
Hassan ibn Naaman, 184
Hauran, 41, 260
Hazor, 67
Hebrew language, 46, 61, 110, 214-15
Hebron (Mamre), 22-23, 39, 48-50, 62, 103, 147-48, 245, 328, 335
Hecataeus, *Apud Diodorus Siculus*, 110
Heine, Heinrich, 216
Hejaz, 168. *See also* Arabs
Hellenisation, 52, 98-99, 101, 111, 117
Henry II (Britain), 200
Heracles, *see* Melqart
Heresy, 161, 164, 167, 181, 197-98, 200-201, 211-13, 216, 219-20, 230, 242, 253 335

INDEX

Herod Agrippa I, 114, 143, 154
Herod Agrippa II, 143-44, 151-52, 154
Herod Antipas, 138, 143, 154, 159
Herod the Great, 129, 131-36
Herodians, 127-39, 143-44, 151, 154, 159, 267, 275
Herodotus, 81
Herzl, Theodor, *The Jewish State*, 258-59, 262, 274
Hezekiah, King (Judah), 73, 80-82
Historians, Arab, 51, 188
History, Sources of, 19-23, 34-37, 39-42, 59, 113
Hitler, Adolf, *see* Nazi persecution *and* Germany
Hittites, 20, 24 *fn.*, 25, 38, 52, 64-65, 232, 243
Hivites, 52
Hope Simpson, Sir John, 281
Horeb, 34
Horites (Hurrians), 20, 24 *fn.*, 38
Hosea, 79
Hugh, St. (Bishop of Lincoln), 200
Huguenots, 219
Hula, Lake, 362
Hulagu (Mongol), 219, 227-29, 237
Hungary, 209, 227, 232, 234, 263
Hurrians, *see* Horites
Husain, Sharif (King), 265, 273, 278
Husain, King (Jordan), 327, 332, 334-35
Hyksos, 24-25, 28
Hyrcanus, John (Hasmonaean), 103, 115, 125, 127
Hyrcanus II, 127-32

Ibn Khaldun, 185
Ibn Saud, 293
Iconium (mod. Konia), 223
Idumaea, 92, 103, 125-32, 135, 139, 144, 147, 151
Il Khanate (Persia), 228-29
Images, 35, 60, 175, 179
Immigration into Palestine, 282, 292-94, 315, 346; into Britain, 316, 346
Immortality, 101, 118
India, 173, 181, 184, 186, 188, 193, 218, 223, 230, 234, 245, 322, 341, 350, 352
Indian Ocean, 65, 173, 218, 234, 343-46, 349-50, 353, 359
Individualism, 111, 113, 117
Indo-Aryans, 82
Indonesia, 186, 343
Industry, 67, 195
Innocent III, Pope, 197, 200-1
Inquisition, 198, 212-14, 242, 251, 292, 335
Integration, 26-28, 30, 38, 50, 53, 61-65, 68, 74, 78, 92, 95, 103, 109, 201-2, 217, 219, 244, 247, 254, 284-85, 321-23
Intellectuals, 162, 164, 188-89, 203, 246, 316. *See also* Liberalism
International area (Palestine), 299, 309
International Court of Justice, 296
Internationalism, *see* Liberalism
International Red Cross, 312, 319
Intolerance, *see* Religious Intolerance
Iraq, 51-52, 78, 223, 227, 234, 264, 289, 307-9, 319, 323, 340, 343, 348
Ireland, 114
Irgun Zvai Leumi, 290-92, 299-300, 302, 307
Isaiah, Prophet, 80-82, 116, 125
Isaiah II, 89
Isfahan (Persia), 101
Ishbaal (s.o. Saul), 62
Islam, 47, 89, 93, 178, 183-85, 200, 203-4, 209, 217-20, 223, 229, 233-34, 242, 245, 345, 348, 350-52, 358
Ismail Pasha (Khedive, Egypt), 347
Ismail Shah (Persian), 232
Isolationism, 92-94, 105, 121, 125, 154-55, 198, 242, 254, 259, 264, 284-85, 316-17, 358
Israel, Kingdom of, 64, 66-67, 73-76, 78, 80-81, 85, 94, 103, 243, 250, 253, 260, 263, 266
Israel, State of, 61, 243, 252-54, 257, 263, 273, 276-77, 285, 290, 298-302, 307-315, 317-20, 323-24, 327, 329-37, 340, 348, 350-53, 358-67
Israeli-Egyptian war, *see* Six-day war
Israelites, from Egypt to Canaan, 25-53; Kingdoms of David and Solomon, 57-69; Assyrian conquest, 73-85; 116-17, 160, 243, 249, 261, 275
Issus (Syria), 95, 345
Istanbul, *see* Constantinople
Italy, 113, 165-66, 186, 193-96, 200-1, 203, 213-14, 217, 241-42, 246, 251, 259, 346-47. *See also* Popes; Roman Empire
Ituraeans (Galilee), 125

Jacob (Israel), 26
Jaffa (Joppa), 98-99, 103, 129, 132, 145, 299-300, 302, 312
James the Righteous, 159-60
Jamnia (Yavneh/Yibna), 147, 152-54, 160, 163
Jannaeus, Alexander (Judah), 125-27
Jason (bro. of Onias II), 99
Jebusites, 48, 52, 64
Jehoiakim, King (Judah), 84
Jehu, 77

INDEX

Jenghis Khan, 209, 219, 225-27, 229-30, 237
Jenin, 299, 309, 314
Jeremiah, Book of, 78, 84-85
Jericho, 41-42, 45, 48, 51, 53, 134-35, 147-50, 302, 357
Jeroboam (of Zeredah), 68, 74, 76
Jeroboam II, 78
Jerusalem, Crusader Kingdom of, 223-28, 245, 279, 281
Jerusalem, international area, 292, 299, 301-2, 309, 330
Jerusalem (Jebusite city), 48, 59, 64
Jerusalem (Judah), 64-65, 76, 80-85, 90-92, 98-99, 101-3, 119, 129-34, 144-54, 159, 167-68
Jerusalem, Temple, 35, 38, 42, 67-68, 74, 81, 84, 89-90, 98-101, 117-18, 120, 129, 134, 138-39, 143-44, 148, 151, 175
Jesuits, 211
Jesus Christ, 138, 159-60, 164
Jethro, 26, 33-36, 39, 42
Jewish Agency, 280
Jewish National Home, see National Home for Jews
Jewries, 109-13, 115, 118, 216-18, 242, 244, 253, 258; world Jewry, 263-64, 274, 316
Jews, international, 109-15, 152-54, 159, 161-68, 178-79, 183-84, 186, 189, 193-205, 209-20, 228, 242-54, 257-69, 273-281, 292, 315-17, 321-23, 357. See also Palestine and Zionism.
Jezebel, 76-77, 99
Jezreel, 76
Jisr al Mejama, 309
Joab, Commander, 62, 64, 66
Job, 36, 117
John the Baptist, 138, 357
Johnson, President, 332, 334
Jonah, 94
Jonathan (s.o. Saul), 59
Jonathan the Hasmonaean, 101-3
Joppa, see Jaffa
Jordan river, 52, 260, 309-10, 328, 359-62
Jordan, Kingdom of, 291, 301-2, 309, 314-315, 319, 327-32, 334-36, 338-39, 348, 359-62
Joseph, 30
Josephus, Flavius, 90, 101, 109, 114, 125-127, 136-38, 144-47, 150-51
Joshua, 46, 48-50, 61, 64, 66, 92, 160, 215, 241
Josiah, King, 73, 84
Judah (Judaea), 50; Kingdom of David and Solomon, 62-67; Assyrian conquest, 74-76; Babylonian conquest, 84-85, 357; post-Captivity, 89-94; Hasmonaeans, 98-105; Herodians, 125-139; Roman rule, 145-55, 159-61, 164, 168; Arab conquest, 204-5, 241; Zionism, 249, 267-68, 274-75. See also Palestine and Zionism.
Judaism, 37, 46, 61, 78, 89-94, 98-99, 104-5, 110-13, 116-21, 152-54, 160-63, 167-68, 263, 269, 275, 316, 323, 357, 358
Judges, Book of, 48, 50-53, 215
Julius Caesar, 90, 129, 131, 293
Juster, J., *Les Juifs sous l'Empire Romain*, 111, 113-14, 119

Kadesh Barnea (mod. Ain Qudeis), 34, 38-40
Karpeles, G., *Heinrich Heine's Memoirs*, 216
Kashgar, 184
Katamon (Jerusalem), 299, 302
Kenites, 33-34, 38-39, 42, 50, 62, 77-78
Kenizzites, 39, 62
Kennedy, Robert, 332
Khadija (w.o. Muhammad), 175, 177
Khaibar (Hejaz), 168
Khalifs, 183, 185, 188, 198, 209, 223, 225, 227
Khan, Great (Mongol), 228
Khazars (Khazaria), 209, 211, 219, 243
Khedive (Egypt), 251, 347
Khurasan, see Afghanistan
Kiev, 227
King David Hotel (Jerusalem), 257, 292
Kitchener, Lord, 247
Knights of St. John of Jerusalem, 234
Knox, Ronald, 50
Kohn, Dr. Hans, 252 *fn.*
Kossovo, 229
Kosygin, 333
Kurds, 223, 259
Kuwait, 340

Lachish, 48
Land purchase (Palestine), 250, 265, 298-299, 310, 317
Languages, 20, 110, 119, 187, 195-96, 214-215, 228, 259, 296, 350
Lansing, R. (U.S. Sec. of State), 278
Laktakia (Laodicea), 60, 98, 350
Latin, 195-96
Law, 38, 42, 84, 89, 92, 110-13, 118-19, 152, 159, 161, 203, 215, 277
League of Nations Covenant, 279, 285
Learning, see Education
Lebanon, 48, 98, 228, 235, 249, 251, 253, 264-65, 309-10, 329, 338, 350

378 INDEX

Lecky, W. E., 193
Lemann, Abbé, *L'Entrée des Israelites dans la Société française*, 243
Lenin, 262
Leon, Henry J., *The Jews of Ancient Rome*, 120
Levant, 19–21, 85, 92, 94, 125, 134, 143, 218–20, 250
Levi, Rabbi Solomon la, 212
Levi, Sylvain, 278, 317
Levin, Harry, *Jerusalem Embattled*, 300–1, 312
Levita, Elias, 203
Leviticus, 89, 93
Liberalism (European), 93–94, 105, 244–246, 254, 257, 318
Liberia, 298
Libya, 95, 113, 293
Lloyd George, David, 262, 265, 273, 276, 316
Local Commanders' agreement, 314
"Lord", The, 38, 45–46, 53, 59, 111, 247
Lorraine, 199
Lovers of Zion, 258
Lowe, Sir Hudson, 346
Loyalties, 263–64, 278
Lusignan dynasty (Cyprus), 228
Lutheranism, 215–16
Lydda, 147, 299, 312

Macalpine, I., and Hunter, R., *George II and the Mad Business*, 136
Macaulay, T. B., *A History of England*, 215, 244
Maccabaeus, Judas, 101, 104–5, 119, 125
Macedonia, 109–10, 113, 229, 293. *See also* Greece
MacMahon, Sir Henry, 265, 273
Magnesia, battle of, 95
Maimonides (Rabbi Musa ibn Maimun), 197
Malik al Nasir Muhammad, 229
Malta, 234, 349, 353
Mamlooks (Mamelukes), 52, 225–34, 236–237, 345
Mamoon Khalif, 186–87
Mamre, *see* Hebron
Manasseh, King (Judah), 82
Manchester Guardian, 262, 267
Mandate, British, for Palestine and Trans-Jordan, 279–85, 290–300, 302, 312–14, 348; Russian, for Libya, 293
Manetho, 26
Mani Ameers (Lebanon), 235
Mark Antony, 129–34

Marranos, 212, 214, 242
Marriage, 52, 92–93, 105, 109, 120, 138
Martel, Charles, 184
Martin of Tours, St., 198
Masada (Idumaea), 132, 144
Mathematics, 187–88, 195
Mattathiah (Hasmon family), 99–101
Mauritius, 292
Mecca, 36, 173–79, 183, 188, 265
Medain, *see* Ctesiphon
Medes, 82–84, 241
Medicine, 187, 195–97
Medina (Yathrib), 168, 177–79, 181
Mediterranean, 65–66, 73, 76; Alexander, 95; Arabs, 173; Muslim-Christian battlefront, 185, 193, 205, 212, 218; competition for naval control, 234, 236, 251, 254, 293–94, 298; Russian opportunity, 329–30, 333, 336; importance of Egypt, 343–47; Russian success, 349–50, 353, 359
Megiddo, 67, 84
Meir, Golda, 327
Melchizadek, King (Salem), 64
Melqart (Heracles), 77, 99. *See also* Baal
Memphis, 25, 89, 109
Mendelssohn, Moses, 244, 246, 253–54, 315
Menelaus (bro. of Simon), 99
Menuhin, M., *The Decadence of Judaism in our Time*, 153, 276
Mercenaries, 65–67, 125, 135, 188, 223, 225
Merchants, *see* Trade
Merneptah, Pharaoh, 38
Merovingians, 166
Mesha, King (Moab), 59
Mesopotamia, 21, 113
Messenger of God, *see* Muhammad
Messiah, 82, 153, 159–61, 164
Mexico, 214
Micah, 81–82
Midas, King (Phrygia), 80
Middle East, 218–19, 227–28, 230, 233, 235–37, 243, 245–46, 253–54, 257, 259, 265, 293, 343–46, 358, 359, 363–64
Middle East Perspective, 340*fn*
Midian (Hisma), 26, 33, 36, 39
Milcom, 60
Military affairs: Hyksos, Egyptians, 28; Israelites, Philistines, 39–42, 48, 51, 53, 57–59; King David, 61–67, 69; Egyptian military colony, 89; Greek phalanx "colonies", 95; guerrilla tactics, 105, mercenaries, 125, 135; battle for Jerusalem, 141–55; Muslim campaigns, 178,

INDEX

185; Mamlooks, Mongols, 225–28, 230–234; militant Zionism, 275, 294; Arab-Israeli war, 307; strategy, 343
Millennium, 118
Millman, H. H., *The History of the Jews*, 152
Mirandola, Pico della, 203
Missionary activities, 117–19, 162, 201
Moab, 38–42, 59–60, 64–65, 76, 85, 89, 94, 160, 241
Modeen (Judaea), 99
Money-lenders, 198–201, 323
Mongols, 209, 219, 225–28, 232, 237, 242, 253
Monophysite Christians (Egypt, Syria), 181
Monotheism, 22–23, 34, 36, 60, 62, 111–13, 117–18, 160, 168, 175–77
Montagu, Edwin, 269
Montefiore, Sir Moses, 249–50
Moore, G. F., *Judaism*, 116–17, 119, 125
Montpellier, 196
Moories, 217
Moriscoes, 214, 242
Morocco, 184, 319, 350
Mosaic Law, *see* Law
Moscati, S., *Ancient Semitic Civilizations*, 20
Moscow, 227
Moses, 26–30, 33–42, 45, 53, 78, 110, 116, 118, 178, 258
Mosques, 35–36, 77, 227
Mosul, 223, 234
Moyne, Lord, 291
Muawiya (Umaiyid), 183
Mucianus, 148
Mufti of Jerusalem, 257, 284
Muhammad, 36, 175–79, 183, 185–86, 188, 241
Muhammad II, the Conqueror (Ottoman), 232
Muhammad Ali, 249–50
Muhammad ibn Qasim, 184
Muhammadanism, *see* Islam
Muntifik tribe (Iraq), 51–52
Murad (Ottoman), 229
Musa ibn Maimun, *see* Maimonides
Music, 187–88
Muslim Empire, 167; Arab Conquest, 177–89; Europe, 193–98, 204–5, 209–14, 218–20; Asia, 222–27, 232–37, 241–42, 343–45, 350–52
Mastasim, Khalif, 227
Mutawakkil, Khalif, 188, 223
Muwahhids (Almohades), 197

Nabataeans, 103, 129, 134–35, 138, 145

Nablus, 299, 309
Napalm, 324 *fn.*, 335
Naples, 166, 214
Napoleon Bonaparte, 236–37, 245–46, 249, 253–54, 345–47, 350–52
Narbonne, 196
Nasser, President, 257, 318–19, 327–37
National Home for Jews, 258–61, 267, 276, 278, 280, 285, 347
Nationalism, 121, 125, 259, 265, 267–68, 274–75, 294, 316–17
Naval power, 67, 95, 173, 186, 218, 234, 236, 250, 293–94, 330–32, 343–47, 349–353
Nazarenes, 160
Nazi persecution, 289, 292, 317–20, 337, 350, 358, 363
Nebo, 60
Nebuchadnezzar, King, 84, 89
Necho, Pharaoh, 84
Nehawand (Babylon), 181
Nehemiah, 92, 104
"Neighbour", 93
Neil, W., *One Volume Bible Commentary*, 33–34, 61, 65, 73–74, 92, 94
Nelson, Lord, 236, 344
Neqeb, *see* Edom
Nero, 143, 145–48, 154, 168
Nerva, Emperor, 154
Netherlands (Holland), 213–15, 242, 345
Neutrality, 209, 242, 350
Nicholas I (Russia), 246
Nicomedia, 229
Nile, 24–26, 29, 236, 346
Nineveh, 84, 94
Nisibin, 227
Nomads, 21–25, 29, 37, 42, 47, 50–53, 66, 74, 77–78, 173–75, 178, 228–29
North Africa, 67, 113, 183–84, 186, 188, 197, 213, 233, 242, 245, 267, 343, 348
North America, *see* United States of America

Octavius, *see* Augustus
Odessa, 258
Old Testament, 20–136, 247, 310
Omri, King (Israel), 76
Onias II, 98–99
Oran (Algeria), 350
Organic Statute (1864), 251
Orkhan (s.o. Othman), 229
Orontes river, 19, 25, 76, 98
Orthodox Christians, 181, 251, 346
Orthodox Jews, *see* Ezra
Othman Khalif (Umaiyid), 183
Othman (Turkman), 229–33

Otho, Emperor (Rome), 147
Ottoman Empire, 52, 205, 211, 213, 215, 220, 229–37, 242, 245, 251, 254, 267, 273, 298, 336, 343–48

Pacific Ocean, 350
Pakistan, 298, 348–49
Palestine, historical geography, 19–20; Abrahamic and Israelite nomads, 21–29; conquest of Canaan, 38, 48–53, 57–62; Israel and Judah, 62–68, 73–78; Assyrians, 78, 80–84; Babylonians, 84–85; Persians, 89–90; Greeks, 94–104; Herodians and Romans, 125–39; Roman control, 143–54; Byzantines, 166–67; Arabs, 180, 185–86, 196, 204–5; Crusader States, 223–25; Mongols, 227; Mamlooks, 228; Ottomans, 232, 234–237; Jews, 245, 247–50, 252, 254; Zionism, 257, 259–68, 358; Mandate, 273–296; United Nations, 296–302; Arab-Israeli conflict, 307–20; Israeli military dominance, 327–29, 335–37; guerrillas, 339–40; strategic importance, 347–48, 350, 363; plans for future, 361–62
Palestine Exploration Fund, 247
Palestine Liberation Organisation, 327–28
Palestine Society, 247
Palmach (regular Israeli troops), 307
Palmerston, Lord, 250
Panium (mod. Banias), 95
Pannonia, 113
Parkes, J. A., *The Conflict of the Church and the Synagogue*, 68, 159–60, 164–65, 167, 215
Parmelee, A., *A Guide Book to the Bible*, 65
Parthia, 104, 131–34, 153–54
Partition, 282–84, 291, 296–99, 301, 309, 312
Patriarchs, 21–24, 33, 215
Paul, St., 159
Paul IV, Pope, 216–18, 220
Pelethites (Philistines), 65
Pella (mod. Kharbet al Fahal), 98, 145
Pentateuch, 45–47, 51, 89, 92
People of the Book, 275, 317
People's Crusade, 199, 205, 215, 241
Peraea, 129, 138, 147
Peres, 327
Perizzites, 52
Perowne, S., *The Life and Times of Herod the Great*, 129, 132; *The Later Herods*, 150
Persecution, *see* Religious Persecution
Persia, 20; Israelite exile, 78; conquest of Babylon, 89; Judaea, 90, 92; decadence, 94–95, 101; Alexandrian community, 109; Jewish communities in, 113–14, 164; war with Byzantine empire, 167–168, 173–75, 181; Arab rivalry, 185, 204; trade route, 209; Middle East communities, 218; Seljuqs, 223–24; Mongols, 225–32; Ottomans, 233–34, 237; tolerance of Jews, 241; "Arab", 319; historical significance, 343–45
Persian Gulf, 345, 348–49
Peru, 214
Peter the Great (Russia), 246
Peter the Hermit, 199
Petra (Nabataeans), 103, 127
Petrie, F., *Palestine and Israel*, 19, 24, 35, 41–42
Pfefferkorn, *Judenspiegel*, 242
Pfeiffer, C. F., *Egypt and the Exodus*, 24, 26
Pharaohs, 34, 38, 66, 84, 343
Pharisees (Chasidim), 103, 125–27, 131, 151, 159
Philadelphus, Ptolemy, 110
Philadelphia, *see* Ammon
Philip of Macedon, 94–95
Philippines, 298
Philips, J. B., *Four Prophets*, 79
Philistines (Philistia), 48, 57–60, 62–65, 80–81, 84, 92, 125, 275
Philo, 113–14
Philosophy, 114, 195, 197, 244
Phoenicia, *see* Tyre
Phrygia (Asia Minor), 80
Pilgrimages, 74, 179
Pius X, Pope, 259
Plagues, 57, 81, 202
Plato, 114
Plekhanov, 262
Pogroms, *see* Religious persecution
Poland, 209–11, 215, 219–20, 227, 242, 246, 253–54, 257, 273, 289, 292
Police, 314
Political power, 110, 125, 179, 193, 228, 246, 259–60, 266
Polygamy, 68, 120, 132
Polytheism, 26, 34, 36, 62, 111, 162, 178
Pompey, 129, 131
Pontius Pilate, 138
Popes, 165–66, 193, 196–97, 199–202, 212–213, 216–18, 220, 242, 253, 259, 284
Population figures, 51, 90, 111–14, 204, 245, 263, 266, 279, 282, 310, 315
Port Said, 335, 350
Portugal, 196, 212–13, 243, 345
Pressure groups, 261, 273
Priests (High), 84, 98–101, 105, 117, 125, 145, 150–52, 159–61
Priest-kings, 64, 125

INDEX

Prisoners, 320
Privileges of international Jewry, 109–10, 114–15, 119–20, 131, 152, 161, 163, 165, 193, 200, 202, 217, 241, 250, 262, 267
Propaganda, 64, 81–82, 119, 244, 275, 307, 312, 316, 318–19, 323, 327
Prophets (Hebrew), 37, 71–82, 116, 177
Prostitution, ritual, *see* Ritual Laws
Protestantism, 197, 216, 234. *See also* Reformation
Protocols of the Elders of Zion, 243
Provence (France), 165, 198
Psalms, 76
Psychological problems, 252–54, 321–24
Ptolemais (mod. Acre), 98, 132. *See also* Acre
Ptolemies (Egypt), 95, 99, 104–5, 110, 114, 199, 241, 293
Publicity organisation, 277, 291, 310. *See also* Propaganda
Punishments, 164
Puritans (Britain), 204, 214–15, 247

Qadasiya, 181
Qairawan (Tunisia), 183, 196
Qarqar, battle of, 76
Qibya, 314
Qoran, 17, 36, 47, 177, 186
Quoist, Michael, *The Christian Response*, 303
Quraish tribe, 173–75, 178–79, 183–84
Qutaiba ibn Muslim, 184
Qutuz, Sultan, 227

Rabbis, 147, 153, 160, 163, 167–69, 196, 203, 211, 216
Rabin, General, 329
Races, *see* Ethnology *and* Integration
Raisin, J. S., *Gentile Reactions to Jewish Ideals*, 90, 92, 111, 135, 152, 154, 197, 200, 202, 211, 213–14, 216, 247
Ramah, 57
Rameses I, 25
Rameses II, 25, 28, 30, 38, 67
Ramleh (Ramle, Ramla), 299, 312
Ramoth-Gilead (mod. Rimtha), 77, 260
Rashdell, *Universities of Europe in the Middle Ages*, 195
Rebellions, 65, 74, 114–15, 120, 127–31, 134, 152–53, 160, 162, 183–85, 198, 223, 241, 257–58, 265, 282, 290
Recared, King, 166
Rechabites, 77–78
Red Sea, 28, 67, 228, 298, 343, 345
Religion, 20–24, 36–37, 47, 101, 111–13, 116–20, 161, 294
Reformation, 197, 215, 219

Refugees, 85, 89–90, 300, 314, 320, 323, 339, 359–64
Regeneration of Palestine, 274
Rehoboam, 74
Religious intolerance, 60–61, 160–61, 164, 166, 215
Religious observances, *see* Ritual Laws
Religious persecution, 88, 99, 119–20, 151–152, 154, 159–61, 163–66, 169, 178, 189–96, 198–203, 211–15, 219, 230, 234, 237, 241, 246–49, 262, 269, 281, 321
Religious reform, 84, 89–92, 118
Religious toleration, 101, 119, 163, 165–67; Arabs, 181–84, 189, 196; France, 197–198, 202; 204, 209–14, 234, 241, 244, 266–67
Renaissance, 196–97, 218
Renan, *Life of Jesus*, 115
Revelation, *see* Spiritual experience
Rhodes, 132, 134
Rhodesia, 336
Richard Cœur de Lion, 200
Ritual Laws, 35, 46, 60, 99, 152–53, 160, 166, 203, 216–17, 241, 284. *See also* Circumcision; Dietary laws; Images
Rodinson, M., *Israel and the Arabs*, 329, 332–34
Roman Catholicism, 215–16, 219, 242. *See also* Inquisition
Roman Empire, 95–101, 104, 111–15, 129–134, 138, 143–48, 151, 153–55, 159, 162–69, 185, 237, 241, 243, 267, 293, 343–45, 357
Roman Law, 119–20
Roosevelt, President, 293
Roth, C., *A History of the Marranos*, 211, 214
Rothschilds, 251–52, 267–68, 278, 317
Roumania, 252
Royal Commission on Palestine, 282–84, 293
Royal Institute of International Affairs, *Great Britain and Palestine*, 291
Royalist propaganda, 81
Russell, Bertrand, 363–64
Russia, 104, 186, 209, 227, 230, 243, 246–49, 251–54, 257–59, 261–63, 266, 269, 289–94, 298, 315–19, 329–36, 338, 346, 348–53, 358–59, 361–62
Russian Orthodox Church, 346
Ruth, Book of, 94

Sabbath observance, 113, 204. *See also* Ritual Laws
Sacrifices, *see* Ritual Laws
Sadducees, 117, 127, 131, 144, 151, 159
Safed, 245, 250

Saladin, Sultan, 223–25, 227
Saleem I, The Grim, 232–33, 236
Samakh (Syria), 309
Samaria (Sebaste), 39, 76–78, 92–93, 98, 103, 131–34, 138, 147, 151, 249, 314
Samarqand, 184, 230
Samua, 328–29
Samuel, Prophet, 57–59, 62–64, 117, 215
Samuel, Herbert, 262
Sanhedrin, 131, 246
Sardinia, 67, 113
Sargon II, 80
Saudi Arabia, 293
Saul, King, 59, 62, 66, 73
Schools, 118–19, 147, 160–61, 165, 167–68, 195, 203, 216, 244
Schurer, E., *History of the Jewish People*, 125
Science, 187–88, 195
Scott, C. P., 262, 267
Scythopolis (mod. Beisan), 98, 103
Segovia, Bishop of, 212
Segregation, compulsory, 216–19, 253, 264
Seleucids, 95–105, 110, 125–29, 160, 241
Seleucus I Nicator, 95, 110
Seleucus IV Philopater, 98
Seljuq Turks, 188, 198, 204–5, 222–23, 228–29, 232–33, 237
Selzer, Michael, *The Arianization of the Jewish State*, 316, 322
Semites ('Semitic'), 20, 24 fn., 61, 211
Sennacherib, 80–81
Sephardo Orientals, 322
Sepphoris (Galilee), 145
Septuagint, 110, 120
Serabit al Khadim (Rephidim), 35, 67, 175
Sexual morality, *see* Ritual Laws
Sextus Caesar, 131
Shaftesbury, Lord, 250
Shalmaneser III, 76
Shalmaneser V, 78
Sharm al Shaikh (Tiran Straits), 315, 332, 361
Sheba, Queen of, 67
Sheba (s.o. Bichri), 66, 74
Shechem (mod. Nablus), 48–50, 53, 147
Shepherds (of Sinai), 24–29, 37–39, 45–47, 61, 69, 74, 78–79
Shihabis (Lebanon), 235
Shiloh, 53, 57
Shrines (Yahweh), 64, 74, 84
Shukairi, Ahmed, 327–28, 333
Sicarii, 143
Sicily, 67, 113, 186, 196, 198, 212
Sigismund I (Poland), 211
Sihon, King (Amorite), 41
Simon the Hasmonaean, 98–99, 103

Simpson, Sir John Hope, 281
Sinai, 24–29, 33–39, 42, 48–50, 53, 61, 65, 69, 77, 90, 265, 273, 275, 315, 330, 347
Singapore, 349
Sin Kiang, 184
Sivas (Asia Minor), 229–30
Six-day war, 330, 332–35, 348–49, 353
Slavs (Khazars), 209–10, 243
Slavery, 120, 151, 166, 193, 211, 225–27, 236
Smith, Dr. G. A., *The Historical Geography of the Holy Land*, 260–61
Social changes, 67–69, 80–82, 110
Sokolow, N., *A History of Zionism*, 214, 245, 249–50, 260, 264, 267–68, 273–75, 278
Solomon, King, 50, 59, 65–69, 73–74, 79–80, 85, 185, 260, 298
South Africa, 259, 261, 298, 317–18, 336
South America, 214, 341
Spain, 113, 165–66, 168–69, 184–88, 193, 196–98, 200, 205, 211–14, 217, 220, 233, 241–43, 251, 253, 276
Spiritual experience (revelation), 26, 29–30, 37, 42, 45, 53, 77–79, 81, 90, 116, 118, 121, 152–55, 160, 162, 175–78
Status of Jews, 257
Stevens, R. P., *Zionism, South Africa and Apartheid*, 317
Stone, I. F., 369
Strabo, 111
Sublime Porte, 236, 245, 250–51
Suetonius, *Lives of the Caesars*, 131, 145, 148
Suez Canal, 28–29, 251, 253, 265, 315, 335, 346–47, 361
Suez, East of, 349, 352
Suqut, 229, 233
Sulaiman the Magnificent, 234
Sultans, 197, 213, 223–27, 229, 232, 235, 258–59
Switzerland, 259, 262, 269
Sykes-Picot agreement, 265
Sykes, Sir Mark, 265–66
Sylvester II, Pope, 196
Synagogues, 77, 110, 118, 197, 199–200, 203, 215
Syria, Hyksos, 24; Egyptians, 25, 51; nomadic shepherds, 26–28; Abraham, 36, 46; religion, 60, 68; relations with Israelites, 74–77; Assyria, 78, 84; Judaean refugees, 85, 89; Persians, 90; Greeks, 94–98, 103, 111–13; Romans, 115, 121, 129–34, 138, 144–45, 148–50; Arab trade, 173, 177; Arab conquest, 181–83, 185–88; Saladin, 223–25; Mongols, 226–27; Mamlooks, 228; Ottomans, 232–37, 241; race, 243; Jews in,

245; Muhammad Ali, 249-51; Zionism and, 260-61, 264; War II, 289, 301-2; Arab-Israeli conflict, 309, 319; defence agreement with Egypt, 327; Syrian-Israeli conflict, 328-34; general, 336, 339, 343-45, 359; French seizure, 347; Russian influence, 349; necessity for neutrality, 350
Syrian-Israeli Armistice, 328

Tabriz, 227
Tacitus, 148
Talmud, 163, 167, 201-2, 242
Tamerlane, 229-30
Tarichae, 145
Tariq ibn Zayyad, 184
Taufiq Pasha, 301
Tawafiq, 328
Tax collectors, 198-99, 212, 217
Taylor, H. O., *The Mediaeval Mind*, 197
Technological skills, 310
Tel al Kabir, 252, 347
Temples (shrines), 35, 38, 42, 68, 74, 81, 84, 89-90, 98-99, 117-18, 120, 129, 134, 138, 143-44, 147, 150, 173-75. *See also* Jerusalem Temple
Terrorists, *see* Irgun Zvai Leumi
Tetrarchs, 132, 138, 143
Theoderic the Ostrogoth, 165, 168
Theodosius I, 165, 169
Theodosius II, 166-67
Thrace, 113, 135, 229
Tiberias, 143, 145, 163, 245
Tiberius, Emperor, 113, 138, 143
Tiglath-Pileser (Assyrian), 78, 80
Times, The (London), 249, 266-67, 364
Timur, *see* Tamerlane
Tiran, Straits of, 330, 332, 361
Titus, 145-51, 168, 227, 241, 247, 357
Torah, 202, 216
Toussenel, *Les Juifs, Rois de l'Epoque*, 243
Trachonitis (Syria), 138
Trade, 67, 76, 173, 185-86, 196, 214, 218, 228, 233-34, 242, 245, 347, 350
Trade Guilds, 201
Trade Routes, 65, 67, 79, 134, 173, 175-177, 205, 209, 228, 298, 332, 343-45, 349
Trajan, 153, 155
Trans-Jordan, 77, 98, 103, 181, 235, 261, 284, 289-91, 299-302, 307-10, 314-15, 319, 327-28, 330-32, 334-36
Trans-Oxiana, 229
Travel, 193, 195
Treaty of London (1841), 250

Tribes, 51, 57, 65, 67, 93, 109, 116-17, 173, 275-93
Tribute, 50-53, 129
Tripoli, County of, 223-25
Truman, President, 293-94
Tryphon (Syria), 103
Tughril Beg (Seljuq), 188, 223
Tulkarm, 299, 309
Tunisia, 350
Turkey, 213, 258, 264-65, 273, 348
Turkish language, 228
Turkistan, 20, 181
Turkman nomads (Ottomans), 229, 232-234
Turks (Turki), 24, 188, 213-14, 220, 223-227, 229-37, 242-43, 251, 253, 259, 265, 273, 330, 346-49. *See also* Hyksos; Mamlooks; Ottomans; Seljuqs; Turkman nomads
Tyre (Phoenicia), 66-67, 74-77, 80, 95, 132, 275

Uganda, 261, 269
Ugarit, 60
Uhud, 178
Umaiyids, 183-85, 188, 209
Union of South Africa, 261
United Nations, Palestine problem debates, 294-302; partition plan, 309, 312; Truce committee, 314-15, 319; Truce supervision, 328; Sharm al Shaikh, 330-333; future role, 359, 361
United States of America, 214-15, 246, 259, 261, 266, 273, 275-78, 280, 291, 293-98, 301-2, 309-10, 315-16, 327, 329-38, 340, 345, 348-50, 352-53, 358-361, 364-67
Universalism, 110-11, 117, 121, 203
Universities, 187, 195-96, 212, 215, 227, 244
Uqba ibn Nafi, 184
Urban II, Pope, 199
Uriah the Hittite, 64
Urmia, Lake, 232
Usque, Samuel, 213
U Thant, 332

Van Horn, General C., *Soldiering for Peace,* 328
Vespasian, 145-48, 151-52, 154
Vietnam, 330, 352
Versailles Peace Conference, 278, 317
Vienna, 227
Visigoths, 166, 168-69, 184, 214, 241
Vitellius, Emperor, 147-48

Vriezen, Th. V., *The Religion of Ancient Israel*, 60, 160

Wadi Araba, 19, 38–39
Wars of religion, 219, 237
Wavell, General, 289
Weil, Simone, 316 *fn.*
Weizmann, Dr. Chaim, *Trial and Error*, 260–67, 269, 273–79, 281, 285, 309, 316, 358
Western Empire (Rome), 166–67
Western Powers, 251, 298, 315, 329
Western press, 328–29, 332–33
Wilhelm II, Kaiser, 258, 350
Wilson, Harold, 332
Wilson, J., *Land of the Bible*, 245
Wilson, President, 273, 276
Wolffsohn, Dr., 262
Wolseley, Sir Garnet, 252, 347
World War I, 262–65, 276, 316, 347
World War II, 289–93, 319, 343, 347–48
Wright, G. E., *The Old Testament against its Environment*, 34, 47, 60

Yahweh, 23, 25–26, 30, 33–42, 45–47, 50, 57–66, 68–69, 74, 77–85, 89, 92, 110–11, 116–17, 120, 241, 247
Yalu, 319
Yathrib oasis, *see* Medina
Yemen, 65, 67, 113, 168, 332
Yost, Charles, 334
Yugoslavia (mod.), 229, 232

Zab river, 185
Zafarti, Isaac, 213
Zaid (slave of Muhammad), 175
Zealots, 147–50, 152
Zedekiah, King (Judah), 84
Zengi, Lord of Mosul, 223
Zeredah (mod. Surdah?), 68
Zeus, 99, 101
Zimri, King (Israel), 76
Zionism, 89, 195, 202, 215, 244–46, 250, 252, 358; Congress, 259–69; methods, 273–81, 284–85, 290–99, 309, 312, 316–318, 337, 353
Zionist Federation (British), 261
Zoroastrianism, 47